D1548411

Jackson School Publications in International Studies

Jackson School Publications in International Studies

Senator Henry M. Jackson was convinced that the study of the history, cultures, political systems, and languages of the world's major regions was an essential prerequisite for wise decision-making in international relations. In recognition of his deep commitment to higher education and advanced scholarship, this series of publications has been established through the generous support of the Henry M. Jackson Foundation, in cooperation with the Henry M. Jackson School of International Studies and the University of Washington Press.

The Crisis of Leninism and the Decline of the Left: The Revolutions of 1989, edited by Daniel Chirot

Sino-Soviet Normalization and Its International Implications, 1945–1990, by Lowell Dittmer

Sino-Soviet Normalization and Its International Implications, 1945–1990

Lowell Dittmer

University of
Washington Press

Seattle and London

MAIN

04762368

To Mark, with affection.

Copyright © 1992 by the University of Washington Press
Printed in the United States of America

All rights reserved. No part of this publication may be reproduced or transmitted in
any form or by any means, electronic or mechanical, including photocopy, recording,
or any information storage or retrieval system, without permission in writing from the
publisher.

Library of Congress Cataloging-in-Publication Data

Dittmer, Lowell.
  Sino-Soviet normalization and its international implications, 1945–1990 /
Lowell Dittmer.
      p.   cm.—(Jackson School publications in international
studies)
  Includes bibliographical references and index.
  ISBN 0–295–97118–5
  1. Soviet Union—Foreign relations—China.   2. China—Foreign
relations—Soviet Union.   3. Soviet Union–Foreign relations—1945–
4. China—Foreign relations—1949–   I. Title.   II. Series.
DK68.7.C5D58   1991   91-15770
327.47051—dc20   CIP

The paper used in this publication meets the minimum requirements of American
National Standard for Information Sciences—Permanence of Paper for Printed Library
Materials, ANSI Z39.48–1984. ∞

Contents

Acknowledgments

I am indebted to many colleagues for their generous help on this study, especially to Peter Berton and to Samuel Kim, who read the entire manuscript and made many valuable comments. Richard Baum and Greg Grossman critiqued earlier versions of chapter 3, Vinod Aggarwal, Robert Powell, and Laura Stoker helped me conceptualize the reciprocal infuence of socialist reform efforts in Part IV, and Kenneth Waltz commented on an earlier version of my discussion of the strategic triangle. I wish to thank Eric Harwit, Y.C. Ha, Rudra Sil, and Bettina Schroeder for research assistance. I am indebted to the Center for Chinese Studies and the MacArthur Group for International Strategic Studies at the University of California at Berkeley for financial support, and to the Woodrow Wilson Center of the of the Smithsonian Institution for making possible a year's research sojourn in Washington, D.C. I also benefited from briefer research visits to the Institute for Slavic and Eastern European Studies of the Chinese Academy of Social Sciences in Beijing and to the Institute of the Far East and the Institute of Oriental Studies of the Soviet Academy of Sciences in Moscow.

Miscellaneous parts of the first three chapters were presented in different form to a Center for Chinese Studies Regional Conference in October 1988 and to a May 1989 Conference with the Shanghai Institute of International Studies in Maanshan, China. Chapters 6 and 7 were presented in modified form at a conference held at the University of Chicago in December 1988 in honor of Tang Tsou, and will appear in a forthcoming book edited by Brantly Womack. I wish to thank the scholarly audiences of these various fora for their comments and criticisms, Cambridge University Press for permission to reorganize and publish this material as chapters 6 and 7, and Routledge, Chapman and Hall for permission to publish chapter 3 in slightly modified form. I am grateful to the University of Washington Press for taking such pains in the editing process.

Finally, on a more personal level, I am deeply indebted to my wife

Helen and son Mark for their support and encouragement during the long and trying gestation period. It goes without saying that only I can claim responsibility for any errors of fact or interpretation that remain.

LOWELL DITTMER
June 1991

Sino-Soviet
Normalization
and Its
International
Implications,
1945–1990

Introduction

The Sino-Soviet relationship over the years has been intense, fitful, and deeply ambivalent. This is perhaps understandable, when both sides have so much at stake. For the Soviet Union, leadership of the international communist movement was at issue almost from the outset, having been raised in the late 1940s by Stalin's ill-fated excommunication of Yugoslavia. China's initial willingness to follow Soviet precepts—especially since Chinese compliance was voluntary, unlike that of the East European "satellites"—added immensely to the USSR's prestige and power. But the People's Republic also had good reason to cultivate amicable relations. For the PRC, its developmental trajectory and political identity were at stake, both of which seemed to hinge on belonging to an international community and adhering to a set of tenets over which Moscow held sway. For both countries, the dialogue involved fundamental values as well as equally basic national security interests vis-à-vis a potent ideological adversary.

China's ambivalence about her great northern neighbor, mother of revolution and leader of international communism, stems in part from the somewhat checkered historical legacy of relations between the two nation-states, and partly from the relationship between parties in the course of the Chinese revolution. The prerevolutionary Russian posture toward China was expansionist in the traditional imperial sense, and although with the famous Karakhan Declaration (July 25, 1919) the Bolshevik regime seemed to have renounced all unequal treaties concluded by the tsarist government as well as all privileges enjoyed by Russia in China, Mongolia, and Manchuria, it was not long before the new rulers repented of their outburst of magnanimity.[1] Expansionist tendencies reappeared: in 1921 the Red Army marched into Outer Mongolia to restore the sphere of influence that had vanished after 1917.[2] In 1929 Moscow underlined its claim to the Chinese Eastern Railway through an armed intervention in Manchuria. Soviet penetration into Northern Manchuria continued, such that the region seemed likely to become a Soviet buffer state—a process that was interrupted by the invasion of a jealous Japan and founding of Manchukuo in 1932. Even Xinjiang fell under Soviet sway in the 1930s; 90 percent of its trade was with the USSR, and there was occasional armed intervention from the north (in 1936 two GPU brigades penetrated as far as Urumqi).

As an outlawed revolutionary force, the Chinese Communist Party (CCP) was not adversely affected by these incursions, and in fact benefited from Soviet aid and advice. Like other communist parties in the world at this time, it was advised and assisted by the Comintern, headquartered in Moscow, and upon dissolution of the Comintern in 1943 more directly by the Communist Party of the Soviet Union (CPSU). The relationship was one-sided and somewhat tempestuous, particularly when the revolution encountered theoretically unforeseen setbacks. Partly because Soviet strategic advice to the CCP was sometimes flawed, partly because the Chinese tended to scapegoat Soviet advisers for their setbacks in what was an inherently tenuous situation, the CCP leadership began to detach itself from Soviet guidelines well before gaining national sovereignty in 1949.

Mao Zedong in particular rose to power without Soviet support, indeed in the face of concerted resistance from the "returned students" most closely identified with the Soviet line (and who, one must infer, opposed Mao with Moscow's knowledge and implicit support). Mao twice made Wang Meng a target for innerparty criticism, once for being excessively "leftist," then for being rightist; but both of these "erroneous lines" seem to have emanated from the Kremlin. Making no secret of his determination to find a distinctive and "self-reliant" approach, first for his party and then for his country, Mao stated as early as mid-1936: "Similarly one can affirm that, although the CCP is a member of the Comintern, this by no means signifies that Soviet China is ruled by Moscow or by the Comintern. We are certainly not fighting for a liberated China in order to hand the country over to Moscow."[3] At the end of the 1930s Mao reasserted his stake in a variant of Marxism specific to China's characteristics: "Thus the Sinicization of Marxism becomes a question that must be immediately understood and solved by the entire Party, i.e., we must make certain that it [i.e., Marxism] is in all aspects appropriate to the special features of China, and that it is applied according to those characteristics."[4] And in 1945, at the Seventh Party Congress, Liu Shaoqi hailed Mao's Thought as the successful realization of that Sinicization: "Mao Tse-tung . . . is a creative and gifted Marxist, who combines the general truths of Marxism—the highest ideology of mankind—with the concrete practice of the Chinese

Revolution. . . . He is the best expression of Marxism applied to a specific nation." [5]

Although consummation of the revolution in 1949 seemed at last to have put Sino-Soviet relations on a stable and amicable footing, the relationship soon turned from sweet to sour, becoming one of the world's most bitter and implacable grudge matches. As we shall see, the 1950s and 1960s were the heyday of the analytical literature on Sino-Soviet relations. Since that time, there have been fundamental changes that call for a fresh analysis. This will be attempted below, in a study focusing on three themes. First, Sino-Soviet "normalization" is real, not a political mirage, and a matter of considerable moment to the Asian-Pacific region and to the international system as a whole. Second, despite reservations on the part of Western strategic thinkers still chary in the wake of the erstwhile threat to Western strategic interests posed by the combination of these two countries, Sino-Soviet normalization need not redound adversely to American interests in the Far East and may in fact result in a more fruitful regional and international balance. Third, this positive outcome is by no means assured, but is contingent upon the satisfactory arrangement of key international economic and security interests—the precise nature of which it will be one of the main tasks of this study to explicate.

The purpose of this introduction is to outline briefly the reasons for the enduring significance of the Sino-Soviet relationship. It will consist of two parts, the first of which reviews the available literature on the topic, while the second attempts to specify and justify the present contribution.

The Analytical Tradition

Western analysts have been at least implicitly aware of the importance of the Sino-Soviet relationship from the beginning, although relatively little was published prior to the public appearance of a schism in the late 1950s. [6] Over the years, a major body of literature in the analysis of Chinese and Soviet foreign policies has gradually accumulated. This literature may be sorted into two broad categories, each of which coincides with a distinct phase of the relationship. The first category seeks to explain the *origins* and causes of the dispute; the second focuses on the *dynamics* of the dispute, now conceived to be a self-perpetuating and essentially immortal process.

The first category, containing the most prolific and voluminous contributions, begins with the advent of the dispute in the mid to late 1950s and follows it to its climax in border warfare between the two countries in March 1969. Noteworthy here are monographs and compendia by Hudson, Lowenthal, and MacFarquhar (1961), Zagoria (1962), Griffith (1964), and Gittings (1968).[7] Although relative emphasis, of course, varies with the particular work in question, each of these studies concentrates on two causal factors in attempting to explain the dispute: ideology and national interest.[8]

Perhaps the dominant tendency among these analysts is to treat *ideology as a dependent variable,* important but essentially derivative from military/strategic or other national interests. Hudson, for example, writing before the ideological dimension had been fully articulated, focused on security issues, noting that Soviet rapprochement with the United States aroused PRC fears of abandonment (as did Soviet overtures to India and Indonesia, on a lesser scale). The Chinese accordingly attacked Khrushchev ideologically in order to waylay or at least inhibit such initiatives. Lowenthal placed somewhat greater emphasis on ideological factors, but his analysis complements Hudson's, rooting ideological accusations in security concerns. Thus revolutionary movements in the Third World were encouraged by the Chinese not only to validate distinct ideological convictions but to foil the amicable relationship the USSR was seeking with the United States, for example. Lowenthal also noted other security concerns in his discussion of the roots of the dispute: a decrease of Soviet military aid in the late 1950s, or a Soviet reluctance to help the Chinese build nuclear weapons.[9] Griffith disavowed any theoretical intention and indeed wrote an essentially descriptive account of the dispute, but also tended to root such ideological differences as the quarrel over the "inevitability of war" with imperialism, or over how best to encourage "national liberation struggles" in the developing countries, in conflicts of national interest. Thus he analyzed the Sino-Indian border dispute, the Cuban missile crisis, and the Soviet-American test ban treaty in terms of the interests of the nations involved, not ignoring ideology altogether but treating it essentially as an ancillary, complicating factor.

Zagoria and Gittings are among the minority who tend to endow ideology with greater causal importance, though its precise function remains obscure. Zagoria seems to suggest, for example, that ideology was both an incendiary factor *precipitating* the dispute (e.g., Mao's desire to become known as a major contributor to Marxist theory after Stalin's death, Maoist China's determination to pursue ideological goals that transcended PRC security) and an adhesive factor *containing* the cleavage and ameliorating tension between the two (on the basis of which he discounted much chance of war, and saw scant likelihood that the United States could ever develop friendly ties with the PRC). While arguing that ideology and national interest are inseparable, Gittings assumed the causal primacy of the former, implying for example that Chinese antagonism to Soviet-American rapprochement was based on ideological premises. He also foresaw no future improvement in Sino-American relations, due to ideologically based CCP hostility to imperialism. Yet only intensified Sino-American rivalry might suffice to heal the ideologically driven Sino-Soviet rift.

By the end of the 1960s, the territorial and security dimensions of the dispute had acquired such obvious salience—dramatized by the series of armed clashes along the border in the spring and summer of 1969—that these came to eclipse ideologically based explanations. Perhaps the most boldly articulated "realist" account was set forth by the journalist Harrison Salisbury (1969).[10] He adduced the dispute to deeply rooted conflicts of national interest, delving into the history of border disputes in the Northeast and Xinjiang over the past several centuries to account for the current security dilemma. As perhaps the first to advocate publicly a diplomatic opening between China and the United States in order to deter the Soviet threat, Salisbury completely discounted the inhibiting force of ideology: "nothing in Chinese ideology, philosophy, or national attitudes precludes [improvement in Sino-American relations] provided only that . . . the United States will act on Taiwan."[11] Other analysts during this period also fasten on the security dimension of the dispute, tracing this either to insatiable Russian and Soviet land hunger or to Chinese territorial revanchism.[12] Yet the unprecedented intensity of the polemical dispute between the two countries during the Cultural Revolution apparently superseded the logic of a historically rooted, security-based explanation, requiring recourse to irrational *qua* ideological explanations during this period as well.

The second broad category of studies, written during the 1970s and early 1980s, accepted and recapitulated (with varying emphases) the explanations of the dispute's origins offered by the first category of studies (thus confirming that this literature had indeed become an analytical tradition), addressing itself in the main now to the dispute's *persistence*. Implicitly assuming the dispute to be self-perpetuating, the investigation focused on those factors that maintain and enhance or reduce tensions, equilibrate or disequilibrate the balance of power. Ideology more or less vanishes from the analytical schema, reflecting both the deradicalization of Maoist foreign policy (the first aspect of late Maoism to be rationalized) and the growing flexibility of the post-Suslov Soviet leadership. In the absence of the old dualism between ideology and national interest, two new analytical perspectives arose to explain persistence of the cleavage: first, the "linkage" approach focused on the relationship between domestic politics and foreign policy in the two countries; second, international structure was introduced as an independent variable, assuming that foreign policy makers in both countries were influenced more by the overall pattern of international relations than by domestic political exigencies.

Although such studies have remained mainly descriptive in content and bilateral in focus, the linkage approach makes an important contribution to our understanding of the dispute's persistence. Attempts to link the domestic political process to foreign policy outcomes typically incorporate elements of the "bureaucratic politics" model, but in view of the relatively weak articulation of distinct bureaucratic interests in both countries and the secrecy shrouding the policy-making process, this model's application is often intertwined with factional analysis. Zagoria and Ra'anan have, for example, both used this approach to explain Sino-Soviet disagreements concerning the Vietnam War, arriving at somewhat divergent explanations. The work of Hinton (1971, 1976), Lieberthal (1978), Gurtov and Hwang (1980), or Harding and Gurtov (1971) might be said to constitute more general and eclectic exemplars of this approach.[13] Aside from the more general drawbacks of the factional model of Chinese politics,[14] its limitations derive from the substantive indeterminacy of factions: unlike a bureaucratic organ, whose interests are defined by its organizational locus and stipulated functions, a faction may decide to pursue any interest, or espouse any ideological line, depending on the personal predilections of its leader. Thus different conclusions are reached by different analysts based on whom they assume to belong to which faction and what rivalries and ambitions they impute to the respective faction chiefs.

Two types of analysis of Sino-Soviet relations in the light of international structure arose in the 1970s and early 1980s. Both capitalize on a watershed development that took place at the end of the 1960s: the internationalization of the dispute. Both the PRC and the USSR, unable to contain their differences within the bloc following the outbreak of border violence and Soviet threats of nuclear blackmail, proceeded to seek support in the international community to resolve the dispute. The first, and still the most fecund line of analysis, fastens on the entrance of the other superpower, the United States, into the fray, thereby erecting a "strategic triangle." First to take this tack seems to have been the eminent Soviet scholar Donald Zagoria, followed by a spate of studies in the 1970s.[15] The strategic triangle had its heyday, both as an analytical tool and as an operational policy, in the early to mid 1970s, when there was much talk of playing various "cards." Since that time, it has been abandoned as a policy (at least ostensibly) by all putative players and has also come under fire as an analytical tool. The most frequently mentioned analytic flaws of the model have to do with two issues: the strategic centrality of the relationship among these three states for the rest of the international system, and the unequal distribution of power among the three.

The second type of analysis based on international structure shifts the focus from the simple lateral relations among "the powers" to the more complex pattern that includes the vertical relationships between each power and its respective client states. This approach reflects the attempts by the two principal disputants (following the American precedent) to build containment or countercontainment networks around each other beginning in the early 1970s, and their competitive efforts to cultivate such clients as India, Pakistan, Vietnam, and North Korea. Scalapino (1982), for example, discusses Soviet attempts to create "buffer" regions around China, and corresponding Chinese overtures to Western Europe, Japan, and the United States.[16] There have also been more microscopically focused studies of particular clientships, notably Vietnam and Korea.[17] This approach tends toward the conclusion that "the tail wags the dog"; which is to say that although bilateral difficulties between the two principals no longer seem intractable, both the Soviet Union and the PRC have invested in lingering patron-client ties that are mutually incompatible, effectively precluding bilateral accommodation.[18]

The Relationship Reconsidered

In the wake of the voluminous literature already available, most of it still worth rereading and a good deal of it still valid, it seems presumptuous to mount yet another entry on this old warhorse. Why write this book—or, more to the point, why read it? Certainly these two countries are large and very important ones, probably more powerful relative to the rest of the world now than when their dispute began. Thus it seems useful periodically to review the most recent developments in their relationship and to reconsider their prior histories anew. The studies reviewed above have admirably performed this service, but they are now out of date. In view of the significant transformation the relationship has undergone since the deaths of Mao and Brezhnev, particularly the most recent developments culminating in full normalization, a reassessment seems timely.[19]

But beyond this inventorial function, there are other good reasons to reassess the relationship. In reviewing the literature, it is interesting to note that the rise of the *problematique* coincides with the schism: Western scholarship did not become concerned with Sino-Soviet relations when they were assumed to be harmonious; the study of the relationship is largely the study of the *conflict*. Moreover, both journalistic and scholarly interest in the dispute (as indicated by the written record) has continued to correlate with its intensity. This is a puzzling coincidence, perhaps having something to do with ideological *Schadenfreude* over this obvious flouting of international class solidarity, perhaps more simply with the greater newsworthiness of conflict as opposed to peaceful cooperation. In any case, this fixation on conflict gives the literature a somewhat monothematic perspective not too well suited to the anticipation of structural change. Most analysts, faced with the opportunity in a "think piece" or concluding chapter to reflect on the past and likely future of the dispute, have tended to extrapolate from the most recent developments in relatively straightforward fashion. Virtually no one anticipated the split, for instance, and even after it occurred there was lingering skepticism about how real it was. Nor were any of the subsequent seismic shifts in the relationship—the outbreak of border warfare, the internationalization of the dispute, the extreme anti-Soviet (and pro-American) Chinese tilt at the end of the 1970s, China's subsequent departure from that stance—foreseen. There seems to be a tendency to "freeze" the relationship into an intellectual construct more rigid than the reality.

Until quite recently, many Western interpretations of the most recent movement toward Sino-Soviet reconciliation were ensnared in the same conventional wisdom: the thaw is more apparent than real—a masquerade designed to enhance China's leverage with the United States, or to serve other limited, tactical purposes. In some of their discussions with Western visitors of the ongoing Sino-Soviet rapprochement, Chinese spokesmen colluded in this construal, routinely calling attention to continuing lack of progress on the "Three Fundamental Obstacles" to deny any perceived improvement in relations.[20] In retrospect it would seem however that "normalization" was an ongoing *process* rather than an outcome, which the Three Obstacles have not so much impeded as masked. Finally, as one Obstacle after another was removed, culminating in "normalization" in May 1989, a basically new stage in the relationship could no longer be denied. Or could it?

It is now time, it would seem, to shift to a new paradigm, one no longer focused exclusively on conflict but also taking into account the prospect of reconciliation—its motives, dynamics, international ramifications, and possible drawbacks or limits. This study is among the first to attempt to reorient the discipline around this most recent shift. Its underlying assumption is that the Sino-Soviet thaw is quite real, that prospects for its continuance are excellent, and that it deserves to be taken seriously. True, it has been inching forward without fanfare and at fairly deliberate pace, and the level of economic and cultural interaction remains below that of the Chinese relationship with the West. But the cumulative upshot has been a multistranded web of interdependency of rather impressive articulation and power. Trade with the Soviet Union has increased more rapidly (from a tiny base) than Chinese trade with any other partner, including the United States. Even though Washington has had "normal" relations with Beijing for a full decade while Moscow has only just realized that consummation, there are five times as many Soviet diplomats in the capital as there are American ones. To be sure, this is not to say that Sino-Soviet normalization will overthrow the international balance of power or even necessarily redound adversely to American interests. But surely the implications of a development of such potential magnitude deserve to be analyzed objectively and without prejudgment.

An additional reason to refocus attention on the relationship has to do with its pivotal position in the formulation of Chinese foreign (and, to a lesser extent, domestic) policy, making it a key to new insights in the evolution of Chinese politics at a time of considerable flux. To this end, the study will seek to exploit rather than ignore the broader implications of the bilateral relationship, to follow tangents wherever they promise to throw light on the implications of this newly emerging political configuration for Chinese foreign policy, the East Asian region, and the international arena as a whole (roughly in that order). The approach is topical rather than historical, focusing in turn on three aspects of the relationship (each of which is internally organized chronologically). Part I looks at the connections between domestic development and bilateral relations. Part II views matters in terms of China's relationship to meaningful international "reference groups." Part III focuses on the security dimension.

Previous literature on the dispute has not completely neglected the "linkage" issue, as noted in the foregoing review, but its application has been elitist, limited for the most part to a factional variant of Allison's "bureaucratic politics" model.[21] The relevance of socioeconomic development to the dispute has rarely been addressed in systematic fashion. Part I seeks to do both, reviving "convergence theory" from its previous incarnation as a model for future capitalist-socialist relations to serve as a paradigm for future Sino-Soviet relations. Use of the convergence scenario opens the linkage model to a more broadly based consideration of domestic inputs into the policy process, including the various functional requisites, political constituencies, and intended or nonintended consequences of economic modernization. Some of the core concerns of comparative communism and political development theory thus merge in a study of international conflict management.

The fact that both China and the Soviet Union (until recently) identified themselves as communist party-states entails that relations between them must differ from those between communist and bourgeois states, or between different bourgeois states. At least this has been the prevailing assumption in both countries throughout most of the history of their relationship; although as "normalization" of relations has progressed, there has been some effort on China's part to deny any such difference in principle. The reason for this prevailing assumption is that communist ideology has been accepted as central and fundamental to the identity of both countries, and this ideology prescribes a class solidarity not felt with states dominated by the bourgeoisie—or even among such states, given the cannibalistic class character imputed to the bourgeoisie. Any discussion of Sino-Soviet relations thus goes to the core of the identity of both nations. The purpose of Part II is accordingly to explore the whole issue of national identity as it relates to their dispute—focusing on the case of China, the source of most of the change in this highly changeable relationship. Parts II and III complement one another in the sense that whereas Part III is concerned with the rational dimension of the relationship, Part II focuses on irrational values and sentiments.

China's engagement in foreign affairs has inevitably implicated the two global "superpowers": the Soviet Union and the United States. Together they make up a triangle of some international consequence. Some of the factors underlying the rise of the concept of a "strategic triangle" were cursorily touched upon earlier, but these will be analyzed more comprehensively in Part III. Although the validity of the concept remains in dispute at this writing, I take it to have pivotal relevance for Chinese (hence Asian) affairs throughout the postwar period, and some pertinence to international developments more broadly conceived during at least part of that period. This section attempts to investigate in relatively systematic fashion both the abstract logic of the triangle and the applicability of that logic to Sino-American-Soviet security interests in the postwar era.

In sum, the purpose of this study is first of all to conduct a fresh inventory of the latest developments in and between two of the more intrinsically interesting countries in the world, and to decide what it all means in the context of cumulatively available information about them. Beyond that, it aspires to make a modest contribution to some of the more general questions that concern students of comparative politics and international relations: Can the processes of industrialization and socioeconomic modernization be expected to have comparable political impact on the two countries? Is there any relation between the way a nation seeks its "identity" and the evolution of its foreign policy? How do Sino-Soviet strategic relations impinge upon Western security interests in the Asian-Pacific region?

Part IV explores conceivable interconnections among the answers these questions elicit. Developments following the crackdown at Tiananmen and the fall of the iron curtain in Europe are taken into account. Events subsequent to the period covered in this book, especially in the Soviet Union, will inevitably have further implications. This is a preliminary attempt to sort out the future of the relationship.

PART I

DEVELOPMENT
AND DÉTENTE

The theory of convergence, which had its heyday in the early 1960s, postulated that the logic of economic development inevitably leads both capitalist and socialist systems to become socioeconomically isomorphic.[1] Socioeconomic convergence would, in turn, eventually have political spinoffs: If conflict between the two systems could be attributed to their structural differences, any diminution of those differences could only facilitate mutual understanding.[2] In short: modernization implies convergence; convergence implies détente.

In the two or three decades since convergence theory was first articulated, how has it fared? The two systems have shared certain trends, such as large-scale bureaucratization; the capitalist states have grown more like the socialist states in their provision of welfare services and some form of planning, while the socialist countries have become more like the capitalist ones in their stratified distribution of material incentives and increasing reliance on markets. Nonetheless, excepting for the moment those East European countries that never experienced an indigenous revolution, the two systems continued until recently to be differentiated by many of the same structural features that distinguished them from the outset (political pluralism versus single-party dictatorship, market versus plan). And they remained international rivals in principle, albeit not incapable of cooperation when it appeared to be in their mutual interest.

Convergence theory is far from defunct as an explanation of emerging relations between command and market systems; indeed, recent developments in Eastern Europe seem likely to stimulate its revival. This section, however, takes the theory in a direction both more original and less ambitious. If convergence theory foundered on the intractability of the political structures in which the socioeconomic system remained caged, the theory would appear to have better chances for confirmation if the political superstructures, too, could be held constant in the systems being compared. This condition appears to have been met in the pairing of the USSR and the PRC. Historically, both were large, economically underdeveloped agricultural empires administered by centralized bureaucracies and led by a hereditary autocrat. Following Liberation, the political structures imposed were essentially identical. The elites who imposed these Leninist structures shared general ideological outlooks as well as the specific objective of a noncapitalist industrialization. They fully expected their duplicate structures to ensure a sense of socialist community between them, and they further expected their developmental paths to converge in the course of modernization.

The developmental experience of the two countries has nonetheless diverged considerably in the four decades since the PRC joined the USSR in the quest for socialist modernity, raising a number of interesting questions. Chapter 1 reconsiders the origins of the rift in the 1950s, to see whether socioeconomic convergence was indeed proceeding at that time, and if so why it failed to ensure political concord. Chapter 2 examines the Chinese attempt to blaze an independent developmental trail in the 1960s and early 1970s, accompanied by an attempt to provoke international hostility at least in part in order to reinforce socioeconomic *divergence*. Chapter 3 considers the currently ongoing joint movement toward détente and convergence, as the two systems undertake socialist "reform." Chapter 4 examines the concerted attempt to build functional bridges between the two countries during the post-Mao period. And Chapter 5 reviews the current pattern of development in light of the prospects for a continuing course along parallel lines.

CHAPTER 1

Socialist Dependency

During the period of China's First Five-Year Plan (FYP), and indeed until Mao's explicit departure from the Soviet model in the Great Leap Forward, the PRC expressly modeled itself after the Soviet pattern in all respects.[1] The relationship was referred to in metaphors of great intimacy as one between "big elder brother" and "little brother," between "father" and "son," between "lips and teeth."[2] Mao (for one) endorsed Chinese emulation of the Soviet "model" explicitly and repeatedly. As he put it on one such occasion: "The Communist Party of the Soviet Union . . . is the most advanced, the most experienced, and the most theoretically cultivated Party in the world. This Party has been our model in the past, is our model at present, and will be our model in the future."[3] Even after Mao had begun to criticize Soviet policy and leadership, he acknowledged the importance of Soviet aid, noting as late as 1962 that in 1949 the Chinese simply did not know how to build socialism on their own.[4]

This dependent relationship was formalized in a Sino-Soviet Treaty of Friendship, Alliance and Mutual Assistance, signed in Moscow February 14, 1950,[5] providing for a loan of U.S. $300 million over five years, plus a supply of mechanical equipment in fifty construction projects, to continue over nine years. In addition to the treaty itself, four other agreements were signed, including: (1) provision for eventual return to China of the Chinese Eastern (Zhangzhun) Railway, together with the attendant property; Mao temporarily agreed to continued Soviet use of the two ice-free naval ports on the Yellow Sea, Port Arthur and Dairen, at Soviet insistence (Moscow recognized Chinese sovereignty over Xinjiang, but there was no mention of Outer Mongolia); (2) Soviet long-term (five-year) credits to China amounting to $300 million; (3) provision for the establishment of joint-stock companies for the exploitation of petroleum and nonferrous metals in China for a projected thirty-year period; and (4) a joint trade agreement. Many of these provisions, such as joint-stock companies (*smeshannye obshchestva*), were part of the familiar repertory of techniques favored by

17

the Soviets at the time to control subordinate members of the bloc (the companies were Soviet controlled, they explained, because the Chinese had no capital to contribute).

Owing to Soviet gratitude for the Chinese role in the promotion of Soviet interests within the bloc as well as beyond it, the post-treaty period saw the Soviets make a series of additional concessions. They withdrew from Dairen in 1950, and in 1952 they forfeited all rights to the Chinese Eastern Railway without compensation; in 1954 they returned shares of four joint-stock companies; in 1955 they remitted the naval port of Port Arthur, accepting compensation. Thanks to Chinese intervention in the Korean War ("It was at the time of the Resist America, Aid Korea campaign," Mao recalled, that Stalin finally came "to have confidence in us."),[6] the Soviet Union relinquished all the residual rights in Manchuria that Stalin had claimed and won at Yalta: this region, then the richest and most developed industrial area in the country, became a staging area for the large "volunteer" armies being deployed in Korea, thereby falling again under uncontested Chinese sway.[7] Only two weeks after the death of Stalin (March 5, 1953), a new accord was reached for Soviet aid to China, enabling the PRC to construct an additional 91 industrial projects.[8] During their first visit to Beijing in October 1954, Khrushchev, Bulganin, and Mikoyan agreed to aid another 15 industrial projects (bringing the total to 156), and to enlarge the scope of aid in the existing 141 projects. Another agreement was signed in April 1956 during Mikoyan's separate visit to Beijing, extending aid to an additional 55 projects.[9] Agreements were reached for the sale of submarines, jet aircraft, and even (in 1956–57) for the transfer of nuclear technology.

Bilateral trade flourished under the terms of the alliance, amounting to 58 percent of total Chinese trade in 1954 and cresting at U.S. $2.097 billion in money value in 1959. Between 1950 and 1961 the Soviet Union provided about 45 percent of China's imports and was the main source of producer goods from the rest of the world; altogether the socialist countries accounted for two-thirds of China's total commerce. Soviet exports to China over this period came to about $7.7 billion, of which about a fourth took the form of complete industrial plants, and another 16 percent that of other machinery and equipment. Most of these the Chinese paid for by means of current exports, but about 27 percent were financed with Soviet credits. The availability of Soviet loans enabled China to run a trade deficit with the USSR from 1950 to 1955, tapping Soviet savings to supplement Chinese investment capital at a time of economic exigency.[10] Trade with the USSR was the largest negative item in China's current balance, with a debt of about $1 billion, including $430 million in the form of two long-term credits; military aid (during the Korean War); and financial obligations dating from World War II (e.g., transfer to China of Soviet shares in joint-stock companies and of the naval installations at Port Arthur).[11]

To be sure, no additional loans were extended after the first half of 1956, and the delivery of existing loans tended to be deferred. This pretermission, which happened to coincide with the emergence of a somewhat more tepid Chinese endorsement of the Soviet model, may have been a diplomatic signal of Moscow's annoyance with Beijing's meddling in Soviet policies toward Eastern Europe.[12] A more likely explanation, however, is that intervention in Poland and Hungary exhausted Soviet eleemosynary capabilities, requiring almost $1 billion in short-term credits to rebuild what had been damaged in the course of the upheaval and its violent suppression. This unforeseen expenditure contributed to premature termination of the Soviet Sixth Five-Year Plan, with the upshot that China—which was in 1956 in the process of drafting its Second Five-Year Plan—was unexpectedly excluded from the Soviet foreign aid program.[13]

In any event, from 1950 through 1966 the Soviets helped the Chinese to construct a total of 256 industrial projects (by Chinese count), or two-thirds of the 320 "complete sets of industrial plant and equipment" that China purchased from the bloc in the 1950s. These projects, described in China's First FYP as "the core of our industrial construction plans,"[14] included the largest iron and steel complex in China (Anshan, in Liaoning province), the largest ball-bearing plant (Luoyang Bearing Plant, Henan), the largest tractor factory (Luoyang No. 1, Henan), one of the largest coal mines (Lingantai, in Heilongjiang), the largest linen mill (Harbin Flax, Heilongjiang), the largest paper mill (Jiamusi, Heilongjiang), the largest manufacturer of heavy electrical equipment (Xian Electrical, Shaanxi), and the largest aluminum plant (Fushun, Liaoning). China acquired whole branches of industry that never existed there before: aviation, automobile and tractor manufacturing, radio, and many branches of chemical production. These projects included aid in all aspects of the construction process, from prospecting for ore to the training of Chinese personnel. In all, Soviet aid projects plus those directly supporting them absorbed over half of all construction investment in the First FYP. Chinese production in 1960 from enterprises built with Soviet technical assistance accounted for 35 percent of cast iron, 40 percent of steel, more than 50 percent of rolled iron, 80 percent of trucks, more than 90 percent of tractors,

55 percent of steam and hydraulic turbines, and so on.[15] Incredible as it may seem, 70 percent of the industrial machinery operating in Chinese factories was still of Soviet or East European provenience as of the early 1980s.[16] Among the major projects constructed was China's first atomic reactor and cyclotron (completed April 1957), which would form the ·basis for all subsequent Chinese research in nuclear physics.[17]

Perhaps even more significant than Soviet material assistance is what has been called "the most comprehensive technology transfer in modern history."[18] It was also more generous: while the former consisted almost entirely of loans (albeit at concessionary interest rates), the latter consisted of grants. The Soviets claim that "it is probably impossible to name a field of science and technology in which the Soviet Union did not share with China, free or at very favorable conditions, its advanced achievements and rich experience."[19] Assistance began even before the first science and technology transfer agreement was signed (October 1, 1954) and continued under two further agreements, signed in January 1955 and June 1961. In addition to these broad intergovernmental agreements, about twenty Soviet ministries and government departments and approximately 160 research and development organizations maintained independent contacts with some 90 of their counterparts in China. In many instances even individual factories, laboratories, and other organizations of the two countries established direct contacts.

The Soviets have contended, no doubt with a certain amount of self-congratulatory exaggeration, that "there is not a single branch of industry that does not produce goods from blueprints, technical specifications, or technological documentation devised in the USSR and transmitted to China."[20] Between 1954 and 1963 the USSR reportedly provided the PRC with over 24,000 complete sets of scientific-technical documents, including 1,400 designs for major enterprises—mostly free of charge.[21] By 1951 China had received 32,000 copies of books and journals published by Soviet academies and educational institutions. By the end of 1952, 3,114 Soviet book titles and thousands of Soviet scientific and technical manuals were translated and printed in China; some three million copies of Soviet books, already translated into Chinese, were imported from the Soviet Union. Interlibrary loan arrangements were instituted, and in 1956 the library of the Soviet Academy of Sciences sent 70,000 volumes of various scientific writings to China.[22] Between 1949 and 1955 over 20 million copies of 3,000 Soviet books on science and technology were published in China.[23] The interchange was not entirely one way: the PRC turned over to the Soviet Union about 2,000 sets of technical documents during the same period.[24] But as the ratio indicates, benefits redounded disproportionately to the Chinese. This was to typify the exchange: the Soviets traded material reward for political loyalty.

Much of the technology transferred was embodied in human resource investment. Some 8,500 technical specialists and 1,500 specialists in science, education, health care, and culture came to China for prolonged visits between 1950 and 1960, most of whom were engaged in economic construction.[25] East European countries sent another 1,200 specialists to train and relate their experiences to the Chinese. Among these visitors were prominent members of the Soviet Academy of Sciences, who helped with problems ranging from the establishment of Chinese research institutes to assistance in drafting the Twelve-Year Plan for Science and Technology.[26] Soviet advisers played a significant role in the drafting of the First Five-Year Plan, for example, and when controversy on the "general line for the transition period" (*guodu shidi zongluxian*) arose over whether "socialist construction" should proceed in small steps or in great leaps, they supported the former.[27] For their part, the Chinese dispatched several hundred delegations, including thousands of Chinese scholars and scientists, to the Soviet Union, where they participated in Soviet professional meetings, toured Soviet scientific installations, and so forth.[28] Between 1950 and 1960 more than 38,000 Chinese "students and trainees" were accepted by leading Soviet industrial enterprises, research centers, and institutions of higher learning. Between 1949 and 1966, about 10,000 Chinese engineers, technicians, and workers, and more than 11,000 students, most at undergraduate levels, completed their course of study in the Soviet Union. An estimated 1,000 scientists from the Chinese Academy of Science also received advanced training in the research institutes of the Soviet Academy of Sciences.[29] An additional 8,173 Chinese traveled to the Soviet Union for practical on-the-job training in connection with the industrial enterprises being built with Soviet assistance.[30]

The entire Chinese educational and research structure was patterned after the Soviet model, and was to retain its original structure—and spirit—with remarkable fidelity long after the relationship broke down. The attempt to train Chinese professionals and educators was remarkably pervasive. The USSR claims that between 1949 and 1960, Soviet experts helped to train 19,000 Chinese instructors (17,000 in China and about 1,700 in the Soviet Union, constituting "about a quarter of the teaching personnel at Chinese colleges"), thereby transmitting their influence to upcoming generations.[31] Russian displaced English as the premier foreign language, and the PRC's decision to "lean to one side" entailed a taboo on "bourgeois" art and literature; thus the authorities prohibited the importation and circulation of American and West European books and publications. For more than a decade, Chinese school children were deprived of exposure to liberal Western culture and scholarship and steeped in Soviet socialism.[32]

Yet this vastly ambitious effort at cultural transfer did not end well. In July 1960, the Soviets suddenly withdrew their 1,390 remaining specialists from China, "tore up 343 contracts and supplementary contracts concerning experts, and scrapped 256 projects of scientific and technical cooperation"; supplies of machinery and equipment were also suspended.[33] By this time only 130 of the 256 projects jointly undertaken had been completed; many projects, such as the massive Sanmen Gorge Power Station, were left uncompleted. Bilateral trade declined precipitously, though it was never allowed to cease altogether.[34] The devastating impact this had on Chinese modernization efforts, overlapping as it did with domestic natural disasters and a border war with India, underlined the value of the assistance hitherto rendered (as the Soviets of course intended that it should).

In view of its mutually disappointing denouement, which would embitter Sino-Soviet relations for the next two decades, the question naturally arises whether the end of the period of close friendship was somehow implicit in the beginning. The Chinese subsequently quibbled about the stinting terms of the alliance. While China received U.S. $300 million at one percent interest, other suppliants were granted larger packages (e.g., Stalin granted Poland $450 million at zero interest), giving rise to the rumor that Mao had actually requested ten times the amount given.[35] Of the total amount lent between 1950 and 1955, 61.5 percent consisted of military aid, much of which the Chinese expended in the Korean War, and the Chinese resented their disproportionate share of this burden. As one Chinese general put it, it was "totally unfair for the PRC to bear all the expenses of the Korean War."[36] When the Soviets returned the naval base at Port Arthur in October 1954, they included an assessment of the buildings and material and other assets in the value of the loan. In the end, only 26.1 percent of the total loan consisted of actual developmental assistance. All credits provided were in rubles, a nonconvertible currency, so Chinese repayments took the form of raw material exports, which were undervalued in the exchange.[37] One estimate for the 1957–59 period calculated that the Chinese returned at least 40 percent of their trade earnings from the USSR to pay the interest owed.[38] The Soviets insisted on continuing to collect debt service installments even during the 1959–62 period, when such payments were severely straining Chinese export capabilities. China even exported grain in 1960, when millions of peasants were starving (the Chinese still managed to complete loan repayments by 1965, without much sense of gratitude).[39] Much of the economic aid was invested in projects concentrated along the Sino-Soviet border, particularly in the northeast, long an object of Russian imperialist interest.

If from the Chinese perspective the Soviets were niggardly and self-serving, from the Soviet point of view the Chinese were manipulative ingrates. Beginning in the late 1950s China expressed more and more interest in the new secret accomplishments of the Soviet Union, particularly in fields with potential military application. Chinese students and scholars in the Soviet Union made special efforts to become involved in classified weapons projects. Sometimes Chinese host institutions even tried to change the lecture topics of visiting Soviet scientists to open up restricted areas of research. The Chinese on the other hand allegedly initiated a policy of "blanket secrecy" about everything pertaining to China, from natural resources to borders (e.g., China forbade Soviet scientists to publish joint research if it included maps). Particularly during the Great Leap Forward, Soviet scientists and technical advisers were cavalierly ignored in the wholehearted Chinese reliance on the ideological enthusiasm of the masses.

If the Sino-Soviet program of technocultural transfer was in many respects disappointing, it was not necessarily unsuccessful. Paradoxically, it seems to have been *both* objectively successful and subjectively disappointing. Success manifested itself first of all in an impressive economic performance. Robert Dernberger, on the basis of "a simple economic model with fixed coefficients," has estimated that China's rate of growth during the First FYP period (1953–57) would have been 20–30 percent less without imports of Soviet capital equipment.[40] It is perhaps not entirely accidental that the duration of the Soviet aid program coincided with the most impressive phase of Chinese industrial growth (during the period of the First FYP, annual industrial growth rate averaged 15 percent, GNP growth 7–8 percent), and that the abrupt cessation of aid coincided with the onset of China's deepest depression. It is also worth noting that most of the Chinese grievances about the aid program were not publicized until after it had been suspended (though early complaints surfaced during the Hundred Flowers).

Notwithstanding Chinese complaints, Soviet aid can hardly be termed ungenerous. If the then current international exchange rate of 1 yuan to 1.7 rubles is used, fully one-third of all Soviet assistance to bloc countries was given to the PRC, amounting to some U.S. $1.56 billion in aid during the eleven years the treaty was active.[41] It is true that most of the aid consisted of loans rather than grants. Yet Soviet payment terms could not be said to be unfair, relative either to the terms of other international aid agreements at the time or to the USSR's ability to afford extensive philanthropy amid efforts to rebuild from the rubble of World War II. No convincing evidence of exploitative pricing has been found; interest rates were in the 1–2 percent range, well below the 5–6 percent on long-term loans charged by the World Bank at the time. To be sure, repayment periods appear to have been significantly shorter.[42] Moreover, in 1956, Khrushchev suggested gradual reduction of Soviet technical advisers in the PRC, and no additional credits were granted over the next two years.[43] On the occasion of the Twenty-first CPSU Congress (February 1959), the USSR offered a seven-year, $5 billion loan that provided for construction of seventy-eight new enterprises, but the political atmosphere had by this time so deteriorated that little of this aid package was actually delivered. An interest-free payments moratorium was granted in 1960, at the height of the famine precipitated by the Great Leap, as was a 1961 interest-free loan of sugar.

What are we to make of this peculiar amalgam of success and disappointment? The immediate success of the aid program seems undeniable from the perspective of either the recipient (in terms of its contribution to economic growth) or the donor (in terms of setting China on a "convergent" course of socialist development). But economic success did not earn enduring political allegiance. No sooner was aid discontinued than the Chinese leadership began grousing about the flaws in the Stalinist model and making tentative steps away from it. The early record of rapid progress toward both socialism and economic development was not to be repeated, as the regime felt constrained to sacrifice the one for the other. An essentially convergent structure has been a more lasting legacy of this early period of socialist solidarity, owing largely to the blunders committed by the Maoist leadership in its efforts at innovation (as we shall see in the following chapter).

Why was such an objectively successful developmental plan so promptly (if ineffectively) spurned? In contrast to, say, the concurrent Marshall Plan, which imposed new structures on shattered economies in the political vacuum left by vanquished and discredited regimes, the Soviet aid program involved a more delicate transfer of institutions to an economy that was no less devastated but led by a victorious and proud political elite. In its hunger for legitimacy the new CCP regime was inclined to commit an elementary attribution error in allocating

praise and blame for setbacks encountered in revolutionary change—
monopolizing credit for successes and blaming the USSR for any lapses.
Moreover, whereas the Marshall Plan introduced political structures
not entirely alien to the national histories of the host countries, a Soviet-
style command economy led by a Leninist political apparatus was quite
new in Chinese political experience, and the impact of its newness was
exacerbated by simultaneous introduction of a crash course in industrialization. There was an understandable tendency to exaggerate Chinese
innovations in the process of assimilation and to downplay the Chinese
model's close family resemblance to the original. For equally understandable reasons, the Soviets took umbrage.

Still, the impact of Chinese departures from the Soviet developmental
model should not be exaggerated in any attempt to explain the split.
Just as the Chinese turn from the Soviet model was based not solely on
the discontinuation of material aid, Soviet repudiation of such Chinese
innovations as the Great Leap Forward and the People's Commune was
based on more than their departure from Soviet precept. Underlying
both was a Chinese disagreement with Soviet foreign policy toward
the bloc and toward the imperialist camp and the Third World, which
in Chinese eyes was based on a fundamental misreading of Marxist-
Leninist doctrine.[44] This disagreement arose not because of but despite
the aid program. From the insight that the Soviet leadership of the
world revolution could be mistaken, it was a short step to the inference
that their approach to economic development might also be wrong.[45]
The Soviets were, of course, highly sensitive to the explosive implications of such a line of reasoning and energetically sought to squelch
it, using ideological arguments, bloc policy, control of the aid spigot,
whatever came to hand. Bitterness and guilt over this cardinal violation of international class solidarity was then "projected" in the form
of mutual recriminations, and historically overgeneralized to discolor
good as well as bad aspects of the relationship. But once the Chinese
had committed themselves to the proposition that it was they who were
right, national pride and the tendency to equate legitimacy with infallibility made it impossible to reconsider their premises objectively.

CHAPTER 2

Divergent Development

The Soviet withdrawal of advisers and other forms of aid was intended to ostracize and punish the Chinese for their ideological and political impudence, and it did in fact drive them into a position of economic isolation. Bilateral trade, after peaking at U.S. $2.09 billion in 1959, continued to decline through the 1960s, reaching its nadir ($4.72 million) in 1970. China might in theory have turned to Western markets and financial institutions. But the increasingly radical ideological preferences that dominated Chinese foreign policy beginning in the early 1960s, spreading to domestic politics with the Cultural Revolution, inhibited contact with contaminating capitalist economies. Thus total value of exports and imports also fell, making a brief recovery in 1966 only to relapse until 1971. Indeed, contact with all Western culture was interdicted, and there were polemics against Western music and dance, and public ridicule and other sanctions for those educated in the West, even for those who had contact with people outside China. The PRC thus in effect adopted an extreme form of import-substitution policy: as a proportion of world trade, PRC foreign trade fell from a 1.4 percent share in the 1950s to 1.1 percent in the 1960s, to a low of 0.8 percent in the 1970s—compared with 32 percent for the developed countries and 23 percent for low-income developing countries.[1]

Yet it would be going too far to say that China's decision to blaze its own developmental trail was simply an invention born of necessity, for there are indications of Chinese dissatisfaction with the Soviet model well before Soviet advisers were withdrawn. "In the early stages of Liberation, we had no experience of managing the economy of the entire nation," Mao noted in 1962. "So in the period of the First Five-Year Plan we could do no more than copy the Soviet Union's methods, *although we never felt altogether satisfied about it*" (emphasis added).[2] Mao's dissatisfaction first became articulate after Khrushchev's critique of Stalin signaled Soviet openness to new experiments and legitimated a reevaluation of the old orthodoxy.[3] Mao focused his criticism on three features of the Soviet model: (1) the doctrine of "primitive socialist accumulation," which Stalin had borrowed from Preobrazhensky;

(2) the "theory of productive forces"; and (3) the Stalinist conception of leadership.

The first public record of Mao's reservations concerning the doctrine of primitive socialist accumulation appears in "On the Ten Major Relationships," enunciated two months after the Twentieth CPSU Congress, in which he criticizes the "lopsided stress on heavy industry to the neglect of agriculture and light industry."

We have done better than the Soviet Union and a number of Eastern European countries. The prolonged failure of the Soviet Union to reach the highest pre-October Revolution level in grain output, the grave problems arising from the glaring disequilibrium between the development of heavy industry and that of light industry . . . such problems do not exist in our country.[4]

Mao faulted Stalin for "concentrating everything in the hands of the central authorities, shackling the local authorities and denying them the right of independent action." This was, he said, "draining the pond to catch the fish"; that is, it did not provide enough material incentives to the peasants, nor sufficient opportunity for political participation. Like capitalism, this resulted in "mercilessly fleecing" the rural masses.[5] Mao rejected the idea of development carried out by a privileged group, proceeding through distinct phases. The whole nation must be engaged at once in the developmental endeavor, leaving none behind. Unified planning and discipline under a strong center were still essential, but not ministerial domination of development through a "tall" bureaucratic hierarchy.

The theory of productive forces, as first formulated in the Soviet Union, maintains that once the relations of production have been socialized (i.e., expropriated by the state), further progress toward the communist utopia would be achieved through growth of the forces of production (i.e., the investment of capital and labor, and the application of advanced science and technology). This theory was incorporated into the resolution of the Eighth Party Congress, which stated that following the CCP's recently completed transition to socialism, "the essence of this contradiction is a contradiction between the advanced social system and the backward social productive forces."[6] Mao seemed to have no quarrel with this formulation at the time, but as it became clear that it implied the neglect ("extinction") of class struggle, he began to have second thoughts. "The basic contradictions in socialist society are still those between the relations of production and the productive forces, and between the superstructure and the economic base," he wrote in the wake of the Hundred Flowers. In this and later statements he made clear his conviction that class struggle had survived the transition to socialism and that society should continue to mobilize around this cleavage, accepting his own definition of the class enemy. Stalin, he said, had failed to take note of the contradiction between advancing forces of production and stagnant relations of production.[7] In counterpoint, Mao argued that at certain periods, the superstructure might be more decisive than the economic base, the relations of production more decisive than the forces of production.[8] This enabled him to attribute continuing bourgeois influence under socialism to an autonomous (and relatively degenerate) superstructure, and to conceive of the next stage of the continuing revolution in cultural rather than economic terms.

While he himself became more ideologically assertive, Mao's notion of the proper role of the party hierarchy beneath him became increasingly populist and egalitarian in his later years. In this context, the Soviet bureaucratic hierarchy was a bête noire. He became acutely suspicious of propensities toward "bureaucratism" (*guanliaozhuyi*), and experimented with various organizational alternatives, notably decentralization and the devolution of responsibility for health care, education, welfare, even capital accumulation, to lower administrative levels. The masses, he contended, were the creators of world history, and elites should learn from the masses rather than attempt to preach or talk down to them. Hence he began to encourage active popular monitoring of the bureaucracy via the "mass line," or "mass criticism."[9] In this context he also questioned the Soviet renunciation of "storming": "This utter repudiation of crash programs and accelerated work is too absolute. . . . If one wants to overtake the advanced, one cannot help having crash programs."[10] Correctly (from a Weberian perspective) identifying bureaucratism with an ethos of impersonal professionalism, Mao rejected it. His comments in the spring of 1958 capture the spirit of this critique:

There are two lines for building socialism: is it better to go about it coldly and deliberately, or boldly and joyfully? . . . In forty years, the Soviet Union has been able to produce only such a little bit of food and other stuff. If, in eighteen years, we can equal what they have done in the past forty years, . . . we should do precisely that. For there are more of us, and the political conditions are different, too; we are livelier, and there is more Leninism here.[11]

Without having conceived of a systemic alternative to the Soviet-style command planning that epitomized the "cold" bureaucratic approach to modernization, Mao thus repeatedly interrupted or superseded plan timetables with spontaneous ("hot") mass campaigns of various sorts. Yet his ideological antipathy to capitalism also led him to reject reliance on the market as an alternative to central planning.

The Maoist attempt to articulate a coherent positive alternative to command planning was most fully realized in practice during the Great Leap Forward, which was conceived as a massive breakthrough against the problems of bureaucratism and relative rural underdevelopment that had been allowed to accumulate during the preceding drive to socialize the means of production. With the Leap, Mao was striking out on a distinctive Chinese path, and the Soviet Union was neither informed of the decision nor consulted. From his comments at the time we may infer that this departure from precedent was quite deliberate. Whereas he began his speech of June 28, 1958, with the admonition, "we should not criticize the Soviet Union," he then made clear that neither did this entail slavish emulation:

We must not eat pre-cooked food. . . . We have learned from the Soviet Union in the past, we are still learning today, and we shall learn in the future. Nevertheless our study must be combined with our own concrete conditions. We must say to them: We learn from you, from whom then did you learn? Why cannot we create something of our own? [12]

Underlining his point with humor, Mao mocked the Chinese excessive deference he had once striven to encourage, recalling that for three years he had not been able to eat eggs and chicken soup because an article had been published in the Soviet Union alleging that eggs and chicken soup were unhealthy. "Whenever a Chinese artist painted a picture of me with Stalin, I was always shown shorter than Stalin." [13]

The Great Leap Forward negated the Soviet model in two ways. First, it substituted spontaneously initiated, mass economic activity for the blueprints worked out by bureaucratic planners. Second, it gave great economic and political authority to local and regional units, specifically the provinces and the freshly minted People's Communes (the regions, which had coordinated the activities of several provinces on behalf of the central party apparatus, were therewith abolished). Mao's goal was an economy in which only major macroeconomic variables and the large-scale modern enterprises would be centralized, leaving other activities to the provinces and the localities to manage, using technologies appropriate to their size and resource bases, on the basis of fiscal "self-reliance." [14]

The Maoist alternative to the Soviet developmental "road" was a strange entity, neither market nor plan, neither democratic nor centralized. In place of an economic market Mao seemed to envisage a political market, in which the leadership (and above all he, personally) would coin the ideological currency, consisting of a set of abstract slogans (e.g., "Walk on two legs," "Go all out, aim high, strive to build socialism faster, better, and more economically"), then allow this currency to circulate, to be "spent" or "invested" with some flexibility on the basis of local circumstances. The relevant actors in this market were not private firms or individual consumers, but work units functioning under the authority of communal and provincial party authorities. The centralized planning bureaucracy was thus largely circumvented, and planned targets were regularly superseded by more ambitious spontaneously generated objectives (spontaneously generated, that is, with Mao's encouragement). The State Statistical Bureau was "captured" by local party authorities intent upon manipulating statistics to "surpass Great Britain and the United States" (*chao Ying gan Mei*). This led to a general inflation of production estimates, which in turn severely impoverished local units when they were forced to forfeit a portion of their harvest corresponding to their predicted rather than their actual output.[15]

This populist assault on bureaucratism entailed a general tendency to devalue expertise, and in fact local enterprise management was sometimes taken over by small production groups of ordinary workers. Any hierarchy of income was likewise assailed, to be replaced (ideally) by distribution in kind, according to need rather than output or merit. The division of labor was disrupted, particularly in the rural communes, in an attempt to approach the communist ideal of a more multifaceted self-realization of the personality. The doctrine of primitive accumulation, which had previously accorded top priority to heavy industry, was nominally revised, giving agriculture first priority, light industry second, heavy industry last. Paradoxically, this was not accompanied by any change in actual budgetary allocations; agriculture and small-scale rural industry were rather encouraged to rely on "labor accumulation" (substituting labor for capital through mass mobilization, mostly for infrastructural projects).[16]

The Great Leap was not deliberately designed to flout the Soviet "leading role" in the bloc, but implicitly the challenge was clear. In the first few months, China began to tout the Leap as a significant theoretical innovation. Bulgaria and Albania, like China relatively underdeveloped agricultural economies, quickly showed interest in the new model, launching their own versions a year or so afterward.[17] In 1959, 127 East European delegations visited the PRC and 104 Chinese delegations visited Eastern Europe to promote the Great Leap Forward and People's Commune.[18] In North Korea, Kim Il Sung's 1958 *Chollima* (flying horse) campaign was clearly modeled after the Leap (though less extreme). Khrushchev was thrown on the ideological defensive.

In a sense, Khrushchev had only himself to blame for this fraternal challenge, for it was he who had initiated the critique of Stalin in 1956, lifting the dead weight of orthodoxy from others as well as disencumbering himself. Mao and Khrushchev were in this sense soul mates. They were also similarly concerned with refurbishing the appeal of Marxism-Leninism as an economic powerhouse for developing economies. Khrushchev had been first within the bloc to broach discussion of the prospect of overtaking capitalism within the foreseeable future,[19] also first to introduce economic hypergrowth as an overriding criterion for successful socialism. Mao eagerly and promptly seized upon both themes when Khrushchev articulated them at the November 1957 international party conference. The obvious Soviet derivation of the Chinese commitment to economic overachievement is evident in Mao's parallel pledge at the same conference. As Liu Shaoqi put it two weeks after Mao's return:

In 15 years, the Soviet Union can catch up with and surpass the United States in the output of the most important industrial and agricultural products. In the same period of time, we ought to catch up with and surpass the United Kingdom in the output of iron, steel and other major industrial products.[20]

Just as Khrushchev revived dormant hopes of the passage to communism within the foreseeable future,[21] so too did Mao suggest such a timetable for China. Just as Khrushchev instituted a wholesale decentralization of the Soviet economic structure in 1957 (with the introduction of the *sovnarkhozy*), Mao's Great Leap resulted in a similar (actually less radical) decentralization.[22]

There were, to be sure, novel elements to the Chinese approach, notably the unleashing of a heaven-storming populism that wound up derogating trained expertise. Still, Khrushchev might have overlooked such national idiosyncrasies and focused on the parallels had it not come on the heels of a series of ideological *qua* foreign policy disagreements, in which he felt his leadership was publicly challenged.

Why was Mao so eager to challenge his patron? Although both men were ambitious innovators, their revolutions were "out of sync," greatly complicating efforts at coordination. In 1956, for example, Khrushchev took his first serious step toward de-Stalinization (in his secret speech to the Twentieth CPSU Congress, to be more closely examined later); this came just as Mao's government was embarking on its effort to complete the collectivization of agriculture and the socialization of the means of production in industry and commerce. China, still under the aegis of a confident first-generation revolutionary leadership, was by 1958 still in the post-Hundred Flowers backlash against bourgeois liberalization that had triggered the antirightist movement and would culminate in the Great Leap, all of which was conceived in terms of continuing the revolution. Khrushchev, having defined his own leadership in contradistinction to the generation of dogmatic old revolutionaries, and weathered the first backlash of right-wing revolts in Eastern Europe and left-wing conspiracy by the "antiparty faction" representing continuity with the past, wished to push his line through to the end once these setbacks had been successfully dealt with. Any Chinese suggestion that Khrushchev represented deviation from orthodoxy could only be viewed as objective collusion with his most dangerous domestic opponents. Thus in a 1958 interview he remarked that the People's Commune was "actually reactionary." At the Twenty-first Congress of the CPSU he dismissed the Leap as "egalitarian communism" that tried to "leap historical stages" (*chao jieduan*).[23] He seemed particularly irked by Mao's presumption that China would arrive at the communist utopia first, pointing out that the PRC as yet lacked the material conditions needed to obviate competition for scarce goods. "If we stated that we were introducing communism at a time when the cup was not yet full, it would not be possible to drink from it according to need."[24] In July 1959 in Poznan, Khrushchev delivered a sharp attack on the notion of a People's Commune, observing that those who had tried something similar in the USSR "had a poor understanding of what Communism is and how it is to be built."[25] That events were to vindicate Khrushchev's critique could not realistically be expected to endear him to Mao, whose own position was thereby doubly jeopardized.

Rarely in human history has a bold and hopeful new venture been so soundly repudiated by its consequences (abetted by fortuitous adverse circumstances, such as inclement weather) as was the Great Leap Forward. During the "three bad years" (1960–62), gross national output dropped by 20–30 percent from the high point reached during the first year of the Leap, per capita income by roughly 32 percent, and industrial production by 40–45 percent.[26] The social ramifications of this great depression have been shown to be even more disastrous than previously assumed, causing mass starvation throughout the country and even having a Malthusian impact on demographic statistics.[27] Although the Leap was never publicly renounced, primarily because of Mao's persisting ego involvement, the attempt to forge a distinctive Chinese approach to economic development had to be relinquished. For the moment, Mao's moderate rivals were allowed to pick up the pieces, introducing *sauve qui peut* policies to salvage the economy. Private plots and rural markets were revived, while the communes were decentralized (i.e., shifting the "unit of accounting" first to the brigade, then to the production team) and somewhat reduced in size. The most ambitious radical experiments (e.g., the communal mess halls, the free supply system, most of the rural small-scale industries, the half-work half-study school system) were ruthlessly "chopped down."

The post-Leap rescue operation could not be systematized to form a coherent program, however, because of various ideological inhibitions. Several economists, the most prominent and penetrating of whom was Sun Yefang, opened discussion of the "law of value" and "commodity production," pressing for reforms in the direction of "market socialism," involving greater ambit for individual enterprise and markets in the countryside, quasi-autonomous enterprises controlled indirectly by parametric planning in the cities. Another group (viz., Liu Shaoqi, Bo Yibo) advocated a GDR-style approach, involving restoration of a renovated command planning system, managed with greater professionalization and efficiency: decentralization of accounting and managerial responsibility to the firm, the organization of "trusts" to coordinate the division of labor and markets along sectoral lines, and distribution of wages according to productivity or meritocratic criteria. Although limited experiments were conducted to promote each of these approaches, neither ever really attained the status of a "line." The continuing anti-Soviet animus precluded open recourse to a neo-Stalinist model, while Mao's growing obsession with "revisionism" and the "capitalist road" constrained the pursuit of market reforms.

Meanwhile, radical self-assurance had been so shaken by the Leap's debacle that none of the Maoists ever really "resolutely grasped" the developmental nettle again. The next stage of Mao's continuing revolution—the Great Proletarian Cultural Revolution—restricted its focus to the cultural superstructure and the relations of production, unleashing the army to suppress the young rebels whenever they threatened to disrupt the functioning of the productive forces. During the early 1970s, the rudiments of the command planning system were restored under the auspices of Zhou Enlai and Deng Xiaoping—albeit amid continuing ambivalence, as indicated by the recurrence of radical criticism campaigns, which demanded that economic policies be evaluated on (radical) political criteria.[28]

Thus the initial Chinese attempt to create an alternative socialist approach to development came to a confusing and desultory end. The attempt to amend orthodox Soviet planning practices to accord with Maoist moral precepts proved unfeasible under conditions of underdevelopment—though it was revamped specifically to cope with those conditions. The conspicuous failure of that attempt set the leadership's planning and developmental agencies tugging and hauling in various directions in their efforts to redefine Chinese developmental socialism. They moved in directions equally divergent from Mao's ideological precepts, but opposite to each other: toward a greater role for the market on the one hand, and toward a new and more technocratically efficient form of centralized planning apparatus on the other.[29] Yet even as Mao's bold departure from Stalinism foundered, his prestige remained sufficiently intact that neither of these alternatives could be fully explored. The Maoist ideological position seemed to harden even as its fallibility as a guideline for economic development became obvious, leaving in its wake a system that was neither very centralized nor very planned. Meanwhile, the Soviets went their own way, repudiating Khrushchev's high-stakes foreign policy adventurism and domestic revisionism ("harebrained schemes") that had so irked the Chinese, and gravitating after the Czech invasion to a more conservative posture under Brezhnev. This left Mao free quietly to abandon his defense of Stalin and shift to a more thoroughgoing radicalism. By the same token, the presence of Maoism to Brezhnev's left may have dimmed the prospects for reform in the USSR. Like two wrestlers circling in a ring, the two regimes would shift ideological postures while remaining diametrically opposed.

CHAPTER 3

Convergence and Its Complications

The premise of this chapter is that if two countries have convergent political systems, they are more likely, *ceteris paribus,* to have amicable bilateral relations than if they do not. It is true that early Sino-Soviet solidarity disintegrated even though it was based on explicit modeling. Yet this was an artificially imposed isomorphism, a Galatea-Pygmalion relationship in which modeling implied mastery, emulation implied self-abnegating subordination and dependency. Surely a convergence voluntarily arrived at, without sacrifice of sovereignty, would in contrast facilitate implicit mutual understanding and more ready agreement? Should not shared structures, shared ideologies, shared goals, in the normal course of things be expected to promote cooperation?

In the era since the original revolutionary vision was tacitly abandoned and the need acknowledged to "reform" Leninist structures, an interest in the prospect of socioeconomic convergence experienced a revival in both countries. The following discussion of this prospect will revolve around two issues: First, have the two countries come to see one another as more alike or more different? Second, how much concord has actually been achieved in reform projects (are the two now on the same developmental "road")?

The Reconstruction of Images

Throughout the history of Sino-Soviet relations, changing mutual perceptions have served as a useful barometer to the emotional climate of the relationship. To the extent that the two countries perceive themselves as typologically generic, they will more easily find points of tangency to interact with and learn from one another.

As we have seen, the early period of fraternal solidarity coincided with celebrations of ideological and structural identity in which any sign of deviation was repressed (by the junior partner). Whereas this was not the sole cause of the parting of ways, the rift at the end of the 1950s did coincide with China's break with the Soviet model and adoption of its own alternative developmental "road." Chinese and Soviet images of one another accentuated these differences and elevated them to the level of principle. Polarization of relations between these two mirror images climaxed in border conflict and nuclear threats at the end of the 1960s. Reversal of this self-reinforcing negative stereotypy was to take more than ten years. We shall examine each side of the polemic in turn.

Chinese Perceptions of the USSR

To Chinese radicals of the 1960s, Soviet "revisionism" was a touchstone of error rivaling capitalism, more insidious because less easily detected.[1] Moreover, these two apparent antitheses (capitalism and Soviet socialism) were found to have an underlying kinship, in the sense that the latter led logically to the former (via a "capitalist road"). The eruption of radical rhetoric in the Cultural Revolution was to a considerable extent a reprise of the anti-Soviet polemics of the early 1960s, in which Liu Shaoqi became "China's Khrushchev." Following the Soviet invasion of Czechoslovakia in 1968, Zhou Enlai made the first Chinese reference to "Soviet social imperialism" (another ideological oxymoron), thereby bringing Soviet foreign policy into play. In the fall of 1968, both Zhou and Mao listed the USSR ahead of the United States in the litany of international threats.[2] The late Maoist conception of the "three worlds" unveiled in Deng Xiaoping's speech to the Sixth Session of the UN General Assembly (April 10, 1974),[3] the first Chinese reformulation of the international order since the concept of two "intermediate zones" was introduced in 1964, conceived of the Soviet and American systems as typologically generic (i.e., both were "superpowers," both sought to impose "hegemony" on the Second and Third Worlds). The model placed the two superpowers in a position analogous to that of the bourgeoisie, China and the rest of the Third World in the position of the proletariat, and posited class struggle between them.[4] Moreover, in a sort of internationalization of Marx's model of capitalist collapse (*Zusammenbruchstheorie*), these two bullying Leviathans were historically doomed to be superseded by those whom they had once exploited.[5] A major theoretical article appeared in the aftermath of CCP's Eleventh Congress in August 1977 which, however, gave the three worlds theory a more specifically anti-Soviet reading, foreclosing any immediate prospect of reconciliation and providing a basis for a broad united front against the USSR.[6] This interpretation was to prevail through the early 1980s.

In early 1979 the CCP circulated a document to officials that concluded that the CPSU should no longer be viewed as "revisionist," that the main threat from the Soviets was merely one of "hegemonism" (military expansionism). This verdict was inadvertently made public in an academic article published in Heilongjiang the same year asserting that the Soviet Union might be termed a "socialist" country.[7] Though that issue of the journal was hastily withdrawn, the antirevisionist polemic was quietly suspended at this time, and the PRC's focus shifted from domestic to foreign policy ("hegemonism"). In early 1980 an article in *Renmin Ribao* (*People's Daily*) repudiated the so-called Nine Commentaries, which had authoritatively defined CCP ideological differences with the CPSU in 1963–64. At about the same time, "Revisionism Street" in Beijing, on which the Soviet embassy is located, reverted to its pre-Cultural Revolution appellation: North Center Street. In fact, though the Soviet Union practiced hegemonism abroad, one commentary opined, "its internal policies remain socialist in nature."[8]

This was a period of policy reorientation within the CCP leadership, during which Hu Yaobang, in an "internal" speech never published, drew attention to the parallels between Khrushchevian "revisionism" and the post-Mao reforms, ruefully concluding that the CPSU might even be due a Chinese apology.[9] Deng rejected Hu's suggestion, and the USSR's socialist status did not receive official recognition until 1984.[10] Nonetheless, one by one, ideological epithets fell by the wayside—the 1982 Constitution dropped "socialist imperialism" and "contemporary revisionism" (both included in the 1978 Constitution)—and in 1982–83 the Chinese muted discussion of the three worlds theory, in apparent deference to Soviet sensibilities. In Hu Yaobang's Report to the Twelfth Congress in September 1982 and Zhao Ziyang's Report to the Sixth National People's Congress (NPC) in June 1983, no united front against hegemonism was mentioned; both emphasized that China pursued an "independent foreign policy" and desired a peaceful international environment.[11] "Hegemonism" was still listed among world threats, but this sobriquet was now shared with the United States. Beginning in the early 1980s, the most likely source of war was no longer "Soviet hegemonism," but "Soviet-American competition." Addressing a press conference in Japan in July 1983, Hu Yaobang said: "We hope for the normalization of relations with the Soviet Union. . . . I think in the end they will go that way. Normalization will be to the advantage of both our peoples and to peace throughout the world." At the Thirteenth CCP Congress in November 1987, antihegemonism was mentioned in reference to past Chinese foreign policy but omitted from a discussion of foreign policy in the future; at the Seventh NPC (March–April 1988), Li Peng spoke hopefully of the prospect of "peaceful coexistence" with the USSR (though he still mentioned antihegemonism).

The newfound Chinese interest in the Soviet Union was based only partly on strategic calculations, and partly on the fact that this was another socialist system whose experiences with the problems of economic modernization might be relevant to the bold reforms on which the PRC was now embarking. As the Soviet interest in reform was slower to awaken than the Chinese, PRC journalists first began to explore new developments in Eastern Europe. Superficial reportage on economic successes and failures in those countries began to appear as early as January 1977, but interest was greatly stimulated by a conference on the Yugoslav economy sponsored by the editorial board of *Shijie Jingji* (*World Economy*) in late May 1978, many of the papers for which were later published in the journal. Interest later shifted to Romania and Hungary, obviously focusing on those countries with which China had amicable relations, but based on the premise that economic reform could spur production and was of possible relevance to the PRC. The delegations that visited Hungary at the end of 1979 and in 1980 were particularly impressed by the three years of preparatory study that preceded their reforms, and by the establishment of a Committee on Reform of the Economic System, staffed by theoretical economists and practical economists, to draw up the blueprint for the New Economic Mechanism before it was launched in 1968.[12]

By the latter half of 1984, there is a conspicuous shift of tone from stressing weak points and crises to a focus on Soviet achievements and the growth being achieved.[13] Most of this reportage was "classified" (*neibu*), perhaps because of concern about American sensibilities, perhaps for fear of the possible domestic demonstration effect of such information.[14] Thanks to the intelligence efforts of Gilbert Rozman, at least a synopsis of some of these articles has become accessible to Western scholars.[15] From this sampling it would appear that ideological impediments to Sino-Soviet rapprochement had by the end of 1985 been greatly mitigated. Among the flattering themes recurring in this literature were that the October Revolution was the turning point in world history, that the Soviet Union played a largely positive role in the Chinese revolution, that China achieved its most rapid economic growth when it was following the Soviet model before 1958, that the Soviet Union has in the 1980s moved toward reform, and that its prospects are good.[16] Both the PRC and the USSR are recognized as socialist systems, and socialism is inherently superior to capitalism, with which it is inevitably in conflict. Capitalism is inherently decadent and historically doomed to be replaced by socialism (whatever the empirical flaws in the latter). Even with regard to foreign policy, where it is acknowledged that the Soviet Union and the PRC have conflicting security interests, the history of Soviet-American relations is largely interpreted in favor of the Soviet side.[17]

Beginning in 1985, Chinese interest in the Soviet Union began to focus squarely on Gorbachev's reform efforts, and to transcend the specialist and *neibu* audience and appeal to a broader range of intellectual interests. Between the April 1985 CPSU Central Committee Plenum and the Twenty-seventh CPSU Congress, the Chinese press was fairly cautious in its reports, focusing mainly on personnel reshuffles in the leadership. This was in the Chinese view a "preparatory stage of *perestroika*" in all spheres.[18] The Twenty-seventh CPSU Congress (February 1986), though not widely heralded among Western observers, kindled in China widespread interest as an event marking a new stage of Soviet development, and since that time there has been extensive Chinese commentary on the nature of Soviet reforms.[19] Chinese observers paid close attention to the parts of the Political Report that outlined the importance of *glasnost'*,[20] and underscored the need "to carry out economic and political reforms together . . . so that the political reorganization creates opportunities for and removes obstacles to economic reforms."[21]

This notion had a vast ripple effect in China.[22] It made its recognizable reappearance in a speech to the Politburo Standing Committee by Deng Xiaoping on June 28, 1986, in which Deng said: "If we only carry out economic reform and not political reform we will not be able to carry the reform of the economic structure through to the end."[23] This statement was sine qua non in licensing a movement that quickly snowballed, becoming the most extensive incarnation of "one hundred flowers blooming, one hundred schools of thought contending" since that policy was first introduced in 1956–57. There was a direct causal connection between this intellectual "blooming" and the abortive student demonstrations that swept Chinese cities in December 1986. And there was a less immediate link to the far bigger Tiananmen movement of April–May 1989, which culminated in bloody suppression on June 4. Clearly Soviet reform had caught the imagination of the avant-garde of Chinese public opinion, and Gorbachev's own charismatic personality also had a measurable impact on the movement when he visited Beijing for the summit during the democracy demonstrations on May 15–18.

Soviet Perceptions of the PRC

The Soviet cognitive transition has been equally profound. During the early 1960s, their polemics tended to descry "petty-bourgeois nationalist deviation" behind Mao Zedong's radical aspirations. During the height of the Cultural Revolution, the critical emphasis shifted from Chinese domestic politics to "nationalism" or "great-Han chauvinism" (implicitly juxtaposed to proletarian internationalism), as specifically exemplified by Chinese refusal to cooperate with bloc foreign policies (e.g., fraternal assistance to Vietnam). Thus in June 1969, Brezhnev denounced China's "departure from Marxism-Leninism and break with internationalism." This theme remained in focus through the 1970s and early 1980s, with various elaborations.[24]

Soviet perceptions of China did not immediately change upon the death of Mao; this becomes clear in an examination of a sample of fifty articles from major Soviet newspapers, such as *Pravda, Izvestiia, Ekonomicheskaia Gazeta,* and *Trud.*[25] We also reviewed a selected sample of articles on Chinese economic modernization in the major Soviet journal *Problemy Dal'nego Vostoka,* as well as other Soviet academic publications.[26] The Soviets of course welcomed the purge of the Gang of Four, but did not deem this to have been decisive in eliminating the roots of Maoism. Deng Xiaoping's rise to power beginning in the spring of 1978 was accompanied by outspoken negative Soviet commentary, which was to continue for as long as Hua Guofeng remained in nominally influential positions. Chinese reform efforts were initially construed wholly from the perspective of Soviet foreign policy interests—as a continuation of militarism, anti-Sovietism, and Asiatic hegemonism: "Maoism without Mao."

Viewing Chinese politics basically in factional terms,[27] the Soviets saw the 1978–82 period as one of conflict between pragmatic Maoists led by Deng Xiaoping and left Maoists; though the former prevailed, they were unable fully to overcome the Maoist legacy.[28] This was indicated by the pro-imperialist, chauvinist platform (read: the antihegemony plank) adopted at the Eleventh Party Congress, and the inadequate reckoning with history by the Sixth Plenum of its Central Committee (June 1981). In terms of institutions, commentators paid keen attention to the state of the CCP after the death of Mao, regretfully noting its loss of influence in industrial management and other areas of decision making (as we have seen in Czechoslovakia and then again in Solidarity Poland, the strength of the communist party has always been for the Soviets a key criterion for determining the bona fides of a socialist system).[29] Likewise lamented was the disruption of the mass organizations.

The overall tone of Soviet commentaries shifts perceptibly in 1982, particularly after the ascendancy of Andropov in 1983. Reporting became more objective and concise, and a number of influential Soviet China-watchers published relatively optimistic commentaries (usually pseudonymously).[30] Modernization issues were decoupled from foreign policy issues and objectively analyzed, even the latter being discussed somewhat more dispassionately. Whereas from 1979 to 1982 the Soviets viewed China as an active participant in building an anti-Soviet alliance with Japan and the United States—looking upon economic reform efforts as part of a conspiracy to cement this alliance,[31] for example—in the post-1982 period they came to view China as a passive victim or dupe of American manipulation (though a lingering bitterness over China's anti-Soviet posture is still detectable).[32] There was also an abrupt decline in the frequency of articles in 1982, suggesting that the issue was under high-level review and debate.

In the 1982–85 period, Soviet views of reform tended to ramify, as was particularly clear in the scholarly literature. Rozman identified two schools of thought, which he calls "defenders of the status quo" and "voices for change."[33] Others draw more complex distinctions, differentiating advocates of "scientific socialism," pragmatic technocrats, "essentialists," socialist pluralists, and so forth.[34] The present study is not primarily concerned with the classification of Soviet scholars but with the overall drift of their thinking, which presumably influences the foreign policy making leadership and ultimately trickles down in somewhat simplified form (through journalistic media) to the Soviet masses. Thus it is pertinent to note that the perspective shifted in the 1980–88 period from a bitterly critical to a much more sympathetic one, but we need not track the relative vertical mobility rates of marginally differentiated schools of thought to infer that the leadership is being presented with a more positive set of options from which to piece together a China policy. It is also worth noting that Soviet China scholarship tends to address characteristically Soviet concerns, though Rozman's "mirror" metaphor probably overstates its subjectivity.[35]

In the beginning, Chinese difficulties with reform were analyzed in excruciating detail. The Chinese "crisis of faith" of the early 1980s was duly noted: bureaucratism, anarchism, factionalism, and, above all, individualism were perceived to be rampant. Obstruction to the reforms had reportedly emerged within the party at both central and local levels.[36] Ironically echoing Mao Zedong's concerns during the Cultural

Revolution, the Soviets expressed apprehension that the foundations of socialism were being undermined in China. Correspondingly, Soviet apprehensions about the future of Chinese socialism tended to draw sustenance from the CCP's more conservative spokesmen: noteworthy was a comprehensive Soviet summary of a talk by Peng Zhen in which Peng eulogized Marxism-Leninism as a revolutionary and progressive philosophy conducive to reform—thereby repudiating as wrong in principle those who viewed Marxism as an outdated worldview inherently inimical to reform.[37] The report on the landmark reform decision of the Third Plenum of the Twelfth Central Committee was particularly ingenious, first reporting objectively on the decision, then recapitulating critical *American* commentary on the difficulties likely to complicate implementation (inflation, unemployment).[38] The internal criticisms of the Chinese were also prominently featured, such as the line of the "grand old man" of Chinese economic policy, Chen Yun: Reform, yes, but only with moderation and caution, and in no case should the steering capability of the state be abridged.

Most of the more specialized commentary focused on the economic dimension of the reforms. In the agricultural sector, the Soviets recognized the increase in output achieved since 1978, but refused to relate this to the reforms.[39] Discussions of agricultural reforms tended to focus on the serious social polarization and welfare problems that these allegedly precipitated.[40] Thus it was noted that in 1980, per capita production in industry and agriculture was 9,000 yuan and 450 yuan respectively; at the same time, in view of the fact that the prices of industrial goods are much higher than those of agricultural products, capital investment in agriculture by peasants becomes difficult. This leads to increasing demands for governmental subvention of capital investment in the agricultural sector. Without solving long-term investment issues, improvements in management and material incentives can only bring about short-term gains.[41] The Soviets contended further that the foundation of collective agriculture has been undermined; because every family is exclusively concerned with reaping short-term payoffs, individual households have no interest in making necessary investments in land and irrigation facilities or in the mechanization of agriculture. Hence in the long run they will ruin the basis for any increase in agricultural productivity.[42]

Soviet criticism of Chinese industrial reforms was more extensive and serious; industrialism is, from the Soviet perspective, the quintessence of modernization. On the one hand, they argued that the decentralization of decision making to the enterprise level has not increased but rather reduced efficiency; in fact, the amount of capital investment actually increases beyond central control, contributing to inflation.[43] The "system of free supplies and floating prices" introduced in late 1984 in China's "second stage" of reform is not working successfully, creating supply shortages (while the proportion of cement, timber, and coal centrally allocated has been reduced from 57 percent to 25 percent, the requests from local enterprises to the center are actually growing), also precipitating localism, failure to fulfill state plans, and attempts to "snatch" more.[44] On the other hand, the introduction of vertically or horizontally integrated trusts is found unnecessarily to complicate the planning process by multiplying the layers of intermediate administrative organs.[45] Rationalization efforts (sometimes referred to in Chinese terms as "readjustment") have resulted in what Soviet analysts consider a sectoral imbalance between heavy and light industry. The closure of allegedly inefficient plants, usually greeted by American commentators as a sign of efficiency, is viewed by Soviets with great consternation (they also see more of this occurring than has the Western press). One article, reporting that more than 2,000 enterprises were closed over an unspecified period, attributed the increase in industrial unemployment (about 25 percent of industrial workers were alleged to be unemployed in 1981) to such capitalistic ruthlessness.[46] For all that, another writer notes, inefficient enterprises were not thereby eliminated (as of 1981, 23 percent of all enterprises were still running a deficit), and the state budget had been burdened unduly.[47] The outlook for the Chinese industrial proletariat, ever a key harbinger for the efficacy of socialism, appeared lugubrious to official Soviet commentators.[48] The rate of increase of manpower is faster than that of jobs. China is ranked 125th in the world in terms of income level, with an average monthly income of U.S. $152 (at time of writing); yet because of inflation, the living standard of the workers has shown no actual improvement since the 1950s.[49]

Another area to receive a great deal of attention was the growth of commerce, particularly the "open door" policy with the West. The latter was viewed on the whole negatively, based on the Marxist assumption that politics is inseparable from economics. Thus China's opening to the world market is the result of a capitalist plot, entangling the country in "the orbit of economic, political and ideological influences of world capitalism,"[50] leading ultimately to "the threat of bourgeois degeneration."[51] The opening to foreign investment invites the reemergence of "imperialism," giving away inappropriate concessions in terms of taxes, profits, markets, prices, and the license to exploit cheap labor. Many more specific problems in the opening policy have been cited, blaming these either on lack of preparation on the Chinese side, or (with increasing frequency) on violations of contracts, trade barriers, or excessive greed on the part of foreign investors. The most serious problem in Soviet eyes (to which their Western counterparts have scarcely adverted) is the negative impact of foreign investment on competing domestic industries. Thus the Soviets attribute the shutdown of many domestic plants, with the concomitant problems of urban unemployment and rising welfare costs, to foreign capital investment.[52]

Following the accession of Gorbachev in early 1985, Soviet reportage became increasingly positive in its assessment of the Chinese reforms, consistent with the incoming party secretary's growing interest in *perestroika*. Since the spring of 1985 the journal of the Institute of the Far East has published a monthly column under the rubric "Economic Reform in the PRC," which focuses on detailed analysis of individual aspects of the Chinese program.[53] Some positive economic results are herein acknowledged, though frequently diluted by criticisms.[54] It is now conceded, for example, that reforms of the incentive structure and the redefinition of responsibility in agriculture have contributed to a decisive improvement of output; at the same time, however, this has led to a weakening of collective institutions and a foreshortening of investors' time horizons.[55] Small-scale industry (which has experienced vigorous growth in many rural areas) is found to have a higher rate of profitability per unit of capital invested; but this also incurs social costs, such as lower wage rates, and infringed worker safety, health, and welfare arrangements.[56]

Following the CPSU's Twenty-seventh Congress, when Gorbachev praised Chinese reform and called for "radical economic reform" at home, China (along with Hungary) surfaced as a positive socialist model.[57] Fedor Burlatsky, after a trip to China early in the summer of 1986 (during which he warned his hosts that his was a minority point of view), wrote a glowing report on the domestic relevance of the reforms.[58] Even with regard to Chinese foreign policy and the Soviet nightmare of joint Sino-American-Japanese security coordination, the Soviets appear to have gained a certain equanimity: weapons purchases from the United States are noted without commentary (whereas Chinese criticisms of the West are reported in exhaustive detail).[59] In 1986 an article appeared reversing Soviet opposition to joint ventures (coincidentally, in 1985 the Chinese announced that they also welcome joint ventures with socialist regimes).[60]

The most recent Soviet coverage has continued to focus on areas of ideological tangency[61] and diplomatic rapprochement (e.g., upbeat reports on the latest session of the ministerial talks, or the new Sino-Soviet Commission for Cooperation in Economics, Commerce, Science and Technology).[62] China is depicted as a supporter of peace and disarmament, which takes a pro-Palestinian and pro-Libyan position and registers condemnation of South Africa (all coincident with Soviet foreign policy preferences).[63] To be sure, a certain reserve is still evident on both sides. Soviet reports still observe (for example, after the 1988 inflationary surge) that Beijing's unorchestrated approach to reform has created chaos, as decontrolled sectors disrupt those still run by the state; and take note of the lack of adequate laws in the PRC to regulate private entrepreneurial activity. Since 1988, the economic setbacks of *perestroika* have led to an intellectual interest in more farfetched models, such as Austria or Sweden—countries with minimum unemployment, small income differentials, free markets, and well-developed social welfare systems.[64] And Chinese correspondents in the USSR write back that grassroots reform is "so slow that little change can be seen here."

All in all, there has been a remarkable transformation in the reciprocal perceptions of both sides since the late 1970s. They have moved, step by step, from a time when each considered the other worse than its ideological anathema, first to an acknowledgment of political kinship, then to an interest in, and finally to qualified support for, the other's reform efforts. As far as Western social science has been able to determine, this has had a modest but perceptible impact on popular attitudes.[65] Since Chinese abrogation of the mutual friendship treaty, the two have been searching for a mutually satisfactory way of relating to each other without simply reimposing hierarchy. The fact that both countries have now embarked on a quest for apparently convergent objectives offers perhaps the best prospect for mutually beneficial socialist cooperation since the 1950s, though it also raises the prospect of invidious comparisons. But now we must inquire: Do their objectives really converge?

Learning Reform

Two broad patterns are discernible in comparing the reciprocal impact of reform in the PRC and the USSR. The first of these is one of Chinese initiative followed by a somewhat more tepid Soviet response. The second pattern has been characterized by relatively bold Soviet initiatives followed by an equivocal Chinese response suggesting indecision or intra-elite controversy. Within the former pattern the emphasis has been on economic reform; within the latter, political and cultural reform

has assumed top priority. Although the two patterns overlap chronologically, the former has tended to prevail during the 1978–86 period,
whereas the latter was dominant from 1986 through 1990. We shall
first examine the pattern of economic reform, then turn to the pattern
of political reform.

Economic Reform

Although there are other models of socialist reform available,[66] it is
natural for the two major Leninist systems to contemplate similar solutions to systemic inefficiencies, owing to their similar size, scale, and
historical experience.[67] The Chinese have by consensus gone further
down the road to economic reform than the Soviets, though the Soviet
economy is by most conventional indicators more advanced than the
Chinese. Whereas this would appear to give each side grounds for reciprocal interest, recent trends place the PRC for the moment in a
more advantageous position. After relatively vigorous growth averaging 4 percent annually from 1928 to 1955 (based on a savings rate
roughly double that of the United States, to offset the low productivity
of capital), Soviet growth has gradually slowed down over the past two
decades, from its peak of 5.2 percent in 1966–70 to 3.7 percent in
1971–75, 2.7 percent in 1976–80, to an estimated 2.0 percent in 1981–
85. Whereas in the twenty-five years following 1949, the U.S. economy
had shown more impressive growth rates on only six occasions, during
the 1976–85 period American growth rates exceeded estimated Soviet
figures in eight out of ten years.[68] By 1985, Soviet GNP was only 55
percent that of the United States and relatively declining, according to
1987 CIA and DIA congressional testimony. Even these estimates may
be too rosy, according to recent statistics divulged by Soviet economists,
who put Soviet output at only 28 percent of U.S. GNP.[69] There has also
been a steady decline in the growth of living standards, with the average annual growth of per capita consumption falling from a peak of
4.3 percent in 1965–70, to 1.7 percent in 1975–80, to an estimated
1.2 percent in 1981–82.[70] There was reportedly even a slowdown in
the rate of increase of Soviet defense procurements in the late 1970s.[71]
More alarming yet, Soviet reforms have not yet alleviated this discouraging situation, nor do reformers harbor much hope that they will do so
in the immediate future.[72] Indeed, the economic situation at this writing
is the worst since Gorbachev took over in 1985.[73]

   In China, on the other hand, although the growth rate during the
Maoist era was on the whole not bad compared with other countries

at the same stage of development (at the price of frozen living standards), reform seems to have had a dramatic positive impact on growth and productivity and an even more pronounced effect on per capita income.[74] China's growth rate for the last decade has been four times that of the Soviet Union (PRC, 7.5 percent; versus USSR, 1.8 percent over the 1976–84 period). If the Soviet growth rate should continue to lag behind that of the PRC at the pace of the 1980–85 period, China may be expected to surpass the Soviet in GNP within the foreseeable future. Even assuming an annual average Chinese growth rate of only 4.7 percent, the Chinese economy is forecast to exceed the Soviet level by 2010, displacing it as third in absolute GNP after the United States and Japan. Assuming that the proportion of GNP allocated to military spending remains constant in both countries, the PRC will emerge as a serious potential security threat to the Soviet flank.[75] China's per capita output will, to be sure, remain at a more humble level—about 10 percent as high as that of the United States or Japan, or one-third that of the USSR.

Considering that Chinese reform achieved an early and quite dramatic increase in production output while the Soviets have far less to show for their efforts, the likelihood that the USSR might be influenced by Chinese economic reform efforts seems greater than vice versa, at least for the moment. The Chinese have hitherto been more willing to innovate, typically beginning by spot-testing experiments locally, then extending them to the nation as a whole. The Soviets have proceeded more cautiously and in monolithic fashion, launching reforms from the top down, under comprehensive central controls. Although like the Soviets the Chinese have proceeded without an a priori plan, "groping from stone to stone while crossing the stream" (*mozhe shetou guo he*), they have had a clear (and felicitous) set of priorities, beginning with agriculture and shifting only later to the more complex urban industrial sector. In retrospect their progress may be seen to have focused on three programs: (1) the recalibration of incentives, (2) the shift from command planning to markets, and (3) the policy of opening to the outside world. We begin our comparison in each case with an examination of the Chinese experience before turning to analogous tendencies in Soviet reform.

The Recalibration of Incentives. We presuppose a shift from "ideal," or ideological, to material incentives, which antedated the onset of reform in both countries. Thereafter, recalibration implies two things. First, these incentives are allocated according to production *outputs* rather than labor inputs; that is, the worker becomes "responsible" for the outputs (thus the Chinese name, "production responsibility system"). Second, the responsible worker is also given *functionally specific autonomy,* to facilitate flexible adaptation to unanticipated problems and motivate workers to make innovative contributions rather than merely serve time. In agriculture, this has meant dividing property into two components, ownership and control, and redistributing control without legal cession of ownership. The 55,000 People's Communes that formed the organizational bulwark of Chinese agriculture for three decades were thus dismantled in 1979–81 and virtually abolished in 1982 (formalized in 1984, to be eventually replaced by rural village councils), and communal farmland has undergone "de facto decollectivization," being redivided into plots leased to individual farm families, on the basis of contracts granting them widespread rights of tenancy (now including the right to inherit or sell their leaseholds) for a period of fifteen years or more. The household responsibility system (HRS) has been an outstanding success in agriculture, although early growth rates have not been sustained since the record 1984 harvest. Chinese peasant income doubled in less than a decade (1978–84), grain production increased by 4.9 percent annually over the same period (compared with 2.1 percent per annum in 1957–78), and output of other crops grew even more rapidly: by 1987 statistics released by the State Statistical Bureau disclosed that the gross value of agricultural output was the highest (in absolute terms) in the world.

In industry, production responsibility involves the devolution of authority both vertically (from the ministerial hierarchy) and horizontally (from the party committee) to enterprise management. Managerial authority has grown incrementally, beginning with experiments with enterprise autonomy under Zhao Ziyang and Wan Li in the early 1980s (then party secretaries of Sichuan province and Anhui province, respectively). Reformers have proceeded to replace government deduction of wages with tax collection [*li gai shui*], more recently adopting the contract system (in which management is given a short-term lease to run a factory autonomously). After considerable debate, an enterprise reform law was finally passed in 1988, containing provision for bankruptcy or merger in loss-making enterprises, and authorization to raise capital by selling stock shares. Despite these efforts, the heavily capitalized, labor-absorptive state enterprises remain among China's least efficient.[76] The responsibility system has been successful in industry and commerce only to the degree that the authorities have followed their own guidelines for "responsibility"; that is, most effective in the private and collective sectors, least in state-owned firms. This type of reform is most easily carried out in the more primitive (i.e., smaller-scale) economic sectors.

Until early 1986 the Soviet observers focused on the drawbacks of the HRS; since that time its success has been conceded, but the Soviets have been hesitant in emulating it. One of the first to refer favorably to the Chinese agricultural reforms was the sociologist Tat'iana Zaslavskaia, who referred to the "collective responsibility family contract system" as a model of what might be done in Soviet agriculture.[77] Soviet peasants have been encouraged to expand their private plots, which account for less than 4 percent of total farm acreage but produce up to half its potatoes and a third of its meat and dairy products. Experiments have been launched with the brigade system and a contract responsibility system popularly known as the "normless link" (*beznariadnoye zveno*), similar to an early incarnation of China's household HRS, consisting of a team of farm households, often family-related or in any case self-selected, who contract to produce a given output while the collective supplies the needed machinery and supplies. Gorbachev himself used this system in Stavropol during his tenure as a *krai* official there. These were, however, initially restricted to certain regions and agricultural sidelines (e.g., Georgia, livestock raising), in a form carefully limiting individual incentives.[78] By late 1988, reformers (e.g., V. A. Tikhonov) were advocating that new "lease contract" collectives similar to the Chinese HRS be allowed to operate independently of the structure of collective and state farms, while conservatives (e.g., Yegor Ligachev, then chair of the Commission on Agrarian Reform) objected that the collective would disintegrate should peasant families be permitted free exit. This conflict seems to have been resolved at a special CC plenum on agriculture convened in March 1989, which dismantled the centralized agricultural bureaucracy (Gosagroprom) and gave private farmers the right to lease state land for up to fifty years and pass it on to their children. Agricultural machinery, now owned by the state and collective farms, may be either leased or sold to private entrepreneurs. Farmers may hire labor so long as wages are not lower than those paid by adjoining state enterprises.

This compromise still refuses to disband the 50,000 state and collective farms (nearly half of which operate at a loss, according to Soviet statistics).[79] The *sovkhoz* and *kholkhoz* (the first of which is in a majority, in contrast to the Chinese ratio) have received somewhat greater financial autonomy (e.g., they may now sell up to 30 percent of their harvest to urban markets and cooperatives rather than the state). "State orders" (*goszakazy*) however continue to be issued, meaning that leaseholders, though not free not to produce what they like, can organize as they please to meet targets arranged with management. It remains to be seen how enthusiastically incumbent *raion* (district) cadres will cooperate in promoting reforms they may well deem ideologically heterodox as well as inimical to their leadership positions.[80] As indicated by the prior history of the "link," the Soviet bureaucracy has become quite effective at thwarting policies deemed threatening to its corporate interests.[81] Rather than banking his prestige on any specific reform, Gorbachev has opted for policy pluralism. The agricultural scene might for the interim evolve in the direction of collective farms with contracts in those regions where the collective farms are still relatively efficient, toward the spread of leaseholds in those areas where the status quo does not work (e.g., the Russian Republic) or where the spirit of peasant entrepreneurialism thrives (e.g., the Baltic Republics and some southern ones).[82]

Although the HRS has been the jewel in the crown of Chinese reform, there are several conceivable reasons for Soviet reluctance to plunge in. The agricultural sector is far smaller in the Soviet economy, whether in terms of its proportionate contribution to GNP or labor absorption (only about 20 percent of the population were employed in agriculture, compared with at least 62.5 percent of the Chinese as of 1985), so improvements in agricultural productivity would have less immediate impact on the economy as a whole. Nationality issues are much more critical in a nation in which the dominant nationality has shriveled to about 50.4 percent of the population (in China, minorities make up only about 8 percent of the populace, and are situated for the most part in remote and underdeveloped regions). De facto decollectivization may well be avoided because of fear of loss of political control in such regions, given that several non-Russian republics, where latent nationalism remains potent, are predominantly agricultural in their economic structure (notably Georgia). In traditional agricultural regions, family farms had been established only tenuously following emancipation of the serfs in the late nineteenth century before Stalin undertook collectivization, moving with such brutal determination that he may have broken the back of peasant entrepreneurship.[83] In those areas in which large-scale resettlement has taken place, on the other hand (about 140 million acres of "virgin lands" were added to cultivation between 1950 and 1960, increasing total Soviet croplands by more than 38 percent), the farmers had no original title to the land, so to redistribute it into family responsibility plots would be as arbitrary as the current organization of ownership. Agricultural machinery is extensively used in these vast and marginally productive regions, and the subdivision of fields might well adversely affect economies of scale.[84] Finally, the CPSU's cumulative success in educating the Soviet citizenry to "socialist" values should not be underestimated. Thus public opinion polls (as well as more impressionistic indicators) do show, in contrast to the climate of opinion in the Chinese countryside, a lack of enthusiasm for any major shift in the agricultural incentive system in the USSR, suggesting that Gorbachev cannot count on popular pressure to echo his calls for change.[85]

Marketization. The shift from command planning to markets does not necessarily entail political liberalization, but it does presuppose two essential freedoms: the freedom of agents to enter and exit the market, and the freedom for prices to fluctuate according to supply and demand. Chinese reformers have undergone an evolution in their satisfaction of these two prerequisites. Concerning the former, the "quasi privatization" of agricultural property in the form of long-term leaseholds has already been noted; at the Seventh NPC (March 25–April 13, 1988), the right was extended to inherit and even to buy and sell leaseholds. China has also legalized private enterprise (denounced and curtailed as the "tail of capitalism" under Mao) in the service, commercial, and even industrial sectors; the latter has quickly become the most rapidly expanding (though still the smallest) of the three forms of ownership (state, collective, and private), followed by the collective sector.[86] More than 80 percent of the restaurants, stores, and repair shops set up since the Cultural Revolution ended in 1980 are privately owned; although most are small-scale affairs, they have been growing in size from an initial limit of seven or eight employees to several hundred.[87] The collective sector includes a considerable number of nonagricultural cooperatives (more than 2.8 million by 1985, employing 70,280,000 people).[88]

China has come to discover that although marketization does not necessarily entail political liberalization, quasi privatization does seem to imply a degree of marketization. The switch to the HRS, and the shift in early 1985 from centralized procurement of farm products to contract and direct market purchases, expanded the sphere of commodity-money relations. Less than 15 percent of the grain now produced in China is sold to the state at the plan price; farmers sell about half their produce privately. By late 1986 there were 67,600 markets in urban and rural communities, with an annual turnover of 90.6 billion yuan.[89] The private sector, of course, has full price-setting autonomy, and the collective sector is also market autonomous after filling state contracts. State plans have been split into command and indicative ("guiding") plans;

command-plan coverage has shrunk (as of the 1984 package) from 120 industrial commodities to 60, and from 29 agricultural commodities to 10. The government's inability to control prices in the growing collective and private sectors[90] has resulted in the advent of what the Chinese call a "dual economy" (actually consisting of a rather disorganized multitiered price system) in which a given commodity may have different prices depending on the market in which it is sold. Grain, for example (in the HRS), may be sold at the base procurement prices (for within-quota produce), the higher procurement price (for above-quota produce), the negotiated price, and the free price; industrial goods may be sold at either the plan price or market price. Thus by 1989 around half of all commodities on sale in China had their prices set by the market to varying degrees.[91] Opportunities for corruption become myriad, as officials take advantage of special access to buy at administered prices and sell at market prices (a form of arbitrage referred to by Chinese as *guan dao*), or to buy abroad (via trading companies) and retail domestically. Chinese attempts to supersede the dual economy and introduce a more thoroughgoing free price system in 1984, in 1986, and again in May 1988, unleashed a mounting wave of inflation (according to official statistics, the retail price index rose 2.8 percent in 1984, 8.8 percent in 1985, 6.0 percent in 1986, 7.3 percent in 1987, 13.5 percent in 1988, and 17.8 percent in 1989).[92]

To mollify irate urban consumers, the government attempted in September 1988 to reimpose fixed prices, postponing price decontrol for at least three years. Since the crackdown on democracy activists at Tiananmen in June 1989 (for whom many reformers had expressed support), the organs of central planning have been reinforced and the degree of latitude permitted market forces tightly constrained, in the name of counterinflationary policy. Still, the Chinese commitment to marketization has held its ground theoretically: whereas in the early 1980s the official ideal was a system in which the planned sector would remain dominant, augmented by markets (Chen Yun's "bird in cage" model), the formulation at the Thirteenth Party Congress (October 1987) was that the state should manage the market while the market should guide the individual firm. At this writing, this formulation still stands—though its patron, Zhao Ziyang, has been evicted from all party and government positions. And in late 1990, the government proclaimed its intention to expand private markets by 10 percent over the next five years.[93]

Gorbachev has shifted with regard to marketization, from an initial position of explicit hostility[94] to one of cautious interest. His early efforts at reform were aimed at "strengthening" the planning apparatus rather than dismantling it; thus he set out to establish seven "super-ministries" similar to those operating in the GDR, creating such organs in agriculture, machine building, and energy development.[95] In August 1986 the Soviets also introduced a new and much larger "basic management unit," called the All-Union Scientific Production Association (VNPO), apparently patterned after the East German *Kombinat*. The Soviets also retained Stalinist budgetary priorities in their Twelfth Five-Year Plan (1986–90), with strong emphasis on the heavy industrial sector most closely linked to the central ministries.[96]

After tacitly abandoning hope of plan-rational reform, Gorbachev moved tentatively toward quasi marketization via administrative decentralization. In June 1987 a draft plan, the "Basic Principles for Radically Restructuring the Management of the Economy," attempted to set forth a comprehensive agenda.[97] This document envisaged that each factory and farm was to be accountable for its profits and losses (*khozraschet*), giving managers and workers an incentive to cut waste and improve quality and output. In a Law on State Enterprise passed January 1, 1988, five-year plans decreed by the central ministries were officially abolished. Rather than following a central plan, each factory director would be free to make his own arrangements with suppliers and retailers. By 1989, every state enterprise could sell up to 30 percent of its output outside the state order framework. Enterprises could no longer count on state budget subsidies, but must finance their operations from bank credits, which must be repaid with interest, or face bankruptcy. Although this program moved well beyond what previous Soviet economic reformers had attempted, the attempt to introduce market flexibility has proved ineffectual without real market options. The ministries remain responsible for overall production, can still place "orders" with a firm, and by retaining monopoly control of raw materials, ensure that these are filled. State orders commonly claimed 100 percent of a factory's production in 1987, declining to nearly 90 percent in 1988 and to some 40 percent in 1989.[98]

The major Soviet reform aimed at improving market access by reassigning property rights has come not (yet) in the form of privatization or quasi privatization,[99] but by giving greater ambit for the growth of economically freewheeling "cooperatives." The first step in this direction came in May 1987, when the state permitted citizens to operate small restaurants, tailor shops, taxis, and other private businesses (including twenty-nine kinds of enterprises), thereby placing this underground economy on legal parity with state enterprises. But regulation

TABLE 3.1.
The Cooperative Sector in the Soviet Union, 1987–89

Year	Output (rubles)	Employees	Cooperatives
1987	330 million	71,000	18,000
1988	6,300 million	1,370,000	67,000
1989	40,760 million	4,600,000	211,000

SOURCE: Data from Vladimir Tikhonov, in a talk at the University of California at Berkeley, May 1, 1990.

remained initially stringent: owners must register with local authorities, quit their jobs in state enterprises, and could not hire labor; they should obtain their supplies from Gossnab (the official state supplier) and not from other private traders. The next step came in September 1987, when the law was extended to include privately run shops and other services. With the new Law on Cooperatives passed by the Supreme Soviet in the spring of 1988 (to go into effect July 1), cooperatives were permitted to engage in virtually any activity, including banking and foreign trade; they could even sell shares and set up joint ventures with foreign companies. Cooperatives are being encouraged to compete with state enterprises even for the fulfillment of state orders, giving them priority in the requisition of rationed inputs. No limits are placed on who joins the cooperative, its size, the industry or service it wishes to enter, or the earnings of members—which may be distributed proportionate to their share of investment as well as labor input. They are free to hire full-time employees and set prices for their products and services. In all these respects, the cooperatives are evolving along the same lines as Chinese collective enterprises, promising likewise to absorb underemployed labor and provide services and consumers' commodities for which there is vast pent-up demand. The cooperative sector has hence mushroomed (Table 3.1), by 1989 accounting for fully 5 percent of the country's GNP.

The cooperatives are perhaps the most successful of Gorbachev's economic reforms at this writing, yet their proliferation has excited popular envy and recurrent regulatory interference, both from the ministries and the legislature. Because Soviet industry faces a labor shortage (versus the Chinese labor surplus) and an aging population in industrially advanced regions,[100] not to mention the Soviet penchant for economies of scale, the cooperative and private sectors may have more limited intrinsic potential than in the PRC—barring a much more sweeping elimination of bureaucratic obstacles than seems in the cards for the present.

Concerning price reform, Gorbachev has been circumspect or even ambivalent. According to the "Basic Principles" adopted at the June 1987 CC Plenum, the Soviets are resolved to encourage private and co-operative activity, a labor market, the abandonment of annual plans, and a shift from command to indicative planning (wherein the authorities manage only important variables of national importance, leaving operational decisions to lower levels). But Gorbachev's announcement at the 1987 plenum that "a radical reform of the pricing system is a most important part of the economic overhaul" led to hoarding and anxious letters to the press. Little wonder: for over half a century, the Soviet government and its ministries have set more than 25 million prices. Some have been in effect for decades. The problem of price reform was hence postponed till 1992, but the issue refused to die. In October 1989, Deputy Premier Leonid Abalkin outlined a switch to a market economy beginning in 1991, which was rejected by Prime Minister Nikolai Ryzhkov in December. The question resurfaced in the spring of 1990 in the wake of inordinately discouraging economic indicators over the past year, only to be debated inconclusively and again deferred. Once again in August–September 1990 Gorbachev considered a plan by a group of reform economists designed to lead the country to a market economy over a 500-day transition period; but after extended public debate, the radical Shatalin Plan was forced into a compromise with the Ryzhkov model.

The Policy of Opening. China's "open door" (*kaifang zhengce*) policy is designed to facilitate Chinese integration into international commodity, technology, and capital markets—particularly to encourage foreign investment in China's Special Economic Zones (SEZs) and other designated coastal enclaves. This has had a quite dramatic impact on both trade[101] and investment.[102] By dint of its size and enormous market potential, China elicits better credit arrangements and terms of trade than most developing countries, and its invitation for capital investment and technology transfer in the early 1980s soon attracted more offers than the bureaucracy could expeditiously process. By 1988 the PRC, which had permitted no direct foreign investment (except for a few joint ventures with the Soviets) during the first three decades of its existence, had become the Third World's biggest recipient of new foreign investment.[103] Though on the whole successful, particularly in the SEZs adjacent to Hong Kong and Taiwan, the policy of opening has not unfolded without controversy. For one thing, the policy has been beset by spontaneous generalization pressures—on the one hand to induce cultural as well as commercial opening (as in the exodus of some 40,000 Chinese students for study abroad, or the internal penetration of tourists, electronic media, and "spiritual pollution"), on the other hand to include domestic as well as international opening (as in recurrent efforts to revive a "hundred flowers" in the cultural and political spheres). The authorities have reacted ambivalently but on the whole restrictively to such tendencies—and when their reactions are severe, the spillover dampens economic opening as well. Thus foreign investment dropped 48 percent in 1987 in response to the antireform backlash that culminated in the purge of Hu Yaobang. Although a new Cooperative Joint Venture Law was passed in April 1988 with more flexible provision for the distribution of earnings, and Zhao Ziyang attempted to extend SEZ provisions to China's entire eastern seaboard, with an area of 320,000 square kilometers and 160 million people,[104] foreign investment plummeted again following the 1989 bloodbath.

China's opening to the outside world was considerably facilitated by its admission to the United Nations in 1971, whereupon it automatically acquired permanent membership on the Security Council and gained entrée to other UN or UN-affiliated organizations, including exclusive (i.e., excluding Taiwan) seats on the World Bank's Board of Governors and the IMF's Board of Executive Directors; more recently, China has also joined the BRD, IDA, IFC, the Multi-Fibre Agreement, and the Asian Development Bank, and applied for membership in GATT (had it not been for Tiananmen, membership would probably have been granted in 1990). Less than six months after being officially granted seats on the governing boards of these leading financial organizations, China succeeded in doubling its own quotas (which determine borrowing rights and voting power) in both institutions, therewith abandoning in practice its traditional advocacy of international financial self-reliance (e.g., in 1976 Maoist China had refused all aid from foreign governments and international organizations in the wake of the devastating Tangshan earthquake). By releasing for the first time its "complete national income statistics" to the UN Committee on Contributions in 1979 and to the World Bank in 1980, China reduced its assessment rate (and required contribution to the UN) from 5.5 percent before 1979 to 1.62 percent in 1983 and finally to 0.88 percent by 1989—based on what many believed to be a deflated per capita GNP of only U.S. $152 (the World Bank's own estimates placed China's 1978 per capita GNP at $460).[105] China has since 1979 requested long-term low-interest loans from Japan's Overseas Economic Cooperation Fund (which really amounts to foreign aid, correspondingly alarming South Korea and ASEAN), and garnered small amounts of technical aid from West Germany and Belgium, as well as substantial assistance from the World Bank (becoming by the mid-1980s its largest borrower).[106] As with private investment, the recent Chinese backlash against political reform seems to have had a temporary chilling effect on governmental grants and subsidized loans. Although these grants and aid were suspended or deferred in the wake of the Tiananmen crackdown, most have since been resumed.

Like the Chinese, the Soviets have expressed interest in integrating their economy into the world market, increasingly lauding "interdependence" and an "international division of labor." The ratio of Soviet imports to GNP, less than 1 percent in the 1930s and about 3 percent in the mid-1960s, had climbed to roughly 5 percent by the beginning of the 1980s. In September 1986 it was decided to facilitate trade by vesting more than twenty ministries and competent departments as well as seventy large enterprises with the power to deal directly with foreign traders, thereby removing monopoly control from the Ministry of Foreign Trade. By April 1989 every enterprise was officially authorized to engage in its own importing and exporting, with chaotic initial consequences. Since 1986 the Soviet Union has voluntarily begun to cooperate with the Organization of Petroleum Exporting Countries (OPEC), and (in the spring of 1990) became an observer at the General Agreement on Tariffs and Trade (GATT), also initiating contacts with the International Monetary Fund and the World Bank; it has also expressed interest in joining the Pacific Economic Cooperation Council (PECC), the Asian Development Bank (ADB), and other regional financial organizations. In order to satisfy the financial prerequisites of such institutions, it has proclaimed its intention to make the ruble convertible with the West sometime in the first half of the 1990s.[107] To attract foreign technology and earn hard currency, the Soviet Union for the first time since 1920 invited foreigners to participate in joint ventures in 1986, a form of cooperation hitherto rejected in principle, initially offering Western investors up to 49 percent of equity and later permitting up to 99.9 percent foreign ownership and a foreign national to act as president. The number of such ventures signed had increased from seven in 1987 to 1,200 by early 1990, though only about 6 percent of these are in operation at this writing.[108] In his speeches at Vladivostok and again at Krasnoyarsk, Gorbachev proposed to take a leaf from the Chinese SEZ experience and inaugurate joint enterprise zones in the Soviet Far East. These proposals have encountered stiff ministerial (and in some cases, military) opposition; as of the spring of 1989 the first economic zone was reportedly still in preparation along the Finno-Soviet border, while plans for a second in Nakhodka in the Far East had bogged down.[109]

Just how successful Soviet overtures for inclusion in the world market will be under current circumstances remains a moot question. The import demand is there, given Soviet interest in Western technology (as indicated by their intensive engagement in industrial espionage in the late 1970s), not to mention continuing agricultural shortfalls. But balance of payments constraints may impinge fairly sharply, even if the upward surge in arms sales to the Third World continues. Soviet hard currency earnings, their preferred way of paying for Western imports, surged with world oil and gold prices after 1973, only to plateau at the end of the 1970s when prices sagged; the Soviet trade deficit to the West almost tripled in 1989 (to U.S. $6.5 billion), because of large unplanned grain imports. The prognosis is that the Soviets will do well to hold hard currency earnings at their present level over the next decade, using natural gas exports to offset a drop in oil exports. Lacking exports to earn hard currency, would the Soviets turn to Western credit markets, thereby exacerbating their trade imbalance? In the past, the Soviets were put off from such deals by American failure to deliver most-favored nation (MFN) treatment (or rather, linkage of this concession to unacceptable demands on Soviet emigration policy), and by recurrent embargoes in response to Soviet military initiatives in the Third World.[110] These impediments seem to have been removed by a remarkable liberalization of emigration policy and by Gorbachev's "new thinking" in foreign policy.[111] But the Soviet estimated foreign debt has risen from about U.S. $21 billion to $70 billion from 1984 to 1991, while the budget deficit has ballooned to at least 10 percent of GNP.[112]

Even if this bid for inclusion in the international economy fares better than the previous one,[113] the Soviets may still have to compete with the East European systems now veering out of the Soviet orbit. Since the early 1980s, Soviet subsidies to East European countries have steadily declined, and there has been a concurrent deterioration of their terms of trade with the Soviet Union.[114] The East European countries—most of whom (viz., Czechoslovakia, Poland, Romania, Hungary, and Yugoslavia) are already affiliated with the IMF—have long considered Western markets an attractive alternative to intrabloc trade. Although several (Poland, Yugoslavia, Hungary) were burned by petrodollar loans in the 1970s,[115] they are now avidly casting competing bids for a limited pool of Western investment capital. In January 1989, Hungary and Poland instituted unprecedented foreign investment laws permitting wholly owned foreign firms (not yet permitted in the USSR); and all East European countries are easing travel restrictions, for both their own citizens and Western tourists. China will also continue to compete for Western venture capital, and North Korea and Cuba have signaled their future intentions by sending delegations to study China's SEZs.[116]

Political Reform

Contrary to popular impression, the Chinese record with regard to political reform has been less than stellar, if we are concerned not only with spectacular initiatives but with systematically institutionalized follow-through. Soviet efforts along these lines antedate Chinese endeavors by a matter of decades, paralleling similar East European reforms. Several East European polities have held multicandidate elections for decades, an innovation not adopted in China until 1980–81 (at the district level). Although the Soviets did not adopt this particular innovation until 1988, they have had extensive experience with legislative reform, including the formation of standing committees, interpellation, and other such devices.[117] The Chinese first set up seven standing committees, each with its own staff, at the Fourth NPC in 1982; by this date the Supreme Soviet, which had first established standing commissions in 1965, had twenty-six such bodies.[118]

Thus it is perhaps not surprising that the major initiatives in the reform of European communism have come not in the economic but in the political and cultural arena, and indeed at a time when economic reform appeared to be bogged down. From the time of his contested accession to power in March 1985 through the end of 1986, Gorbachev was preoccupied with the consolidation of his own position, primarily through the time-honored mechanism of the "renewal of cadres" (read: purge). In his first year in office, Gorbachev removed 47 of 121 regional party secretaries and replaced more than half of the CPSU Central Committee; half the membership of the Council of Ministers (42 ministers) was also cashiered.[119] By the Twenty-seventh Congress in February 1986 half the Politburo and Secretariat members had been appointed within the previous year, there had been major changes in military leadership, and a third of the republic and regional first secretaries had been replaced.[120] Although he seems to have then been placed on the defensive (by Chernobyl, among other things), beginning with the pardon of Sakharov in the summer of 1986, he introduced a more tolerant stance toward intellectual dissidents. This policy of "socialist pluralism of opinions" (*glasnost'*) has resulted in an intellectual ferment redolent of, but more far-reaching than, Khrushchev's "thaw."[121] Long-suppressed works such as Pasternak's *Doctor Zhivago* and Rybakov's *Children of the Arbat*, or the anti-Stalinist film *Repentance*, were approved for release. With the convention of the January 1987 CC Plenum (after three postponements), Gorbachev endorsed "radical reform" (*radikal'naia reforma*) vis-à-vis the Brezhnev legacy and began to introduce his own positive agenda for "restructuring" (*perestroika*). He called for "democratizing" the political system by introducing multicandidate elections for local soviets and party posts, involving more nonparty personnel in the government and economy, and expanding the sphere of private economic activity. The June 1987 CC Plenum sought to extend these initiatives to the economy, by reducing central planning and giving more independence to managers of enterprises, promoting competition, and improving the level of services. Albeit ambitiously conceived, Gorbachev's reforms failed to catch fire, however, and from the fall of 1987 to April 1988 he suffered another series of setbacks, including the Yeltsin affair and the outbreak of interethnic strife in Transcaucasia.

Only when he returned to the political arena was Gorbachev able to recover momentum. He did so by convening a massive all-union Party Conference (the first held since 1941) in June 1988, followed a month later by a CC Plenum. A raft of reforms was introduced, including limited tenure (two five-year terms) for all elective party and government officials, the right to a multicandidate slate for every elective office, the right of recall, and, most important, preparations for an ambitious restructuring of the Soviet legislative apparatus. Constitutional reforms were introduced by the Supreme Soviet in November 1988 to clear the way for a general election in March 1989 to a new and more powerful Congress of People's Deputies, involving contests between candidates in single-seat constituencies. This election was held on schedule, and although not all candidacies were contested (384 of the 1,500 districts saw party hacks running unopposed), the number of upsets it precipitated testifies to its efficacy. The Congress of People's Deputies convened its first session in April 1989 to select a working parliament and elect Gorbachev the country's first executive president. The Supreme Soviet became the first standing parliament in Soviet history, convening each fall and spring for three to four months. Still a bicameral structure consisting of a Council of the Union and a Council of Nationalities, the legislature has been significantly downsized (to a total of

542 deputies—remarkably close to the size of the American congress!), making true deliberation, rather than mere "rubber stamp" endorsement, possible.[122] Although opposition was not legally sanctioned until early 1990, two informal groupings of noncommunist deputies have already coalesced informally, the so-called interregional group in support of more vigorous reform and the Soiuz (Unity) group favoring a more cautious approach. The CPSU, too, is scheduled to have an election campaign to reelect all party committees—from shop-floor level to Central Committee—also in multicandidate elections. Hungarian and Polish reforms announced in early 1989, followed by similar moves in East Germany and Czechoslovakia, have of course gone further still, for the first time permitting opposition parties to participate in free electoral competition. The initial results (spring 1990) amount to a stunning repudiation of communist party hegemony in Hungary, East Germany, and Czechoslovakia; only by preelectoral arrangement was the Polish United Workers' Party (PUWP) spared a similar fate. At the CPSU Central Committee Plenum in February 1990 it was also decided to abolish the constitutional article which enshrines its "leading role."

Whereas the Chinese have in the past also introduced promising initiatives toward political reform (e.g., "Let a hundred flowers bloom, let a hundred schools of thought contend," and the concept of "nonantagonistic contradictions," both introduced in the context of post-Stalin thaw; the Great Proletarian Cultural Revolution also aspired to ambitious political reforms, albeit unsuccessfully), implementation has been sporadic and uneven, still falling within the ambit of "continuing the revolution under the dictatorship of the proletariat," which tended to undermine institutionalization.[123] Despite periodic crackdowns and reverses, the East Europeans have thus over time realized a more open political and cultural climate than the Chinese, and even the Soviets seem to have surged ahead since 1986. While Deng's regime did introduce a series of political reforms beginning in August 1980 (including multicandidate elections at local levels, limited tenure for nonparty posts, standing committees within the NPC, and a generous voluntary retirement program for veteran cadres), these have been modest in conception and carried out without much conviction. Since 1984, as Chinese reform efforts became complicated by the more difficult problems of the urban industrial sector and ensnarled in the struggle to succeed Deng Xiaoping and his generation of Long March veterans, the CCP's enthusiasm for political reform has grown still cooler. For example, in the summer of 1986, Chinese public opinion was enlivened by discussion of the need for political reform as a prerequisite for further progress in economic reform—a discussion directly stimulated by Gorbachev's initiatives in the Soviet Union, as previously noted. But when this discussion precipitated a wave of sympathetic student demonstrations in December, the veteran leadership firmly suppressed the demonstrations and purged Party General Secretary (and heir apparent) Hu Yaobang for having failed to do so. For the next several months a countercampaign was launched against "bourgeois liberalism." Although the reformers appeared to have made a convincing comeback at the Thirteenth Party Congress (October–November 1987), reform momentum had by the summer of 1988 once again flagged, and in the spring of 1989 the same scenario played itself out with far more tragic consequences. Upon the death of Hu Yaobang on April 15 the students rallied to his cause, aiming not to overthrow the regime but to seek common cause with the reform wing of the leadership in an effort to regain momentum. By eschewing mob vandalism and blatant indiscipline, the demonstrators were able to forestall a regime crackdown for nearly a month while their own numbers mounted to unprecedented proportions, swelled by popular concerns about inflation and elite corruption. By mid-May, the issue of how to respond had split the leadership. The hard-line majority may have then felt it expedient to suppress the demonstrators even more vigorously than necessary in order to discredit their soft-line opposition. It seems unlikely that the shocked international reaction to this well-publicized bloodbath had been fully taken into account.

Thus 1986 marked a shift from the pattern of Chinese reform and cautious Soviet response to a new pattern of Soviet initiative and Chinese ambivalence or even violent reaction. In the Soviet case, economic reform had been able to make no headway at all before running up against insuperable bureaucratic obstacles, necessitating political reform in order to make even a bare beginning. In the Chinese case, economic reform was able to make far more impressive strides before political reform seemed called for, but at this point any attempt to broach the question provoked a violently aversive elite response, as the very success of the former ironically made the need for the latter seem moot. In both cases, economic reform alone proved insufficient, either bogging down in an institutionally enforced ideological morass after initial successes or proving unable to move beyond the prologue. Whereas Soviet elites adopted a low-key but apparently effective passive resistance to economic reform while accepting unexpectedly sweeping political reforms, even when these jeopardized their own tenures, Chinese elites seem to have been much more receptive to pragmatic economic reforms but adamantly opposed to any political reforms that might conceivably threaten their own positions.

The reasons for these contrasting elite responses to the problems of socialist reform have partly to do with the fact, as noted above, that the European communist systems have more extensive experience with constitutional engineering and other forms of nonviolent political change than have the Chinese. The Chinese experience with political reform has been after all both violent and humiliating, and, in the Chinese expression, "once bitten by a snake, one fears even a coiled rope." Both countries endured prolonged bouts with charismatic leadership, but the legacies of the Stalinist and Maoist eras are in many ways quite different. Stalin was a traditional autocrat who ruled through a vertical hierarchy, enhancing his power by skillfully playing one apparatus off against another, and ruthlessly using that power to precipitate a "revolution from above." Mao was, in contrast, a populist who seems to have lost (or felt he had lost) organizational control of the "commanding heights" of the party-state apparatus relatively early (say, by 1960), and was able to regain command only by mobilizing the "revolutionary masses" to criticize, even to "smash" and "overthrow" the "Party persons in authority taking the capitalist road." Many of those leading party figures who bore the brunt of mass criticisms (e.g., Peng Zhen, Deng Xiaoping, Chen Yun) managed to survive the Cultural Revolution and to reemerge as leaders in the post-Mao reform movement. On the one hand, this implied that in areas under Stalinist rule, the democratic impulse, even the willingness to disobey bureaucratic authority, was virtually eradicated—via such object lessons as the permanent (blood) purge, forced collectivization, secret police, and concentration camps. In areas under Maoist rule, on the other hand, the willingness to challenge bureaucratic authority was tolerated and even encouraged, notwithstanding the intolerance of the regime for explicit ideological deviance. The Soviet apparatus was terrorized from within, but its hierarchical integrity was never violated; whereas the Maoist apparatus was frontally challenged and (to all appearances) "smashed" in a searing experience that left its legitimacy in ruins. In China, the excesses of the Cultural Revolution had more fully discredited ideology than in the Soviet Union; when Gorbachev took over, neither Stalin nor Brezhnev could be criticized in public. This has meant that post-Stalinist Soviet leaders have had much more difficulty stimulating the initiative of the masses than the post-Mao Chinese leadership, and have had to resort to more dramatic concessions in the political arena to win both support for their reforms and innovative zeal in implementing them.

The outlook of the party vanguard in the wake of the Stalinist and Maoist epochs emerges quite differently. The leaders of the Soviet reform effort tend to conceive themselves, rightly or wrongly, to have suffered personally under Stalinist autocracy, and hence harbor enduring fear and loathing of any concentration of power. Thus they seized upon the succession as an opportunity to deliver themselves from that particular nightmare. The leaders of China's reform effort have their own *via dolorosa* to look back upon—not, however, of having been terrorized by a repressive police state (which has tended, in fact, to deal relatively leniently with the party leadership), but of having been humiliated by the unleashed fury of the masses. Whereas Stalinism left a pervasive control apparatus in its wake, which its legatees tinkered with to enhance their own security but never squarely challenged,[124] Maoism bequeathed a particularly disruptive pattern of mass participation. This is not to say that China's post-Mao defenders of Mao's legacy retain this populist impulse, nor that democratic activists remain radical Maoists; but it has meant that reform leaders continue to adopt a much more cautious, even paranoid stance toward political liberalization than their counterparts in Eastern Europe or Gorbachev's Soviet Union. While Soviet and East European reformers use political reform to generate support for seemingly unpopular economic reforms, Chinese reformers use political centralization, even occasional repression, to rein in economic reforms (and their political-cultural spillover) whose enthusiastic supporters might otherwise cause to career out of control.

Thus the correlation between economic and political reform is quite different in the two cases. In both systems, political reform appears to be a means to the end of economic reform, rather than an end in itself. The success of economic reform without political reform seems at least for the moment to have encouraged CCP elites to assume that the latter may be dispensed with altogether. Hence their enthusiasm for the concept of "new authoritarianism" borrowed from the postwar history of the Asian NICs (newly industrialized countries), which would preserve elite authority and prerogatives while promoting continued economic development. Should economic reform instead generate its own economic constituency and social momentum in favor of political reform, as it has in the NICs themselves since the early 1980s or at Tiananmen, the CCP seems (from current evidence) prepared not only to block political reform but to rescind dangerous aspects of economic reform as well. The Soviet case is quite different. There the utter failure of economic reform has perhaps led the CPSU elite to overload political reform with aspirations for a comprehensive transformation of the system that it cannot perhaps sustain. Political reform becomes the independent variable, economic reform the dependent variable. This causal sequence has rarely been encountered empirically, and studied even less. But little evidence is at hand indicating that democracy per se enhances economic efficiency. The risk for the Gorbachev leadership is that if *demokratizatsiia* and *glasnost'* do not eventually give rise to perceptible improvements in Soviet living standards, the masses will look on with passive indifference while the whole reform experiment is cast in history's dustbin by some reinvigorated authoritarian leadership prepared to violate liberal sensibilities in order to recover a sense of political control and economic momentum.

Another aspect of political reform, conceived in a broader sense, is the reconceptualization of the regime's ideological legitimation in the light of perceived economic imperatives. While it is fair to say that theory has followed rather than led reform in both countries, both have endeavored to revise Marxism-Leninism to rationalize and facilitate modernization. The Chinese have made their boldest demarche on behalf of economic reform, with the concept of a "socialist commodity economy" that borrows not from the sparse prognoses of classical Marxist texts concerning the future postcapitalist economy, but places Chinese socialism together with capitalism in the category of commodity economies, thus subject to the same universally valid laws (as outlined in *Capital*) governing any economy under conditions of shortage. Thus Chinese reform theory envisages an economy of independent but interacting producers for the market who decide in relative autonomy on the production and exchange of commodities and who are subject to pressure to improve efficiency via the "law of value." The watchword for "developing the socialist market" is the principle of "separating ownership from management," which implies that while (large-scale) enterprises remain social property, their management is nominally free to operate as if private or collective property arrangements prevailed (the downside is a "soft budget constraint"). State planning regulates not the firm, but the market, through various fiscal and monetary mechanisms; the party's role should be limited to ideological suasion. While contemporary China is thereby realigned in terms of Marxist categories, the bolder Chinese literature goes still further by throwing open to question the infallibility of the laws governing the relationships among these categories.[125]

The Soviets have also begun more recently to rethink Marxism-Leninism, moving in many of the same theoretical directions traversed by the Chinese. Their conceptual innovations have been perhaps less dramatic, as the excesses of the Cultural Revolution had discredited ideology more thoroughly in China than gradual stagnation did under Brezhnev. Beginning with the rectification of the past, Soviet intellectuals have undertaken a reassessment of the New Economic Policy, with its legitimation of the market and small private enterprise;[126] in this connection Bukharin and Rykov, two prominent Bolshevik NEP supporters later executed in the purge trials, were politically rehabilitated in January 1988. In a speech to the Central Committee the following month, Gorbachev called for updating those elements of communist doctrine that were outdated and calcified.[127] Gorbachev's critique of the (Brezhnevian) "period of stagnation" focuses on systemic failure: not only do the relations of production (including state ownership) no longer correspond to the forces of production, they have imposed a "braking mechanism" on the further development of the productive forces, slowing the rate of economic growth and impeding scientific-technological innovation.[128] Anticipating (perhaps inspiring) the subsequent Chinese self-definition at the "primary stage of socialism" at the Thirteenth CCP Congress, Gorbachev in January 1987 replaced the doctrine of "developed socialism" with "developing socialism," acknowledging the need to postpone ideological aspirations in the name of economically realistic development. Yet this is no longer Stalinist development, mobilizing the masses by raw terror and crude propaganda, but a new era of "intensive development," when human creative powers must be fully tapped. Workers are found to be "alienated" under existing (socialist!) working conditions.[129] Thus historical necessity merges with the dictates of Marxist humanism, as in the name of the "human factor" it is deemed necessary to grant greater decentralization, increased scope for private initiative, and the toleration of economic, political, and social activities that would have been anathema only a few years ago. In foreign policy, Gorbachev's dramatic innovations have been premised on "new political thinking" (*novoe myshlenie*), which stresses "common human values" rather than class interests as a basis for foreign policy, mutuality of security, and international interdependence.

Whether such rethinking draws the two countries closer together remains to be seen, but it is noteworthy that key Soviet reformers are confident that it will. "I am deeply convinced that Gorbachev has already launched the country on a path of reform comparable to that of the Chinese," said Fedor Burlatsky of the Soviet Academy of Sciences. "But here the obstacles will be greater because there is a group within the political leadership who will struggle against the reform."[130]

CHAPTER 4

Building Functional Bridges

Sino-Soviet diplomatic relations reached their nadir in the late 1960s, inspiring predictions of a major war between these former allies. Up to the end of 1965, despite the escalation of polemics, both sides still paid lip service to ideological unity. But on November 11, *Renmin Ribao* published an editorial stating that the two sides had absolutely nothing in common: "The chief task for the CCP is now to totally demarcate itself from the CPSU both politically and organizationally." Though party-to-party relations lack official character, this probably marks their lapse. During the Cultural Revolution's high tide (1966–68), the two countries even came perilously close to a rupture of diplomatic relations, as Soviet diplomats were driven into exile by rampaging Red Guards, and both countries reduced relations to the chargé d'affaires level.

A beginning was made in bridging the yawning diplomatic chasm only when the point had been reached that the prospect of war was clearly in view, and the uncertain and no doubt mutually catastrophic consequences of such an outcome could be fully appreciated (see Chapter 11). The Chinese agreed to negotiate in the wake of the 1969–70 border clashes under Soviet nuclear blackmail. Zhou Enlai and Kosygin agreed in their preliminary talks at the Beijing Airport to drop the Chinese precondition that existing treaties be described as "unequal," also to cease armed provocations along the border. This series of talks contained the dispute, giving both sides a regular forum (the talks met biannually in Moscow) in which to articulate their suspicions and even broach a few new proposals (see Table 4.1). Although the Chinese dropped the issue of acknowledgment of the "inequality" of the treaties imposed on them by the tsarist government as a precondition for talks, they continued to raise it during the talks, notwithstanding an intransigent Soviet response.

Although discussion deadlocked over this issue, it cannot be said that the talks were utterly fruitless. The arms buildup along the frontier stabilized, trade increased slightly, the Soviets offered *in camera* to accept the thalweg (midline down the main navigable channel) to demarcate

TABLE 4.1 Border Talks

Dates	Outcome
February 25 to August 22, 1964	PRC calls tsarist treaties "unequal," but agrees to accept them as the basis for negotiation. USSR refuses to concede treaties unequal, or even that there are "disputed areas." Talks break down.
October 20 to December 14, 1969	Talks convened under duress. PRC demands prior acknowledgment of "unequal treaties" and "disputed areas," proposing mutual withdrawal of border forces from the latter. USSR refuses all preconditions. Talks break off.
January to April 1970	USSR proposes border compromise based on territorial status quo without further discussion of treaties' historical legitimacy; downplaying boundary issues, suggests "overall" improvement in relations featuring economic, cultural exchanges. PRC refuses.
Mid-January to Summer 1971	USSR repeats offer of territorial compromise, including acceptance of the thalweg to demarcate Heilong (Amur) and Wusuli (Ussuri) rivers (except Heixiazi Island). Also proposes secret draft treaty eschewing use of force. PRC refuses.
March 20 to mid-July 1972	Rehashing of old arguments. No progress.
March 6 to June 30, 1973	USSR repeats offer for mutual nonaggression treaty. PRC declines.
June 25 to August 18, 1974	PRC tacitly drops references to treaties' "unequal" status, agrees to sign mutual nonaggression treaty if USSR agrees to mutual withdrawal from disputed areas. USSR refuses.
February 12 to May 5, 1975	Talks overshadowed by commotion over Soviet helicopter intrusion in Xinjiang.
November 27, 1976, to February 28, 1977	Deaths of Mao Zedong and Zhou Enlai encourage USSR to suspend polemics, suggest partial settlement. PRC refuses.
May 4 to June 1978	"Heated" talks; suspended by mutual agreement.

riverine boundaries (in 1973), and made certain other territorial concessions.[1] Both sides concurred with the nonaggression concept in principle and tacitly agreed to accept the status quo on the border until exact boundary locations could be mutually accepted. Yet the Chinese insisted on the issue of unequal treaties in principle, leading the Soviets to suspect they were holding out for more, unspecified but potentially vast concessions, and they grew exasperated. The death of Mao in 1976 raised their hopes, only to see them dashed against the equally adamant stance of the Hua Guofeng regime, and talks were broken off at the spring 1978 session. The relationship began to veer out of control again, as violence promptly erupted at two strategic points along the Chinese perimeter: on Christmas Day, 1978, the People's Army of Vietnam (PAVN) launched a blitzkrieg attack against Chinese client Kampuchea (Cambodia), and the following month China launched a "self-defensive counterattack" against Vietnam; in December 1979, Soviet troops invaded their own client, Afghanistan (assassinating their troublesome puppet Amin in the process). The Soviets at around this time undertook an ambitious second stage in their Far Eastern arms buildup, now focusing primarily on air and naval (including nuclear arms-bearing) forces. In retrospect it seems plausible that the talks had served at least a stabilizing function.

Progress toward "normalization" ironically (or perhaps not?) resumed just after the consummation of diplomatic relations with the United States at the beginning of 1979. On April 3, 1979, Foreign Minister Huang Hua met with Soviet ambassador to China J. S. Shcherbakov to give formal notice that his government had decided "not to extend the Sino-Soviet treaty beyond its expiration" (April 11, 1980), on grounds that the "international situation had changed drastically." Since Brezhnev had warned the Chinese in January 1979 that if they did abrogate the treaty, they should bear responsibility for the consequences, this seemed a rather audacious move. But in the context of the same notification, Beijing announced its willingness to engage in talks "on a separate basis from those on the border" for the solution of outstanding issues in the improvement of relations between the two countries. The PRC had implicitly suspended its insistence on acknowledgment of the "inequality" of existing treaties and prior withdrawal of Soviet troops from "disputed areas" before negotiations could be held. Though obviously irked by the Chinese decision to abrogate the treaty, Gromyko accepted this offer promptly (April 17), both sides agreeing to suspend the hopelessly deadlocked border question and focus instead on the normalization of state-to-state relations.

Bilateral normalization talks at the vice-ministerial level commenced September 27, 1979, and continued through October 12, without making much headway. Unlike the 1969–78 talks, all of which were convened in Moscow, the resumed talks began in Moscow and henceforth met on an alternating-site pattern between capitals (see Table 4.2). Although the Chinese had agreed to negotiate without preconditions, within the negotiations they immediately raised three demands—two of which had to do with reduction of Soviet troops along the northern borders, the third with Soviet aid to Vietnam. Whereas the Chinese insisted on tight linkage between Soviet movement on these demands and the normalization of bilateral economic and cultural relations, the Soviets wished to proceed with the latter irrespective of progress on the former. Because of the Soviet invasion of Afghanistan three months hence (leading the Chinese to add this to their foregoing demands, comprising the famous Three Fundamental Obstacles), the talks were not resumed on schedule after the fall 1979 session. But following the death of Mikhail Suslov (the CPSU's ideological "grand inquisitor," and leading veteran of the 1960s polemics) in January 1982, the ailing Brezhnev made some conspicuously favorable overtures, leading to the resumption of talks in the fall of 1982.[2]

The Chinese now effectively agreed to the Soviet demand for delinkage, permitting trade and cultural exchanges to slowly accelerate in the course of negotiations. During the next six years, there would be a total of fourteen rounds of vice-ministerial talks, held on a biannual basis with even-numbered sessions convening in Moscow and odd-numbered sessions held in Beijing. This was not the first forum to be opened for regular contact between the two countries, for formal trade agreements or their equivalent had been signed each year throughout the dispute. And, with one or two exceptions (including 1968), the Sino-Soviet Joint Commission for Frontier River Navigation has met every year since 1951. But these were relatively low-level contacts unqualified to settle the fundamental issues between the two powers. Held in executive session, the normalization talks have not been the occasion for dramatic announcements, but they no doubt contributed to the public agreements, declarations, and exchanges that punctuated the intermissions between rounds. Within this well-institutionalized context, relations slowly but steadily improved, despite apparent lack of progress in removing the Three Fundamental Obstacles that China defined as foreclosing such improvement.

The normalization talks provided a nexus to which new ties were

TABLE 4.2. Normalization Talks

Round	Date	Place	Outcome
1	September 27 to November 30, 1979	Moscow	Chinese demand reduction of Soviet troop deployments on Sino-Soviet border and in Outer Mongolia, end of aid to Vietnam. USSR proposes cessation of polemics, regular meetings, expansion of trade, cultural exchanges; refuses to discuss "third countries" (Vietnam, Mongolia). With Soviet invasion of Afghanistan, talks are broken off *sine die.*
2	October 5–21, 1982	Beijing	PRC articulates Three Obstacles to improved relations, but agrees to improve relations anyhow: cultural exchanges, tourists, trade increase. "Unequal treaties" issue quietly dropped. Supreme Soviet adopts new border law endorsing thalweg as riverine border demarcation.
3	March 1–15, 1983	Moscow	USSR repeats nonaggression pact offer; PRC reinvokes Three Obstacles. Student exchanges initiated, SS-20s discussed, border trade resumed.
4	October 6–20, 1983	Beijing	Both sides agree to double trade over the coming year, increase student exchanges from ten to one hundred over time.
5	March 12–27, 1984	Moscow	Some cultural exchanges, but apparently heated talks discussing Sino-Vietnamese border fighting, Reagan visit; Arkhipov visit postponed.

TABLE 4.2. (*Continued*)

Round	Date	Place	Outcome
6	October 1984	Beijing	These talks, preceded by foreign minister talks, agree to proceed with economic and cultural exchanges while differing on political issues.
7	March 1985	Moscow	Little progress, though Hu Yaobang says the PRC is willing to "upgrade" talks, and Chernenko expresses Soviet desire to normalize relations.
8	October 3–13, 1985	Beijing	Gorbachev's accession to power brings a warming trend, but Deng complains that the Chinese are still awaiting a "first decisive step," growing impatient.
9	March–April 1986	Moscow	PRC reinvokes Three Obstacles; still, agreement is reached to resume border negotiations at vice-ministerial level.
10	October 1986	Beijing	Gorbachev's Vladivostok speech preceding talks offers new concessions; Deng hints at summit if Cambodian issue resolved. Although USSR agrees for first time to discuss Three Obstacles, talks deadlock on Cambodian issue.
11	April 1987	Moscow	Talks preceded by Soviet withdrawal of a motorized division (10,000 troops) from Outer Mongolia. New consular agreement formalized.
12	October 1987	Beijing	Cambodia remains pivot of discussion; no agreement reached.

TABLE 4.2. (*Continued*)

Round	Date	Place	Outcome
13	January 1988	Moscow	Two sides commence discussion of withdrawal of troops from Sino-Soviet border.
14	August 27 to September 2, 1988	Beijing	Talks focus on Cambodia: agreement reached to divide the problem into "international" and "domestic" phases (the former concerned with troop withdrawal, the latter with setting up new Cambodian government).

linked incrementally (see Table 4.3). A "new channel" of vice-minis-terial discussions was begun in September 1983 with the visit of Vice Foreign Minister Mikhail Kapitsa to China (actually his fourth visit in as many years, but the first at the invitation of the Chinese gov-ernment), which *Xinhua* hailed at the time as the "first high-ranking Soviet government official to come to China on an official visit in over twenty years." In December 1985 Kapitsa visited Beijing once again to brief the Chinese on the recently concluded Geneva summit. He led yet another delegation to China in August 1986, a month after Gorbachev's Vladivostok speech, to arrange for the resumption of vice-ministerial border talks.

A third series of talks (actually a fourth, if we count the Frontier River Navigation Commission) was commenced in December 1984, at the still more elevated level of deputy premier, with the visit of First Vice-Premier Ivan V. Arkhipov to China. The most senior official to visit China since Kosygin (and erstwhile leader of the Soviet advisory staff during the heyday of Sino-Soviet cooperation), Arkhipov was festively received by Zhao Ziyang, Peng Zhen, and Chen Yun (though not by Deng Xiaoping). Arkhipov and Chinese Vice-Premier Yao Yilin signed three major agreements: one on economic and technical cooperation; one that established a Joint Commission for Economic, Trade, Scien-tific and Technical Cooperation; and a third that dealt with trade and scientific and technological cooperation. Tentative arrangements were made for a five-year trade agreement to cover the 1986–90 period and to provide for Soviet industrial assistance. In July 1985 the Arkhipov visit was reciprocated by Vice-Premier Yao Yilin (the highest-ranking

TABLE 4.3. "New Channels"

Forum	Date	Outcome
Vice-minister visits	September 1983	Soviet Vice Foreign Minister Kapitsa visits Beijing to discuss cultural exchanges, "secondary" issues. Agreement reached to increase trade, exchange students, teachers, tourists, various educational delegations.
	December 1985	Kapitsa returns to Beijing, but attempt to arrange foreign ministerial summit miscarries. He briefs Chinese on Geneva summit.
	September 1986	Kapitsa leads another delegation to Beijing for briefings.
Vice-premier visits	December 1984	Soviet Vice-Premier Arkhipov visits Beijing, to warm reception; signs three major agreements on technical and economic cooperation. Tentative arrangements made for five-year trade agreement.
	July 1985	Chinese Vice-Premier Yao Yilin visits Moscow; two agreements are signed, providing for the USSR to send advisers and equipment to help refurbish seventeen plants originally built with Soviet assistance, and to build seven new plants. Trade agreement signed, integrating trade into the five-year plans of both countries.
	July 1986	Arkhipov visits Beijing with advance copy of Gorbachev's Vladivostok speech. His delegation makes proposal on settling issue of Heixiazi Island.
	August–September 1986	First Vice-Premier Talyzin visits Beijing to sign first consular agreement in two decades. A new trade agreement was reportedly signed (but not pub-

TABLE 4.3. (*Continued*)

Forum	Date	Outcome
		lished) providing for even higher levels of bilateral trade. Delegation member V. Karpov briefs Chinese on SALT II and INF talks.
Joint Commission for Economic, Trade, Scientific and Technical Cooperation	March 1986	Meeting in Beijing, at vice-Premierial level, brings protocol agreement on exchange of working personnel, educational exchanges; helps facilitate Soviet assistance to Chinese plant renovation.
Joint Commission	May 1987	Meeting in Moscow discusses possible Soviet participation in joint ventures to develop the northeastern part of China. Soviet participation in Chinese nuclear power development, possible sites for joint hydroelectric dam across the Amur. The two sides agree to exchange detailed information about their reforms.
	January 1988	Meeting in Beijing of a working group of the Joint Commission, to exchange experiences on economic planning and development.
Foreign ministerial meetings	September 21–22, 1984	Foreign Ministers Gromyko and Wu Xueqian meet prior to the UN General Assembly in New York (the first meeting on this level since 1969). Results not publicly disclosed.
	March 1985	Foreign Ministers Wu and Shevardnadze meet again in New York at the UN General Assembly session.
	September 1986	Wu and Shevardnadze meet again at UN General Assembly session in New York, where they agree that border talks should resume at the vice-ministerial level in early 1987.

TABLE 4.3. (*Continued*)

Forum	Date	Outcome
	December 1988	Foreign Minister Qian Qichen visits Moscow (for first such visit since 1956) to discuss Cambodia, plan summit.
	February 1989	Shevardnadze visits Beijing, to reciprocate Qian visit and make final preparations for summit.
Summits	May 1989	Party General Secretary and President Gorbachev visits Beijing, to complete normalization process.

Chinese official visit to the Soviet capital in seventeen years). The USSR pledged in two significant agreements to provide advisers and equipment to help refurbish seventeen plants originally built with Soviet help in the 1950s, as well as to build seven new plants; bilateral trade was slated to increase by an annual rate of 14 percent, effectively doubling within five years.[3] For the first time, trade was placed within the long-term planning cycles of both economic systems (previously it had been arranged on a year-by-year basis). The Soviets also indicated willingness to provide loans to the PRC on favorable terms, even to invest in joint enterprises there, like capitalist entrepreneurs.

A fifth channel was opened with the establishment of the Sino-Soviet Committee on Economics, Trade, Scientific and Technological Cooperation during the Arkhipov-Yao exchange. These talks, also at the vice-premier level, first convened in Beijing in March 1986. At the first session the two delegation leaders, Arkhipov and Li Peng (subsequently to be replaced by Nikolai V. Talyzin and Yao Yilin), signed a protocol concerning the conditions for exchanging working personnel in connection with projected Soviet assistance in building the seven new projects and reconstructing 17 (now 24) of the 130 Soviet-built factories abandoned after the 1960 break. At the same time, they jointly determined "new approaches and new forms" of enterprise cooperation, economic and scientific exchange, agreeing that Moscow would send several hundred experts to the PRC and that Beijing would send technicians to the USSR for training. They also set up a Scientific and Technological Cooperation Permanent Subcommittee to promote scientific and technological cooperation. This group first convened in January 1988 when a Soviet delegation led by S. A. Sitarian, first vice-chairman of the Soviet State Planning Commission, arrived in Beijing; the two sides agreed to exchange experience on economic planning and development.

Meanwhile, the Chinese in 1986 opened a consulate in Leningrad, the Soviets one in Shanghai. In July the PRC held its first large-scale industrial and trade exhibition in Moscow in thirty-three years, provoking considerable interest; the Soviets reciprocated with their own exhibition in Beijing in December. In May 1986 the two countries concluded a two-year cultural cooperation accord to expand cooperation in science, education, culture, art, the film industry, journalism, publishing, broadcasting, television, sports, health, and other areas. In June of the same year, the Chinese and Soviet Academies of Science signed an agreement on scientific cooperation and a program for implementing scientific cooperation in 1987–88. Exchanges of journalists, academics, and officials quickly ensued.

Border talks, which had broken off eight years earlier, were resumed at the vice-ministerial level in Moscow February 9–23, 1987 (see Table 4.4). Both sides agreed at the first session to discuss demarcation of the border, beginning with the eastern quadrant; the Soviet side also finally agreed that Zhenbao (site of fierce fighting in 1969) belonged to China. At the second session, a panel of experts was set up to work out the details; the session also agreed to use the river for transport and trade as well as joint hydroelectric projects. Border talks were held again from mid-February to mid-March 1989, but certain issues have hitherto resisted resolution. One of these is the status of Heixiazi [Black Bear] Island, situated on the convergence of the Heilongjiang (Amur) and Wusuli (Ussuri) rivers. Although on the Chinese side of the thalweg, Heixiazi is the gateway to Khabarovsk, and has been fortified for its strategic importance. The Soviets have been seeking to exchange the Pamir plateau in the West, which is of no great value to them but penetrates like a knife into the Xinjiang Autonomous Region, for Heixiazi Island.[4]

With that, the two sides had established no fewer than six channels of communication, at different levels of institutionalization, some meeting regularly and others more episodically, but all procedurally formalized. This proliferation of diplomatic ties even in the absense of movement on the Three Obstacles seemed to place time on the side of the Soviets. But the Chinese, by withholding party-to-party ties, dragging the pace of economic-cultural exchange, and complaining publicly about the lack of progress on political issues, were able to apply sufficient pressure for further concessions. In addition, the accession of Gorbachev seems

TABLE 4.4. Border Talks (Resumed)

Date	Place	Outcome
February 9–23, 1987	Moscow	PRC asserts but does not insist on inequality of treaties. USSR agrees to discuss entire alignment of boundary, beginning with the Ussuri-Amur region and eastern Mongolia. The two sides set up a committee to draft a comprehensive water development plan for boundary rivers— hydroelectric power generation, flood control, navigation, fishing.
August 7–21, 1987	Beijing	Focused on technical demarcation of border near Khabarovsk, working on the basis of existing, "unequal" treaties. The two sides agree to set up a panel of experts to delineate the eastern sector. Regular air service between Harbin and Khabarovsk is agreed upon; USSR announces plans to reopen Leninskoye port, upstream from Tongjiang, to river trade.
October 20–31, 1988	Moscow	The two sides settle on the position of most of their eastern border and expand talks to the western frontier. Military teams set up to take aerial photographs and map border.

to have stimulated Soviet strivings for a diplomatic coup, as relations with Washington remained initially cool. These two factors combined to facilitate a further acceleration of the rapprochement process, as evidenced first of all in a shakeup of the Soviet foreign policy making apparatus, and second in substantive Soviet concessions on the Three Obstacles.

For many years the conservatives (i.e., defenders of "scientific socialism") had been firmly entrenched in the China field: Oleg Rachmanin, first deputy secretary in charge of the Ruling Communist Parties of Asia (who also wrote China commentaries under a pseudonym for *Pravda*); Ivan Kovalenko, deputy chief of the Oriental Division of the CC's International Department (a Japan specialist); Sergei Tikhvinsky, rector (recently promoted) of the Foreign Ministry's Academy; and Mikhail Kapitsa, vice foreign minister. As a new broom, Gorbachev made a sweeping purge of this crew of veterans, appointing eleven new vice foreign ministers within his first two years. Boris Ponomarev, a hard-line ideologue who for many years chaired the CPSU's International Department (successor to the Comintern in charge of relations with nonruling communist parties, national liberation movements, and so forth), was replaced in 1986 by long-term ambassador to the United States, Anatoly Dobrynin. Since 1986, Vadim Medvedev has chaired the Department for Liaison with Socialist Countries, which was recently (1988) shifted to the International Department. Rachmanin was replaced in late 1986 by a former deputy chief in the same department (Georgii Shaknazarov), who in his written work presents a softer exterior. M. I. Sladkovsky was replaced by the younger and more moderate M. L. Titorenko as director of the Institute of the Far East, and Kapitsa was replaced by the experienced China specialist Igor Rogachev as vice foreign minister with responsibility for Asian-Pacific affairs (Kapitsa was shuttled to leadership of the Institute of Oriental Studies). The appointment of Oleg Troyanovsky (former Soviet UN ambassador) to the Beijing embassy symbolizes an enhancement of the China connection, as does the recent reorganization of the Foreign Ministry to give greater organizational weight to Asia.[5]

Meanwhile, in the PRC, the process of generational change has brought to the helm a third generation of Chinese leaders far more sympathetic to Soviet interests. Many among the generation poised to succeed Deng Xiaoping's Long Marchers were educated in the USSR: the so-called Russian returned students (*liu Su pai*) have seniority over the potentially more numerous American returned students (*liu Mei pai*), and may be relatively comfortable with a form of socialist modernization more carefully crafted to reinforce the pillars of the Leninist party-state. Since the Seventh NPC (March 1988), Premier Li Peng has presided over a cabinet in which one-third of the ministers are Soviet-trained, including foreign minister Qian Qichen.[6] The potential constituency favoring improved relations with the USSR would include not only such returned students but many in the central foreign trade apparatus who find their monopoly over trade slipping away as economic decentralization proceeds, those in the planning apparatus who find it easier to deal with a planned economy than with the uncertainties of a free market, and those in the propaganda apparatus and security organs who find reform policies eroding their functions. The potential pro-Soviet lobby would transcend the central party-state apparatus to include the remote Western provinces, which find themselves neglected by capitalist investment preferences and wish to cultivate economic ties with the Soviet Far East, as well as enterprises and ministries elsewhere which produce goods with no market or stiff market competition in Western markets. This coalition may plausibly argue that ties to the USSR need not come at the expense of China's ties to the West, and might in fact induce the United States to render the PRC the respect it deserves.[7] Whether this will still be true when (and if) Soviet reforms achieve takeoff remains to be seen. Chinese leaders were quite taken aback by the Soviet abandonment of Eastern Europe.

Substantively, the Soviets began to respond in July 1986, when Gorbachev, in his Vladivostok address, made key concessions toward resolution of Chinese security concerns as well as the border dispute (to be examined in greater detail in Chapter 15). Although the initial Chinese response was suspicious, the Soviets were in the course of the next two years able to remove, "basically," all Three Obstacles. This cleared the way for certain Chinese concessions, culminating in the 1988–89 exchange of foreign ministerial visits, and finally in the May 1989 Gorbachev summit in Beijing. Diplomatic normalization has now been fully consummated, in an almost Pyrrhic context to be more amply considered in the concluding chapter.

The summit has made still other forms of collaboration feasible in turn. The Sino-Soviet Commission for River Navigation, never defunct, has been revitalized (Rogachev, now vice foreign minister in charge of Asian affairs, was an interpreter for the first such commission in 1955). By 1989 its meetings had resulted in efforts to construct a large, joint hydroelectric facility that would help control flooding in the Heilongjiang and Wusuli River valleys.[8] Military-to-military talks resumed in April 1988, and in November 1989 talks began on the demilitarization of the border. In 1989, after the United States had (ostensibly) discontinued all official contacts in response to the Tiananmen crackdown, China and the USSR exchanged reciprocal visits of their NPC and Supreme Soviet leaderships, several foreign ministerial meetings in Paris and New York, the leading officials of both parties' Propaganda Departments and International Departments, leaders of unions, youth groups, women's associations and friendship associations.

Functional Interdependence

Within the protective diplomatic context described above, bilateral trade has begun to mushroom, growing more than tenfold between 1981 and 1988 (from a value of U.S. $300 million in 1981–82 to $3.25 billion in 1988), far outpacing both China's overall trade expansion

FIGURE 1. Chinese Trade with the Soviet Union, the United States, and Japan, 1950–1980.

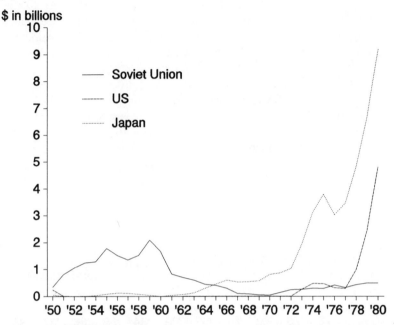

SOURCE: Statistical Yearbook of China, 1981. State Statistical Bureau. Hong Kong: Economic Information Agency, 1982.

and its trade growth with any other single trading partner. During the 1970s, the value of trade hovered at around $200 million per year. In 1978–85 it grew at a rate of about 23 percent per year. Coinciding with a fall in world market prices, bilateral trade declined in 1987, but recovered smartly in 1988, reaching four times its level of the year before.[9] Future growth seems assured, as China committed (under five-year trade agreements with the Soviet Union and Eastern Europe) to at least double trade with every member of the bloc by 1990. Sino-Soviet trade is not yet equal to that with the West (Sino-American trade in 1990 is estimated at U.S. $20 billion), but has expanded according to plan, without need to adjust to a world of unpredictably fluctuating currency exchange rates and trade balances (see Figures 1 and 2, for an overall comparison). Moreover, Sino-Soviet trade contains no risk of "spiritual pollution," as does traffic in Western consumer goods, and could (until January 1991) be arranged through barter agreements,

FIGURE 2. Chinese Trade with the Soviet Union, the United States, and Japan, 1978–1988

$ in billions

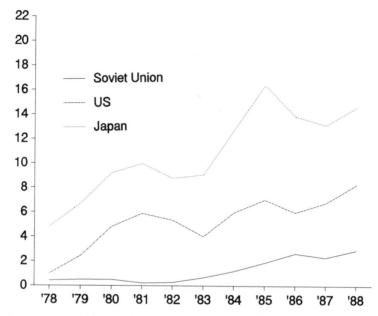

SOURCES: 1978–1980 Statistical Yearbook of China 1981. State Statistical Bureau. Hong Kong: 1982. 1981–1988: Almanac of China's Foreign Economic Relations and Board of the Almanac, Beijing: Water Resources and Electric Power Press.

sparing precious foreign exchange.[10] The Soviets are not above advertising their relative advantages:

The U.S. has imposed restrictions on 33 of China's commodities . . . ; our country, however, has not erected such tariff barriers. Generally, China suffers large trade deficits with the U.S.; however, China enjoys a trade surplus with the Soviet Union. . . . The geographical proximity of the two countries lessens transportation costs, and the similarity in the structure of foreign trade management between the two countries is also conducive to the signing of contracts.[11]

And there are indications that they do not lack an appreciative Chinese audience.[12]

In terms of composition of trade, the USSR is one of China's natural partners, offering raw materials as well as heavy industrial products in exchange for China's agricultural products and light manufactures.

The USSR has a huge machine-building industry with considerable excess capacity, while China produces large amounts of relatively low-quality light industrial goods and agricultural products it cannot sell on Western markets. The Soviet cumulative overemphasis on heavy industry has created a vast untapped market for consumer goods—kitchenware, haberdashery, stationery, rubber and plastic goods, and above all clothing and footwear. In exchange, the Soviets offer industrial and mechanical equipment, trucks and cars, aircraft, fertilizer, minerals, and precision instruments—all at prices considerably lower than those of machinery and equipment made in the West (though often of lower quality).[13] It is true that the USSR cannot provide the level of financing nor can its technology compare with the advanced computers, integrated circuits, and modern industrial designs available from the United States, Japan, or West Germany. But China cannot afford new turnkey plants from the West—a fact underscored by the cost overruns of the ultramodern Japanese-German built Baoshan steel plant near Shanghai. The Civil Aviation Administration of China (CAAC) purchased nineteen TU-154 aircraft (the Soviet version of the Boeing 727) in 1985, for example (delivery began in 1986); the jets are not fuel efficient and their engines need maintenance more frequently, but they were about a third the price of those purchased on international markets.[14]

The Soviet economic nexus offers many advantages beyond complementarity, short supply lines, ideological affinity, and low cost: in certain areas Soviet industry offers superior quality. China will be particularly interested in Soviet steel-making and metal-processing technologies, nuclear and thermal power generation, hydropower equipment, hydraulic coal mining (China has the largest coal reserves in the world), and long-distance power transmission technologies—all areas in which the Soviets excel.[15] The Soviet Union has a barter contract with China to supply two nuclear power plants to Liaoning province, for example, and agreement was finalized at the summit for a sale of nuclear technology for China's second atomic power plant at Daya Bay near Hong Kong—a bold move after Chernobyl.[16]

As noted above, in 1985 the Soviets agreed to provide technical assistance to upgrade and modernize seventeen major Chinese industrial plants and provide assistance in seven new complete plant projects. In February 1989 an agreement was signed for the joint restructuring of the Jiamusi Paper Mill, China's largest, in this connection. The Soviets also agreed in 1989 to provide technology to modernize the Baotou Iron and Steel Works in Inner Mongolia, another project originally built with Soviet technical assistance in the 1950s. Economic cooperation has forged ahead on diverse joint ventures, including Chinese thermos-making enterprises in the USSR. The most important of these is a U.S. $400 million paper pulp mill to be built in Heilongjiang, which will use logs from the Soviet Far East as well as a great deal of Soviet equipment and technology, and Chinese labor; the Chinese will repay the investment in the form of paper pulp shipments to the Soviet Union. By May 1989, about fifty such ventures had been signed, worth $200 million, with more than four hundred more under negotiation; China also had seven joint projects under way in the USSR (mostly hotels and restaurants).[17] Soviet loans were agreed upon in 1988 for two projects: completion of the Urumqi-Alma Ata link of the Sino-Soviet Railway (see below), and a $125 million credit in conjunction with Soviet renovation of the Baotou Iron and Steel Works.

Regional Complementarity

With the prospect of economic cooperation in the offing, China's 4,200-mile border with the Soviet Union (including the Sino-Mongolian segment), the longest in the world, may cease to be seen as a barrier and become an avenue for peaceful cooperation. Heretofore, Soviet economic relations with the countries of the Asian-Pacific Basin have been minimal, accounting for only about 4 percent of Soviet exports and 8 percent of imports (in contrast, U.S. trade with Asia surpassed its trade with Europe in 1980, and now accounts for more than a third of total trade volume).[18] Since the closure of forced labor camps during the Khrushchev era, it has been difficult to attract population to this remote and climatically forbidding region, and the population suffers from a severe shortage of housing and consumer goods. Although Siberia and the Soviet Far East account for about 57 percent of the Soviet land mass (nearly four million square miles), two-thirds of the area is covered with permafrost, with winter temperatures falling to −60°C. Only about 7.9 million people live there, and Soviet economic planners seem to have resigned themselves to leaving labor requirements at the minimum needed to staff various resource-development projects.

Yet Soviet leaders ambitious for Herculean undertakings return obsessively to this forbidding frontier. Over 80 percent of the Soviet Union's total reserves of primary energy are in the Soviet Far East (roughly estimated—less than 10 percent of East Asian Siberia has been adequately surveyed), in addition to rich deposits of nonferrous metals, gold, asbestos, fluorite and magnesite, diamonds, platinum, cobalt, lesser deposits of copper, tin, and tungsten, and an enormous potential for hydroelectric power.[19] As fuel resources in European Russia dwindled, the Tenth Five-Year Plan (1976–80) assigned Siberia to provide all planned increases in oil production, with output slated to rise from about 30 percent in 1975 to half the increased national output by the end of the planned period; similar increases for natural gas and coal output were foreseen. Thus by the 1980s Siberia was absorbing one quarter of the entire capital investment of the USSR, despite possessing less than 10 percent of the population.[20] And these ambitious quotas were met: petroleum output of the Minsk oil field increased from 28 million tons in 1970 to 357 million tons in 1983; the proportion of its petroleum output to the country's total rose from 10 percent in 1970 to 60 percent in 1983.[21] By 1988, two-thirds of the country's petroleum and half its natural gas supply came from Siberia. The Baikal-Amur Mainline Railway (still under construction at this writing after remarkable delays and cost overruns) is expected to further promote the economic development of the region. Gorbachev declared in September 1985: "Accelerating the development of the productive forces of Siberia and the Soviet Far East is an important component of the Party's economic strategy." And following his July 1986 tour of the region, a 200 billion ruble project (about $359 billion) was drawn up for investment in the Soviet Far East by the year 2000. The Politburo adopted a "Far East Development Plan" in July 1987, which aims for "a growth tempo higher than the entire country for the Far Eastern region," calling for new housing and cultural facilities.[22] In 1988 V. Lutsenko, a ranking official in the Soviet Far East, promised: "In the next fifteen years we will invest in the region's economy an amount equal to the previous half century."[23] Cash investment will triple, with heavy emphasis on building infrastructure, also in developing export industries, so that exports would eventually shift from natural resources and raw materials to processed goods, such as machinery.

Skeptics point out, however, that there is a certain vagueness in the Soviet Far East development plan, for several reasons. The rate of return for investment is very low because of high transportation costs, and the region lacks the most basic infrastructure—roads, dependable electricity, telephones.[24] None of the seven Soviet jurisdictions to be granted economic autonomy in an experiment beginning in 1990 are in the Soviet Far East, despite Gorbachev's frequent mention of this intention to open up the region to external markets.[25] According to some Western Siberiologists, the functional exigencies of the Soviet economy will push Gorbachev in the direction of renovating and replacing existing capital stock in the fully developed regions rather than allocating scarce funds to the undeveloped and forbidding eastern frontier.[26] Even in the worst-case scenario, however, the Soviets will have ample economic incentive for greater integration into the Pacific economy. If the country is to remain self-sufficient in energy, it must increasingly rely on its vast Asian frontier; and to fully exploit the latter, Moscow must turn to neighboring countries for consumer goods, and attempt to attract foreign investment (perhaps from Japan or South Korea).

As Soviet Far East development proceeds, it may thus integrate the USSR more successfully into the region's dynamic economy, helping to offset the hitherto conspicuously disproportionate Soviet military presence in the Far East. The region's potential has led some to expect the USSR to exploit its extractive industries to pursue export-led growth within the Pacific Basin economy. This has not yet occurred, with foreseeable resource production increases already bespoken by domestic needs or by markets in Eastern (and Western) Europe, but development has led the Soviets to diversify trade beyond their alliance network. Japan has become the largest Soviet trading partner in the region in absolute terms, monopolizing nearly 50 percent of total Soviet trade (amounting to U.S. $5.9 billion in 1988). The USSR has risen to fifth place among China's trade partners, while China has moved into second place among Soviet trade partners in Asia (crowding out India and Vietnam), increasing its share of Soviet imports from Asia by five times in 1970–85.[27] The Soviets have sought new business ties in South Korea, Taiwan, the Philippines, and Thailand, also pursuing membership in regional economic groups like the Asian Development Bank and the Pacific Basin Economic Cooperation Council.

In June 1983, local border trade was resumed for the first time since 1969 at three locations in Xinjiang and Heilongjiang provinces. Border trade increased nearly 4,000 percent between 1983 and 1988, reaching some U.S. $700–800 million by 1988.[28] Heilongjiang has set up over a hundred offices to handle Soviet trade, accommodating a steady stream of trade delegations. The value of Heilongjiang's border trade has grown from $18 million in 1984 to over $40 million in 1987 (at current exchange rates); the Soviets accounted for 70 percent of Heilongjiang's foreign trade in 1989, compared with 9 percent the previous year. By 1986, under the expanded authority granted by the central government, Heilongjiang expanded its trade by developing cooperative relations with other provinces wishing to trade with the Soviet Union; Shanghai, for instance, has begun to pursue new opportunities created by the opening of regional barter trade, signing barter agreements in 1988–89 under which the Soviets supply fertilizers and refrigerators in exchange for garments, thermos bottles, shoes, and wallpaper produced in Shanghai. Xinjiang's trade has grown from $12 million to nearly $30 million over the same period. Between 1983 and 1986, total border trade increased by nearly twenty times (amounting to about 16 percent of total bilateral trade); it more than doubled in 1988, reaching the equivalent of $274 million. The regional economies dovetail: China's low-cost food-processing industries and livestock can supplement the meager diet of residents of the Soviet Far East and Siberia. As the provincial trading companies are licensed to negotiate local trade arrangements with their Soviet counterparts outside the state plan (as of 1987), profits are retained in the province. In 1988 permission was granted to local Soviet enterprises to engage in foreign trade autonomously, resulting in a boom in cross-border barter trade. But Soviet officials complained that Soviet enterprises were incurring losses in the exchange, so in March 1989 Moscow clamped down, forcing each enterprise to get a license to trade from a ministry in Moscow. Beijing retaliated by proposing that bilateral trade be placed on a cash basis, a proposal promptly adopted by Moscow.[29]

The most important factor limiting Sino-Soviet trade in Central Asia has been transportation. A regular air service between Harbin (the regional center of northeastern China) and Khabarovsk has been agreed upon in the border talks, with service scheduled to begin in 1990; the Soviet Union also announced plans to reopen Leninskoye port, upstream from Tongjiang, to river trade. Unlike Heilongjiang in the east, the rest of Central Asia has no through rail links to the Soviet Union; yet the distance between Urumqi and the nearest Chinese seaport is more than 3,000 kilometers, so such links make economic sense. Poor roads mean that only small trucks can be used. Work on a link between Urumqi and the Soviet line between Alma Ata and Semipalatinsk began in 1958 but halted when relations soured. In the spring of 1986, Beijing and Moscow agreed to resume reciprocal utilization of inland communications lines, and by 1989 tracks had been laid for 269 of the 460 kilometer stretch between Urumqi and the Soviet border. This is part of the Eurasian Continental Bridge, to connect the Pacific and the Atlantic, from the port city Lianyungang in eastern China to the Black Sea, the Baltic Sea, the Mediterranean, finally to Amsterdam. It will save 20 percent on transportation costs, and the time will be about half that of sea transport (via the Indian Ocean and the Suez), making large-scale foreign investment in Xinjiang economically feasible for the first time. This line should be opened to traffic by 1991. Early in 1988 China's State Council approved a plan to designate Xinjiang's Urumqi and Qinghai's

Xining counties as Special Economic Zones to attract Soviet investment and trade.[30]

The Chinese labor surplus constitutes a natural complement to the Soviet labor shortage, now that Soviet fears of demographic inundation have been allayed; China has already begun exporting technocrats and skilled labor for work abroad, to help generate foreign exchange. Labor export to the USSR and other bloc countries looks particularly attractive, as the risks of defection are low there and the political system is supportive. Most of the bloc has already signed labor agreements with China. The GDR signed a ten-year contract in 1986 for the use of Chinese labor, to be paid for in local currency, and by 1989 some 80,000 Chinese workers were helping offset the chronic labor shortage there.[31] The Soviets had already made arrangements to import tens of thousands of Vietnamese and North Korean workers to this sparse and gelid region; in 1988 they imported their first 1,200 Chinese workers to work in Siberian timber projects. That number increased to 10,000 in 1989 (hailing from the three northeastern provinces), and is slated to reach 50,000 by 1992. During the last half of 1988 alone, China signed labor contracts worth $100 million.[32]

CHAPTER 5

Parallel Development?

To the Soviets, the relationship with the vast socialist country sharing its longest border has always presented an opportunity and a challenge. As an opportunity, the PRC represents a major augmentation in the global significance of that ideology to which Soviet national interests were attached. The challenge has been that of ensuring Chinese co-operation in the pursuit of ideological *qua* bloc objectives, as the CPSU has defined them, in the absence of the brute power to enforce such cooperation that it could wield in the last resort over Eastern Europe.

To meet this challenge, the Soviet leadership has in succession pursued three different strategies, which they have sometimes mixed. The first was to cultivate material dependency, adhering to a functionalist logic, offering relatively generous aid and trade arrangements to spin a web of interdependence so that Chinese developmental prospects would remain hostage to cooperation on international issues. When the PRC boldly defied that logic by striking out on its own path, in both foreign and domestic policy arenas, even managing to survive the considerable hardship that the consequent severance of material dependency entailed, the USSR resorted to its second strategy. This was to rely primarily on negative sanctions, including ideological invective and ostracism, to coerce Chinese cooperation. This simply resulted in a polarization of relations, climaxing in border clashes that brought the two countries to the brink of war. Reliance on negative sanctions might have succeeded had the USSR been able to contain the dispute within the bloc and preclude U.S. involvement. But China is after all not Czechoslovakia; when the Chinese found themselves faced with the threat of an application of Soviet strategic superiority, they opted to secede from the bloc rather than capitulate, successfully stalemating this threat through diplomatic realignment.

The 1969–79 decade was a transitional one, during which the Soviets adopted a "mixed" strategy of intimidation and negotiation. Although nothing more positive than stalemate was achieved, the dangerous escalatory dynamic toward mutual demonization was at least broken.

Since 1979, they have reverted to the strategy of cultivating dependency by multiplying ties in accord with the old functionalist logic, while gradually reducing the level of military intimidation. But there is at least one important difference from the pattern of the 1950s. Having apparently learned from their previous experience that the economic "base" in any Leninist system is but a dependent variable, they have taken pains to augment economic interdependence with a carefully constructed network of diplomatic, cultural, and other exchanges at the level of "cultural superstructure." With full appreciation of the fact that the Chinese now have other options, they have proceeded step by step, with scrupulous respect for Chinese nationalism. This strategy seems to have been quite successful. Negotiating forums have proliferated, both material and symbolic exchanges have mounted steadily, and both physical and polemical conflicts have been brought under control. The sprawling Soviet Embassy compound in Beijing houses some five hundred Soviet citizens (by far the largest diplomatic contingent in the PRC), and it is still growing. Nor is anything looming on the horizon to impede this convergence. The Three Fundamental Obstacles had been "essentially" removed by the fall of 1988, in Chinese eyes, permitting the climactic foreign ministerial and leadership summits the following spring. And considering that the USSR has now joined the PRC in the quest for "reform" or "restructuring," having given up its attempt to play China's ideological or developmental preceptor, the construction of socialism need no longer divide them.

The Chinese have long held ambivalent attitudes about their powerful northern neighbor. After having been both closely allied with the Soviets and on the brink of war with them, the Chinese are now seeking a "normal" relationship, one in which interdependence and mutual advantage can be cultivated without lapsing into dependency. And the USSR seems eager to reciprocate. As far as the two countries' developmental needs are concerned, this would seem to be to their mutual advantage; other aspects of the relationship will be examined in the following chapters.

As of this writing, the pattern of development in the two countries might be said to be neither convergent nor divergent, for neither is preceptor or "model" for the other, but rather *parallel*, in the sense that both systems have now adopted the same vocabulary of motive and built their discourse around it. This is the language of "reform socialism." The language of orthodoxy having been bankrupted in the course of the polemics of the 1960s, both have resorted to a language that means little more than that each country will be flexible, tolerant, and pragmatic about its own policies as well as about the other's. Yet the fact that both use the same political language, for all its imprecision, is significant. It signifies that they again belong to the same reference group (a term to be more thoroughly explored in the next section)— that the policies each experiments with will be accorded a higher degree of interest and face validity than policies adopted by nonmembers of that group. This does not mean those policies will necessarily be adopted, of course; there has been at least as much policy divergence as convergence since June 1989. But it does mean those policies will be carefully considered as possible options, either to be endorsed or repudiated. Chinese diplomats have even begun to talk of a new alliance to replace the friendship treaty Beijing abrogated in 1979—an alliance no longer centered on "common action" to foment revolution abroad, but on collaboration to reform socialism at home.[1]

And indeed, such collaboration could be mutually beneficial. China's experience with economic reform has been much more successful than that of the Soviet Union, which has however exposed itself much more boldly to popular demands for political reform than China has, inviting an "exchange of experience" concerning reform. Both systems approach politics with similar backgrounds, organizational maps, and expectations. Both have imperial traditions with little taste of democracy, both have experienced indigenous revolutions whose impact on political culture has been profound and lasting, and both have powerful, reliable military-security apparatuses whose role in future political crises it would be naive to discount. In view of these parallels, it is perhaps more likely that both will remain members of this reference group longer than their former comrades in Eastern Europe.

Yet despite obsessive Soviet attempts to impose some sort of procedural order on the relationship via the proliferation of institutionalized communications forums, there is still a certain "lag" in the process of parallel development, as each side tends to hypostatize its image of the other and respond to obsolescent notions. This time lag, a likely consequence of the imposition of a political freeze-frame on information flows, results in systematic misperception and misunderstanding: Mao, for example, became a fervent Stalinist only after Stalin's demise. Just as the Maoists continued to criticize Khrushchev's "revisionism" during the increasingly orthodox Brezhnev administration, those in the current Chinese leadership most attracted to the Soviet model seem to take their cue not from Gorbachev but from Brezhnev or even Stalin. Even now, as the two countries move ever so hesitantly into each other's arms, their different conceptions of socialist reform make their embrace a bit awkward—as was most recently evident during the May 1989 Gorbachev summit in Beijing, amid admiring democracy protesters (and embarrassed hosts).

PART II

CHINA'S SEARCH FOR A NATIONAL IDENTITY

The premise of this section of the book is that at least one of the factors determining a country's foreign policy is the way it comes to define its "national identity."[1] The notion that a nation-state in the course of development acquires a distinctive "identity," which in turn comes to influence its subsequent evolution, is an old one. National histories typically accept, and seek to demonstrate, this (generally tacit) assumption. The extreme cases illustrate its plausibility most effectively: it is as difficult to imagine the rise of Caesarist leadership in, say, Samoa, as it is to imagine stable parliamentary democracy flowering in post-tsarist Russia. Even ideologically and organizationally homogeneous political phenomena may take quite different forms because of divergent national "identities," as in the case of "fascism" in Italy, China, and Germany, or socialism in Russia, Vietnam, and Cuba. The problem for the social scientist is to transform the intuitively plausible notion of a distinctive collective experience into a semantically precise concept which might, at least in theory, form the basis for systematic comparative inquiry and even theoretical prediction.

Some of the confusion might perhaps be dispelled by eliminating the conceptual overlap between "national identity" and "political culture," and drawing a clear distinction between the two.[2] The concept of political culture would be properly concerned with the political beliefs, attitudes, and values of individual citizens, and the relationship between these and collective entities—less through the empirical mechanisms subsumed by the concept of "interest aggregation" (electoral participation, pressure groups, and so forth), which remain the object of traditional political analysis, and more through such psychocultural processes as the articulation of symbol systems and popular identification with them.[3] The concept of national identity, drawing on the Durkheimian insight that a collective representation has an existence independent from (if not "more than") the sum of its constituent parts, would be concerned exclusively with the properties of the *collective* entity. These might be expected to derive, in turn, from the cumulative historical experience of the nation-state in question.

A second conceptual innovation might be introduced from the social psychological literature that, together with the Eriksonian neo-Freudian tradition, has made significant contributions to our understanding of identity formation.[4] Whereas the Eriksonian interest remained focused on the individual psyche, on "the sameness and continuity of one's [in this case, the state's] meaning for others,"[5] thus attempting to identify a sense of thematic coherence over time, the social psychological focus has been the discovery of meaning within a group. Within this tradition, "identity" is closely related to role theory. A "role" is formed through the accretion of meaning via interactions with "significant others."[6] And, just as "lying" does not deny the truth-value of speech, but rather depends on it for its effectiveness, even the deliberate manipulation of a role for political ends assumes the significance of role relationships. An "identity" is at least in part a compilation of mutually complementary roles, adapted to meet a variety of social expectations and task environments. Yet integral to a fully realized identity is also a sense of its uniqueness, which derives from the willingness to *detach* one's identity from its social milieu.[7] From this perspective, then, an identity is an amalgam of "fitting in" and "standing out," the product of socialization into and/or identification with selected reference groups of significant others, yet at the same time a combination of characteristics destined to impart a sense of distinctiveness and integrity, defying reduction to those reference groups.

National identity thus consists of at least two facets. On the one hand, there is a basket of more or less interrelated meaningful themes—certain equal rights, say, or the fable of the old man who moved mountains —that have some coherence and continuity over time. These themes are central to the people sharing an identity, embracing certain common values, norms, and substantive (including territorial) goals. These collective aspirations are inherently somewhat elastic, but it should be possible to delineate certain minima and maxima, on the more precise demarcation of which rival political groups might be expected to form and compete. Or, given a more authoritarian political tradition, one dominant group might superimpose a particular variant of these collective values and goals, as in the case of the socialist or fascist national myth. In addition to this perceived continuity of values in pursuit of core policy desiderata, a national identity is based on a set of patterned relationships with other nations—just as an individual "role" is formed through interaction with significant others. In any nation's attempt to arrange a "meaningful" relationship with others in its international environment, there is a tendency to reduce a confusing welter of states into a few categories or national "types" (e.g., bourgeois democracies, developing nations, oil sheikdoms) which come to represent particular values, opportunities, and dangers. Like the individual, the nascent nation-state selects a *reference group* from among these national types to which it can usefully relate.

A reference group serves two functions in the process of national self-definition. First, *legitimacy:* discovery of a like-minded group beyond national boundaries allows one to maintain that the principles on which one's domestic political arrangements and development are based have generalizable validity. This is particularly vital in new nations without ready resort to the sanction of a domestic tradition, which bolsters more established orders. Second, *leadership:* the country assumes itself to have an intimate, fraternal relationship with those nations in its reference group, implying that the latter will welcome suggestions, even vigorous leadership in the pursuit of mutually beneficial joint international objectives otherwise beyond realistic hope of attainment. This need not imply that the "leader" *coerces* its "followers" to obey, only that the latter do so.

In many, perhaps most, cases both functions are served by the same international reference group. Thus for the Soviet Union, its position as the vanguard of the international communist revolution provides both legitimacy and international leadership, reinforcing the "leading role" of the CPSU domestically. As for the United States, its self-appointed role as leader of the "free world" serves both legitimating and leadership functions, though there has been considerable ambiguity about what values and needs this particular reference group has in common (democracy? capitalism?) and what sort of leadership it requires. Those nations whose size and resources do not permit them to exercise leadership over their reference groups still have several options. First, they may reconcile themselves to the role of (sometimes reluctant or even nominal) followers and endeavor from this less visible position to induce their reference group to adopt policies beneficial to their interests, as in postwar Japan and West Germany. Second, they may attempt to usurp leadership, compensating for objective incapacity with an especially compelling vision of a joint project or a charismatic personal candidate, as in India under Nehru or France under De Gaulle. Third, they may secede from their original reference group, as the Albanians have done (twice). But the need for an international reference group is so strong that a secession is usually soon followed by identification with a new group: either swinging to the opposite "side," as in Castro's Cuba or Egypt under Sadat, or attempting to assemble a new group, as in the nonaligned bloc organized by India, Yugoslavia, et al. in the 1950s, or the (less successful) attempt by Indonesia's Sukarno to organize a rival United Nations of New Emerging Forces in 1965.

Once firmly established, a national identity may be expected to provide a basis for reasonable expectations concerning the range of feasible coalition partners or even the nation's future international comportment under various conditions. If, on the other hand, the nation in question has difficulty establishing a national identity, its international behavior is likely to be unpredictable, perhaps even dangerous. The nation may "try out" various identities, alternating between regimes striving to lead it in quite different directions. In a situation of national identity crisis, the nation's leadership may seek to forestall identity diffusion or other perceived perils by preemptively defining national identity in an unambiguous, "extreme" way, and coercing its citizenry to fit this Procrustean bed. Lacking a patterned, well-integrated relationship with other states in the international environment, a state may in extreme cases lose its sense of proportion and launch inappropriately ambitious, even "crazy,"[8] unilateral foreign policy initiatives.

This section of the book will interpret the PRC orientation to world politics from the perspective of China's search for national identity. Inasmuch as revolutionary China repudiated its cultural legacy with unusual vehemence and may thus be assumed to have cut the ties of domestic policy continuity on which a sense of identity normally rests, the focus will be on international as opposed to domestic factors, new as opposed to old reference groups, in China's search for national identity. Whereas other, more parsimonious explanations may perhaps be found for discrete events in Chinese foreign policy development, the quest here is for a pattern that makes sense of a series of policy choices. Contextual determinants of international relations are also important in the choice of identity—the ninety-five pound weakling and the football hero have different options—but again, that is not the focus of this analysis.

Almost from the beginning, the PRC has been afflicted with a national identity dilemma. Approaching the modern international system with memories of a glorious traditional identity as regional hegemon, followed by the status degradation of defeat and parcelization at the hands of perceived inferiors, China was accustomed to a position of international leadership which political resource depletion and economic backwardness made it impossible to sustain. This sense of sudden national status deprivation gave rise to an ambiguous attitude of admiration and indignation vis-à-vis the dominant Western powers.[9] Inhibited in discussing these issues explicitly by the Marxist denial of nationalism, they transposed the problem to the selection of external reference groups, identifying on the one hand with the communist bloc and on the other with the Third World.[10] The decomposition of identity due to ambivalence about available reference group options is perhaps not unique, but China's "split" has been unusually clear-cut and protracted. From the Chinese perspective, the bloc provided ideological legitimacy, but Soviet monopolization of the "leading role" foreclosed any prospect for international leadership. Perceiving itself as the most important of the new nations—with the largest population and land area, first to acquire nuclear capability, the only one eventually to gain a permanent seat on the UN Security Council—it was easy for China to see itself in a leadership role among developing countries, with whom the PRC identified as a fellow victim of imperialist exploitation. But it was less facile to derive system legitimacy from such an amorphous and heterogeneous grouping, which included communist, capitalist, feudal-monarchical, democratic, militarist, and diverse mixed systems. So China identified with both categories.

Why was this a dilemma? Of course China *is* in fact both a socialist nation under the leadership of the Chinese Communist Party and a developing nation, and these two identities are not necessarily mutually exclusive. It is tempting to infer that the PRC arranged itself among its reference groups hierarchically, adopting the bloc as an "ego ideal" and the Third World as a "negative identity"—but that would be an oversimplification.[11] The Soviet Union was clearly a role model at an early, formative stage, but Chinese feelings were already more ambivalent than appeared at the time; the Third World represented not so much a negative identity (a role usually played by capitalism) as a throwback to a prerevolutionary stage (with whom the PRC might thus identify in its travail and to whom it might offer helpful developmental advice). The PRC attempted to integrate the two reference groups ("straddle two boats," in the Chinese expression) by way of organizing its own self-concept, sometimes successfully rationalizing its bifurcated identity theoretically, sometimes shuttling between identities when their fates seemed irreconcilable or a clear-cut choice seemed imperative. While this ambivalence has permitted considerable flexibility in the pursuit of Chinese national interests, it has also rendered Chinese participation in either group somewhat marginal (but, as we shall see in Part III,

China has sometimes been able to use its very marginality to strategic advantage).

We shall first examine China's evolving role within the communist bloc, then turn to the PRC relationship with the Third World. In constituting the two reference groups, for those countries (other than China) which might legitimately be subsumed by either category (e.g., Vietnam, North Korea), bloc affiliation is assumed to take precedence.

CHAPTER 6

China and the International Communist Movement

The communist bloc first became a geopolitical reality in the post–World War II period, when the Soviet Union seized the opportunity to install communist parties in the power vacuum left by retreating Axis forces in Eastern Europe while the Chinese Communist Party seized power from the tottering Kuomintang (KMT) in China. Altogether this constituted a rather impressive international empire. The CCP had consistently adhered to the discipline of international democratic centralism despite occasional misgivings during the revolutionary era (for example, agreeing at Moscow's behest to release Chiang Kai-shek from house arrest when he fell into their hands at Xian), and now that the revolution had triumphed the PRC submerged its national identity relatively completely in the socialist community.

During a time of frigid cold war, tight bloc alignment was deemed sine qua non for national survival by most bloc members, and discipline was taut. The East European countries, having been devastated by the Nazi invasion and the Soviet counterattack, exhibited a temporary power vacuum, into which the CPSU quickly inserted émigré communist party leaderships more beholden to Moscow than to indigenous constituencies. The highly centralized distribution of power within the Soviet Union during the late Stalinist period thus found its echo in a similar arrangement within the bloc.

The CCP leadership, having come to power based on its own resources with little indebtedness to outside aid, nevertheless not only accepted but reinforced this asymmetric distribution of power—eager as it was to shift from a negative and ambiguous identity ("half-colonial, half-feudal") to full integration within a positive reference group. The CCP fully endorsed the excommunication of Tito, for example; party theorist Liu Shaoqi devoted a long article to the rationalization of that decision as early as 1948.[1] Sino-Yugoslav relations were to remain strained for many years thereafter (much longer than Soviet-Yugoslav relations); Beijing and Belgrade did not even exchange ambassadors (China simply ignored Yugoslav recognition) until January 1955, and by the fall of 1957 relations between the CCP and the Yugoslav party had been severed, not to be restored until 1980.

Once Stalin's initial suspicions had been overcome, the CCP was accorded special deference within the bloc, as its largest constituent party with jurisdiction over the world's biggest population and third largest land mass. Stalin's death in March 1953 enhanced China's status, as symbolized by Zhou Enlai's selection as the only non-Soviet pallbearer at his funeral and by a doctored photograph appearing in *Pravda* just five days after his death, showing Malenkov with Stalin and Mao.[2] Indeed, during the period from October 1954 to the first half of 1956, the Soviet attitude toward the PRC changed from one of hegemon-to-satellite to one of relatively equal partners.[3] The Soviets frequently cited with pride Lenin's several references to the importance of China, such as the following passage from an article first published in 1923:

In the last analysis, the outcome of the struggle will be determined by the fact that Russia, India, and China, etc., constitute the overwhelming majority of the population of the globe. And it is precisely this majority of the population that during the past few years, has been drawn into the struggle for its emancipation with extraordinary rapidity, so that in this respect there cannot be the slightest shadow of doubt what the final outcome of the world struggle will be. In this sense, the final victory of socialism is fully and absolutely assured.[4]

But by the latter half of the decade, China's sense of having its identity securely anchored in the socialist community and value system had become unhinged. The seeds for this alienation were sown in the famous "secret speech" Khrushchev delivered to the Twentieth CPSU Congress in February 1956. Although Khrushchev recalls that Mao's initial reaction was favorable—that Mao, too, began to criticize Stalin[5]—in the long run the Maoist leadership found that Khrushchev's bold departures took international communism in a direction inimical to Chinese interests. Khrushchev introduced three important ideological innovations at this conference that were to set the parameters for the conflict that would rage for the next twenty years. These innovations signaled what Zagoria has termed a shift from *continental* to *global* strategy: rather than focusing on the consolidation of the bloc countries in the Eurasian heartland, Moscow turned its attentions outward toward the rest of the world, attempting to foster détente with the developed countries and to solicit clients among the developing nations in Asia and

Africa, whose decolonization struggles had given rise to a certain sympathy for anti-imperialist, anticapitalist perspectives.

First, Khrushchev introduced the theoretical possibility of establishing "peaceful coexistence" with the capitalist world, particularly the United States. (At the Twenty-second CPSU Congress in 1961, he would extend this doctrine further, saying not only that "capitalist encirclement" was at an end but that the danger of global wars would cease within a generation.) Ideologically, this entailed what Chinese polemicists would deride as the "extinction of class struggle": because of the development of nuclear weapons, war between blocs would annihilate people of every class background, making no difference whether a country was socialist or imperialist.

Second, he supported nationalist struggles among the decolonizing new nations who were not yet under the control of communist parties but evinced a certain sympathy for Soviet foreign policy objectives, or some inclination toward a Soviet pattern of domestic economic development.

Third, he liberalized socialist authority relationships, both among member parties of the bloc (by endorsing "many roads to socialism") and between masses and party elites domestically (by renouncing the "cult of personality"). In the same context he endorsed a "transition to socialism by parliamentary means," in an evident play for nonruling communist parties endeavoring to compete in democratic electoral contests.

Some of the broader implications of these theoretical innovations receive fuller attention in the following chapter. As far as China's attempt to resolve problems of national identity via identification with the international communist movement is concerned, it posed both short-run tactical difficulties and long-term systemic problems. The tactical difficulty was that the leader with whom Mao had personally identified in order to bolster his ascendancy within the CCP had been shorn of his legitimacy. The central thrust of Khrushchev's speech, explicitly in point three but implicitly in points one and two as well, was to repudiate the Stalinist personality cult. While this served Khrushchev's immediate interest in discrediting his (Stalinist) rivals within the Soviet Politburo, it also had the troublesome side effect of splitting all the satellite leaderships between those who had identified with (thereby benefiting from) Stalin's personal ascendancy and those who had suffered either under Stalin or his local surrogates. In Eastern Europe this led to the rehabilitation of leaders who had been victims of Stalinism and to demands for political and economic reforms of Stalinism as a system.[6] In China it undermined the leadership of Mao Zedong. At the CCP's Eighth Congress (held only a few months after the Twentieth CPSU Congress), not only were all references to Mao Zedong Thought deleted from the Party Constitution (at the motion of Peng Dehuai, promptly endorsed by Liu Shaoqi), but a new position of "honorary chairman" (for which there could be but one conceivable candidate) was created. The provision contained in the 1945 (Seventh Congress) Constitution permitting the party chairman to hold the concurrent post of chairman of the Secretariat was rescinded, and a separate Secretariat was created under a new secretary-general named Deng Xiaoping, who was authorized not only to handle the daily work of the Central Committee (CC) but to convene Central Work Conferences—ad hoc convocations with the functional competence to displace CC plenums (which could be convened only by the chairman) during the 1962–66 period.[7] This cleavage would endure at least a decade, emerging clearly in the purge pattern of the Cultural Revolution. Its mimetic pattern illustrates one of the perils of such intense identification with another national leadership.[8]

The systemic problem was that Khrushchev's doctrinal innovations, together with the dissolution of the Cominform in April and a meeting with Tito in June, unleashed fissiparous tendencies throughout the bloc: the community into which the PRC was trying to integrate began to disintegrate. In March 1956, one month after the secret speech, riots erupted in Soviet Georgia, Stalin's birthplace; in June, civil unrest broke out in both Poland and Hungary; by October, a much more sweeping insurrection had swept through Hungary, which would require Soviet military intervention to suppress.

The CCP leadership seems to have played an equivocal role in these developments. Susceptible to the same nationalist impulses that roiled Eastern Europe, the Chinese initially welcomed a more loosely integrated bloc, maintaining through the end of 1956: "A serious consequence of Stalin's errors was the development of dogmatism."[9] Mao advocated that the relationship among socialist countries be regulated on the basis of his theory of contradictions among the people and the Five Principles of Peaceful Coexistence (as distinguished from the principles of proletarian internationalism emphasized by the CPSU), even going so far as to urge Khrushchev to withdraw all Soviet troops from Eastern Europe.[10] Then an uprising erupted in Poznan, Poland, resulting in election of a new Politburo from which all Stalinists were excluded, and the release from prison and meteoric rise (to the position of party first secretary, without Soviet approval) of reformer Wladyslaw

Gomulka. Rubbing salt in the wound, the Poles further demanded the removal of Marshal Konstantin Rokossovsky, a Russian who had been installed as Poland's defense minister in 1949. Zhou Enlai intervened to mediate Polish-Soviet tensions, helping to prevent armed Soviet intervention or ideological ostracism à la lito. During Edward Ochab's visit to Beijing for the Eighth Chinese Party Congress in September 1956, Mao expressed sympathy for the liberal faction of the Polish Communist Party (now rechristened the Polish United Workers' Party, or PUWP), advising Moscow against intervention in a personal letter the following month.[11] A Polish observer reported that during the tense Polish-Soviet negotiations of October 19 (when Khrushchev flew to Warsaw, with Soviet troops ringing the city), CCP support during and after the Eighth Plenum of the PUWP in October helped the Poles to sustain their will and not make concessions under duress.[12]

The Chinese also at first opposed the intervention into Hungary, hoping that the Polish compromise had definitively solved the "many roads" problem; the Chinese press hailed the Polish-Soviet agreement with the prediction that it also would correct "whatever was wrong with relations between the Soviet Union and Hungary."[13] The CCP leadership hesitated so long to condemn the reformers that the rumor emanated from Budapest: the Chinese are with us.[14] When the situation in Hungary nonetheless got out of hand, the Chinese changed course 180 degrees and actively advocated intervention, even adjuring an allegedly uncertain and vacillating Khrushchev to "go to the defense of the Hungarian revolution."[15] The deciding factor for the CCP seems to have been Imre Nagy's announcement on November 1 of Hungary's unilateral withdrawal from the Warsaw Pact, declaration of bloc neutrality, and endorsement of multiparty democracy; Nagy seems to have been hoping for a settlement along the lines of the Austrian State Treaty of 1955. All mention of Hungary was removed from an October 31 Chinese government commentary when it was published in *Renmin Ribao* on November 2, and an editorial the following day roundly denounced the rebellion.[16] Taking advantage of Western preoccupation with the Suez crisis, the Soviets attacked on November 4; on November 5, Liu Shaoqi arrived in Moscow in a demonstration of Chinese support for Khrushchev's "fraternal help," which "respected the territorial integrity and sovereignty of the Hungarian People's Republic."[17] In early 1957, Zhou Enlai visited the Soviet Union, Poland, and Hungary in an effort to restore bloc unity. (These broad shifts of "line" at the intrabloc level would have their subsequent domestic echo in the CCP's decision in the spring of 1957 to "Let a hundred flowers bloom, let a hundred schools of thought contend," followed shortly by the repressive "anti-Rightist movement.")[18]

These experiments with liberalization seem to have frightened the leaderships of both countries, while at the same time unveiling the unpopularity of unreconstructed Stalinism.[19] However abortive, they were not to prove politically fatal to either Khrushchev or Mao, though the two reacted quite differently to their failure. In the case of the former, the uprisings in Poland and Hungary gave birth to an opposing coalition of strange bedfellows, ranging from unreconstructed Stalinists such as Molotov and Kaganovich to erstwhile liberals such as Malenkov, in the face of which Khrushchev at first had to give ground, declaring in December 1956, "We are all Stalinists now."[20] But having disarmed his opposition by firmly repressing the Hungarian uprising and restoring bloc unity under Soviet leadership, Khrushchev was able to purge the "antiparty group" (Malenkov, Molotov, Kaganovich, and Marshal Zhukov) in the summer of 1957, and seize the premiership (while retaining the position of party first secretary) by March 1958. He then proceeded to sanctify his reforms by rewriting the official history, in three documents: Fundamentals of Marxism-Leninism (October 1959), the Declaration of 81 Communist Parties (December 1960), and the new Soviet Party Program (the first new program since 1919), endorsed by the Twenty-second CPSU Congress (October 1961)—thereby, however, also formalizing his doctrinal differences with the CCP.

To Mao Zedong, on the other hand, emergence of a rightist opposition critical of his radical policies and his somewhat autocratic leadership style had hardened his conviction that "class struggle" still existed (contrary to some prematurely optimistic observations he and other CCP leaders had made at the Eighth Party Congress in 1956), and he turned vigorously to the left. Despite his initial (privately expressed) misgivings about Stalin and Stalinism, he came now to his public defense, reflexively shifting to the critique of "revisionism" that would preoccupy him for the next two decades.[21] In this context he introduced the theory of "continuing the revolution under the dictatorship of the proletariat," developing the notion that the seizure of power marked the beginning rather than the end of the revolution and that the superstructure tended to lag behind the base, the relations of production behind the forces of production—rather than the other way round. Those class enemies still extant after socialization of the means of production had been completed were now labeled "rightist," "bourgeois," or "revisionist," not necessarily because they had a bourgeois class background but because they opposed Mao's "socialist revolutionary line," making them "objectively" bourgeois. This (plus the discrediting of the right in the Hundred Flowers) freed him to undertake far more radical domestic programs—notably, the "Three Red Flags" of 1958–59 (the Great Leap Forward, the People's Commune, and the General Line). When early opposition to this utopian experiment surfaced under the leadership of Peng Dehuai, Mao denounced (and purged) it under the ideological epitaph of right revisionism.

The CCP's post-Hundred Flowers turn leftward would put it on an eventual collision course with Khrushchev's CPSU, but for the moment, China's rejection of "revisionism" propelled it toward reintegration of the bloc under strong Soviet leadership. The CCP became during this brief hiatus puritanically orthodox, endorsing a laager mentality that would subordinate the interests of contending bloc members to those of the bloc as a whole. Thus during what would be his last visit to Moscow (to attend the Fortieth Anniversary of the October Revolution, November 14–16, 1957, followed by a conference of leaders from socialist countries and an international conference of communist parties, the reports of which have not been published), Mao declared that the Soviet Union was not only head of the bloc, but that it was absolutely imperative to "strengthen international proletarian solidarity with the Soviet Union as its center."

Our camp must have a head, because even the snake has a head. I would not agree that China should be called head of the camp, because we do not merit this honor and cannot maintain this role, we are still poor. We haven't even a quarter of a satellite, while the Soviet Union has two.[22]

"Bourgeois influence constitutes the domestic cause of revisionism," he inscribed into the text of the Conference Declaration, "and capitulation to external imperialist pressure constitutes the external cause."[23] Gomulka, to whom support had been extended only the previous year, was now criticized for being "too weak" (*trop de mollesse*) concerning revisionism; Yugoslav revisionists were denounced in a series of widely publicized articles for having refused to sign the 1957 Moscow declaration of the communist parties of the socialist countries, for "following the imperialist reactionaries," and for "venomously" attacking the "proletarian dictatorship in the Soviet Union and other socialist countries."[24] Criticism of the Yugoslav League of Communists (YLC) intensified upon its publication of an April 1958 Congress Program forecasting a world "evolution" to socialism. Whereas the crisis in Hungary could previously be attributed to the failings of the Socialist Workers'

Party leadership, now it was due to the pernicious influence of Yugo-slav revisionism. This new Chinese line was not well received in either Eastern or Western Europe, where it stultified an incipient freedom of movement.[25]

The moment when Beijing and Moscow could stand together on a platform of unquestioned Soviet bloc hegemony was to prove fleeting. When Mao's strategy for the realization of national identity premised on rapid, simultaneous achievement of nationalist and communist aspirations ran aground (efforts at the completion of national unification were frustrated by the U.S. Seventh Fleet in the Taiwan Strait, and the Great Leap Forward foundered on organizational disarray and inclement weather), he refused to relinquish his dream, reasserting its essential correctness in the teeth of adversity, blaming failure on class enemies foreign and domestic.[26] As if abruptly thrown back by these losses to an earlier stage of development, PRC politics underwent re-radicalization. Diplomatic overtures to the West (cf. Zhou Enlai's polished performance at Geneva in 1954) gave way to provocative challenges, as in the repudiation of Soviet-American nuclear arms limitation talks, support for the reviving Viet Cong insurgency, public derision for Khrushchev's embarrassing setback in the Cuban missile crisis. Revisionist tendencies were found to be ubiquitous; deviation from orthodoxy was soon discovered in the sanctum sanctorum itself (first in Moscow, then even in Beijing). Meanwhile, Khrushchev took Soviet foreign policy in the direction most apt to excite Chinese apprehensions: toward détente with the West. Just two years after restoring unity to the bloc at the 1957 Moscow conference, Khrushchev became the first communist leader to visit the United States, amid considerable fanfare.

This fateful parting of ways is partly attributable to the different menu of opportunities and dangers posed by the international system at the time, partly to the different developmental background from which the two states were emerging. The Soviets, having precariously consolidated their power over forty tempestuous years, despite the sacrifice of some nine million in the revolutionary civil war and more than twenty million in the Great Patriotic War (not to mention millions more in self-inflicted catastrophes—collectivization, forced-draft industrialization, the great purge), had finally arrived at the status (symbolized by Sputnik) of a leading world power. Now proudly looking back on an economic growth rate that averaged 7.1 percent per annum between 1950 and 1958 (a growth rate nearly 50 percent higher than that of the United States during the same period), and sitting on a (somewhat illusory) lead in the arms race, they had every reason to be confident in their economic future and by the same token chary of risking conflict with a still formidable military adversary.[27] Increasingly they turned their attention to the United States, not only as principal adversary but as a role-referent for the USSR's emerging national identity as a global "superpower."[28] Khrushchev's 1959 trip to Camp David was in this sense a turning point in Soviet history, visible recognition that the USSR now ranked with the United States as a joint arbiter of world affairs. The Chinese, on the other hand, despite an impressive beginning at socializing and modernizing their country, still saw the world very much from the perspective of a "have-not" power (whereas the Soviets had a multiethnic empire and a host of satellites, the PRC had not yet recovered all its former territories), with less to lose and more to gain from provoking strategically superior opponents. That strategic and economic inferiority was accompanied not by humility and patience but by militant self-confidence and even occasional rhetorical bravado may perhaps be attributed to the unlikely (and to some extent fortuitous) victory of CCP arms over vastly superior forces during their own revolution.

The CCP's deviation from Moscow's foreign policy line had the effect of obliging the CPSU to pay more attention to the bloc over the next several years, which became the audience before whom an increasingly vitriolic polemic was played out. Following dissolution of the Comintern (1943) and Cominform (1956), the Soviet Union began to try to coordinate and control world communism by organizing conferences of the international communist movement. These were meant to function analogously to national party conferences: the CPSU would act as the leading party among leading parties, setting the agenda, selecting participants, prefiguring policy outcomes. There were altogether three world conferences of the communist movement, held in Moscow in 1957, 1960, and 1969. Their final documents are still accorded the status of binding agreements by the CPSU and its loyal followers. But the CPSU's ability to control the agenda diminished over time, as we shall see. Indeed, the ideological controversy became so effervescent that it tended to overspill the designated forum, as member parties availed themselves of courtesy invitations to various national conferences to attend and rejoin the fray. The Twenty-first CPSU Congress of January 27 to February 5, 1959, was still relatively civil. Although Zhou Enlai made no mention in his address of Khrushchev's innovative proposal for a nuclear-free zone in the Far East and Pacific, no outward sign of tension appeared. In retrospect it seems clear that an ideological cleavage had already emerged, though it was successfully veiled by good will on both sides.

The first visible break was at a meeting held in June 1960 in conjunction with the Romanian Communist Party Congress, where Khrushchev (fresh from the failure of the Paris summit) clashed with the Chinese delegation (led by Liu Shaoqi) concerning the inevitability of war. The Soviets (promptly rebutted by the Chinese) had already breached etiquette by sending documentation to all communist parties outlining their ideological positions on the eve of the conference. Practically all the attending communist parties took the side of the CPSU. (This conference was immediately followed by the unilateral Soviet decision to withdraw all 1,600 Soviet advisers from China.) The dispute resumed at the second conference of representatives of all communist parties (except the Yugoslavs) held in November 1960. Although the Soviet perspective prevailed on most issues, Khrushchev's attempt to isolate China was frustrated, for Albania supported China to the hilt, while the Indonesian, North Korean, and North Vietnamese delegates remained neutral, inclined toward the Chinese point of view. The final declaration bore the scars of the dispute, awkwardly combining divergent positions on peaceful versus nonpeaceful paths to socialism, peaceful coexistence versus class war, and other central issues. In October 1961, at the CPSU Twenty-second Congress, to which the Albanians had not been invited, Khrushchev attacked Albania (read: China) for opposing the line agreed upon by all at the Twentieth Party Congress. Zhou Enlai objected vociferously, walked out, laid a wreath on the tomb of Stalin (whose body was removed a few days later from the Lenin Mausoleum), and left Moscow.[29] Only two-thirds of the parties represented at the Congress endorsed the attack on Albania; all the Asian parties remained mute.

Until 1962, both sides refrained from attacking the other directly, instead "pointing at the mulberry bush while cursing the locust" (to use a Chinese expression). The CCP directed its thrusts against "revisionism" in general and Yugoslavia in particular, sometimes also assailing the Italian Communist Party (at that time led by Palmiro Togliatti). The Soviets attacked "dogmatists" in general and (after the breach with the Albanian Communist Party in 1961) the Albanians in particular. The issues remained basically those defined in Khrushchev's 1956 speech: the question of war or peace (with the Chinese still insisting on the inevitability of international class war), the approach to the Third World (with the Chinese espousing wars of national liberation, the Soviets urging communist parties in the developing countries to form a united front with the postcolonial "national bourgeoisie"—as they had once urged the CCP to form a coalition government with the KMT), and the possibility of a "parliamentary road" to socialism (the Soviets in support, the Chinese remaining firmly opposed). These issues however became personalized, especially after the Albanians began calling for Khrushchev's resignation in 1962. In the fall of that year, the CCP dispatched a delegation to the congresses of the communist parties of Bulgaria, Hungary, Czechoslovakia, and East Germany to defend the Chinese-Albanian position on this and other issues.[30]

The heat of the ideological exchanges at these interparty forums, combined with the inability of the dominant side to prevail conclusively and ostracize the defeated minority, eventually led to their paralysis. Proposals for a new international conference were put forth at the beginning of 1962 by the communist parties of Indonesia, North Vietnam, Great Britain, Sweden, and New Zealand (with Soviet endorsement), but the CCP killed the motion by proposing numerous preconditions: the cessation of public polemics, the holding of bilateral talks between parties, and the restoration of normal relations between the Soviet and Albanian parties (which had been broken off in 1961). During the fall and winter of 1963–64, Khrushchev called for an end to public polemics and convocation of a world communist conference; if there were still differences between the Soviet and Chinese parties, "let us allow time to have its say as to which viewpoint is more correct"—implicitly suggesting (in Chinese eyes) an imminent showdown, in which the CPSU was confident of a majority.[31] After protracted stalling, resumed polemics, and a futile Romanian attempt at mediation, this meeting also had to be abandoned (in 1965), owing to Chinese rejection and the consequent inability to reach preliminary consensus.

Not until June 1969 did the Soviet Union succeed in holding the long deferred third international conference, in the shadow of the invasion of Czechoslovakia. By this time the nonparticipation of China could be assumed. Moreover, there were no representatives from Albania, Japan, Indonesia, North Korea, or indeed from any East or Southeast Asian communist party; and some of those delegations who did attend defended the Chinese and Czech right to dissent.[32] Although Brezhnev attacked Mao by name for violating the principles of scientific communism and struggling to gain hegemony within the world communist movement, there were no critical references to the CCP in the joint basic document issued by the conference.[33] As of this writing, this remains the final meeting of the "communist world movement": Moscow proposed a fourth conference in 1981, but this was firmly rejected by the Chinese, Yugoslav, Vietnamese, North Korean, Italian, Spanish, Japanese, and other communist parties. Beijing rejected a CPSU call for a world conference of communist parties in January 1985, and in June 1986, Jaruzelski (presumably acting for Gorbachev) revived a proposal to convene a conference on the themes of "peace and disarmament," but it has gone nowhere.

Given the paralysis of world communist party conferences, the CPSU turned to the international organizations of the bloc that it still controlled, the Warsaw Treaty Organization (WTO) and the Council of Mutual Economic Assistance (CMEA), who accordingly saw their heyday in 1956–71.[34] This permitted a distinction to arise within international communism between Soviet-controlled and non-Soviet controlled networks, which we shall refer to respectively as the internal and external blocs. In 1961–62 the Soviets moved to transform the CMEA into a supranational planning organization (CMEA had been dormant until roused to handle economic aid to Hungary in 1957), and in 1965 they reorganized the WTO to permit coordination of foreign policies as well as joint security planning. The Comprehensive Program agreed upon at the July 1971 meeting of the CMEA, stressing voluntary coordination of national economic plans and joint economic forecasting, was an important step toward economic integration. Gorbachev initially endeavored (unsuccessfully) to continue or even accelerate this movement, as indicated in the "Comprehensive Program for Scientific and Technical Progress" adopted in December 1985, which attempts to include scientific as well as economic and cultural integration. He also dramatically increased the number of CMEA and WTO meetings convened, as well as summit meetings with various party leaders. Since his succession, he has visited every one of the East European states, some more than once. Finally, on April 26, 1985, the WTO was extended for another twenty years, plus a further ten unless notice of withdrawal is given a year before expiry.[35] It is ironic that this grandiose aspiration should be followed so soon by the collapse of communist party hegemony in the front-line East European states (in 1989–90), auguring the imminent disintegration of both WTO and CMEA.

Despite incapacitating the (external) bloc, the CCP's principled dissent may paradoxically have expanded its influence within it: "In retrospect, one may say that it was from 1960 to 1965 that China experienced the greatest influence within the socialist camp."[36] Difficult as it is to measure influence, in view of the CCP's previous subordination of national demands to international solidarity, its willingness to disagree, and even to campaign for leadership of the bloc (claiming the CPSU had betrayed socialism, and indeed was no longer a socialist country), seems to have enhanced its ideological status, even among those who disapproved—meanwhile also greatly impressing both superpowers.[37] Although remaining a minority, the Maoist faction split the bloc ideologically and to some extent geographically, gaining the occasional to regular support of Albania, Cuba, North Korea, and North Vietnam; even Poland opposed CCP expulsion. While sharing the ostensible interest of the CPSU in greater intrabloc pluralism and a less confrontational approach to the noncommunist world, many smaller parties were loath to support excommunication of the second most powerful bloc member, whose unpunished assertion of dissident views eroded the ideological authority of the CPSU and tacitly enhanced their own margin for maneuver. Thus in the early 1960s, many Soviet troops and advisers were withdrawn from Eastern Europe, leaders were no longer appointed directly from Moscow, and more mutually advantageous cultural and economic ties were developed.

The schism also had spillover effects beyond the bloc, spreading to nonruling communist parties in Europe, Japan, and the developing countries. In 1963 the CCP began to call for the formation of pro-Chinese fractions in all countries where the local party leadership supported the CPSU. Thus, for example, in their "Proposal for the General Line of the International Communist Movement" (June 1963), the CCP articulated twenty-five points to define the world movement in what it considered an ideologically correct way, challenging communist parties throughout the world to overthrow their existing leadership and avoid revisionism. This call was not without consequence. In the spring of 1964 the communist parties of Hungary, Bulgaria, Czechoslovakia, and the GDR reported Chinese-inspired "Stalinist" plots had attempted to split their respective parties and seize control of the leadership; in the fall the PUWP alleged that "pro-Chinese communists in Prague" had been caught circulating rumors against the Gomulka regime, and a group of six "Stalinists" was arrested.[38] The Belgian Communist Party was "reconstituted on a national level on the basis of Marxism-Leninism"; pro-Chinese parties or fractions were also organized in Spain, Italy, Austria, France, Great Britain, West Germany, Switzerland, Holland, Ireland, Denmark, Norway, Sweden, and Finland.[39] In the Third World (e.g., Argentina, Brazil, India, Chile), pro-Chinese parties were formed to parallel and compete with pro-Soviet parties. To be sure, these "Maoist" fractions were of dubious diplomatic value, their radical orientations as likely as not reflecting domestic political issues rather than a conscious ideological choice between rival worldviews, and the CCP was unable to control them. It was at this time that the CCP also left most of the international communist front organizations because they were under Soviet control.

By the late 1960s, however, China seems to have lost its bid for ideological leadership of the bloc. China's bout with "crazy" foreign policy radicalism during the Cultural Revolution reduced China's stature among all but the extreme left wing of the international communist movement, at the same time eviscerating the PRC's own diplomatic cadre structure. During this period, the Maoist leadership repudiated the existence of a socialist camp and depicted the Soviet Union as what Mao called a "negative model" of socialism (thus for example linking the highest CCP purge victims, Peng Dehuai, Liu Shaoqi, and Lin Biao, with pro-Soviet conspiracies). As West Germany's Ostpolitik bore fruition in the late 1960s under Brandt, the Soviets shifted the role of scapegoat and bogeyman from the German neo-Nazis to China in their efforts to maintain discipline within the WTO.[40] The PRC thus functioned no longer as an outer limit for permissible dissent but as an *exemple terrible* to preclude the slightest deviation. Most important, WTO suppression of the Czech "socialism with a human face" experiments in August 1968 (which Beijing indignantly protested, despite its contempt for the "revisionist" Dubček), and Brezhnev's ensuing declaration of his doctrine of "limited sovereignty," had a pervasive chilling effect, and China came closer than ever to complete excommunication. It was in response to this threat that the PRC broke out of the bloc in a search for geopolitically useful support. China was concerned not only with possible application of the Brezhnev Doctrine to China, but with possible Soviet intervention elsewhere in Eastern Europe—particularly in light of the mild American response to the invasion.[41] The ensuing attempt to build an international united front against the Soviet Union was eclectic, even promiscuous, tending to detract from China's ideological credibility. The opening to the United States was difficult for those communist parties still friendly to the CCP to comprehend, further mitigating Chinese influence within the international communist movement.

As China emerged from self-imposed isolation under the stimulus of Soviet nuclear threats in the early 1970s, the split came to revolve around power-political rather than ideological considerations. At the Tenth CCP Congress in 1973, the leadership announced that "the socialist camp has ceased to exist," labeling the Soviet Union a "social imperialist superpower." The CPSU's forcible reassertion of hegemony in

Eastern Europe in 1968 brought out the geopolitical dimension of the schism: by the end of the 1960s, aside from Albania and Romania,[42] most supporters of the CCP line (the Cambodian, Thai, Malaysian, Indonesian, and New Zealand communist parties) were in East Asia. The CCP's 1974 inauguration of its three worlds schema exacerbated this regionalizing tendency by dissolving the socialist "camp" (an ideologically based category) in favor of the Third World (a more regionally based, ideologically catchall category) as the main revolutionary axis in the struggle against the superpowers. It was over this reconceptualization that the Albanians chose to split with the "insincere, perfidious, malicious and treacherous" CCP, though they did not announce their disagreement until several years later.[43] Seven further parties took advantage of the dispute to declare their neutrality, including in addition to the Yugoslavian, the North Korean, Japanese, Vietnamese, and Laotian parties; the regional trend is also noticeable here. While trying to preserve their regional hegemony over the Asian communist movement, the Chinese adopted a policy toward Eastern Europe analogous to that of the Americans, encouraging any tendency toward greater autonomy in foreign policy regardless of its ideological thrust. Between 1968 and 1971 Beijing cultivated Sino-Yugoslav relations (ambassadors were exchanged in October 1969 for the first time in eleven years), though not until Mao's death could this bitter enmity be fully reconciled. In August 1977 Tito visited Beijing, and in March 1978 party-to-party relations were restored (further exacerbating Sino-Albanian difficulties). In 1971 it was revealed that Romania had functioned as a diplomatic channel for contacts leading to the Nixon visit (at American rather than Chinese initiative), and in June 1971 Ceausescu himself became the first Warsaw Pact member to visit the PRC since the Sino-Soviet rift.[44]

While the Chinese were thus nurturing their garden of Asian socialism and cultivating outposts of resistance in the Soviet backyard, the Soviets were no less assiduous in courting defectors on the Chinese periphery. Geopolitically considered, the opening and growing warmth between China and the Western capitalist countries (particularly the United States) had placed the smaller socialist countries on the Asian rimland (North Korea, Vietnam) in a tenuous position. Already exposed to American naval and air power from the Pacific, they suddenly felt their continental rear area being undermined. The Vietnamese were first to experience this type of geopolitical squeeze in the early 1970s. Indeed, that was one of Nixon's major goals in his opening to China. As far as China's support of Vietnam was concerned, his efforts were not without impact, having an alienating effect on Sino-Vietnamese relations. In the case of North Korea, the PRC's growing involvement in sub rosa trade with South Korea in the 1970s and 1980s (by 1989, Chinese trade with South Korea amounted to more than U.S. $3 billion, ten times more than that with the North) was acutely resented by the latter, as well as the waning of Chinese military support (moral or material) since the Rangoon *attentat* against Chun. The security dimension of these developments will be explored more fully in Chapter 14, but in both cases the political impact was a shift of patronage from Beijing to Moscow—emphatic and public in the case of Hanoi, more subtle and tentative in the case of Pyongyang.

The CCP discovered Eurocommunism toward the end of the decade, its own incipient domestic reform program helping to arouse mutual interest. Again, however, this effort was primarily prompted by a desire to outflank the CPSU rather than any deep ideological affinity. In 1971 Spanish party secretary Santiago Carrillo arrived in Beijing, bearing a secret letter from Enrico Berlinguer proposing a resumption of party-to-party relations with the Italian party (the Chinese could not agree). Jiri Pelikan, a Czech dissident and member of the European Parliament, came to China shortly after the invasion of Afghanistan and the Vietnamese occupation of Cambodia, when Chinese sensitivities about encirclement had been aroused. It was at about the same time that Chinese media began to refer more neutrally to the communist parties of Italy (PCI) and Spain (PCE), and to suspend their polemic against "revisionism." A major benchmark was the visit in April 1980 of Berlinguer, who was now warmly received and had numerous meetings with Hua Guofeng, Deng Xiaoping, and Hu Yaobang. In his April 16 speech at Peking University, Berlinguer denied the existence of a unique model for all communist parties. He said that each party must find its own road, based on its historical background, while all parties shared certain ideal interests, especially concerning peace and justice. The renewal of interparty relations between the CCP and PCI, Berlinguer insisted, should not be at the expense of any third communist party. Hu Yaobang could not entirely agree at the time, insisting on the need to "mobilize the working class in the struggle against the hegemonists." Echoing Mao's original critique of "revisionism," the Chinese also professed their belief in the inevitability of war and their reservations about the "parliamentary road." Whereas Berlinguer (along with most Eurocommunists) had abandoned the concept of the "dictatorship of the proletariat" in favor of "structural reform," the CCP still deemed the former indispensable.

Since the outset of the Sino-Soviet "thaw" (particularly since the cooling of Sino-American relations in 1981–82), the PRC has accelerated efforts to make new friends in the international socialist movement. The major innovation has been that the search for coalition partners no longer so obviously pivots on an anti-Soviet axis. Indeed, the Sino-Soviet rapprochement now often opens the door to reconciliation. Although no longer seeking to drive a wedge between Eastern Europe and the Soviet Union, Beijing is not above taking advantage of the nationalism of these countries to score some points, particularly regarding Cambodia and Afghanistan, noting that "socialist fraternal assistance" to these countries entails opportunity costs for their own economies. Santiago Carrillo and Babis Dracopoulos, general secretaries of the Spanish and Greek parties, visited Beijing in November 1980 and restored party relations. A French Communist Party delegation visited in 1982, followed by Georges Marchais six months later, restoring party relations broken since 1965; the (likewise pro-Soviet) Dutch Communist Party restored relations the same year. The following year the CCP established relations with the Belgian, Swiss, Mexican (Socialist Unity Party), and Swedish parties, delegations traveling in both directions to formalize ties. In April 1983 relations were established with the Communist Party of India (Marxist), when its general secretary, E. M. S. Namboodiripad, visited the PRC, followed by representatives of the parties of Australia, Norway, Portugal, Austria, and Finland. China refrained from condemning Jaruzelski's December 13, 1981, imposition of martial law in Poland, and, instead of joining the West in imposing sanctions, signed a trade agreement with Poland in early February 1982. (In 1987 Deng Xiaoping made clear his support for Jaruzelski's crackdown, when faced with an analogous situation in China.) Since the Sino-Soviet trade agreement was signed in July 1985, each East European country has signed a similar long-term trade agreement with the PRC, together with intergovernmental commissions and agreements for the exchange of films, cultural shows, scientific and technological cooperation, and the reciprocal opening of consulates. It was at this point that Sino-East European trade first began to revive after its long hiatus. Although the USSR remains the principal communist trade partner, PRC trade with the bloc countries since that time has also waxed, maintaining a consistently favorable balance.

Broadening its ambit beyond those East European states that have pursued an independent foreign policy, China normalized relations with Hungary in 1984 for the sake of the "exchange of experience in the construction of socialism."[45] With the visits of Honecker and Jaruzelski to Beijing in the fall of 1986, and the visits of several vice-premiers from

Hungary, Poland, Czechoslovakia, and Bulgaria, China resumed official contacts with the East German and Czechoslovak parties and official relations with the PUWP, thereby moving decisively toward normalization of political relations with even the most loyal satellites—still insisting that this had "no direct links" with Sino-Soviet relations.[46] In 1987 the PRC received Czechoslovak Premier Lubomir Strougal, Hungarian Party Secretary János Kádár, and Bulgarian Party Secretary Todor Zhivkov, while Premier (and Acting Party Secretary) Zhao Ziyang reciprocated in June with a tour of Poland, East Germany, Czechoslovakia, Hungary, and Bulgaria. China remains closest to its earliest, hence "special friends," Yugoslavia and Romania, but has displayed keen interest in Hungary, the GDR, and Poland—Hungary because of its reform experience, the GDR due to its economic achievements, and Poland because its economy is perceived to be complementary to the Chinese (and perhaps because of its experience with riot control and martial law).

As a theoretical criterion for establishing party-to-party relations, the leadership has replaced antihegemonism with the so-called Four Principles, first set forth in the section on interparty relations of Hu Yaobang's Report to the Twelfth CCP Congress in 1982 and reiterated in the new Party Constitution. These are: (1) independence of each party, (2) complete equality among parties, (3) mutual respect, and (4) noninterference in each other's internal affairs.[47] Their basic assumption is that the tendency toward independence among communist parties has become the "mainstream" in the international communist movement (Marx and Engels are retrospectively found to have opposed attempts by German social democrats or French socialists to impose their views on other parties). Not only is the Brezhnev Doctrine thereby repudiated, Deng Xiaoping even went so far as to disavow the universality of the Chinese "model." The Chinese revolution had succeeded by applying universally valid principles of Marxism-Leninism to the concrete reality of China, but this should not lead to the expectation that "other developing countries should follow our model in making revolution, even less should we demand that developed capitalist countries do the same."[48] Socialism has no unified pattern, and each nation must determine its own road of development.[49] The value of socialism is in practice, as Hu Yaobang put it in a speech to a PCI Conference in June 1986 in Rome, and thus it is necessary to respect and learn from one another's practical experience.[50]

This latitudinarian Chinese redefinition of socialist internationalism permits the opening of relations with all types of "worker parties," spanning the ideological spectrum. The CCP has not only established relations with some eighty communist parties, but with more than two hundred vaguely leftist parties and organizations in other countries, including socialist, social democratic, and labor parties, and various associations in the Third World, divided into political parties and national liberation movements. The International Liaison Department of the CCP's Central Committee has therewith expanded its sphere of competence beyond the currently shrinking ambit of communist parties. Relations have been taken up with the French Socialist Party, the German Social Democratic Party (SPD), the British Labour Party, and the Italian Socialist Party. During Willy Brandt's visit to China in May 1984, he was asked (and agreed) to give the CCP observer status at meetings of the Socialist International. The CCP has begun to send delegations to selected meetings of international front organizations, as observers. Former Maoist splinter groups have not been forsaken in this eclectic reconciliation: the French Communist Party (Marxist-Leninist) received notice two months after the Marchais visit that they too were invited to Beijing, and a half year later (July 1983) a delegation of the French Revolutionary Communist Party was received in Beijing by Hu Yaobang. In March 1988 the CCP's relations with the Communist Party of India were restored after twenty-five years. Only the Japanese Communist Party has remained out in the cold, largely because it has shown no interest in reviving relations (for doctrinal reasons); but the CCP does have cordial relations with the Japanese Socialist Party.

In Southeast Asia, the CCP has continued to balance its relations with the nonruling communist parties there against its diplomatic ties with the indigenous governments, as well as competing bids for control by the CPSU or the VCP. In 1974 the PRC normalized relations with Malaysia, and in 1975 with the Philippines and Thailand—without, however, renouncing support for the (illegal) communist parties in those countries. In his 1978 tour through Southeast Asia, Deng Xiaoping, while refusing to abandon relations with the local communist parties, nonetheless made a slight concession in declaring that China would not allow party-to-party relations to interfere with the improvement of state-to-state relations.[51] Zhao Ziyang went somewhat further during his August 1981 visit, emphasizing that his concern was with strengthening state relations, and that China's relationship with local communist parties was only "political and moral." The Chinese have, however, been loath to sever all ties to the Burmese, Malaysian, and Thai communist parties, no doubt anxious lest they shift allegiance to Hanoi or Moscow. Thus, for example, the PRC-based Voice of People's Thailand and Voice of the Malayan Revolution radio stations, longtime supporters of guerrilla insurgencies in those countries, were shut down in July 1979 and June 1981 respectively—only to be succeeded by new, albeit less powerful, transmitters no longer on Chinese soil.

In sum, the CCP has provided a model for an alternative form of co-operation within the world communist movement, a "new unity" which acknowledges differences as unavoidable and even useful and denies the concept of a "center of leadership" or "leading party," thereby mini-mizing the possibility of hegemonism and even making "joint action" problematic. The paradoxical consequence is that the more the CCP integrates itself into the bloc, the more its inclusion tends to dissolve the bloc. In fact the CCP, unlike the CPSU, no longer attributes priority to cooperation or solidarity between communist parties as a privileged group. Whereas Hu Yaobang had reaffirmed (in his 1982 Report to the Twelfth Party Congress) the CCP's "adherence to proletarian interna-tionalism," that concept is now extended to all forces that advocate national independence and progressive change on the basis of equal rights. "We no longer use the term of fraternal party relations in refer-ence to other communist parties," CCP spokesman Wu Xingtang told a news conference in October 1986. "Our relationship with the other communist parties is one of moral relationship."[52]

This notion of proletarian internationalism tends to disregard the nature of the social and class structures in other countries, but is rather (like the recent practice of the CPSU) a function of Beijing's national interests and objectives. The bloc and its meaning are interactive with China's foreign policy behavior. While retaining the term "interna-tional communist movement," the Chinese have hitherto avoided any organizational solidarity on the international or regional levels, limit-ing relations with other communist parties to a series of bilateral ties. On questions involving previous debates within the world commu-nist movement, the CCP has only seldom and quite vaguely taken a position—partly, no doubt, in order to avoid publicly contradict-ing (and thereby calling attention to) previous positions now deemed embarrassing.

This new Chinese bloc policy has many points of tangency with that of other communist parties that have sought autonomy from Soviet guidelines, although there are also differences among them. The Roma-nians joined the Chinese in placing the main emphasis not on class relations but on the defense of the national interest. The Yugoslav and Italian parties are like the CCP in attempting to articulate a conception of international relations that goes beyond the confines of the interna-tional communist movement, in fact tending to negate that movement.[53]

The French Communist Party, although tending to gear its foreign policy relatively closely to Moscow's line, nevertheless has come out in favor of a "new internationalism," the essence of which it sees in each party's right to self-determination.[54] All of these tendencies objectively undermined Moscow's attempts to enforce a stricter alignment of the international communist movement with the CPSU, but the CCP line was perhaps more vexing than that of other dissidents, because of the party's size (with some forty-three million members, the largest in the world). The CCP not only maintains a distinction between internal and external bloc policies, but within the former it distinguishes between Soviet and East European policies—sometimes inciting Soviet accusations of pursuing a "differentiated policy," like the United States, in order to undermine the unity of the bloc.

Although the Soviets have taken no official notice of recent Chinese ideological pronouncements and activities in the field of interparty relations, since the accession of Gorbachev they have gradually come to permit greater leeway within the bloc in hopes of undercutting the appeal of the CCP and other maverick parties. By replacing Comintern veteran Ponomarev with the diplomat Dobrynin as head of the International Department, Gorbachev signaled his intention to rely on diplomacy and avoid sterile ideological disputes about first principles. The program of the Twenty-seventh Congress (February 1986) still attempted to preserve an "international communist movement," but made no claim that the CPSU is the center of orthodoxy in world communism. Although initially most concerned with halting tendencies toward bloc fragmentation and promoting further integration in economic, cultural, and scientific-technological spheres, since the spring of 1987 Gorbachev has emphasized intrabloc tolerance: "Each individual country can act independently," as Yegor Ligachev put it during an April visit to Hungary. In April and November 1987, Gorbachev endorsed "unconditional and full equality" among communist parties, and claimed there was "no 'model' of socialism to be emulated by everyone."[55] The latest edition of Deng Xiaoping's *Selected Works* (published in late 1987, and immediately translated into Russian) was reviewed favorably and at considerable length in Soviet journals. The reformist newspaper, *Moscow News*, carried a particularly laudatory review praising Deng's effort to combine the universal truths of Marxism with "China's specific features" and implicitly criticizing the (previous Soviet) effort to hold up the experience of a particular country as universally relevant.[56] Finally, during a visit by Gorbachev to Yugoslavia in March 1988, the two countries issued a formal document enjoining the USSR from undertaking the kinds of invasions it conducted in Hungary in 1956 and Czechoslovakia in 1968.[57]

Though wary of Western reactions, the CCP had begun to evince cautious interest in some form of revival of the international communist movement in the late 1980s. The CCP declined to send a delegation to the Twenty-seventh CPSU Congress on grounds that "there are no interparty links between the Soviet and Chinese Communist Parties."[58] When Mongolia invited China and other Asian communist parties and working-class parties to a meeting in Ulan Bator in 1987, the CCP again declined, explaining that they deemed any multilateral meetings among communist parties inappropriate at this time. But the CCP did send a delegation to the celebration of the seventieth anniversary of the October Revolution in 1987, and when Gorbachev invited the delegation to an informal meeting (promising: "The meeting will be attended by communists as well as the representatives of other political parties. The meeting will not pass any document and will draw no conclusion"), the CCP delegation accepted and attended.[59] When the CPSU sent a message of congratulations to the CCP on the occasion of the Thirteenth Congress (November 1987)—the first such message since the Eighth CCP Congress in 1956—it received honorable notice in Renmin Ribao.

This brief review of the vicissitudes in China's relationship with the socialist community leads one to doubt that anything about it is fixed. What is needed to reintegrate the bloc (an increasingly remote likelihood), in view of the declining credibility of authoritative command by a self-appointed bloc leader, is a revival of its collective mission that would inspire categorical identification. Only then might closer affiliation with the international communist movement regain the domestic legitimating function it once provided. As suggested in Part I, the reform movement may offer such a common program, once it becomes clear that it can succeed and exactly what policies and consequences it entails. Since the early 1980s, the CCP's affiliation with international communism has been so loose it is questionable to what extent it serves its function of legitimizing its own "leading role" domestically.[60] Never was the CCP so loyal to the international communist movement than when the European parties proceeded to abandon it in 1989.

CHAPTER 7

China and the Third World

From the very beginning, the CCP has considered itself especially well qualified to promote the cause of socialism in the developing countries. Emerging from a background of relatively egregious imperialist depradations ranging from the Opium War through Japanese invasion, and miraculously snatching victory from the jaws of annihilation with relatively little outside aid, the CCP was proud of having achieved victory via "people's war," a form of guerrilla warfare based on indigenous martial traditions. The Chinese revolution did not immediately lead to a proletarian dictatorship but to New Democracy, implying completion of the bourgeois-democratic revolution under communist leadership. This the CCP took to be a relevant model for the phased but uninterrupted transition of other precapitalist, preindustrial societies from colonialism to socialism. In adjacent countries with strong indigenous communist movements, the CCP thus adopted a posture of militant activism, sending "volunteers" to fight "American imperialism" in Korea, also providing crucial moral and material support to the Viet Minh in their national liberation war against the French.

Even in countries with relatively weak communist parties, the Chinese enthusiastically propagated their own "model" of revolution. In the report to the Seventh Congress in 1945 in which he so lavishly praised Mao's contributions to the Chinese revolution, Liu Shaoqi contended that Mao's Thought had relevance for the emancipation of people everywhere, "particularly the peoples of the East."[1] Marx and Lenin were Europeans who wrote about European problems and seldom took China or Asia into account, Liu observed in the spring of 1946, whereas Mao was an Asian who had transformed Marxism "from a European to an Asian form."[2] And it was also Liu Shaoqi who made a famous statement in November 1949 outlining the CCP claim that "the path taken by the Chinese people in defeating imperialism and its lackeys and in founding the People's Republic is the path that should be taken by the people of various colonial and semicolonial countries in their fight for national independence and people's democracy."[3]

121

Nor did the CCP's claims to relevance go unheeded by communist parties in neighboring new nations. In India, the pro-Soviet communist leadership was overthrown in early 1948 by a pro-Chinese faction led by B. T. Ranadive, and the Maoist strategy of a multiclass (united front) alliance for a two-stage revolution (New Democracy followed by transition to socialism) was accepted.[4] The Malayan Communist Party praised the Chinese revolutionary strategy, and the Indonesian, Japanese, Burmese, and Thai parties were also influenced to some degree by the Chinese model. But the Soviets were loath to accept such an abridgment of the relevance of the classic Leninist model of proletarian revolution to the developing countries. Ranadive was obliged to recant in 1949, and in 1950 an editorial in the Cominform journal, while conceding the relevance of the Chinese revolution, advised the CPI to formulate a strategy that would "draw on the experience of the national liberation model of China and other countries."[5] That November, at a conference at the Soviet Institute of Oriental Studies, the principal speaker, one Ye. Zhukov, said: "It would be risky to regard the Chinese revolution as some kind of 'stereotype' for people's democratic revolutions in other parts of Asia."[6]

Over the next several years, after the Chinese intervened in the Korean War and subsequently became domestically engaged in socialization of the means of production and simultaneous economic reconstruction, all of which sorely taxed domestic resources and required Soviet assistance, the CCP became less outspoken concerning the special form Marxism must take to deal with the problems of Asia and the Third World. All discussions of "Mao's road" ceased by late 1951, and the flow of Soviet arms aid rose markedly thereafter.[7] To be sure, this retreat may have been merely tactical, as Khrushchev suggested in writing about his first encounter with Mao in 1954: "Ever since I first met Mao, I've known—and I've told my comrades—that Mao would never be able to reconcile himself to any other Communist Party being in any way superior to his own within the world Communist movement. He would never be able to tolerate it."[8]

Upon settlement of the Korean War (July 1953), the CCP indeed soon reasserted its special calling to lead the Third World. The Chinese opening to the Third World now shifted from an emphasis on propagating its revolutionary model to a "united front" style of diplomacy. As early as 1946, Mao made a seminal contribution to the Marxist conceptualization of the Third World, referring to the developing countries as a nonhostile buffer zone rather than a part of the capitalist encirclement.[9] At that time he introduced the notion of an "intermediate zone" between the two camps, characterizing it as a "vast zone which includes many capitalist, colonialist and semi-colonial countries in Europe, Asia and Africa."[10] He said the United States would first have to subjugate this zone before threatening the Soviet Union, implying that the zone's current status was undecided and not necessarily anticommunist. China dropped this line of interpretation in 1947 in the light of Zhdanov's more militant "two camps" worldview, but returned to it upon Zhdanov's (and Stalin's) departure from the scene.

The Korean War ended in July 1953, only a few months after Stalin's death. The PRC, exhausted and drained by some thirty years of virtually incessant strife, subdued its emphasis on people's war in favor of a more discreet approach to the prospect of revolution in the "intermediate zone." Zhou Enlai's evident objective was to establish a "neutral belt of states as the 'zone of peace' between the Western coalition and China,"[11] accordingly endeavoring to redefine "neutrality" as opposition to U.S. influence and rejection of anti-Chinese alliances, rather than anticommunism. Lenin's phrase "peaceful coexistence" was first revived not by Khrushchev, but by Zhou Enlai, in his political report to the national committee of the Chinese People's Political Consultative Conference (CPPCC) in February 1953. Having finally negotiated a cease-fire at Panmunjom, the PRC also sought truce in Indochina, which was achieved in April 1954 at Geneva, the first time the PRC was represented in an international conference. Thanks largely to the diplomatic efforts of Zhou Enlai, the Viet Minh (whom the PRC had previously aided in their insurgency) acceded to a compromise settlement in Geneva that it would subsequently regret.[12]

Following the close of the Geneva meeting in June, the PRC delegation visited India and Burma on its way home. (India had been the first "capitalist" country to recognize China in April 1950, the leading nonbloc proponent of the immediate seating of the PRC in the United Nations, and China's only available channel to Washington and other Western powers during and after the Korean War. Relations were at this time quite cordial.) As a result of Zhou's talks with Nehru and Burmese Prime Minister U Nu, joint communiqués were issued emphasizing that relations between the PRC and these two countries would be based on the Five Principles of Peaceful Coexistence: mutual respect for territorial sovereignty, mutual nonaggression, mutual nonintervention in internal affairs, equality and mutual benefit, and peaceful coexistence. These principles were further propagated at the Conference of Asian Countries in New Delhi in April 1955, followed by the Conference of Asian and African States at Bandung, Indonesia. On his journey to New Delhi in June 1954 to sign the understanding, Zhou appealed to Nehru to exclude the United States and the Soviet Union from Asian affairs; Chinese leaders also successfully opposed Soviet participation in the Bandung Conference. At Bandung Zhou called upon all overseas Chinese to adopt the citizenship of their resident countries (which was particularly appreciated by Jakarta), pledged peaceful coexistence with Laos and Cambodia, and offered direct negotiations with the United States (which began at the ambassadorial level in August 1955 in Warsaw). From November 1956 through January 1957, Zhou visited eight Asian states, further extolling the Five Principles. The Third World, Asian states in particular, greeted "new China's" bid to seek peaceful solutions to common problems (rather than sponsoring revolution) with great relief.

Alert at this time for promising innovations to distinguish his leadership from the Stalinist policies to which his Politburo rivals remained wedded, Khrushchev moved quickly to co-opt this Chinese initiative, not only generalizing the principle of peaceful coexistence to the United States and other developed capitalist countries (as noted in chapter 6), but adopting nonmilitant, gradualist tactics to promote (Soviet) communism among developing nations. As a result of the emergence of the communist camp and the weakening of colonialism, he maintained (borrowing Mao's concept of an "intermediate zone"), "a vast 'zone of peace,' including both socialist and nonsocialist peace-loving states in Europe and Asia, has emerged in the world arena," and this zone might play a "progressive" role in weakening "imperialism" and strengthening the communist world. Thus the neutralist, even capitalist, nations on the periphery of the communist bloc were not to be treated as objects of fear and suspicion, but as opportunities to be exploited by a more flexible foreign policy. In October 1954 the Soviet Union issued a joint communiqué with China affirming application of the Five Principles of Peaceful Coexistence to their relations with Asian countries. In 1955, Soviet theorists began to redefine Soviet doctrine on the role of the bourgeoisie in "bourgeois nationalist" revolutions and the possibility of nonalignment in states without communist governments.[13] Khrushchev and Tito incorporated the Five Principles into their Belgrade Declaration of 1955 and their Moscow Statement of June 1956. (Still more ironic is the fact that Nagy cited the Chinese position against military blocs in announcing Hungary's exit from the WPO in 1956.) To be sure, the CCP was duly credited for its contribution to this reorientation of socialist policy toward the Third World.[14] In Molotov's foreign policy report to the Supreme Soviet in February 1955, he noted that the Five Principles announced in the Sino-Indian and Sino-Burmese communiqués should be respected—the first time these principles were mentioned in official documents issued by the highest Soviet authorities.[15] In one section of his report to the Twentieth CPSU Congress, Khrushchev himself said:

The great historical significance of the famous Five Principles, put forward by the PRC and the Republic of India and supported by the Bandung conference and world consensus, lies in that they have provided the best form of relations among nations with different social systems under the present situation. Why should not these principles become the basis of peaceful relations among all nations in all parts of the world? If all nations accept these Five Principles, it would be in the self-interest and at the desire of the people of every nation.[16]

And in November 1957, the Five Principles were formally endorsed by the Conference of Twelve Nations' Communist and Workers Parties, which convened in Moscow. At this meeting, Khrushchev recalled:

I think during the Moscow conference . . . we suggested that the task of the international Communist movement would be more readily accomplished if we adopted some kind of division of labor. Since the Chinese Communist Party had won a great revolutionary victory in Asia, we thought it would be a good idea for the Chinese to concentrate on establishing closer contacts with the other Asian countries and Africa. We were primarily concerned about India, Pakistan, and Indonesia—three nations with economic conditions similar to China's. As for our own Party, it seemed to make more sense for us to be responsible for keeping in touch with the revolutionary movements in Western Europe and the Americas.

Yet according to Khrushchev, Mao just as graciously declined this gracious invitation:

When we presented this idea to the Chinese comrades, Mao Tse-tung said, "No, it's out of the question. The leading role in Africa and Asia should belong to the Soviet Union. The Communist Party of the Soviet Union is the Party of Lenin; its cadres understand Marxism-Leninism more profoundly than anyone else. We of the Chinese Communist Party look to the Soviet Union for guidance. Therefore I think the CPSU should be the one and only center of the international Communist movement, and the rest of us should be united around that center." [17]

Apparently taking Mao at his word, Khrushchev resumed what seemed at the time to be a highly promising Soviet demarche toward the Third

World, ignoring the increasingly tepid (after 1957) Chinese engagement. Soviet theoreticians went beyond Mao's Five Principles in hypothesizing that preindustrial societies not only offered favorable conditions for socialist inroads but that they might become socialist without having to pass through the successive stages prescribed by orthodox Marxist theory. Such an evolution was feasible if the countries in question first opted for a "noncapitalist" route of development, moderately socialist and nationalist in character.[18] This approach, not foreseeing the divisive impact that nationalism would have on the Soviet empire, now deemed it "progressive," in hopes that it might undermine the Western alliance structure (as in de Gaulle's withdrawal from NATO).

Under the protective cover of a policy of détente with the West, Soviet diplomatic and technical advisers of various types fanned out into the Third World, focusing on those regimes offering the best prospects for "noncapitalist" development. Did they practice land reform? Were they "progressive"? The visits Khrushchev and Bulganin made to India, Burma, and Afghanistan in 1954–55, where they repeatedly emphasized Soviet friendship with those nations that took a neutral position in world affairs, marked the beginning of both the Soviet foreign aid program and the Soviet Union's special relationship with India. The arms deal with Egypt the same year was the first to be concluded as part of a new policy of military aid to noncommunist countries.[19] By the end of 1956, fourteen economic and military assistance agreements had been signed with various new developing nations, often on terms more generous than those granted the PRC. Thus by 1961 Soviet non-military loans to India amounted to more than twice the total amount given China from 1949 to 1961.[20] It has been estimated that by the time of Khrushchev's fall in 1964, about U.S. $3 billion worth of arms had been delivered to thirteen noncommunist developing countries in the preceding decade, amounting to nearly half of total Soviet aid during the same period.[21] Several Third World regimes (e.g., Egypt, Algeria) declared themselves to be socialist, welcoming Soviet advisers (e.g., the engineers who constructed the Aswan Dam) along with arms and developmental aid.

Although the CCP might thus be said to have originated the first concerted communist campaign to win the allegiance of the Third World, Chinese support for the program did not survive the radicalization of Mao's Thought that followed the abortive Hundred Flowers campaign. From Mao's impatient perspective, Bandung had not borne fruit: only four nations established relations with China during 1955–57, most important of which was Egypt; meanwhile the UN embargo ensuing from the Korean War remained intact. In its newly discovered concern for the perils of revisionism, the CCP suddenly began attaching much more stringent criteria to underwriting protosocialist regimes, groups, or tendencies in the Third World. Instead of concerting foreign policy with moderate leaders such as Nasser or Nehru, the PRC began promoting violent national liberation movements and supporting radical programs for international reorganization (e.g., following Sukarno's indignant 1965 withdrawal from the UN, Foreign Minister Chen Yi called for a "revolutionary United Nations"). There are at least three conceivable reasons for this shift.

First, according to the "theory of uninterrupted revolution" adopted in this more radical phase of Mao Zedong Thought, revolutions were expected to move more quickly from the national democratic to the socialist phase than previously assumed, while under the leadership of the communist party. This meant that bourgeois nationalist regimes such as the United Arab Republic (UAR, then including Egypt and Iraq, under Nasser and Kassem respectively) were unworthy of assistance, not to be trusted. The China-India-Egypt alignment was thus replaced by the so-called Beijing-Jakarta-Hanoi-Pyongyang axis, as the PRC shifted from a policy it now scorned as "class collaboration" to internationalized class war. It was also at this time that China articulated its "intermediate zone theory," [22] according to which imperialist attacks would not be directed against the formidable ("The East Wind prevails over the West Wind") socialist camp, but concentrated against the vulnerable "intermediate zone." It was hence incumbent upon socialist countries to support anti-imperialist, anticolonial struggles in the "intermediate zone."

Second, although Nehru was first to endorse PRC entry to the United Nations, even in the context of the Korean War, India's surge to the forefront of the nonaligned bloc and emergence as China's main rival for Soviet patronage in Asia seems to have awakened a Sino-Indian rivalry and perhaps a competitive differentiation of platforms in a campaign for leadership of the nonaligned bloc, with the CCP perforce advocating the more militant strategy while the Indians maintained their insistence on nonviolent resistance. As early as 1958 Beijing was annoyed to find that when Khrushchev proposed a five-power summit to devise ways of relieving international tension, China was not included, while India, "one of the leading states of the world" (according to Khrushchev), was.[23] This rivalry was exacerbated by Indian support for Tibet in its 1959 insurrection against Chinese occupation forces, and its granting of sanctuary to the Dalai Lama and his followers when the PRC crushed that uprising. This, in turn, precipitated intense border friction.

Third, there seems to have been a serious disagreement over the likely imperialist response to the instigation of relatively low-level violence in the Third World. Although the Chinese flaunted their endorsement of class war to an exaggerated degree, reaching an eventual rhetorical zenith with Lin Biao's extrapolation of the Chinese civil war to the entire world,[24] experience proved them to be correct in assuming that socialist states could venture more support for national liberation wars without touching off massive and instant nuclear retaliation than the Soviets were at this point prepared to risk. China thus supported Viet Minh forces in Indochina with large amounts of military and economic assistance, also offering rhetorical support and smaller amounts of material aid to communist movements in Thailand, Burma, Indonesia, Malaya, and the Philippines. Beyond Asia, the PRC supported liberation struggles in Guinea-Bissau, Angola (UNITA during the 1960s, then to the FNLA through 1975), Mozambique (FRELIMO), Zimbabwe (ZANU), and Southwest Africa (SWAPO), the PLO and PFLOAG in the Middle East, as well as the Naxalite movement in India. In Algeria, Beijing was the first to extend official recognition to Ben Bella's insurgency. Khrushchev had warned against this line, arguing that such brushfires might escalate into nuclear conflagration, devastating the East as well as the West (not to mention inhibiting neutralism and leading to the repolarization of the Third World).[25]

The militant revolutionary phase of Chinese Third World policy, which lasted with some variations from the late 1950s through the late 1960s, had mixed results. It certainly seems to have impressed both superpowers, leading the United States to overestimate the Chinese military threat, and causing the USSR gradually to revise its own Third World policy in the direction of tendering military aid to national liberation wars.[26] In Africa, the PRC managed to establish diplomatic relations with about ten new nations, most important of which were Ghana, Guinea, Mali, Algeria, the UAR, the Congo (Brazzaville), and Somalia. Cultural agreements were signed, trade developed, and economic assistance was given (the Chinese showed skill in allocating their limited funds and technicians to maximum public relations effect). Zanzibar, Tanzania, and Zambia turned increasingly to Beijing for support and assistance, and the construction of a few high-profile projects, such as the Tan-Zam railway, paid high dividends in good will. In Latin America, the PRC established relations with Castro on September 2, 1960, also setting up a *Xinhua* press office (with branch offices in Argentina, Brazil, Colombia, Ecuador, Peru, and Venezuela).

The adverse consequences of the Chinese pursuit of international class struggle began to become apparent just before the outbreak of the Cultural Revolution, when that line had become most radicalized. Zhou Enlai undertook a tour of Africa in January 1964, which seemed to be proceeding successfully enough until he declared that "revolutionary prospects" were "excellent" in Africa, whereupon he began to encounter such a frosty reception that his travels had to be prematurely concluded.[27] A number of African countries decried China's policies (including Niger, the Ivory Coast, Upper Volta, and Madagascar), while some even broke diplomatic relations (e.g., Ghana, Burundi), reducing the total number of African states with whom China maintained ties from eighteen in 1964–65 to thirteen in 1969. The second Conference of Nonaligned States in Algeria had to be canceled in 1965, because of an irresolvable rivalry between China and the USSR (each of whom wished to attend, but the PRC only if the USSR were excluded—which India resisted). In Latin America, China's stock declined when Castro opted to side with the USSR in the Sino-Soviet dispute. Even in Asia, China suffered a setback when the Indonesian Communist Party (PKI) was brutally suppressed following an ill-advised and abortive coup attempt (in which the CCP may have been implicated), decimating what had been the largest communist party outside the bloc. Even the three contiguous socialist states (Outer Mongolia, North Korea, North Vietnam) began to lean, more or less, toward Moscow rather than Beijing.

Nevertheless, the early phase of the Cultural Revolution (1966–68) was characterized by the heightening rather than curtailment of radical tendencies: Beijing increased its support for several Maoist groups and organizations seeking revolution in various parts of the world, also engaging in vicious assaults on some Third World countries previously deemed special friends, such as Burma; there were also more concerted attempts to manipulate overseas Chinese communities on behalf of revolutionary objectives (as in Hong Kong). By late 1967, China had become ensnarled in controversy with more than thirty countries.[28]

Soon after the Red Guard phase of the Cultural Revolution had been terminated in late 1968 and the foreign policy making apparatus reconsolidated, China hastened to establish relations with the Third World on a more ecumenical basis—greatly encouraged in this effort by border fighting and nuclear strike threats from the Soviet Union. Its efforts were again greeted with great relief, and rewarded by prompt diplomatic recognition from a veritable wave of Third World countries. China's successes were facilitated by the decline of America's prestige among the new nations of Asia and Africa owing to its embroilment in Vietnam, as well as the unease among many smaller Third World states about the USSR's expansionist proclivities (e.g., Soviet advisers were expelled from the Sudan in 1971, from Egypt in 1972)—all of which fostered a certain mistrust of both superpowers. Also, whereas many were frightened and repelled by the Cultural Revolution, it should not be forgotten that many were also impressed at the time. The claims of Chinese propagandists to have eradicated poverty, corruption, and inequality received widespread credence.[29]

Thus when China opened the door, the response was surprisingly forthcoming. Dropping all ideological prerequisites to political normalization except "antihegemonism," skillfully using banquets and tourism as well as conventional diplomacy, the PRC achieved almost universal diplomatic recognition in the early 1970s; but the real breakthrough was achieved in the Third World, with which China reaffirmed its identification as never before.[30] In addition to renouncing most ideological prerequisites for normalization, the PRC at least nominally abandoned its pretensions to lead the Third World toward revolution, now claiming only fellowship in this group. "Like the overwhelming majority of the Asian, African and Latin American countries, China belongs to the Third World," announced Qiao Guanhua, head of the Chinese delegation to the twenty-sixth session of the UN General Assembly on November 15, 1971. Mao confirmed this (June 22, 1973): "We all belong to the Third World, and are developing countries."[31]

China also redrafted its ideological worldview, for the first time recognizing the Third World as such. During the 1950s and 1960s, the Third World had been a mere "intermediate zone," characterized by its nonmembership in either of the two "camps" rather than by any more positive attributes. A slight modification was introduced in late 1964, when, apparently encouraged by Gaullist France's recognition of the PRC in January, this intermediate zone was perceived to be subdivided into two. "At the present time, there exist two intermediate zones in the world," Mao maintained to an audience of Japanese socialists. "Asia, Africa and Latin America constitute the first intermediate zone. Europe, North America and Oceania constitute the second. Japanese monopoly capital belongs to the second intermediate zone, but even it is discontented with the United States, and some of its representatives are openly rising against the U.S."[32] Because the "second intermediate zone" was "subjected to U.S. control, interference and bullying," it had something

in common with the socialist countries and the peoples of various countries.[33] The definitive reformulation of this worldview was articulated
in Deng Xiaoping's speech to the UN General Assembly in 1974, which
perceived not one world but three: the two superpowers comprised
the First World, having in common their attempt to seek world hegemony, bring the developing countries under their control, and "bully"
the other developed countries. The superpowers were the "biggest international exploiters and oppressors of today," sharing a form of "monopoly capitalism" as the basis of their respective social systems. Developing countries are hence adjured to maintain "equidistance" from the
two superpowers.[34] The Second World consisted of the other developed
countries of both the East and the West, who exploited the developing
countries but were also in turn exploited and bullied by the two superpowers. The Third World, consisting of the developing nations of Asia,
Africa, and Latin America, was exploited and oppressed by both of the
others, but nevertheless held the key to the future.[35] With three-fourths
of the world's population, three-fifths of the area, and a large share of
the natural resources, markets, and investment opportunities, the Third
World was Mao's "blank sheet of paper" on which the most beautiful
characters could be written. This was the first time the Third World
had been recognized for its own distinctive properties, rather than as
an intermediary zone or hotbed for socialism. Aside from permitting
a harsher critique of the Soviet Union than hitherto (as not only nonsocialist, but protocapitalist and "social imperialist"), this formulation
permitted the theodicy and eschatology of Marxist salvationism to be
projected internationally, to China's symbolic advantage.[36]

Since the launching of China's reform program in late 1978 and
the commencement of Sino-Soviet normalization talks soon afterward,
China's overtures to the Third World have continued, but with three
modifications. First, the PRC has suspended or at least drastically curtailed its own foreign aid program: Chinese aid commitments dropped
from U.S. $366 million in 1975 to less than $200 million for 1976,
1977, and 1978, declining further since then.[37] There has been a revival
of Chinese military and developmental assistance to Africa since 1982–
84, focusing particularly on Zambia, Tanzania, and Zaire, though this
has not matched previous Third World disbursements. Second, Deng's
market reforms have facilitated China's integration into the international trading and financial systems, a tendency that has continued even
after the early enthusiasm with the American connection cooled. In
its role as active participant in the international (Western-dominated)
economic system, the PRC has tactfully opted to play down the three

worlds theory, with its implications of international class war. This has been particularly true since proclamation of China's "independent" foreign policy at the Twelfth Party Congress in 1982, which brought with it a revival of appeals to the Five Principles of Peaceful Coexistence. Third, Sino-Soviet normalization talks have permitted China to drop antihegemonism as a prerequisite for normalization with various socialist Third World countries. The functional extinction of the "antihegemony" plank was confirmed by its inclusion in the communiqué of the May 1989 Sino-Soviet summit.

China's continued identification with the Third World has now shifted to the international legislative forums where such politics are now most actively played. Throughout the 1960s, China had criticized the United Nations, World Bank, and International Monetary Fund, and its relationship to these organizations (from which it had, to be sure, been ostracized) was generally hostile. In 1971, making skillful use of a compromised American position,[38] China gained entré into the UN General Assembly, thereby also acquiring permanent membership on the Security Council and admittance to other UN or UN-affiliated organizations. China's voting behavior in the United Nations reflects its Third World identification. In 1983, China voted for the draft resolution of the General Assembly condemning the invasion of Grenada, for example, and abstained on the U.S.-sponsored draft resolution condemning the Soviet shooting down of the KAL airliner (in the other nineteen Security Council resolutions of 1983, China voted with the United States). Analysis of China's General Assembly roll call votes shows the PRC to have voted more frequently against the U.S. position than in favor, probably in deference to its Third World reference group, which now holds a clear majority in the General Assembly.[39] In October 1981 at the Cancun conference, Zhao Ziyang made an ambitious proposal for the creation of a new world economic order, according to which the developing countries should have full access to Western markets without protectionist barriers or disadvantageous terms of trade; indeed, the distinction between North and South in the international division of labor should be eliminated altogether, and the developing countries given "full and eternal sovereignty" over their own natural resources. In 1982, China publicly associated itself with the basic principles espoused by the Group of 77. (China has not however joined the Group, nor has it joined the nonaligned movement, determined as it is to adhere to its "independent"—not merely neutral—foreign policy.)[40] Nor has it chosen a significant leadership role in any of the international governmental organizations (IGOs) that service Third World demands and needs. It has, rather, sought to join those IGOs still assumed to be under the control of the First World, in apparent pursuit of its own national interests. By 1983, the PRC had joined some 340 international organizations, tacitly underlining its commitment to the international organizational status quo.[41]

The leadership's apparent purpose in becoming such an avid IGO "joiner" has been to facilitate access to credit, capital, and technology markets. China's membership in, and application for aid and concessionary loans from, various international eleemosynary institutions has placed the PRC in direct competition with other members of the Third World. Like many developing countries, China is a net exporter of primary products, including cotton, rubber, and wood. Indonesian oil has been squeezed out of Japan by Chinese oil exports, for example, because of Beijing's pressure on Tokyo to maintain a balance of trade. Growing concern (particularly in regions on China's periphery) about Chinese competition in traditional markets has thus to some extent qualified general approval of China's self-appointed role as Third World advocate:

As China modernizes, there is a growing tendency throughout the Third World to view Beijing in South-South terms as an economic competitor and ascendant great power. In North-South terms, however, China is increasingly viewed as a champion of Third World views on economic and financial issues. Moreover, the success of its economic reforms, in the face of many Third World economic failures, makes China something of a role model.[42]

Inasmuch as China's economic relationship with the Third World is now an economically competitive one, it has been argued that its real interests lie with the First World, with the industrially developed countries, not with the Third. China's trade with advanced industrialized countries has risen from 46 percent in 1966 to 64 percent in 1975 and over 70 percent in 1979. Its large merchant marine gives Beijing a common interest with the United States and Japan in defending freedom of the seas. Its offshore oil deposits give China an interest in extended territorial limits, rather than in an internationalized seabed.[43] According to the Chinese timetable, the PRC's sojourn in the Third World is in any case only temporary, as China is scheduled for arrival in the developed world by 2050, according to Hu Yaobang's report to the Twelfth CCP Congress (September 1–15, 1982). Although the composition of China's trade with the First World parallels that of other developing nations, the composition of its growing trade with the Third World is analogous to that of other First World countries. The latter trade balance has been consistently favorable to the PRC, averaging some U.S. $5.9 billion per year through the 1980s. Among other things, the PRC has become the world's fourth leading arms merchant (in contrast, during the Maoist period China would only give, never sell, weapons—and only to ideologically "correct" beneficiaries), plying this trade almost entirely with other developing countries.[44] Beijing has also begun to send tens of thousands of contract workers abroad, especially to Iraq and the oil countries, where remuneration for their services helps generate needed foreign exchange.[45] China also seeks to attract investment capital from the more prosperous Third World countries—the United Arab Emirates, Kuwait (before 1990)—to prospect and drill for oil in China and on its continental shelf, for instance. According to incomplete data, more than ninety economic cooperation projects involving capital from Singapore, Thailand, the Philippines, and Malaysia had been built by the mid-1980s, including both jointly operated enterprises and those wholly owned by Third World businesses.[46]

China's growing integration into world markets is justified à la neo-functionalist theory in terms of its positive political spillover effects. This functionalist perspective on the international system is inconsistent with the class struggle still implicit in the three worlds model, and accordingly the latter has fallen into desuetude. The PRC has since 1983 descried a "new era" in world affairs in which countries with "various social forms" become increasingly interdependent within "one world market," improving the prospects for peace.[47] In place of the (not yet explicitly repudiated) theory of three worlds, a "peace and development line" has emerged, according to which all nations may rise to full development according to their merits.[48] In this connection it is interesting to note that, since 1984, the PRC has taken a more favorable view of the "Pacific Basin" concept, which it had in 1982 dismissed as a mask for North-South exploitation.

China's relationship with the developed First World is one of would-be exporter to import market, precisely analogous to the relationship between the other successful East Asian developing countries (NICs) and the West over the past two decades or so—but at a time when there is enhanced concern in the developed countries (particularly in the United States) about a structural trade deficit with the NICs. The PRC's ambition is to follow the trail blazed by the NICs toward wealth and power, at a time when that trail has become crowded and perhaps more difficult to traverse. Under those circumstances, the relationship with the advanced industrialized countries seems likely to be delicate, necessitating occasional to frequent political negotiation or "triangular" leverage. The Chinese have tended to inject the same nationalist intensity into mundane economic matters, such as balance of trade or tariff barriers, that is more typically associated with symbolic issues.

By embarking on its long march toward normalization with the USSR, the PRC has suffered no real losses in the Third World (where only one or two ideological confreres had been able to seize and retain power anyway) while in effect disarming the gatekeeper to the harem of socialist or protosocialist developing nations. During his December 1982–January 1983 visit to eleven African countries, Zhao Ziyang thus announced that the PRC no longer necessarily opposed Soviet policy on that continent; he also met with PLO chief Yasir Arafat, with representatives of SWAPO, and with leaders of the ANC and the Pan-African Congress, thereby demonstrating China's continuing support for those Liberation movements enjoying wide support in the region. In May 1983, Zhao withdrew Chinese support for the national liberation front guerrilla movement of Holden Roberto in Angola and officially recognized the (Moscow-backed) MPLA government of that country. In January 1983, China established diplomatic relations with Luanda; and in October 1983, Beijing even received the foreign minister of Cuba, the first time since the days of Ché Guevara that a high Cuban official had been received in China. The Chinese later explained that "Cuba has gradually readjusted its foreign policy," and was no longer deemed a dangerous accomplice of "social imperialism."[49] In 1986, the PRC established diplomatic relations (in return for diplomatic recognition) with the Sandinista government in Nicaragua. The way seems clear for improved relations with various other previously shunned Soviet clients, such as Libya, Mozambique, South Yemen, Syria, and Ethiopia—perhaps subtly offering these countries an alternative "road to socialism." But traces of the old rivalry are still visible in Chinese support for Somalia (which opposes Soviet-backed Ethiopia) and the Sudan (dating from Nimeiri's survival of a Soviet-sponsored coup in 1971).

Whereas this opening to the socialist developing countries may serve to bolster the coalition China seems intent on building in the UN General Assembly, no African leftist regime can yet be expected to turn to China as a serious alternative to the USSR as a source of military support.[50] Any serious Chinese attempt to compete with the USSR for the patronage of socialist developing nations is likely to founder on the same philanthropical incapacity that has crippled such efforts in the past. On the other hand, China's interests in the Third World may coincide with those of the Soviet Union to a greater extent now than when the Sino-Soviet dispute was in full flower—at least outside of East Asia, where the two still compete for geopolitical spheres of interest.

In sum, the PRC's identification with the Third World reflects China's sense of being unjustly suppressed and exploited by those more powerful, bespeaking a deep underlying sense of vulnerability and grievance.[51] This identification is not the assumption of a negative identity, for the Third World has remained a positive reference point, but rather identification with the victim, as a way of kindling the moral indignation and revolutionary ardor of the Chinese masses vicariously.[52] This identity as helpless victim was internalized early in the history of China's debut in the modern international system, and has survived as a *Doppelgänger* to the nation's positive identity as a highly self-confident, world-transforming revolutionary-modernizing force. While determined to transcend their "victim" identity as soon as possible, the CCP leadership has balanced that ambition with recurrent assurances of its determination to continue to identify with those in this category even after their material interests diverge, and to "never become a super-power"—by which it seems to mean, never a victimizer. Whether that vow will be kept remains to be seen, but it is worth noting that identification with the less developed has always been a marked feature of PRC foreign policy, and remains at this writing a relatively focal theme in an admittedly much more pragmatic and multifaceted, less rhetorically exuberant approach to world affairs. It has become the basis for Marxist eschatological assumptions that the "weak shall inherit the earth," whereby the PRC may continue to see itself as member of a vanguard group and thereby exert symbolic international leadership; this accrues increasing relevance in the wake of declining faith in orthodox stage theory.

Since June 1989, China has intensified its rhetorical identification with the Third World in the context of growing alienation from both superpowers—from the United States due to its public sympathy for the democracy demonstrators suppressed at Tiananmen, from the USSR because it refused to crack down on analogous tendencies in Eastern Europe and the breakaway Soviet republics. This has been accompanied by a revival of propaganda themes from the 1960s—anti-imperialism, protests against foreign interference in China's domestic affairs, the reassertion that "socialism will save China" (sarcastically transposed on the grapevine to "China will save socialism"). Thus a recent article criticized the Soviet Union for abandoning its ties to the Third World and siding with the United States on such issues as the need for democratic elections: "Meanwhile, the U.S. and Western countries are now considering diverting UN aid from traditional Third World recipients [including China?] to the Soviet bloc."[53]

CHAPTER 8

Realizing National Identity

This section has argued that national identity is a dimension of foreign policy worth taking into account in trying to explain otherwise inexplicable diplomatic gyrations. It is certainly not the only dimension worth considering, nor is it necessarily the most important factor in any given case; but it should not be neglected in interpreting the overall pattern of development. The PRC's foreign policy has been marked by unusually dramatic shifts over the past four decades, giving China an international visibility transcending its resource base (like Germany before 1945, another country with unusually severe identity problems). These vicissitudes, however, begin to seem somewhat more rational in the context of a proud but humiliated old culture's search for a new national identity. Whereas the foregoing chapters have been exclusively concerned with the international dimensions of that quest, an attempt will now be made to integrate that with a cursory sketch of parallel domestic developments.

At its inception, the new leadership immediately manifested a pronounced need to repudiate the negative and diffused identities of the recent past and embrace a new identity, along with an evident confusion about its precise contents. This confusion was not explicitly articulated, owing to the ideologically decreed spuriousness of nationalism, but appeared in the choice of mutually incompatible policy objectives (e.g., support for national liberation wars versus an international united front). The most that could be said was "China has stood up"—but for what? The PRC quickly launched an ambitious domestic program for both revolutionary transformation and economic reconstruction, while simultaneously affirming its membership in the communist bloc and affiliating with the still loosely defined group of decolonizing new nations. The country's repudiation of domestic foreign policy traditions led to a relatively strong emphasis on external reference groups in the quest for an acceptable place in the world, even though such modeling has always been inhibited by suspicion of outside referents. The picture was further complicated by the fact that China adopted not one but two reference groups, the communist bloc and the Third World, which stand for quite different things to the Chinese. These roles were reconciled by the conviction that socialist revolution represents the route whereby underdevelopment could be most efficiently overcome, and that China, as the world's largest developing country, might act as a functional specialist within the bloc on how to lead other new nations toward socialism.

Nevertheless, by the end of the 1950s, China had experienced its first national identity crisis. A number of factors seem to have brought this about. First, completion of the transition to socialism (including transition from New Democracy to the Dictatorship of the Proletariat) much more rapidly than planned, amid unexpectedly rapid increases in economic production, brought the process that had most preoccupied the leadership since Liberation to a successful conclusion. There is persuasive evidence that this achievement, temporarily depriving this goal-rational movement of its raison d'être, precipitated intense debate within the leadership on issues of future direction and ultimate values. This debate probably also included several issues raised and deferred in the course of that transition—such as Mao's cultivation of a (now discredited) "cult of personality," the flaws of the Stalinist model, how to encourage an intellectual "blooming" without undermining the legitimacy of the regime, and so forth. The debate was sharp, even "antagonistic," and resulted in the purge of a group of dissidents (led by Peng Dehuai) followed by a major departure from existing policies in the early 1960s that could not be ideologically admitted, a form of covert "revisionism."

On the international scene, events also conspired to force a reassessment. Because of its revolutionary primacy and ideologically authoritative status (then acknowledged by both parties), the USSR seems to have hitherto represented a sort of international parent figure, to be emulated and internalized. But a parent must allow the child to grow up. Having apparently graduated from the status of a maverick pupil to full partnership in the bloc, the CCP discovered from the 1956 reversal of verdicts on Stalin, and the ideological innovations coinciding with that reversal, that their sensibilities were not really considered on major decisions affecting them. Nor were Chinese interests taken into account in the Soviet management of bloc security: despite the major enhancement of Soviet strategic capabilities represented by the launching of Sputnik I and II and the world's first ICBM, the Soviets promptly threw themselves into the open arms of the imperialist archenemy (the "spirit of Camp David") rather than utilizing their advantage on behalf of the national aspirations of less advanced socialist countries and peoples (read: China). A parent should not only provide guidance and discipline, but nurturance and protection—neither of which Khrushchev was doing, in Chinese eyes.

Finally, whereas in the early 1950s the Chinese introduced a more accommodative approach to the decolonizing nationalist regimes among the developing nations, and seemed to have carved out a niche as socialist leader of this nonaligned bloc, they then watched in hapless dismay as the Soviet Union co-opted their initiative and, with its more ample eleemosynary capabilities, assumed the major socialist role in Third World diplomacy, effectively marginalizing Chinese efforts in this area. In the international communist movement, Chinese partnership became irrelevant as the CPSU set the ideological agenda unilaterally and used physical force to discipline East European dissidents. Like the children of overbearing parents, the Chinese seem to have found it difficult to find their own distinct identity in the international arena, living as they were in the shadow of a dominant power that claimed the right to make all significant decisions on their behalf, to co-opt all potentially useful initiatives, and to do all of this without much consultation. This generated strain between divergent strivings: strain between the high sense of efficacy achieved at home and the complete frustration of nationalist aspirations abroad, strain between boundless (perhaps ill-founded) confidence about the international future of the bloc and the growing pusillanimity of its leadership in defense of mutual interests. These strains led to the PRC's first crisis of national identity.

An identity crisis of course tends to precipitate a search for identity. A search for national identity may be exhibited in relatively adventurous behavior on the international scene designed to test the limits of the politically possible and to "try out" different identities. A country afflicted by an identity crisis may thus experience a certain amount of domestic cultural turmoil, as in the West during the 1960s, where self-selected groups of concerned citizens engaged in random searching behavior. In more authoritarian systems, the leadership may curtail such random searching, superimpose an "ideal type" of identity and rigidly demand universal conformity to it—Hitler's "New Order," and the concomitant attempt to exterminate all Jews, communists, gypsies, and other assumed deviants while dramatically expanding national boundaries represents the most extreme and consequential implementation of this approach.

Many of the policies or actions the PRC pursued during the late 1950s, which might seem puzzling or irrational in terms of a means-ends calculus, become more comprehensible when construed as an attempt to resolve an identity crisis. The break with the Soviet Union appeared so irrational that neither the Soviets nor outside observers would credit it at first, assuming that the Chinese would eventually conform to the logic of the situation. Already the Soviets had made a massive investment in the country, creating ties of economic and techno-logical dependency that could be cut only at great cost. But Soviet and bloc inhibitions on Chinese national self-realization were felt to be so constraining that they had to be cast off nevertheless; the Chinese self-estimate was still so high at this point that they may have discounted the cost of a break.

The Maoist leadership then engaged in a *preemptive resolution* of the national identity crisis, not by physically eliminating rival contes-tants but by creating a bandwagon momentum behind a symbolically freighted policy "line" and intimidating potential opponents.[1] In the Three Red Flags (Great Leap Forward, People's Commune, and Gen-eral Line), the leadership proposed to achieve their maximal domestic program for a new national identity at "one slice of the knife," making a dramatic breakthrough toward economic modernization and the com-munist utopia simultaneously. Because the class enemy was still active, as demonstrated during the Hundred Flowers, unprecedented pres-sure was applied during the foregoing anti-Rightist movement (some 300,000 intellectuals purged) to compel strict ideological conformity to a Marxism-Leninism that now began to emphasize its distinctively Chinese features, thereby equating itself with patriotism. On the world stage as well, the Chinese leadership sought a role commensurate with its emerging self-definition. Toward the class enemy abroad, the regime indulged in what can only be deemed provocative behavior (e.g., the 1958 Sino-Indian border dispute and simultaneous Taiwan Strait im-broglio), betraying an unrealistically, even dangerously optimistic self-estimate.

Forgoing for the first time any empirically extant model to embark on a quest for a more explicitly revolutionary identity, China's bold experiment brought only misfortune. The Great Leap Forward failed catastrophically, resulting in mass starvation in many regions. The Tai-wan Strait probes were repulsed by American nuclear threats, exposing Soviet promises of extended deterrence to be empty bluffs.

For the next several years the Chinese sense of national identity might be loosely characterized as "schizoid." Rhetorically, Chinese ideologi-cal and foreign policy pronouncements continued to reaffirm a com-mitment to radical transformation, while in practice more moderate policies were introduced domestically in an effort to deal with the economic aftereffects of the Great Leap's failure. The upshot of the Hundred Flowers experiment had shaken the elite assumption that the new socialist identity had won consensual popular acceptance, but this unhappy consciousness was left in quiet abeyance pending recovery from economic difficulties and the correction of more easily specifiable forms of corruption. There seems to have been a clandestine and somewhat murky intra-elite struggle concerning basic values and national identity, but the "revisionists" never publicly articulated their point of view, contenting themselves with the practical implementation of concrete policies. This latent contradiction was ironically brought to a head by the failure of "revolutionary" policies on the international scene, the last remaining arena in which they held uncontested sway. This defeat seems to have crystallized Mao's determination to resolve China's identity crisis once for all, before his own anticipated demise, by launching the Great Proletarian Cultural Revolution.

The Cultural Revolution was (among other things, such as an elite power struggle and massive purge) an attempt to define the core values of a revolutionary Chinese identity "dialectically," or critically (i.e., in terms of what was being opposed—Soviet revisionism, Confucian humanism), without having a clear idea about how a constructive solution to ideological maladies should be put into effect or even what such a solution would look like. The Cultural Revolution might be said to represent what Dror called "crazy state" behavior, in the sense that a new and radically autonomous national identity was being sought on the basis of a critique of a value system (Marxism-Leninism) without having fully transcended that value system. Little wonder that this vast and tumultuous upheaval succeeded in achieving only an artificial transformation of identity that veiled serious unresolved "contradictions" in education, culture, economics, foreign policy, and many other facets of life. As the movement unfolded, the radical critique became increasingly anarchic, meaninglessly vandalistic (the "fight, smash, steal" syndrome), as in the cold light of workaday economic exigencies and constrained cost-benefit tradeoffs it found nowhere to go. This radical "solution" could be sustained through 1976 only by force of Mao's accumulated charisma.

The PRC thus experienced a second identity crisis in the 1970s, but this was a crisis of a different sort. The break with the Soviet Union at the end of the 1950s had led to an effort to superimpose a self-reliant, *revolutionary fundamentalism*. China would build its own identity, giving aid and ideological accreditation to other progressive forces in the Third World, but otherwise isolate itself from contaminating influences—in defiance of both meddlesome superpowers. Domestically, this "line" reached final bankruptcy in the Cultural Revolution. Abroad, its inherent limits were clearly signaled by the Sino-Soviet border clash and subsequent Soviet nuclear threats. The resolution to this crisis consisted of the dawning awareness that national identity cannot be constructed purely in accord with revolutionary ideals, but must make expedient compromises with political reality. It was reached in two stages: in foreign affairs it was manifested in the ideologically indiscriminate search for supporters that culminated in Chinese entry into the UN in 1971 and the Nixon visit in February 1972; on the domestic political scene, not until the death of Mao and the rise of pragmatic reform politics under Deng Xiaoping in 1978 was the revolutionary dream expressly relinquished.[2]

Deng's pragmatic program was meant to supplant Mao's focus on revolutionary purity with the vision of a long march into the promised land of modernity, where China would emerge as a nation of wealth and power. To achieve this end, means could be compromised, including the introduction of such hitherto taboo practices as market allocation of commodities (or even means of production), substantial privatization or quasi privatization of property, and experiments with labor mobility and commercialization. These innovations were introduced incrementally, sometimes under stealth, but nevertheless pointed ultimately toward a profound identity shift. The rapidity with which the population was willing to abandon revolutionary slogans testifies to the tenuousness with which they had been held, but emancipation made certain groups uneasy, particularly those to whom the socialist aspects of the PRC's identity remained meaningful, either because their political interests were implicated or simply because they had deep value commitments. Even among the young people most apt to abandon the old ways and gravitate to new if still vaguely defined ones there was a subjective sense of a "crisis of faith," which seems to have been particularly acute toward the end of the 1970s.

During the early 1980s, the juggernaut of economic reform seemed to belie these signals of cognitive dissonance by forging ahead with such rapid and convincing strides. But the "second stage" of reforms launched in the fall of 1984 encountered much more formidable economic difficulties. Although the GNP growth rate remained high, agricultural production stagnated following the record 1984 harvest, and the attempt to reform the more complex urban industrial sector touched off price inflation and the spread of "spiritual pollution." This led to a pause in the reform momentum, during which the forces of orthodoxy seemed to gain a second wind, while the reform forces shifted the spearhead of their attack to the political structure they deemed to be impeding their efforts. The controversy precipitated a split between generations, in which senior cadres clung tenaciously to the political bulwarks. In terms of national identity, the dilemma was essentially one over the introduction of selected elements of a system ("capitalism") hitherto thought to be not only alien but antagonistic and subversive. The pretext for this infection had ironically been provided by Deng's prior shift to a "modernization" paradigm, in which the implicit model was no longer the Soviet Union but the United States; the advanced industrial democracies thus became a quasi-legitimate reference group. This engendered a sense of ambivalence analogous to the 1950s split between socialist and developmental reference groups. The forces of reform sought to use privatization, markets, and other economically successful bourgeois imports as a bridgehead for the introduction of democratic electoral procedures, parliamentarism, civil rights, and so forth; the forces of orthodoxy, in counterpoint, referred to the unintended adverse consequences of reform—wherein they included pervasive corruption and vice, spontaneous protest movements, distributive inequality, and a general decay of authority—as good and sufficient reason to retreat from reform to an economic system more consistent with the nation's socialist identity.

From this perspective, the crackdowns of January 1987 and June 1989 may be viewed, among other things (such as the resolution of an elite power struggle), as an attempt to resolve an identity dilemma that would otherwise give rise to an intolerable sense of cognitive dissonance. From the perspective of the hard-liners who masterminded the 1989 crackdown, previous attempts to eradicate the negative concomitants of reform and screen out the "flies and worms" who were coming through China's open door had been insufficiently thoroughgoing, and they vowed that the 1989 rectification campaign would be much more definitive in setting the nation's future course. Although the fact that this campaign was presaged by the most sanguinary military crackdown in PRC history would seem to betoken resolute determination, there are at least two reasons to suspend judgment. First, the great retreat is still in progress at this writing, and while a political crackdown is perhaps consistent with policies of economic retrenchment and deflation, it remains to be seen whether rapid growth can be regenerated without the liberalization entailed by a resort to market forces, or whether political stability can be maintained without rapid growth. Previous periods of political repression and economic retrenchment have always steered clear of rescinding such basic reform innovations as the household responsibility system, or the spread of markets, in view of the likely economic costs and political resistance such a step would entail. To be sure, the policy of opening to the outside world has been seriously jeopardized by the crackdown, and the private sector set back by the campaign against corruption. Yet there are also signs at this writing that the forces of orthodoxy have reached their limits: they may impede, but cannot substantially reverse, the reform process. Second, those in power are all advanced in age, and in view of Deng Xiaoping's apparent failure to institutionalize his political reforms, it seems no more certain that his attempt to prescribe the nation's future will survive his own passing (and that of his fellow gerontocrats) than was Mao Zedong's attempt to immortalize the revolution. The succession scenario has been thrown completely awry by the most recent purges, and further turmoil over that issue seems likely.

Thus the uncertainties of pragmatism seem to have led China full circle, as the same two reference groups by which the PRC first set its course return to play a significant role in that nation's self-definition. Through identification with the developing and socialist worlds, China seeks to deny or compensate for her economic and security dependency on the West. Although Gorbachev's bold moves toward political reform and *glasnost'* have complicated matters considerably, identification with the socialist bloc still poses less threat to the domestic legitimacy of the CCP than bourgeois consumerism, and some of the hard-liners have reportedly advocated greater reliance on the Soviet alternative in the face of widespread ostracism by Western democracies following Tiananmen. Whereas the Third World can offer neither security nor significant economic advantage, and offers little more clue to China's future identity than a Rorschach ink blot, this reference group continues to provide an abstract point of reference for the Chinese identification with the poor and afflicted that has been so consistently emphasized in the Maoist variant of Marxism (though there has been a perceptible shift in the post-Mao era from "underdeveloped" to "developing" countries—the NICs). There have also been recurrent attempts to integrate these two reference groups and identifications, forging a link between East-West and North-South axes of conflict: "Victory in the world-wide struggle against hegemonism and victory in the international proletariat's struggle for socialism and communism are identical as far as fundamental interests are concerned."[3]

The major difference in the most recent period is that China's approach to both reference groups is cooler, more detached, more imbued by China's own specific economic and security interests. Why? Although currently available empirical evidence does not permit any certain conclusions at this point, one possible explanation is that the domestic popular appeal of the officially endorsed reference groups is increasingly tenuous. Identification with the Third World points backward developmentally rather than forward, and the socialist world is in considerable disarray at present without a clear or convincing vision of its future. Neither category seems to offer the key to the country's most pressing economic or security needs. There is hence the suspicion that the leadership is simply manipulating these reference groups to forestall a spontaneous identification with the bourgeois democracies that might otherwise imperil the CCP regime's domestic political legitimacy and international freedom of maneuver. If this supposition is correct, another identity crisis is predictable. To truly consolidate national identification with the officially sponsored reference groups, however, would require a major reorientation of the nation's economic, cultural, and strategic affiliations that the present regime lacks the legitimacy to achieve.

PART III

THE STRATEGIC TRIANGLE

The strategic dimension of the Sino-Soviet relationship has always perforce included a third party: the United States. At first this was because this leading bourgeois democracy was perceived as their mutual ideological antithesis and chief security concern. Later, as the Sino-Soviet alliance deteriorated, the United States emerged as a potential alternative coalition partner, first for the Soviets, then for the Chinese. Other nations have also become involved in the calculus, beginning with Taiwan and Korea, later Vietnam and India and, indirectly, Japan, Southeast Asia, and even Afghanistan and Pakistan. But these other actors have usually been deemed peripheral and, to some extent, functional dependents of one or another of the three principals. In this sense, the "strategic" (or security) dimension of the Sino-Soviet relationship may properly be defined as "triangular." And, because the three countries involved in this relationship are large and powerful, and so geopolitically situated that their interactions necessarily impinge on the interests of many other countries in their mutual vicinity, this triangular relationship is also "strategic" in another sense: it is internationally pivotal. Whether anything more definite than this may be said about the "strategic triangle" can more easily be ascertained at the end of this inquiry than at the beginning.

The purpose of this section, then, is on the one hand to describe the strategic relationship between the United States, the Soviet Union, and the People's Republic, as it has evolved over the past four decades, and on the other hand to try to explain that relationship. In order to both describe and explain, a formal model will be presented below, and applied to historical "reality" in the subsequent chapters. This model is based on the assumption that the relationship among three actors may be reduced to a relatively limited number of possibilities—more than are possible in a bipolar arrangement, but fewer than, say, a pentagon might permit. The roles that each actor may play in a triangular relationship are similarly limited. Creation of a formal model permits us to explore the political implications of a limited set of conceivable relationships that have been temporarily detached from the chaotic welter of international causal influences. Yet if the model has successfully grasped the logic of the relationship, its explanatory power will not be entirely vitiated by the greater complexity of empirical reality.[1]

The Model

There are two different types of "rules of the game": the first are "rules of entry," the second are "rules of play." The first define which players may compete in the game; the second indicate which moves are possible, for what stakes, risking what penalties. Rules of entry may consist of either "objective" criteria (as defined by the analyst), or "subjective" criteria (as defined by the players). Objective criteria may refer either to some measure of material assets, or to the performance of some functional role in the international system. In terms of material assets, such as geographic or demographic resources, economic development, military strength, and so forth, it has (quite plausibly) been argued that China does not qualify for inclusion in the game.[2] Only the Soviet Union and the United States can fully qualify as global strategic actors, and the structure of the international system is hence essentially bipolar. In terms of the fulfillment of functional role requirements, too, it has been argued that China cannot qualify.[3] A global actor must by definition fill a "managerial" role in the international system, which means that it must have the power to affect the foreign policy calculations of all other members of that system. Again, only the United States and the Soviet Union have the international power-projective capability to play this role.

If material assets are to serve as entrance requirements, it is quite easy to demonstrate that China is less strategically significant than either the United States or the Soviet Union. In per capita terms, China may still be classified as a developing nation, with low levels of per capita output, income, scientific development, and a significant technological lag in various categories of weapons. It lacks the power-projective capability to influence strategic developments in far-flung corners of the globe; indeed, the People's Liberation Army (PLA) is now estimated to be capable of conducting military operations beyond its own borders only with great difficulty. Yet China enjoys the status of a great power if aggregate indices are used: the country is first in the world in size of population; second in grain output and now in size of standing army (since the 1985 decision to retire one million troops); has the third largest navy and air force, and is third also in strategic nuclear forces, space satellites, cotton, raw coal, and steel output; fourth in total commercial energy output; sixth in GNP, and in crude oil output.[4] In view of recently improved chances for superpower disarmament, China's relative strategic position seems likely to improve.[5] Population size has sometimes been discounted as a meaningful index of military strength in view of low per capita income, but it would still provide a useful reserve of cannon fodder in case of a protracted conventional conflict: if China were to deploy the same proportion of men in the 18–45 age group as does the United States, its standing army would rise to 8,470,000; any attempt to match the USSR's deployment ratio would bring that figure to 12,074,000.[6] Moreover, that population is less vulnerable to nuclear attack than the more urbanized populations of economically developed countries, dispersed as it is throughout the countryside. China's lack of industrial development implies that its key industries could be quickly knocked out by a nuclear strike, but also the more primitive, small-scale rural economy might survive more tenaciously than the relatively capital-intensive economies of the developed countries. While it is true that China lacks carrier task forces and other such power-projective capabilities, the Soviet Union also lacked such capabilities until the mid-1970s. Yet both have been successful (up to a point) in promoting their ideologies and developmental models without military logistic backup.

Whereas it must be conceded that there is a wide gap between the strategic capabilities of China and the two superpowers, there is also a gap between the superpowers: Soviet technological development lags in many areas, and Soviet gross domestic product (GDP) is less than 60 percent that of the United States;[7] even by a strictly military calculus, the USSR did not achieve strategic parity until the end of the 1960s. Despite this gap, China is clearly the *third* most powerful strategic actor in the world, with a significant lead over any contender (by the late 1970s, China had surpassed France and England, and now has a nuclear weapons inventory greater than that of both combined).[8] Japan and Western Europe have more powerful economies, but less military-strategic heft than the PRC, for different reasons. Japan has a small, high-tech "self-defense force" consisting of an air-defense and antisubmarine network around its periphery. While Japanese military prowess should not be underestimated (the military budget claims only about 1 percent of Japan's GNP—about U.S. $30 billion in 1988—but that is 1 percent of the world's second largest GNP, giving Japan the eighth largest military force), Japan's lack of nuclear capability entails that it can figure in the strategic calculus only in alliance with the United

States. Western Europe is at this point still politically fragmented and loosely tied to one of the superpowers—just as Eastern Europe has historically been bound to the other. India, a nonaligned state loosely associated with the Soviet bloc since 1971, is a power whose strategic interests are essentially regional.[9] As the third most powerful strategic actor in the world, situated in the heart of Asia with borders adjoining more nations than any other country in the world, able to exert considerable influence in the region and sometimes well beyond it by dint of ideological proselytization and often skillful diplomatic efforts, with a permanent Security Council seat and high visibility in other international organizations and a fully developed position on most international issues, China's influence has often transcended her military or economic limitations.[10]

In addition to these objective factors, there is the subjective criterion: do the three principals take one another to be engaged in a triangular game? If the players themselves act on this assumption, the triangle becomes a self-fulfilling prophecy: "That which is perceived as real is real in its consequences," as W. I. Thomas put it. Operationally, the subjective factor can be defined in terms of positive answers to four questions: (1) Do all three *recognize the strategic salience of the three principals*? (2) Does each player *take into account the third player in managing its relationship with the second*? (3) Would the "defection" of any player be perceived to *shift the strategic balance* between the other two? (4) Is each player always open to the prospect of a *realignment of its relationship* with the other two? (Thus the Soviet-American-European and Soviet-American-Japanese relationships are not subjectively "triangular," although the defection of either Europe or Japan would shift the strategic balance fundamentally, because long-standing alliances and mutual expectations make such a shift incredible.)

As far as subjective criteria are concerned, there is no question that both the United States and the Soviet Union have perceived themselves as leading world powers since World War II, but the inclusion of the PRC is more recent. The Chinese have consistently denied that they are a "superpower" or ever intend to become one, but this seems to be because the Chinese term has pejorative *moral* connotations.[11] Like the Soviets, the Chinese have denounced the metaphor of a "card" game, understandably in view of the fact that most such scenarios would relegate one or both powers to the role of passively manipulated pieces in another player's game plan.[12] Yet leading Chinese foreign policy figures have at various times indicated that they are familiar with the logic of the "game." In a 1984 speech in Wuhan, high-level Chinese strategic adviser Huan Xiang referred to "great triangular relations" as "what really determines the development of the world situation."[13] In other comments, Chinese leaders—including Deng Xiaoping himself—have displayed keen appreciation of their country's strategic leverage within the triangle.[14]

Not only do the Chinese understand the game, their actions indicate that they consider their country a fully accredited player, daring militarily to confront, even provoke each of the others from a position of apparent strategic inferiority. And the two superpowers, in turn, have at various times indicated that they take China's seemingly presumptuous self-estimate quite seriously. China is the only country in the world (aside from the superpowers themselves) to have been threatened by each of them in turn with nuclear attack.[15] Each superpower has deemed it highly advantageous to be aligned with China, each in its turn experiencing euphoria, almost a national love affair during the early stages of entente; contrariwise, each has deemed China's realignment to be a traumatic event severely jeopardizing its international security (for the United States, China's "loss" helped touch off the spasm of national paranoia and internecine recrimination known as McCarthyism, which further exacerbated the cold war). When the United States began construction of an antiballistic missile (ABM) system in 1967, it was in order to defend against a Chinese, not a Soviet, nuclear strike (the Chinese were at the time deemed too irrational to respond predictably to deterrence).[16] To the Soviet Union, the China threat is so serious that it has for the past two decades devoted an estimated 25 to 33 percent of its military budget to that contingency; about 52 of its 184 divisions are deployed along the Sino-Soviet (including the Outer Mongolian) border, and some 170 of its 378 SS-20 IRBMs were (at least until the 1987 INF agreement) in the Soviet Far East, most of them aimed at Chinese targets. Garrett and Glaser, by interviewing Soviet military elites and reviewing available war planning literature, found that Soviet strategic planners anticipated that a nuclear exchange between the two superpowers might be inconclusive, leaving the motherland devastated and thus acutely vulnerable to Chinese intervention with conventional forces in the postnuclear phase.[17]

The analytical possibilities for rules of entry range along a continuum. At a maximum, the model might be pivotal to the international balance of power. At a minimum, the model might define the formal "rules of the game" for the three participants, without asserting necessary implications for the rest of the world, or indeed for any actors beyond the three principals. The modicum position adopted here is that the model *pertains to the power balance within the greater East Asian region* (i.e., the Pacific Rim, or Pacific Basin), but not necessarily to other regions. The entrance rules are *objective* criteria, according to which these three qualify as the most powerful strategic actors in the region. Subjective considerations, though not criteria for inclusion, are important variables affecting the relations among members. Using the Kantian language Marx also found useful, we might distinguish between a triangle "in itself" and a triangle "for itself." A triangle "in itself" persists as long as the objective criteria pertain; a triangle "for itself" becomes clearly visible during security crises, or when the configuration of the triangle is in flux. To repeat, this model defines the triangle on objective criteria within a regional context, and aims to provide a logically exhaustive—indeed, tautological—analysis of the possible relations among the three main strategic actors within that arena.

All the same, the ramifications of triangular permutations sometimes transcend the regional arena, for two reasons: (1) The Asian region includes the two global superpowers and two quasi or potential superpowers—China and Japan—and the implications of any shift in the power balance among them is obviously likely to have wide-ranging implications. (2) The international significance of the region in relation to other regions has increased considerably in the past four decades, largely because of very rapid economic development there.[18] That economic growth—as well as the region's commensurately growing political significance—is likely to continue for the foreseeable future.[19] It seems legitimate to draw attention to the transregional implications of shifts in the Asian triangle when these appear obvious.

Before going into the "rules of play," some of the game's underlying assumptions should be made explicit. First, it is assumed, as in the previous section, that the same vocabulary of motives used to explain individual actions may also validly characterize those of collective actors (e.g., nation-states); that is, that Allison's "rational actor" model still applies at the level of the international system.[20] This involves at least a "translation" from the language of individual motives or bureaucratic interests into the language of unit-actor policies. I would argue that this involves no real distortion, for the justificatory rationale for the latter—not to mention the decisions themselves—are explicitly tailored to "fit" the interests of the nation-state in question, whatever their parochial origins. Second, it is assumed that each player has a disposition toward the other two players which may be simply but not inaccurately characterized as either positive or negative. A positive disposition will tend to be reciprocated in kind, while a negative disposition will invite various hostile countermoves: in international relations as in affairs of the heart, "unrequited love" (or hate) is unlikely to endure. That such a characterization often involves a "reduction" of complex and ambivalent relationships is no less true than the fact that regimes are often required to make such a determination, and to orient their own moves accordingly.

Based on these grounding assumptions, four different ideal-typical configurations are logically conceivable. These are the *ménage à trois,* consisting of positive relationships for all three players; the "romantic triangle," consisting of positive relationships between one "pivot" player and two "wings," but a negative relationship between the two wings;[21] the "stable marriage," consisting of a positive "spousal" relationship but negative relationships between each "spouse" and a third "pariah"; and a "unit-veto" triangle,[22] consisting of negative relationships between each player and the other two. These configurations are graphically depicted below:

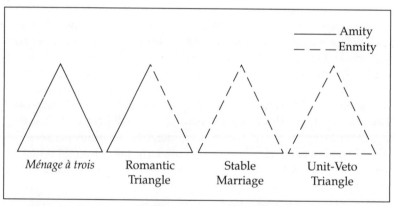

While each of these configurations is logically possible, each is not equally probable empirically. The unit-veto triangle has occurred relatively infrequently empirically. When there is enmity between all three players, there is little to hold the triangle together or make it a meaningful basis for international strategic organization, and it threatens to disintegrate. The *ménage à trois* is relatively "introverted" and tends not to be "strategic," given the absence of negative relationships (unless it is simply a coalition of the three against some outside threat, in which case it is not really a triangle but at least a quadrangle). Despite difficulties of coordination due to the virtual foreclosure of vigorous leadership and the endemic suspicion of collusion, the *ménage* has been known to function reasonably effectively (*vide* the Trilateral Commission), and should not be altogether discounted. From a systemic perspective, it is the optimal configuration, though it is perhaps suboptimal from the perspective of the individual player. For practical purposes the two most commonly encountered configurations are the stable marriage and the romantic triangle. And the romantic triangle seems to be less stable than the marriage, in view of the instability of the pivot position. The main reason for variant stability has to do with the invidious distribution of structural advantages to different roles, which will now be considered.

Each role in each configuration has certain inherent advantages and disadvantages, although in any specific political situation these would be affected by the identity and respective strengths of the players, the nature of their interaction, and other empirical variables. Assuming that all players wish to maximize their national interests, each player will prefer at a maximum to have positive relationships with both other players, and minimally to have a positive relationship with at least one other player (i.e., to avoid negative relationships with both other players). Assuming all players wish to minimize possible risks, each player will try to prevent malign collusion between the other two players. Hence a rational player's ranking of role preferences would be: (1) "pivot" in a romantic triangle; (2) "wing" in a *ménage à trois;* (3) "spouse" in a stable marriage; (4) "wing" in a romantic triangle; (5) "wing" in a unit-veto triangle; and (6) "pariah" in a stable marriage. The reason (1) is ranked higher than (2) is the difficulty of detecting and monitoring collusion, which is minimized if relations between the other two players are clearly negative. Similarly, the reason (5) is ranked higher than (6) is the absence of malign collusion in the case of the former.

Historical Permutations

Since the end of World War II, the relationship between China, the United States, and the Soviet Union has undergone seven permutations: (1) The period from 1945 to 1949 was one of an unstable and deteriorating *ménage à trois,* undergoing a transition to bipolarity. (2) The period from 1950 to 1959 was one of relatively stable "marriage" between the Soviet Union and the PRC, confronting the American pariah with an apparently monolithic "communist bloc." (3) The 1960–70 period, although somewhat more difficult to classify, was essentially a unit-veto triangle. (4) The 1971–76 period was a "romantic triangle," in which the United States played "pivot," dividing its favors between

Soviet and Chinese "wings." (5) From 1977 to 1981, a brief and relatively unstable "marriage" was consummated between the PRC and the United States, casting the USSR in the role of "pariah." (6) From 1982 to 1985, there was a return to the "romantic triangle," in which the "pivot" role was assumed by the PRC, consigning the United States and the USSR to "wing" positions. (7) During the still emergent post-1986 period, there has been a reversion to the *ménage à trois* configuration with which the triangle began.

Each of these configurations deserves more detailed analysis within its historical context. It is worth investigating specifically which strategic considerations were uppermost in the formation of each, and what disfunctions were then responsible for the dissolution of that configuration and its transformation into a new one.

CHAPTER 9

Ménage à Trois, 1945–1949

During the interregnum between dissolution of the Big Five alliance following the unconditional surrender of the Axis powers and the rise of a "two-camp" division of the postwar world, the three powers might be said to be characterized by rapidly deteriorating mutually positive relations, a decadent *ménage*.

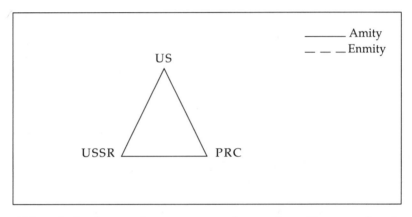

Although the three nations were part of a wartime alliance, and each had some interest in sustaining good relations with the other two, the common threat that had sustained their collaboration had been vanquished and a host of hitherto suppressed internecine conflicts soon surfaced. The fact that two of the three had been ravaged by Axis invasion forces left an imbalance of power among them, placing the United States in a position of unprecedented paramountcy. China was also devastated by the war and eager to compensate for past deprivations, but the eruption of civil war between Communist and Nationalist forces further complicated matters. While exhausted American forces proceeded with postwar demobilization, their national strength and security now apparently ensured, still vulnerable Soviet forces swiftly filled the power vacuum left by the retreating Axis, grasping for territorial compensation as a form of insurance against a third European invasion; in China an unlikely coalition between CCP and KMT forces held by a thread.

Certainly there is evidence of CCP interest in an opening to the West in this immediate postwar period, when the Red Army was still in a vulnerable military position and the CCP was hopeful of gaining power peacefully. At this time, the CCP purported to believe that American capitalism was becoming more enlightened and that Soviet-American cooperation during the war represented a permanent trend toward "peace and democracy." While on the one hand indicating that the CCP also had a Soviet option, Mao assured John Service during the latter's 1944 mission to Yanan that China would not follow the Soviet model, but would open its market to Western capitalists and cooperate with the United States against Japanese imperialism.[1] Socialism would be impractical in China for the foreseeable future given the country's low level of economic development, Mao confided; he had even considered dropping the word "Communist" from the party's name, but had decided against it because its program was so moderate that even conservative American businessmen could find nothing objectionable to its policies.[2] If the United States pursued a "correct" policy, Soviet rule in China "should be secondary to that of the U.S."[3]

As Soviet-American relations visibly deteriorated, CCP spokesmen began to play on the rivalry. Thus Zhou Enlai, shifting the onus westward for any disruption of relations, told U.S. officials in 1946, "Of course we will lean to one side, but how far depends on you."[4] Not wishing to compromise their availability for an American offer, CCP leaders were careful to conceal from Service the extent of direct Soviet presence at Yanan.[5] Simultaneously, the CCP leadership acted to reassure Moscow of its unswerving loyalty.[6] It is, however, perhaps conceivable that early CCP protestations of continuing interest in good relations with Washington may have assumed continuing Soviet-American amity. The Soviets may have even shared these optimistic assumptions, as Molotov submitted a memorandum to Acheson on January 3, 1945, requesting a commercial loan of U.S. $6 billion.[7]

But with the fall of Czechoslovakia and the Berlin blockade (both in 1948), Soviet-American relations went into a tailspin; in China, the CCP engaged in the delicate maneuver of defeating a government that had cultivated good relations with Washington without jeopardizing those relations. The CCP sensed that Sino-American relations might be adversely affected by the deterioration in Soviet-American relations— an apprehension the Soviets also shared, as indicated by Zhdanov's September 1947 revival of the "two camps" worldview and the founding (at the same meeting) of the Cominform. (The vision of a monolithic communist bloc was not monopolized by Western anticommunists!) The CCP, which had already initiated an anti-American campaign in June 1946, enthusiastically endorsed the Soviet stand, stressing the impossibility of remaining neutral in a bipolar world.[8] This line was to persist more or less unchanged for the next two years. Relations were further aggravated in 1948, when American consular officials in Mukden were placed under house arrest for more than a year on charges of espionage, and then were tried and expelled from China.[9] The right argued for a resolute American response, but Acheson treated the matter with delicacy, arguing that the United States should take no steps that might enhance the position of "pro-Moscow" Mukden communists.

What is intriguing and perhaps more significant is that the CCP again evinced interest in a rapprochement with the West in the spring of 1949, when the Red Army could see the light of victory at the end of the tunnel of civil war and Soviet-American relations had already polarized. Yet it must be said that this "last chance" was, according to the best information presently available, highly ephemeral, perhaps ultimately chimerical. Although the underlying motives are difficult to read, CCP behavior was equivocal, simultaneously expressing interest in good relations with both Washington and Moscow. In the immediate postwar period, when Soviet-American relations were still intact, this was perhaps plausible; but even after 1949, when polarization became inexorable, the CCP continued to try to play both sides. Is there any way to tell which courtship was "sincere"? It is noteworthy that whereas the CCP *publicly* declared its loyalty to the communist bloc, accompanied by sotto voce indications of disagreement, CCP signals of interest in a rapprochement with Washington were transmitted sub rosa amid continuing public avowals of ideological enmity. What was Washington reasonably to infer—that the United States was being offered a clandestine dalliance but no marriage?

Meanwhile, if signs of Sino-Soviet disagreement were invisible to outside observers at the time, they have since become impossible to ignore. Even after the Japanese (whose Kwantung Army had blockaded the entire Chinese coastline) had been evicted in 1945, Stalin's assumption was that Chiang would retain power by dint of American patronage, so he advised the CCP that "conditions were not ripe for an uprising in China," [10] and "that we should not have a civil war and should cooperate with Chiang Kai-shek, otherwise the Chinese nation would perish."[11] Moscow's attempt to rein in the CCP was premised on the suspicion that Mao was pursuing a deliberately provocative policy liable to foster friction between the Soviet Union and the United States; if the KMT were seriously threatened by defeat, the United States would intervene, crush the CCP, and establish bases on the Soviet border.[12] Stalin did not wish strife in China to upset his working relationship with the Allies at a time when he was still consolidating Soviet control of Eastern Europe. Moreover, as Stalin told U.S. envoy Averell Harriman in 1945 (explaining why he had recognized the KMT instead of the CCP as government of China), he wished to avoid "exorbitant demands for the industrialization of China"—which, he added, "Soviet Russia could not meet."[13] Even when CCP forces met with unexpected success, "Stalin urged through Liu Shaoqi that the Chinese Communists continue guerrilla war and refrain from pushing their victory to a decisive conclusion," suggesting (in July 1948) that they hold the line at the Yangtze.[14]

An unspoken factor helping to account for Stalin's restrained enthusiasm for immediate CCP victory is the fact that he had just reached a settlement with the Allies and the KMT regime quite favorable to Soviet territorial interests. In the terminal stages of World War II he availed himself of the perceived Allied need for Soviet help in the struggle against Japan to seize back those privileges Russia had held in Northeast China (then Manchuria) under the tsars, and also induced the KMT to recognize the "independence" of Outer Mongolia and renounce all Chinese claims[15] (thereby preemptively denying one of Mao's earliest requests, that Outer Mongolia revert to China). Stalin also attempted less successfully to absorb Inner Mongolia into Outer Mongolia in 1948. In May the Soviets extended their agreement with the Nationalist government on joint rights in Xinjiang province for five more years, and even apparently attempted (unsuccessfully) to have Xinjiang proclaim its autonomy from China.[16] For his part, Chiang reluctantly acquiesced in Soviet demands for hegemony over portions of Chinese territory that he could not control in any case in exchange for Soviet neutrality in the Chinese civil war. Thus he conceded the "independence" of Outer Mongolia, agreed to Soviet participation in the operation of the Chinese Eastern Railway, to joint Sino-Soviet use of the naval base of Port Arthur, and to the internationalization of Dairen, as formally acknowledged in the Sino-Soviet Treaty of Friendship and Alliance signed August 14, 1945. In return, the Soviet Union recognized the legitimacy of the Nationalist regime and promised "to render to China moral support and aid in military supplies and other natural resources, to be entirely given to the Nationalist Government as the central government of China."[17]

Chinese signals of interest in friendship with the United States, on the other hand, were emitted under the table in the context of hostile propaganda broadsides. In late May 1949, Zhou Enlai informally delivered a message to the Americans (via the UPI) requesting economic assistance from the U.S. government, in return for which China would play a neutral role between West and East.[18] American ambassador John Leighton Stuart, who had been cultivating numerous contacts with CCP diplomatic officials and wished to accept an invitation to pursue these at the highest levels during an unofficial trip to Beijing in the spring of 1949, was denied permission to do so by Dean Acheson; yet the invitation was clandestine and deniable, interspersed by public CCP testimonials to international communist solidarity and denunciations of Western imperialism. In early June 1949, Liu Shaoqi published a speech (written in November 1948) adopting the Zhdanov "two camps" worldview and denying any prospect of China's finding a third way,[19] while Mao reacted to the creation of NATO by declaring (on April 4, 1949) that in the event of Soviet-American war China would side with the USSR.[20] Still more definitive was Mao's speech, "On People's Democratic Dictatorship," published under a June 30 dateline, in which he uttered the famous statement: "The Chinese people must either incline to the side of imperialism or towards that of socialism. . . . It is impossible to sit on the fence; there is no third road; neutrality is merely a camouflage; a third road does not exist."[21] Indirectly alluding to a leadership wrangle on this issue, Mao renounced any interest in American aid, at the same time leaving open the possibility of accepting it while denying any reciprocal obligation to the donors:

"We need help from the British and U.S. Governments." This, too, is a naive idea in these times. Would the present rulers of Britain and the United States, who are imperialists, help a people's state? Why do these countries do business with us and, supposing that they might be willing to lend us money on terms of mutual benefit in the future, why should they do so? Because their capitalists want to make money and their brokers want to earn interest to extricate themselves from their own crisis—it is not a matter of helping the Chinese people. The communist parties and progressive groups in these countries are urging their governments to establish trade and even diplomatic relations with us. This is goodwill, this is help, this cannot be mentioned in the same breath with the conduct of the bourgeoisie in these same countries.[22]

Nor did Mao seem seriously interested in Western recognition: "As for the question of recognition of our country by imperialist countries, we should not be in a hurry to solve it now and need not be in a hurry to solve it even for a fairly long period after nation-wide victory," he said in his report to the Seventh Central Committee (March 5, 1949).[23] Yet again, this expression of public defiance was softened by informal diplomatic assurances to the effect that this was a "political line" that did not preclude "give-and-take" in economics.[24] When Anastas Mikoyan made a secret trip to meet with Mao in early 1949 and inform the CCP leadership of Stalin's excommunication of Tito the previous June, the Chinese assured him of their wholehearted support for Soviet leadership of the bloc. Soviet leaders later contended that for the PRC to have abandoned their Soviet patrons in favor of a dalliance with the United States at the time would have been out of the question: "We would never have permitted Mao to have taken the Party toward the United States, and we had the means—both in terms of friends within the CCP that would have adamantly opposed any such trend and in terms of our material resources in the area—to prevent this."[25]

If we read between the lines, CCP terms for the establishment of formal diplomatic relations with Washington emerge fairly clearly: in addition to an economic aid package, the CCP would demand severance of ties with the KMT regime in Taiwan (and noninterference in the planned PLA invasion of the island), plus American acceptance of close ideological and diplomatic links between the PRC and the Soviet Union.[26] In return, the CCP leadership was prepared to offer low-profile diplomatic relations and an opportunity for dialogue, probably without opportunity for investment or significant economic relations for the time being, given the concern with eliminating vestiges of imperialism and proceeding with socialization of the means of production.

On the American side, there was also debate, pitting the "defense perimeter" concept first proposed by George Kennan and defended by Acheson and the State Department against an "Asian Rim" containment policy that found favor among the Joint Chiefs of Staff, MacArthur's SCAAP Headquarters in Tokyo, and segments of the State Department (Dean Rusk's group et al.).[27] The defense perimeter school advocated dissociation from the KMT and tacit acceptance of a victorious PLA completion of the civil war, in hopes of encouraging a division between the Soviet Union and China which the United States could exploit. To this end, the United States should lower its profile in China and try to avoid inciting xenophobic feelings (meanwhile also straining the Sino-Soviet link by exacerbating Chinese economic dependency through an economic blockade).[28] The Asian Rim school countered that certain geopolitical "exceptions" to the "defense perimeter" notion (e.g., bases on Taiwan, Korea, Japan) might enable the United States to maintain a military presence on the Asian rimland from which further Chinese Communist expansion might be "contained." Until the summer of 1950, the advocates of a "defense perimeter" seem to have prevailed. The United States did not, however, normalize relations during this hiatus, as the public behavior of the incipient PRC regime remained too hostile to justify such an accommodation in the face of increasingly anticommunist American public opinion.

The CCP's seizure of power was immediately followed by a redistribution of spoils and headlong pursuit of comprehensive political transformation that exacerbated tensions with all bourgeois democracies with residual interests in China. CCP authorities placed direct pressure on American diplomatic officials, as already noted, in addition to which private U.S. business, religious, and journalistic groups felt a variety of constraints.

First, foreign investment in pre-Liberation China had exceeded U.S. $150 million, about half of which was British, a fourth American. CCP pressure on private investors included heavy taxes, including direct levies, and the forced employment of redundant labor in order to relieve unemployment. Foreign businessmen suspected that the CCP policy was to squeeze out all foreign firms without nationalizing them in order to avoid compensation (China denies this). In some cases, there was outright expropriation (i.e., without compensation), as in the seizure of Economic Cooperation Administration stocks in 1949. During the 1952 "Three-antis and Five-antis" campaign, businessmen were requested to submit a detailed report on their backgrounds and their thoughts were reviewed; those with foreign contacts were either investigated or arrested.

Second, there had been a highly visible Western religious presence in pre-Liberation China, led by some five thousand Catholic and four thousand Protestant missionaries. About half the Catholic and a fourth of the Protestant clergy stayed on after Liberation. The CCP authorities restricted them to the premises, and put pressure on Chinese Christians to have no contacts with foreign missionaries; the ties of the Chinese Catholic hierarchy to the Vatican were forcibly severed. During the first Campaign of Suppression of Counterrevolutionary Elements, churches were closed down and foreign missionaries expelled from the country; many members and others with foreign contacts were treated as spies.

Third, a great number of intellectuals who were educated in the West were purged and subjected to thought reform. Western culture and art, music, and dance began to come under criticism. The English-owned press in Shanghai was subjected to heavy censorship.[29]

These areas of friction made it difficult for any "imperialist" powers to establish amicable relations with the new regime. Any attempt to do so would have involved politically expensive concessions: the "loss" of Taiwan, a policy of passivity during "socialization of the means of production" that would also affect residual Western interests, possibly the forfeiture of Korea and Vietnam. The British, who under Labour leadership sought to accommodate the CCP,[30] managed to retain formal relations at the chargé d'affaires level, but these remained almost as cool as Sino-American relations until the 1970s.

Meanwhile Sino-Soviet relations were blossoming into formal alliance. The CCP victory over the Nationalists prompted Stalin to concede his initial misjudgment (though he continued to harbor suspicions in the wake of Tito's defection).[31] Mao's first trip to Moscow, in the dead of winter (Zhou Enlai and others joined him—after rather involved negotiations with the Soviets—on January 21), coincided with Stalin's seventieth birthday celebrations; and the Kremlin, according to available sources at the time as well as subsequent Soviet accounts, accorded him rather special treatment. Mao stood to Stalin's right hand in the congratulation ceremonies, and was selected to speak first. He stressed that the Chinese people were "deeply aware of Comrade Stalin's friendship," and hailed the "great Stalin—leader of the world working class and of the international Communist movement." When Mao and his party attended an all-star ballet performance at the Bolshoi Theater on the eve of the signing of their treaty, the Soviet audience gave them a "standing, prolonged, shouting ovation. . . . Mao and party appeared exhilarated by the thunderous enthusiasm."[32] Upon his departure from Moscow, Mao gave a farewell address at the Yaroslav station, where he said: "People can see that the unity of two great nations, China and the Soviet Union, reinforced by the treaty, will be eternal, indestructible, and that nobody will ever be able to tear us apart."[33]

After the fact, allegations have surfaced that Sino-Soviet relations were already severely strained; Khrushchev, for example, claimed that the two "came to the verge of a split," as Stalin declined even to meet with Mao until the latter let it be known that if the situation continued, he would leave.[34] This seems to have been a slight exaggeration,[35] though there were indications of mutual distrust. A preliminary delegation led by Liu Shaoqi was sent clandestinely in May 1949, and seems to have been quite successful (Liu met with Stalin five times). Mao himself had wished to visit Moscow as early as April 1948, and even formed a delegation and sent a cable, but Stalin demurred, instead sending Mikoyan as his plenipotentiary. Contrary to reports that Stalin refused to see Mao, the latter was immediately ushered in to meet Stalin upon his arrival in December, and the two exchanged wary compliments. Stalin was launching his last great purges (a trial was under way in Sofia of the latest batch of East European party leaders accused of Titoist sympathies) at the time of Mao's appearance.[36] As Mao (who would later defend Stalin's reputation) recalled in his speech to the Tenth Plenum of the Eighth Central Committee (CC) in October 1962: "After the victory of the revolution he [Stalin] next suspected China of being a Yugoslavia, and that I would become a second Tito. Later when I went to Moscow to sign the Sino-Soviet Treaty of Alliance and Mutual Assistance, we had to go through another struggle. He was not willing to sign a treaty."[37]

Finally, after what Mao later characterized as a "series of struggles" lasting more than two months, the two concluded the Sino-Soviet Treaty of Friendship, Alliance and Mutual Assistance.[38] There is little empirical information about the nature of these "struggles," but it seems to have been difficult for Mao even to bridge the hierarchical communications gap. Evidently intimidated by the older man (Mao was younger than Stalin, older than Khrushchev), who was then riding the crest of his cult of personality, Mao masked his intentions. "We have come here this time to complete a certain task," he said mysteriously. "A certain thing has to be made, and it must be both beautiful and tasty." He then refused to elaborate. Stalin, who appeared "notably guarded and terse," refused for his part to be drawn out.[39]

The question whether there was a "lost chance" in China, and who lost what, will no doubt continue to inspire controversy. Our task is not to second-guess foreign policy makers, but to describe and explain the shift in the configuration of the triangle from *ménage* to "marriage." If we can contribute anything here it is the insight that "America's failure" must be seen in a triangular perspective, not as a strictly bilateral disturbance. From this perspective the primary factor was the polarization of Soviet-American relations, as the USSR sought to compensate for an overwhelming sense of vulnerability and the United States eventually scrambled to stem a slide from absolute to relative international hegemony. In this context, the Chinese Communists were forced to choose. From the American perspective, the course they took could only be viewed as an additional blow. Although the PRC seems to have made some effort to engineer a shift from a *ménage* to a "romantic" configuration (with Beijing at pivot), the CCP's ideological identification with what was still at this time a relatively intact bloc undermined its credibility as a fair broker, and the PRC was too weak to resist the application of bloc discipline should it have come to that, too needy to decline Soviet aid in the context of Western isolation and American blockade.

CHAPTER 10

Sino-Soviet Marriage, 1950–1960

Upon formal establishment of the PRC, China and the USSR were joined in a "marriage" confronting a hostile and defensive United States. They were united not only by ideology but by formal alliance. This treaty—part of the web of such pacts that made up the bloc—defined their mutual obligations as well as their common security needs (and putative adversary, the United States). For the Soviet Union, it satisfied security requirements in terms of a continental strategy, based on the acquisition of buffer areas in Eastern Europe and East Asia; for the PRC, it provided extended nuclear deterrence.[1] The configuration may be depicted as follows:

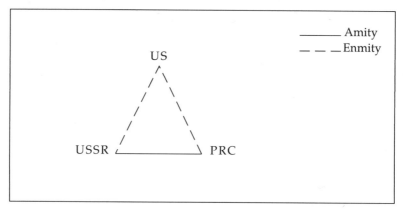

From the perspective of the United States, this was the least advantageous configuration available, permitting Communist domination of the Eurasian heartland and obliging Washington to halt disarmament and prepare for possible conflict with two large and apparently formidable adversaries in widely dispersed theaters. Although a relatively powerful, undamaged economy (in 1946, the U.S. economy produced over half the gross world product!), temporary monopoly on deliverable nuclear warheads, and virtually unchallenged mastery of the seas would permit the United States to protect its global interests for the foreseeable future, this rude reversal of international fortunes, coming so soon after the euphoria of victory over the Axis powers, touched off a major domestic trauma. Communist claims to inherit the future seemed borne out by the vast potential of the two countries, soon hailed by zealous revolutionaries from Vietnam to Guatemala.

If the Sino-Soviet treaty provided the legal basis for the marriage, the experience that more than any other bonded the relationship, according to scholarly consensus, was the Korean War. Truman reacted to the June 25, 1950, invasion by immediately committing American air and naval support, followed by ground troops; he then proceeded to obtain a UN Security Council decision to provide military assistance via a UN "police action." Apparently neither Stalin nor Mao had anticipated these countermoves. Although Truman in January 1950 disclaimed any interest in bases on Taiwan and Acheson announced (and repeated as late as June) that Taiwan lay outside the U.S. defense perimeter, on June 27, two days after the North Korean invasion of the South, Truman decided to dispatch the Seventh Fleet to "neutralize" the Taiwan Strait, making a PRC invasion practically impossible. This move, putting Taiwan and South Korea within the same perimeter, helped to embroil China in the Korean invasion. A shocked Beijing perceived this as fresh evidence of American aggression and mounted a nationwide hate-America campaign. "All these counterrevolutionary activities are engineered from behind the scenes by imperialists, particularly by American imperialists," Mao declared.[2]

In view of the fatefulness of the decision that was to bring the two powers into armed conflict, locking the PRC into a pro-Soviet and anti-American stance for at least the next decade, China's decision to intervene might profitably be reexamined. It has been argued in retrospect that the decision was manipulated by its chief beneficiary, the Soviet Union.[3] There were two junctures in the decision-making process that may be distinguished for closer scrutiny: first, the North Korean invasion of the South in June, and second, the massive influx of Chinese "volunteers" in October. As to the former, reconsideration of the evidence reveals that although the Soviets were certainly advised of the Korean invasion plan, Moscow had *less* control than previously believed. The North Korean decision to invade the South was made in Pyongyang, and its timing seems to have had to do with Korean rather than triangular politics.[4] Beijing seems to have been caught "unawares" by the invasion, but was in any case preoccupied (since autumn 1949) with plans to invade Taiwan and initially unconcerned with what it considered a sideshow.[5]

So far as the subsequent Chinese intervention is concerned, it seems clear that the decision was made in Beijing, largely in order to prevent an American military presence on the Chinese border,[6] despite the fact (unknown in advance, of course) that the expedition would incur appalling Chinese sacrifices because of the technological superiority of American weapons. When in mid-September 1950 MacArthur landed at Inchon, in conjunction with a breakout of UN forces from the Pusan perimeter, the North Korean Army was routed, driven from the South within two weeks. Kim Il Sung sent a supplicant letter to Stalin, to which the latter replied noncommittally; in fact, Stalin seems to have written off the DPRK, and he warned Mao that the Chinese might soon be called upon to host a government in exile.[7] Soviet military advisers were precipitately withdrawn that fall, and it became clear that no troops would be sent; Stalin sought to limit the Soviet role to diplomatic efforts and some air support. Under these circumstances Mao's decision to intervene and fill the exposed breach in Communist defenses was a courageous (or foolhardy) one that did not even win immediate firm backing from Stalin, who was concerned about the possible American retaliatory threat to a weakly defended Siberia. When Zhou went to Moscow to discuss the matter, Stalin expressed apprehension lest "our action would anger the United States, thus triggering World War III."[8] Mao was opposed within the CCP Politburo as well, by Chen Yun and others (including some military officers) who preferred giving top priority to economic reconstruction.[9] Nor were the fears of Stalin and other more cautious Communist strategists entirely unfounded; although the Chinese invasion achieved complete surprise and inflicted a severe initial setback on UN forces, one considered American response involved expanding the war to China, and the Americans resorted to nuclear blackmail in their efforts to impose a truce. Eisenhower threatened China with nuclear attack immediately after assuming office in February 1953, using the Panmunjom peace talks as the most direct of several channels through which to convey this threat. And there seems little doubt that the threat was credible: only objections from the U.S. Army dissuaded him from employing tactical nuclear weapons on the battlefield without advance warning to Beijing.[10] Whether it was decisive in concluding the war remains uncertain, however.[11]

The Chinese intervention marked a sea change in presumptions of Sino-Soviet solidarity, both for the Soviet Union and the United States. For both, this ordeal by fire represented consummation of a stable marriage. This fusion effect should, to be sure, not be overstated. China did not simply dissolve its national sovereignty in the communist bloc, nor did American foreign policy-making elites make such a naive assumption. Recently declassified documents indicate that American policy makers remained cognizant of Chinese autonomy, and deliberately set about trying to drive a wedge between Moscow and Beijing by pushing a soft line toward the former and a hard line (referred to by Dulles as a "closed door" policy) toward the latter.[12] While this differentiated policy was ultimately to have its desired payoff, creating strain within the alliance (the Soviet leadership gained a rosier view of the class enemy than the Chinese, and this manifested itself in interparty differences over the inevitability of class war, and so on), Washington was equally clear that the alliance remained strong and that great patience would hence be required. One high-level American intelligence analysis of the mid-1950s concluded:

The heavy dependence [of China] on the USSR for the realization of her industrialization program and for the support and modernization of her armed forces is well established. This dependence is virtually complete as regards heavy industrial equipment, machine tools, motor transport, heavy weapons, aircraft, destroyers, submarines, and high-grade fuels. Thus, through manipulation of material support alone, the USSR is patently capable of governing not only the rate of growth of the Chinese economy, but also the effectiveness and scale of any Chinese military effort. . . . the Soviets would be able to *apply pressures, including curtailment, or withdrawal if necessary, of Soviet economic and military aid in order to obtain Chinese conformity to Soviet views* (i.e., Soviet vital interests vs. Chinese vital interests). [Emphasis in the original.][13]

As late as 1959, the CIA cautioned that it would be a "grave imprudence" to assume major discord within the "Moscow-Peking axis."[14]

All the available evidence emitted from the bloc supported the impression of tight solidarity, as China supported virtually every Soviet diplomatic initiative. As Mao put it as late as 1956:

The policy of China's leaning to the side of the Soviet Union is a correct one. At present there are still people who are doubtful of this policy, and say "Don't lean." Even some consider that [China] can adopt a neutral position, stand in between the USSR and USA, and serve as a bridge. This is the Yugoslav way. This means that [we] can get money from both sides, that is, from this side and that side. Is it a good way? I think it is not a good way to stand in between, it is not good for this nation, because one side is a powerful imperialist and China has been oppressed by imperialism. It looks good to stand in between the USSR and USA. [To lean to one side] looks isolated, but it will not be isolated in the end.[15]

Yet while the Korean War functioned to enhance bloc solidarity, subsequent episodes of interbloc polarization tended to precipitate intrabloc friction. This was owing at least in part to the differentiated American response. Throughout the 1950s, the CCP leadership took it upon itself to launch a series of unilateral military probes similar to the Korean intervention along its borders, usually small in scale but often accompanied by propaganda broadsides designed to magnify their impact. The United States typically responded with military countermeasures against the perceived aggressor and simultaneous diplomatic overtures toward Moscow designed to settle the dispute. In a sense the differential treatment was a natural response to a differential threat perception. Moscow tended to waffle at this point, reassuring Beijing of its resolute support while at the same time seeking to accommodate the other side. This was also in a sense natural, for Soviet national interests were not at stake.

Moscow's increasing discomfiture with Beijing's provocations was due to what the Soviet leadership now viewed as a squandered opportunity for diplomatic initiatives, from the standpoint of a basic Soviet post-Stalin shift from a "continental" to a "global" strategy (reviewed in Chapter 6). From the Chinese perspective this shift was incompatible with "continuing the revolution" in foreign affairs, which Beijing identified first and foremost with some form of armed mass insurrection. Thus the PRC was the major supporter of Ho Chi Minh at this stage, contributing significantly to the Viet Minh's unexpected 1954 triumph at Dien Bien Phu. After the Geneva Conference (April–July 1954), Khrushchev effectively abdicated any major role for the Soviet Union in Indochina (indeed, in all of Southeast Asia), deferring to growing Chinese influence in Hanoi.[16] The PRC also sought to develop a guerrilla war against the neutral government of Burma and supported a major insurgency in Malaysia. In the summer of 1950, China invaded Tibet and was apparently preparing to invade Taiwan when the Korean War intervened.

Owing in part to the countermeasures undertaken by the two superpowers, partly to the defensive response of the developing countries at whom the initiatives were aimed, they proved on the whole counterproductive. Eleven days after the Korean cease-fire (August 7, 1953), a U.S.–South Korean Mutual Defense Treaty was signed. The initial shelling of Jinmen (Quemoy) immediately preceded convention of the Manila Conference, called to discuss a Southeast Asian Collective Defense Treaty; SEATO was signed September 8, 1954 (Beijing approved an order to begin national military conscription the same day, in protest). At about the same time the United States entered into negotiations with the Kuomintang for a mutual defense treaty (signed December 1954, in the midst of the first Taiwan Strait crisis). Strategic parity between the superpowers was still remote: while the United States had a first-strike capability, the Soviets did not explode their first H-bomb until autumn 1955. It was the 1954–55 Taiwan Strait crisis that elicited the first movement toward Soviet-American collaboration: in an exchange of letters between Eisenhower and his old comrade-in-arms, Marshal Zhukov, the two came to an understanding that if the Americans restrained Chiang, the Soviets would leash Mao. This tacit quid pro quo, leading to an agreement between Dulles and Soviet Foreign Minister Molotov, provided the basis for the first Soviet-American summit (Geneva, summer 1955).[17] It is not surprising in view of the meager (indeed counterproductive) upshot of these early revolutionary initiatives that they were to give way to the two-year diplomatic respite known as the Bandung period (see Chapter 7).

Two of China's revolutionary foreign policy initiatives were particularly effective in causing the two superpowers to revise their perspective of China from that of a socialist revolutionary to that of an essentially nationalist force, a change in perception that was necessary for them to bridge the ideological chasm that divided them and make possible a shift in the triangular configuration. These were the territorial disputes with India and Taiwan—in both of which there was considerable overlap between contemporary and traditional foreign policy objectives (and a rather imperfect fit between national and "revolutionary" objectives). Although they overlapped chronologically, we shall look at them in sequence.

Despite early Indian overtures to the PRC, the Chinese invasion of Tibet in the summer of 1950 laid the grounds for friction between these two great Asian powers. During Khrushchev's first visit to Beijing in the fall of 1954, Mao asked him to recognize the Indian subcontinent as falling within the Chinese sphere of influence (according to subsequent Soviet accounts), also asserting various Chinese territorial claims against India.[18] The issue again became salient upon Chinese suppression of an insurrection in Tibet in 1959. The Indians sympathized openly with the Tibetans and offered sanctuary to the Dalai Lama and other refugees. But when Zhou Enlai asked for Soviet support following the October 1959 frontier clash at Ladakh, Khrushchev viewed this as an attempt to challenge his policy of peaceful coexistence and refused to support the Chinese position, arguing that the area in dispute was uninhabited and without strategic significance.[19] The ensuing increase in Sino-Indian friction discountenanced Soviet overtures to India, an obstacle the Soviets sought to surmount by privately urging compromise on the Chinese[20] and by declaring their neutrality in the dispute the following year. As Sino-Soviet and Sino-Indian relations deteriorated, Soviet-Indian relations improved commensurately. Military aid was first offered in 1959 in the form of transport aircraft, culminating in the summer of 1962 in an agreement for the delivery of a dozen MiG-21s to the Indian Air Force, as well as in the construction of a factory for their production under license.[21] Although Khrushchev issued statements expressing solidarity during the early phase of the border crisis, when the Chinese refused to support the Soviet position in the Cuban missile crisis in early October, he abruptly shifted his sympathies. Border fighting broke out along the Sino-Indian border and in Ladakh on October 20, 1962, with Chinese forces achieving an unexpectedly swift victory. The Soviets repudiated the attack, complaining that China had invaded "without even informing the USSR beforehand."[22] The Sino-Indian dispute thus not only hamstrung Chinese diplomatic entrée into the nonaligned bloc (as indicated in Chapter 7), it came to symbolize Sino-Soviet ideological differences over how revolution should be conducted in the international arena.

But the issue that fused together Chinese nationalist and revolutionary aspirations more than any other was Taiwan, an issue that also brought the other superpower into play. The islands of Jinmen (Quemoy) and Mazu (Matsu), both within artillery range of the mainland, with about 20 percent of the Nationalist Army garrisoned there, proved to be a convenient lightning rod, about which two storms were to gather, the first in 1954–55, the second in the summer of 1958. After attempting unsuccessfully to invade the island in 1949, China launched its first bombardment of Jinmen in September 1954. After ascertaining that the Dachen Islands along the coast farther north were beyond the range of Taiwan-based air support, the administration persuaded Chiang Kaishek to evacuate these islands in return for a U.S. pledge to defend Jinmen. Eisenhower did not announce this understanding publicly, however, stating only that the United States would intervene if a PRC attack appeared to be preliminary to an assault on Taiwan, without specifying which islands he would defend. Under the assumption that the fall of Jinmen would have a devastating effect on KMT morale, the United States did aid in the defense of Jinmen, resupplying the island from outside the three-mile limit with the help of armed landing craft and threatening once again to use nuclear weapons. In January 1955, Eisenhower submitted the Formosa Resolution to Congress, giving the

President the right to use military aid in defense of Jinmen and Mazu. In February 1955, Dulles stated at a SEATO meeting in Bangkok that the United States was considering a nuclear strike against China; this was confirmed by a national speech on March 7 in which he declared that the United States considered nuclear weapons "interchangable with the conventional weapons" in its arsenal.[23] The Chinese took these threats seriously and had begun to prepare for hostilities when Zhou Enlai announced (at the Bandung Conference) that his government wanted no war with the United States and was prepared to negotiate. It was in the context of these threats that the Chinese leadership decided (in January 1955) to launch China's own nuclear program.[24] As regards Taiwan, however, the PRC shifted to a "peaceful liberation" policy from 1955 to 1957.

In May 1957, accompanied by the rise of the doctrine of limited war, the United States announced the introduction of tactical nuclear weapons to South Korea and Taiwan in the form of Matador missiles (under U.S. operational control), and began constructing an airport with a long runway that could accommodate B-52 strategic bombers.[25] Despite this enhanced risk, Beijing undertook preparations early in the summer of 1958 for a second confrontation over the Strait. Taking advantage of the American intervention in Lebanon in July 1958, the leadership decided at an enlarged Politburo meeting held August 17–30 to launch a naval blockade and artillery bombardment of Jinmen and Mazu. This began on August 23, with the apparent intention (following the Dachens precedent) of at least seizing the offshore islands.[26] On August 27, Eisenhower made a statement indicating that he intended to exercise the power entrusted him under the Formosa Resolution to assist Taiwan in defense of Jinmen and Mazu, and by mid-September the United States had amassed the largest concentration of nuclear support forces in history, under the protection of which they proceeded to escort supplies to the besieged islands.[27] On September 4 the PRC announced a twelve-mile limit on their territorial waters, in an effort to keep the U.S. Navy from convoying Nationalist ships to Jinmen; Dulles promptly responded with a statement expressing determination to defend Jinmen with whatever force necessary.[28] Mao had apparently not anticipated that his initiative would provoke such an escalation of the crisis and, in the absence of strong Soviet backing, he had no choice but an embarrassing diplomatic climb down. Mao convened a Supreme State Conference, and on September 6 Zhou Enlai proposed without preconditions the resumption of Sino-American ambassadorial talks, signaling subsidence of a serious Chinese invasion threat. The crisis did have one favorable outcome, from the PRC perspective: on October 23, Dulles and Chiang signed a joint statement in which the KMT pledged not to use force as the primary means to recover the mainland.

Sino-Soviet relations seem to have been seriously damaged by what the crisis revealed about the limits on their alliance. As in the later Cuban missile crisis, the junior partner evinced an early propensity to take greater risks, under the assumption that extended deterrence would provide shelter from escalating tension between the two super-powers. The superpower being challenged tended, however, to localize the crisis by focusing on the smaller adversary (in the case of Cuba, this would include threats of surgical air strikes and invasion of the island; in the case of China, the threat of nuclear attack on PLA shore batteries), while pressing the opposing superpower to compromise. In both cases, this strategy proved effective. Soviet public statements in the early phase of the Taiwan Strait crisis sought to reassure both sides; one statement emphasized that "the Chinese people have sufficient strength to counter the aggressors fully." Not until September 7, immediately following American acceptance of the Chinese offer to resume ambassadorial talks, did Khrushchev write a letter to Eisenhower stating that "An attack on the PRC . . . is an attack on the Soviet Union," noting that "if war should break out in the Far East, neither you nor I would be able to escape from it." [29] And not until his second letter (September 17) did he explicitly warn that the USSR would respond in kind to a nuclear attack on the PRC.[30] During and immediately after the crisis, various Chinese officials expressed warm thanks for Soviet support, but after relations soured in 1963, PRC officials ridiculed Soviet efforts, claiming that the USSR had come to China's defense only when it was clear that the crisis was over.

It is in fact the case that in stark contrast to the impressive American demonstration of military resolve in the Strait, the Soviets did not accompany their statements of support with any force movements whatever. The evidence suggests that the Soviets informed the Chinese that their alliance was limited to the contingency of an unprovoked attack on the mainland, and did not necessarily cover Chinese "adventurism." When Khrushchev later (during his 1959 stopover on the way home from Camp David) suggested that the PRC in effect relinquish exclusive claim to Taiwan, this only aggravated Chinese resentment.[31] The crisis was thus resolved (at considerable Chinese loss of face) by resolute American demonstration of local military superiority (as well as strategic, though this was less clear at the time) abetted by a Soviet decision not to respond to provocation.[32]

How can this provocative Chinese initiative and apparently feck-less Soviet response be accounted for? In part it was a rational Soviet response to the lower perceived stakes and threat involved. Soviet-American relations were in early thaw, in the context of which Washington began adopting a differentiated policy toward the bloc, moving toward accommodation with Moscow while continuing to regard Beijing as dangerous and irrational. Thus Dulles warned that Chinese Communism posed a graver threat to new nations than the Soviet version, as it controlled a larger population and possessed a cultural prestige not shared by Russia in either Europe or Asia.[33] This perception, exaggerated as it seems in retrospect, resembled contemporaneous Soviet preoccupations and illustrates the degree to which the two superpowers were drawn together by their common apprehensions concerning Beijing's perceived appeal to volatile, have-not, nonwhite international forces.

Yet for all that, mutual Russian and American apprehensions should not merely be dismissed as a relapse into racism.[34] Why should the strategically vulnerable Chinese be more willing to provoke the Americans than their more formidably armed patron? Wang Bingnan, in his memoirs, recalls two motives: to "punish the reckless activity of Chiang" and the "bluster" of the United States, and to counter indirectly Khrushchev's appeasement policy.[35] It would seem that the Chinese, finding themselves unable to dissuade Moscow from an accommodation with the West that would leave Chinese national interests unsatisfied, deliberately sought to aggravate Soviet-American relations by provoking a confrontation with the United States from which the USSR could not easily extricate itself. If successful, Mao could prove to Khrushchev that his critique of "appeasement" was correct by demonstrating that the Americans would back down if confronted;[36] if unsuccessful, presumptive Soviet nuclear superiority would cover his risk. The evidence for this is circumstantial, but cumulatively quite persuasive. The Chinese launched their attack on the offshore islands immediately following the signing of a Sino-Soviet communiqué on August 3, concluding a summit meeting between Mao and Khrushchev in Beijing. That communiqué spoke of complete unity of views on both sides to "problems of struggle for peaceful settlement of international problems and defense of peace in the whole world," but made no specific mention of Taiwan. The Soviets insist that (as in the Sino-Indian dispute) "the USSR was not informed of the PRC's decision to unfold military activities in the Taiwan Straits," despite Beijing's obligation to do so under the terms of the treaty of alliance.[37] Under the circumstances, inclusion of the phrase alleging "complete unity of views" and the timing of the military initiative immediately after its announcement certainly lent plausibility to the Soviet claim that "Peking tried to create an impression as though the probe of force undertaken by it was performed after consultation with the USSR."[38] And since the bombardment came right after the meeting, American intelligence indeed assumed that the Soviets were involved.[39] Khrushchev was understandably irate at being manipulated in this way, on behalf of objectives he probably considered trivial or at least well shy of being worth a nuclear war.

Why did the Chinese endeavor to place their patron in such an awkward situation? Essentially, it would seem, because the Soviets had already quietly made clear their reluctance to join the Chinese in a confrontation with the United States on this issue, leaving them little alternative (as they saw it) to unilateral action. In a speech delivered December 12, 1957, Khrushchev proposed to the United States as part of his policy of peaceful coexistence the abandonment of ideological confrontation and an agreement not to change the status quo by force, which of course would have left satisfaction of Chinese irredentist claims hanging in permanent abeyance.[40] The Chinese were further chagrined that the Soviets had previously agreed to provide sufficient weaponry for the Chinese to achieve this objective on their own without fear of nuclear blackmail, but were now backpedaling on this promise as well. When Mao reminded him of this commitment during Khrushchev's July 1958 visit, the latter replied that such weapons were unnecessary in the light of China's inclusion under the nuclear umbrella of the Sino-Soviet friendship treaty. "Well, then, we shall cope with the American 'paper tiger' on our own," Mao told Khrushchev.[41] So Mao decided to test the umbrella.

The Soviets had of course raised Chinese expectations for the international advancement of socialism with their launching of two Sputniks and the world's first ICBM in the fall of 1957. Mao's last trip to Moscow came on the eve of this achievement, and his enthusiastic support of Khrushchev's leadership position within the bloc coincided with the signing of an agreement to share the technology.[42] The occasion seems to have put Mao in a buoyant mood, for during the 1957 visit he proceeded to discount in rather cavalier fashion the possible risks of nuclear war, observing that even if war should occur, it might at worst destroy half of mankind, thereby wiping out imperialism so that "the whole world would become socialist."[43] Khrushchev recalls in his memoirs how Mao "urged" him during a secret visit to Beijing in August 1958 to go "spear against spear" with the United States, promising the backing of "hundreds of Chinese divisions." When Khrushchev sent Soviet Foreign Minister Andrei Gromyko (accompanied by M. S. Kapitsa) to Beijing in early September on a fact-finding mission,[44] Mao reportedly told him that he anticipated an American attack on China as a result of continuing tensions over the Taiwan Strait, whereupon the PLA would retreat into the heartland of China, and the USSR should then "catch them with all its means" (Gromyko claims to have been aghast).[45] When reminded on another occasion that he himself had invoked slogans of world peace in the immediate postwar period, Mao retorted that there was a difference between the use of such slogans for tactical purposes and actually believing them.[46]

The Soviets profess to have been shocked: Did the Chinese really regard nuclear weapons as a "paper tiger," no different from conventional weapons? Such comments were not apt to inspire great confidence in Chinese strategic prudence. To the Chinese, this reaction seemed more than a little hypocritical. After all, had not Khrushchev's Twentieth CPSU Congress adopted the line that if a new world war were unleashed, it would be neither the whole world nor mankind but imperialism that would perish?[47] True, since this formulation was first articulated the Soviets had chosen not to elaborate, while Mao quite frequently dilated upon it.[48] The Soviets evidently were having second thoughts, either because they had not anticipated their own political "satellites" might touch off such a conflagration, or because the advent of ICBMs had inspired them with a more acute sense of their own vulnerability. Superpower summitry beckoned. Nevertheless, when the Chinese asked for submarines and other advanced military equipment to facilitate the invasion of the offshore islands, Khrushchev agreed to send designs and experts and help choose a suitable site.[49] In return, he proposed Chinese cooperation with Soviet efforts to expand their naval power in the Pacific, in an arrangement similar to that reached with Warsaw Pact forces in Eastern Europe. Specifically:

(1) In April 1958, the Soviets proposed establishment of a long-range radio broadcasting station on Chinese soil for communication with offshore submarines, to be jointly owned and operated. This was intended to facilitate Soviet naval operations in the Pacific and Indian oceans.

(2) Three months later, the Soviets proposed establishment of a joint Sino-Soviet fleet, operating in Chinese territorial waters and using Chinese ports (with a mixed high command, probably dominated by Soviet officers).[50]

(3) In response to Chinese requests for aircraft, long-range artillery, and air force advisers (to facilitate a second Taiwan Strait operation),

Khrushchev countered with an offer to station Soviet interceptor squadrons on Chinese territory.[51]

These demands reportedly prompted convocation of a CCP Politburo meeting on August 17–30, where the Soviet proposals were indignantly rejected and the final decision reached to bombard Jinmen and Mazu unilaterally. True, the Chinese themselves had asked for what they now spurned, but had not anticipated that there might be strings attached. They seem to have been most concerned about Soviet attempts to limit their freedom of action: "The question of sovereignty may not be bargained or negotiated to the slightest degree," Mao declared.[52] He subsequently characterized the Soviet offer as an attempt "to block the China seacoast, to launch a joint fleet in China to dominate the coastal area, and to blockade us."[53] Whereas the Chinese Army training program published in January 1958 had spoken of the need to incorporate Soviet advanced experience, including training troops in the conditions of atomic bombs, chemical warfare, and guided missiles, by the end of August, *Jiefangjun Bao* (*Liberation Army Daily*) was saying that the Soviet experience was of little use for the PRC.[54] Although security conditions were approved in October 1958 for anticipated delivery of a prototype bomb the following month, the bomb never arrived. At last, in June 1959, Moscow rescinded the 1957 agreement.[55]

The reason Moscow reneged on the agreement was only partly because of Mao's perceived recklessness, and partly because an understanding with the United States, the USSR's chief security concern, seemed at hand. Thus immediately after his Camp David meeting with Eisenhower (September 26–27, 1959), Khrushchev announced a unilateral reduction by one-third of total Soviet armed forces, and talks were set in motion toward bilateral disarmament.[56] The issue of nonproliferation was given high priority in these talks from the very beginning: if the two superpowers were to disarm, the nuclear threat to them from nonsuperpowers must also be controlled. In March 1958, the Supreme Soviet passed a resolution to discontinue all nuclear tests, and in April Khrushchev followed this up with letters to the American president, the British prime minister, and other world leaders (including Premier Zhou Enlai). This, however, aroused the (justified) presentiment among the Chinese that they stood to be deprived of nuclear capability preemptively. In a resolution of the National People's Congress Standing Committee of January 21, 1960, the PRC formally denied the right of any other state to bind it in the disarmament field without its consent.

But the Chinese attitude toward nonproliferation was visible even before this. As Soviet China scholar and diplomat Mikhail Kapitsa recalled, Mao wished to develop "a huge military rocket nuclear program as fast as possible," thereby attaining parity with the two superpowers. "But the Soviet leadership considered this unreasonable from an economic and a military point of view, that it would complicate the struggle for disarmament and the preservation of peace and that the Soviet Union (already) had sufficient military power to defend all socialist countries."[57] The Soviets were at this time attempting to induce the United States (via threats to West Berlin, inter alia) to convene a summit meeting at which a peace treaty could be negotiated guaranteeing that West Germany—an historically dreaded Soviet antagonist—would never acquire nuclear weapons. The implicit quid pro quo would have been a joint renunciation of nuclear weaponry to superpower clients: Germany for China. Nuclear-free zones in Central Europe and in the northern Pacific might then be created, sealed by a nonproliferation agreement.

As things turned out, the Americans proved to have greater leverage to impose such an arrangement on its client than the Soviets. Whereas the FRG was rearmed, in due course becoming the cornerstone of NATO defense arrangements, with many thousand tactical nuclear weapons and hundreds of cruise missiles and IRBMs (now being removed again), the United States was able to preserve monopoly control over the "trigger," relegating the host country to the status of warehouse and launchpad. (At about the same time, incidentally, the United States was also able to reinforce its quarantine of Japanese nuclear power via the Japanese-American Security Treaty.) The Chinese were able to resist such an arrangement, at the cost of only a slight postponement in the acquisition of nuclear capability. Meanwhile, Chinese suspicions of the malignly collusive character of Soviet-American collaboration seemed to have found their first empirical corroboration.

The PRC has steadfastly denied the Soviet account of this episode, and it is indeed conceivable that Mao did not really intend to touch off a Soviet-American conflagration, in which his own country was also likely to sustain heavy collateral damage. In the wake of the triumphant launching of Sputnik I and II and the world's first operational ICBM in October–November 1957, Mao's assessment of the "correlation of forces" was understandably optimistic, as indicated by his public comment at the November conference that the east wind was now prevailing over the west wind. A more benign interpretation of his behavior in the Taiwan Strait crisis would be that he assumed he could bank on the imputed Soviet strategic preponderance to bluff the Americans, or at least to bluff Taiwan, and that his objectives could be accomplished short of war. Mao's previous experience at boldly confronting apparently superior adversaries had encouraged him to believe that this might well succeed.[58]

In any case, Khrushchev declined to play the role Mao envisaged, in part, no doubt, because he disliked being manipulated, but probably also because he feared that the bluff might be called. Sputnik had created an international impression that the Soviet Union had suddenly leapfrogged to technological and military preeminence, which was not altogether accurate.[59] The Soviets had won the race to Sputnik and the ICBM by utilizing a technologically inferior liquid-fuel propulsion system, which the overconfident Americans had bypassed in favor of a more advanced (less volatile, more easily stored, more quickly launchable) solid-fuel system. The ICBM launched in 1957 was not a deployable weapons system (firing preparations required days, and the fuel could be stored only for short periods, as cryogenic materials were used) and the Soviets remained vulnerable to an American first strike. Khrushchev nevertheless encouraged the impression of Soviet economic, technological, and strategic superiority in order to capitalize on the immediate political advantage, thereby misleading both the Americans and the Chinese.[60] As Cuba would publicly demonstrate, the "missile gap" existed, but to American rather than Soviet advantage.[61] The regional balance was even more disparate, for the Soviets could not begin to challenge American naval and air forces in the Pacific at this time. The personally ebullient, even bumptious Khrushchev was hence quite chary of military confrontation, particularly when no vital Soviet interests were at stake. The Soviet strategy was to reduce the size of the Red Army in response to a national labor shortage, while shifting emphasis to less costly strategic nuclear forces, freeing budgetary resources for the civilian economy. Preferable to Khrushchev at this stage was competition via economic growth rates. It was to this prospect that he was referring when he boasted, "We will bury you."

In sum, the Sino-Soviet marriage was beset by serious strains in the course of the 1950s, to which it of course ultimately succumbed. The only thing that continued to hold it together through the decade was ideology, which oriented the two countries toward certain commonly held values and goals, and against a commonly defined international adversary. Yet these ideological cognates were insufficient to bear the strain of conflicting geostrategic interests, which pulled the two in quite different directions. With its postwar breakthrough to industrialization, acquisition of windfall territorial gains, and a buffer zone, the USSR had become a "have" power, and the achievement of apparent strategic nuclear parity made it even more protective of existing gains and chary of bold risks, despite its enhanced prowess. China's revolutionary initiatives were intentionally provocative, seemingly designed not only to spread the revolution and confront the forces of imperialism but to challenge Soviet leadership of the socialist cause. The United States responded flexibly to threats to its international interests in a way that may have reinforced fissiparous tendencies, but the Eisenhower administration's differentiated policy should not be construed as some sort of *primum mobile* that caused the Sino-Soviet split. Despite their analytical awareness that the two socialist adversaries remained sovereign entities with distinct national interests, in practice American policy makers tended to assume a greater degree of coordination between Moscow and Beijing than was in fact the case, and when a split occurred they did not exploit it or even perceive it accurately.

CHAPTER 11

Unit-Veto Triangle, 1959–1969

The 1959–69 period was somewhat ambiguous, but may be character-ized in essence as a unit-veto triangle, which maximized the risks of all three participants. From the Chinese perspective, it was a period of "opposing two sides" (that is, both superpowers) and supporting the forces of revolution in the Third World, with which China identified its own long-term interests. Thus the relationship between China and the United States remained essentially negative, despite the first explora-tory contacts since Panmunjom. The relationship between China and the Soviet Union was also negative, moving from a somewhat synthetic masquerade of camaraderie to increasingly bitter public enmity, despite the continued maintenance of formal treaty relations and the claim of each to adhere to the same ideology. As the Soviet Union gained stra-tegic parity and China a minimal nuclear deterrent during this period, the configuration became unit veto:

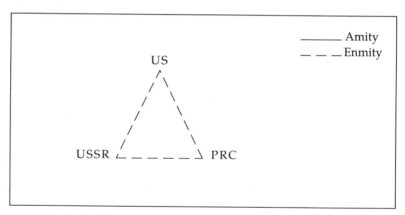

Although this is on the whole a rather thankless configuration, efforts to regulate the arms race and to cultivate various positive contacts (commercial, cultural exchanges) showed signs of assuaging Soviet-American relations (while further exacerbating Sino-Soviet enmity). This flirtation was never really consummated, however, because of recurrent conflicts of interest over Cuba, Berlin, Indochina, the Middle East, and other peripheral crisis points.

According to one interesting recent reconstruction, the triangular configuration during this period was actually a romantic triangle in which the Soviet Union played pivot.[1] In the 1960s, the Soviet Union began moderating its foreign policy, according to this interpretation, seeking a middle road between China and the United States. And because it was the only great power to have viable relationships with both wing players, Moscow qualified as pivot. It is true that Sino-American relations remained adversarial, for reasons to be explored further below. Yet Sino-Soviet relations also remained antagonistic throughout this period, rendering any Soviet attempt to play pivot out of the question. Thus the Soviets were induced to lean Westward, toward détente, in order to solve their China problem—not to the center.

Although the previous period had culminated in a certain momentum toward Soviet-American condominium, the U-2 incident had already derailed the "spirit of Camp David" before Eisenhower left office, and the advent of the Kennedy administration inaugurated a revival of the cold war. During the early 1960s, the frigid summit at Vienna, followed by the Bay of Pigs, construction of the Berlin Wall, and the Cuban confrontation, indicated that prospects for reaching a Soviet-American understanding were in abeyance for the time being. Triangular logic would in any case dictate that the pariah show some interest in pursuing a tryst with the *junior* partner. Kennedy in fact made an offer to sell wheat to the PRC during the three years of famine in the wake of the Leap, while instructing his government not to oppose similar sales by Canada and Australia. The Americans also managed to conduct negotiations with the Chinese at Geneva without major confrontation, and indicated to the Chinese, after the Taiwan Strait crisis flared up yet again in June 1962, that it would not support a Nationalist effort to recover the mainland.

This American initiative was, however, not reciprocated by the PRC (for example, they spurned American grain, despite the starvation of some 20 million Chinese in the aftermath of the Great Leap), for at least three reasons. First, although ideology no longer provided a basis for Sino-Soviet solidarity, it continued to inhibit the Chinese from seeking a rapprochement with the leading force of capitalist imperialism. At a time when the Soviets were seeking to free themselves from ideological dogmatism in order to find ambit for reform, the Chinese intensified their grasp on fundamentalist first principles in a quest for ideological legitimacy during their apostasy from the bloc, becoming "more Catholic than the pope." The caustic Chinese critique of Soviet "revisionism" had the effect of also inhibiting a positive Soviet response to American overtures. As John F. Kennedy put it, "A dispute over how to bury the West is no grounds for Western rejoicing."[2] Or, in the words of Dean Rusk:

The principal arguments within the bloc have to do with how best to get on with their revolution. In Peiping, for example, they appear to want to take a more aggressive, more military approach to these questions—to go back to some of the—shall I say the more primitive aspects of Leninism. In Moscow they're more subtle and sophisticated. They talk about peaceful coexistence. They are using such instruments as economic assistance and things of that sort. This is chiefly an argument of technique.[3]

Second, the PRC's policy of providing both moral and material support to national liberation struggles within the region and endorsing such low-level conflicts throughout the Third World greatly complicated Western counterinsurgency efforts in Malaya, Vietnam, and Laos, causing Western strategic analysts to attribute major importance to the Chinese threat.[4] An indirect ramification of the more audacious Chinese support of Third World insurgencies was to stimulate the initially cautious Soviets to increase their own aid efforts. This competition in support of Third World revolutionary movements—in which the Soviets soon overtook the Chinese, taking advantage of their vastly superior military-industrial complex, plus the depleted Chinese aid capability in the wake of the post-Leap depression[5]—considerably aggravated the processes of decolonization and modernization, from the Western perspective.[6] Third, China's determination to acquire its own independent nuclear strike force confronted American (as well as Soviet) defense planners with a potentially complicating shift in the configuration of the triangle.

The Chinese evinced interest in the acquisition of nuclear weaponry as early as April 1955, shortly after being stymied by nuclear threats in the Taiwan Strait, when they concluded an agreement for the peaceful exchange of atomic technology. This agreement, though explicitly addressed to the civilian sector, did not preclude the transfer of technology for military purposes. According to Nie Rongzhen (administrator of the Chinese nuclear weapons development program), the Soviets limited themselves initially to training Chinese students. After the Hungarian uprising (the suppression of which China staunchly supported), they became "more flexible." In October 1957, the PRC and the USSR signed a New Defense Technology Pact, according to which the Soviet Union agreed to supply China with "new technology for national defense," including what the Chinese called the "two bombs": nuclear weapons, and missiles to deliver them.[7] Over the next two years, the Soviets began construction of a gaseous diffusion plant capable of producing bomb-grade uranium, which actually went into operation in September 1958. In accord with the 1957 weapons-sharing agreement, the Soviets sent "a couple of outdated missiles, planes, and other military equipment along with relevant technical data, technicians and experts," Nie Rongzhen recollects condescendingly. "Although these things were outdated, they helped us improve our research."[8] In fact, the Soviets provided a sample MRBM minus its atomic warhead, a G-class ballistic missile submarine without its missiles. They sold China TU-16 Badgers, and Chinese nuclear scientists were trained at the Joint Institute for Nuclear Research at Dubna. In 1956, Beijing began construction of its first MRBM rocket assembly factory, presumably with Soviet assistance.[9]

Not even at this early point relying entirely on the Russians, the Chinese also agreed in 1955 to resume Sino-American ambassadorial talks in Warsaw. Although the main point of these talks was to resolve the first Taiwan Strait crisis, the Chinese quickly reached an accord for mutual exchange of civilians. This provided an avenue for badly needed Chinese-American scientists to return home, including two internationally renowned physicists who had suffered discrimination during the McCarthy years, Qian Xuesen and Deng Jiaxian, specialists in ballistics and in nuclear weapons technology respectively.[10] Soon after the Soviets unilaterally abrogated their October 1957 agreement to provide nuclear weaponry, China set up a fifteen-member specialized committee under the State Council (in November 1962) and resolved to construct a primary design for an atomic bomb within two years (the prototype bomb was code-named "596," after the Chinese rendering of the date of Soviet rescission of their original aid agreement, June 1959). On October 16, 1964, the Chinese succeeded in exploding their first experimental atomic bomb. The PRC then in rapid succession launched an MRBM with nuclear warhead (October 1966), a hydrogen bomb dropped from a high-flying TU-16 (June 1967), an IRBM (1969) and its first satellite (April 1970).[11] The Chinese intention was a minimum deterrent: "Once I have six atomic bombs, no one can bomb my cities," as Mao told André Malraux in 1965.[12] By the mid-1960s, they had one.[13]

The revival of Soviet-American cold war in the early 1960s seems to have been premised on the one hand on Khrushchev's assumption that Kennedy was a callow young millionaire who could be bullied or bluffed with impunity, on the other by Kennedy's own revival of anticommunist militancy in the context of his New Frontier. It was to continue until the October 1962 Cuban missile crisis. Following this episode in brinkmanship, which seems to have given pause to both men, Soviet-American détente made a resurgence. On June 10, 1963, Kennedy gave a speech at the American University commencement in Washington, D.C., in which he called for reconsideration of the cold war and declared that the United States would "not conduct nuclear tests in the atmosphere so long as other states do not do so." This speech was republished in full in the Soviet press. In a speech and an interview, Khrushchev welcomed Kennedy's initiative, and gave notice that Soviet production of strategic bombers would be halted. A process of reciprocal gestures was thereby set in train that covered multiple problem areas: on August 5, 1963, an agreement was concluded partially banning nuclear testing, which was swiftly ratified by the U.S. Senate; in October an understanding (UN Resolution of October 19) was reached not to station nuclear weapons in space; on June 20 an agreement established a "hot line" between the two executives; the USSR withdrew its veto preventing UN observers from visiting Yemen; and the United States in turn withdrew its veto blocking readmission of the Hungarian delegation to the General Assembly. Finally, the United States approved a wheat sale, valued at U.S. $65 million, to the USSR, establishing the first meaningful commercial contact between the two countries since World War II.[14]

The reciprocation of gestures of good will between the two antagonists was given a more institutionally stable basis in the form of an arms control regime, including delegations that met regularly to arrive at agreements to be approved by the legislative machinery of both countries. On July 25, 1963, representatives of the Soviet Union, the United States, and Great Britain initialed in Moscow the partial nuclear test-ban treaty, the first major step toward mutual nuclear arms control. From the Chinese perspective, any movement toward Soviet-American strategic collaboration could only be viewed with suspicion; on July 31, the PRC issued a statement passionately denouncing this treaty as a "dirty fraud" designed to preserve "nuclear monopoly." Through the rest of 1963 and into 1964, the CCP and CPSU exchanged the most strident polemics in the history of the international communist movement.[15]

As it became evident that the Soviet Union now lacked the power to enforce a nonproliferation agreement, discussion soon shifted to possible joint extralegal steps to sidetrack or even derail Chinese access to the nuclear trigger—to which the Chinese may have been privy, through well-placed intelligence sources.[16] As early as 1962, Defense Secretary McNamara had thought seriously enough about the question to commission a feasibility study for a surgical attack on Chinese nuclear plants, only to find that the U.S. nuclear strike force lacked "clean" bombs; the smallest weapon would have caused millions of fatalities from fallout.[17] Averell Harriman reportedly asked Khrushchev in 1964 what the Soviet Union would do if Washington decided to eliminate the Chinese nuclear sites, and this suggestion apparently evoked interest.[18] The Soviets also lacked a "surgical" capability, but nonetheless expressed interest in coordinating a preemptive strike. On the same day the Chinese protested the test-ban treaty, the American National Security Council submitted the following confidential memorandum:

(1) We are not in favor of unprovoked unilateral U.S. military action against Chinese nuclear installations at this time. We would prefer to have a Chinese test take place than to initiate such action now. If for other reasons we should find ourselves in military hostilities at some level with the Chinese Communists, we could expect to give very close attention to the possibility of an appropriate military action against Chinese nuclear facilities.

(2) We believe that there are many possibilities for joint action with the Soviet Government if that Government is interested. Such possibilities include the warning to the Chinese against tests, a possible understanding to give up underground testing and to hold the Chinese accountable if they test in any way, and even a possible agreement to cooperate in preventive military action. We therefore agreed that it would be most desirable for the Secretary of State to explore this matter very privately with Ambassador Dobrynin as soon as possible.[19]

These prophylactic schemes never approached operational level, and the two would-be nuclear oligopolists returned to the conference table. The Soviet delegation now began to emphasize the desirability of a complete test ban. According to the Soviet proposal, the United States, Great Britain, and the Soviet Union would negotiate a total ban on nuclear testing and then ask other nuclear powers to adhere to the agreement; if they refused, the three signatories could renounce the treaty. Eventually these efforts bore fruit in the Treaty on the Non-Proliferation of Nuclear Weapons, signed in July 1968 (to enter into force in March 1970) by the three depository governments and by fifty-eight other states (including both Germanies). Although they had by now already broken into the nuclear club (having exploded a device before January 1, 1967, the PRC qualified as a Nuclear Weapons State), the Chinese seemed to consider this agreement aimed at them and denounced it vociferously.

While Soviet-American relations were thus improving on the basis of mutual suspicion of the PRC, Sino-Soviet relations deteriorated correspondingly. In the wake of the intensification of ideological polemics during the Cultural Revolution, tension began to manifest itself in a joint military buildup along the Sino-Soviet border. It was not until the Ili incident of April 1962 that both sides began to reinforce their garrisons in the border areas, although border friction antedated that. Previously, the Chinese stationed some twenty-four divisions in the Military Districts adjoining the border, in addition to some border guard units; the Soviets maintained only twelve to fourteen regular divisions in the Far Eastern Military Districts. In 1966, reports appeared that the Soviets were transferring highly trained Soviet forces from Eastern Europe, together with the latest equipment. The USSR signed a twenty-year defense pact with the Mongolian People's Republic (Outer Mongolia) in January 1966, and by early 1967 the Soviets had moved nearly 100,000 men into the MPR, supplemented by tank and missile units. Based along the Sino-Mongolian frontier, these were ideally situated for an attack on the Chinese capital, only a few hundred kilometers away.

With Sino-American relations still in deep freeze, the PRC was moving into the position of pariah in a potential Soviet-American condominium, a possibility whose risks were dramatized by concurrent developments in the south. The Tet offensive in February 1968 brought about a major increase in U.S. troop strength in Vietnam (549,500 authorized), raising the possibility of confrontation with two superpowers on two different fronts. Then however the United States, under the newly elected presidency of Richard Nixon (but already anticipated during the final year of the Johnson administration), opted to move toward negotiated withdrawal rather than further escalation; signals were conveyed to Beijing and Moscow to that effect as early as November 1968. The Chinese indicated their interest by requesting resumption of the Warsaw ambassadorial talks, which they had broken off six months earlier. Nixon's Guam speech (July 25, 1969), one of his first major foreign policy statements, made clear that while the United States would keep its treaty commitments, the security burden in East Asia must increasingly be borne by the Asian nations themselves. The policy of "Vietnamization," involving gradual withdrawal of American troops under cover of reinforced ARVN forces, was set in train, coincidentally removing the threat to China's southern flank.[20]

As the unwonted prospect of Sino-American rapprochement beckoned, Sino-Soviet tension further intensified. The first indication that the Soviet Union had shifted to a tougher posture toward its "satellites" came in the form of the Warsaw Pact invasion (under Soviet leadership) of Czechoslovakia in August 1968, precipitately ending "socialism with a human face."[21] Though quite unsympathetic with Dubček's reform efforts, which from the Chinese perspective were "revisionist" *à out-rance,* the CCP denounced the invasion for its interference in the internal affairs of a sovereign state. Addressing the Polish United Workers' Party Congress on November 12, Brezhnev attempted to justify such interference in terms of a theory of "limited sovereignty," which in effect gave the USSR the sovereign right to determine the foreign and domestic policy limits of all bloc members and left the latter a choice between compliance and military occupation. The Chinese were indignant and probably alarmed by the implications of this doctrine, and it is not coincidental that the Red Guards were demobilized and rusticated in the same month, spelling the end of the Cultural Revolution (at least its spontaneous mobilizational phase). CCP Vice Chairman Lin Biao enunciated the Chinese critique of what became known as the Brezhnev Doctrine in his report to the Ninth Party Congress in April 1969.

Bringing the more menacing Brezhnev posture "home" to the PRC was the simultaneous escalation of the border dispute. China first broached the territorial issue as early as August 1960, proposing negotiations for "boundary delineation"—but the proposal went nowhere. Mao bruited the issue publicly in 1962 in the context of a spiraling repartee with Khrushchev: in response to Mao's blunt and scornful characterization of the Soviet "Munich policy" in Cuba, Khrushchev had retorted (in a major speech to the Supreme Soviet on December 12, 1962) that if the Chinese were so intrepid, why had they failed to recover two "colonial outposts" (Hong Kong and Macao) in their own backyard? Not to be outdone, Mao pointed out that the Chinese had indeed suffered grievous losses to imperialism, most of which were in fact inflicted by tsarist Russia.[22] Khrushchev quietly proposed a conference at which the border question could be discussed. After successively concluding border agreements with Burma (1960), Mongolia (1962), Nepal (1961), and Afghanistan (1963), excepting only India in the south, the Chinese agreed to convene the first round of Sino-Soviet boundary negotiations in February 1964. In July, however, Mao held a talk with a visiting Japanese Socialist Party delegation, in which he summarized Chinese accusations of Soviet territorial encroachment in the following terms:

The Soviet Union has occupied too much territory. At the Yalta Conference they [i.e., the Allies] gave Outer Mongolia nominal autonomy, in reality it fell under the control of the Soviet Union. The territory of Outer Mongolia is in comparison with your Kurile Islands much larger. At the time we raised the question whether it would be possible to return Outer Mongolia to China. They said it would not. We made this proposal [again] to Khrushchev and Bulganin during their trip to China. They also took a piece of Romania, called Bessarabia. They took parts of Germany, namely a piece of East Germany. All the German inhabitants were chased into the Western sector. Also they took a piece of Poland and added it to Byelorussia. Another piece they took from Germany and gave it to Poland as compensation for the parts of Poland they annexed and gave to Byelorussia. Finally they also annexed a piece of Finland. Whatever they could take, they took. Many claim they also wanted to annex Xinjiang and Heilongjiang from China. They increased their troop strength on the borders. In my opinion they should not have annexed so much territory. The territory of the Soviet Union is already big enough, with over 20 million square kilometers for a population of only 200 million.[23]

A month after publication of Mao's remarks the first session of the talks was adjourned *sine die,* not to be resumed until October 1969—under circumstances far less propitious for resolution.

As relations deteriorated in the course of the Cultural Revolution, both sides stepped up their aggressive patrolling of the disputed areas. The Chinese claim that more than four thousand border incidents were initiated by Soviet border forces from 1964 through 1968[24] but the first serious incident took place on March 2, 1969, on the disputed island of Zhenbao (Damansky), which is on the Chinese side of the main channel in the Wusuli (Ussuri) River, which demarcates the Manchurian-Soviet border. The initiative seems to have come from the Chinese side, despite the fact that military preparedness had been severely impaired by the army's involvement in quelling domestic unrest.[25] The reasons for this Chinese provocation remain uncertain, and hypothetical scenarios abound, but the most likely explanation is that Chinese leaders calculated that a sharp, short warning blow would deter future Soviet encroachments and force them to reassess their border policy.[26] A high-level defector provides a firsthand account of the Kremlin's reaction:

The events on Damansky had the effect of an electric shock on Moscow. The Politburo was terrified that the Chinese might make a large-scale intrusion into Soviet territory. . . . A nightmare vision of invasion by millions of Chinese made the Soviet leaders almost frantic. Despite our overwhelming superiority in weaponry, it would not be easy for the U.S.S.R. to cope with an assault of such magnitude.[27]

The Soviets opted to retaliate in force, inflicting over a hundred Chinese casualties in the second clash two weeks later.

This miscalculation marked the beginning of a six-month crisis. Subsequent clashes occurred along the Manchurian border on March 15, May 12–15, 25, and 28, and in the west along the Xinjiang border on April 16, 25, May 2, 20, June 10, and August 13. The Soviets, still smarting from the public relations setback their intervention into Czechoslovakia the previous August had precipitated, seemed anxious to reconcile the dispute, sending a telegram relatively free of polemics demanding immediate resumption of border talks during the CCP's Ninth Congress. But the Chinese, either because they apprehended that reconciliation might entail compromise of Chinese interests or because they wished to exploit the propaganda advantage of their underdog position (or simply because they wished to avoid buckling to superior force) declined these overtures, refusing even to receive a telephone call from Kosygin.

At this point, the CPSU adopted a much harder line. On September 16, 1969, Victor Louis wrote an article for the London *Evening News* that had probably been vetted by the International Department of the CPSU Central Committee, which implied that the Soviet Union was prepared to extrapolate the Brezhnev Doctrine to the China problem. (The Chinese could perhaps also recall the nonchalant American response to the original application of the Brezhnev Doctrine: the United States continued throughout the Czech crisis to insist on its commitment to détente, and Rusk made a public statement emphasizing that no action was contemplated in defense of Dubček's government.) Soviet rockets were quite ready to destroy China's nuclear center at Lop Nor (Xinjiang), he asserted, and "the world would only learn about it afterwards." Louis claimed that anti-Maoist forces were emerging in China which "could produce a leader in China [Lin Biao?] who would ask other socialist countries for fraternal help."[28] Other sources confirm that the Soviet leadership seriously considered a preemptive strike at this point, with Defense Minister Andrei Grechko advocating the use of nuclear "blockbusters" to "once and for all get rid of the Chinese threat" (an extreme position).[29] In June 1969, Soviet bomber fleets were brought from the western USSR to Siberia and Mongolia to engage in mock attacks against targets made to resemble nuclear facilities in northwestern China.[30] Soviet intelligence reported that Chinese military facilities and arsenals were vulnerable to attack, that the air-raid shelters and cellars constructed on a crash basis since the Zhenbao incident had not been built in accord with the requirements of nuclear warfare.[31] By 1969 Moscow had completed an ABM system oriented against China, reducing the risk of a counterstrike.[32]

At the very moment Louis's article appeared, Kosygin was meeting in confidential discussions with Zhou Enlai at the Beijing Airport, where he, as a relatively moderate member of the CPSU leadership selected to symbolize complete Soviet consensus on this point, reiterated the Soviet nuclear threat.[33] Zhou Enlai responded (according to a disinterested third-country observer) by stipulating as a precondition for further talks that the ideological polemic would not be stopped and that the Chinese atomic bases must not be attacked, for that would mean all-out war.[34] Moscow had meanwhile further disseminated such warnings through various diplomatic channels, putatively to underscore the credibility of the threat and gauge the likely Western response.[35]

After months of frustration, the Soviet resort to strategic intimidation appears to have had some impact. The Chinese had just begun deploying their first operational missiles at this time and were acutely vulnerable to a preemptive strike. On September 7, the PRC agreed in principle to enter into border negotiations. The Chinese reasserted that they would not be first to use nuclear weapons (a pledge first publicly announced in the wake of the 1964 nuclear test), that differences with the USSR would not prevent normal state-to-state relations on the basis of the Five Principles of Peaceful Coexistence, and that the boundary question should be settled peaceably.[36] This statement was followed in short order by an agreement to resume border talks (October 7) and by the actual convention of talks on October 20.

Successfully averting further border conflict solved neither the territorial dispute nor any of the other issues cleaving the two powers, marking only a deescalation from crisis to a less volatile level of stalemate. Polemics revived, in the wake of Lin Biao's September 1971 coup attempt (with implied Soviet complicity) and the December 1971 India-Pakistan War (which embroiled opposing client states). For the Soviets, perhaps less important than what was being said was that it was now being said *in camera*. Resumption of the talks contained the border issue within a regular diplomatic forum without resolving any of the underlying issues. This limited success however seems to have reinforced the Soviet reliance on military threat, and over the next two years the USSR further strengthened its military forces in the region at a rapid pace. Immediately after the incident the Soviets moved nuclear-equipped divisions to within two miles of the border, and American intelligence reported seeing (presumably via satellite) "hundreds of Soviet nuclear warheads stacked in piles. Eighteen thousand tents for their armored forces erected overnight in nine feet of snow." [37] By the end of 1969, the Soviet Union had augmented its troops east of Lake Baikal from fifteen to twenty-one divisions, including some eight tank divisions. In addition to long-range and intermediate-range strategic nuclear strike forces, the Soviets deployed hundreds of tactical nuclear missiles and bombers along the eastern sector of the boundary. In response to Chinese complaints of "nuclear blackmail," they offered proposals for treaties of nonaggression and nonuse of force, also calling for a summit meeting with Mao or Zhou.[38] By 1971, Soviet regular combat forces along the border had increased to about thirty divisions, at least two of which were armed with tactical nuclear weapons, three of which were deployed in Outer Mongolia.

The Chinese, though still reeling from the Cultural Revolution and internally divided over the purge of Lin Biao, countered these threats with reciprocal countermeasures. By 1970, the PRC had apparently increased its troops in Inner Mongolia to four regular divisions, in addition to border guards. In late 1970, another four divisions were added to Beijing and Shenyang, bringing the total of Chinese troops to about thirty-two divisions in these two Military Districts. China's total troop strength jumped from sixty combat divisions in 1968 to ninety by 1971 (about half of which were located in the Military Districts adjacent to the border) and to a peak of 109 by mid-1973, thereafter remaining on a plateau. The minuscule Chinese strategic nuclear force was redeployed: beginning in 1971, the first DF-4 missile units moved to Qinghai and other sites in northwestern China, closer to Soviet targets. Chinese strategy in the early 1970s was based on the concept that the PLA could prepare fortified positions in depth to protect key areas, while mobile forces could cover the gaps created by the great length of the Sino-Mongolian-Soviet border.[39] Whole populations were evacuated from the border areas, a considerable number of factories were transferred from the northern areas of China to other provinces; under the slogan, "dig tunnels deep, store grain everywhere and never strive for hegemony," the entire population in large cities was conscripted to build gigantic bomb shelters, and regular training was given in civil air defense. In response to the Soviet threat, Mao launched a thirteen-year "Third Front" campaign to develop defense and heavy industrial production in the interior provinces, especially southwestern China. At its peak, in 1965–70, the program absorbed over half the entire national capital investment.[40]

As the stakes were raised, the spillover effects of the dispute for the first time began to transcend the Communist world. The Soviets, still dominant within the international communist movement, were relatively cautious in their international coalition-building efforts, continuing to focus attention on members or potential members of the bloc. At a world convocation of communist parties held in Moscow in June 1969, Leonid Brezhnev introduced the concept of an Asian collective security pact (to be examined more closely later), a proposal he would pursue with great consistency and modest success for the next dozen years. It was during the early and mid-1970s that Soviet-American détente reached full flower, and the Soviets repeatedly attempted to convert this into a *cordon sanitaire* against the Chinese. The PRC, finding itself dangerously isolated after a ten-year losing campaign to capture intellectual leadership of the world communist movement, began to shop more boldly for support beyond the bloc, beginning with the ideologically sympathetic (but strategically useless) new nations. Chinese attempts to mobilize Third World support in 1969–70 proved useful in gaining entry to the United Nations (as indicated in Chapter 7), but just as Brandt had discovered in the late 1960s that Ostpolitik required an admission fee to the Soviet gatekeeper, Beijing learned in the early 1970s that the road to Western Europe and Japan passed through Washington. More to the point, to deter Soviet nuclear blackmail only the help of the other superpower would suffice.

CHAPTER 12

Romantic Triangle, 1969–1976

The romantic triangle came into being as a result of Chinese attempts to break out of impending Soviet encirclement and launch a counterencirclement of the USSR, plus U.S. attempts to extricate itself from an unwinnable neocolonial conflict by utilizing internal fissures to prize apart the opposing combination. With proclamation of the "Nixon Doctrine" heralding a retreat from a forward role on the Asian rimland, the United States no longer posed an immediate threat to Chinese security interests in Asia, and offered even to provide extended nuclear deterrence against the prospect of a Soviet preemptive strike until China had developed its own assured second-strike capability. "Better two against one than one against two," as Mao reportedly quipped in explaining his decision to skeptical military colleagues. The result was a shift to a romantic triangle in which the United States played pivot:

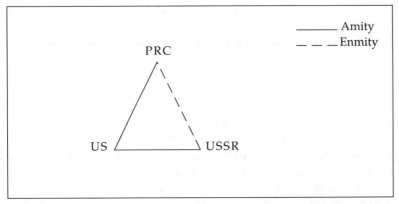

The logic of the new relationship was stated most clearly by Kissinger: "Our relations to possible opponents should be such, I considered, that our options toward both of them were always greater than their options toward each other."[1] Thus the two positive sides of the triangle were implicitly premised on a negative relationship between the Soviet Union and the PRC—a negative relationship about which the

United States seemed somewhat ambivalent: "Triangular diplomacy . . . must avoid the impression that one is 'using' either of the contenders against the other; otherwise one becomes vulnerable to retaliation or blackmail. The hostility between China and the Soviet Union [nevertheless] served our purposes best if we maintained closer relations with each side than they did with each other."[2] In addition to this ambiguity of motive (should the pivot encourage enmity between the wings, while at the same time pretending not to do so?) was another one: Was Washington seeking merely to balance the two wings, or to concert with one against the other? While Nixon announced on the eve of his departure for Beijing his intention to treat China and the Soviet Union "even-handedly" (with regard to trade issues), and Kissinger insisted that rapprochement with China was not viewed by Washington as "inherently anti-Soviet," his own account includes a memo to Nixon stating: "Pressure on the Russians is something we obviously never explicitly point to. The facts speak for themselves."[3] Triangular logic also involved alerting the Chinese to the Soviet threat (perhaps even exaggerating its magnitude). On the other hand, the motives of none of the participants were pure, as we shall see, and the pivot had a greater structural interest in equilibrium than either wing.

The new triangular configuration was initiated by the pivot, by accommodating the need of the former pariah for succor while taking care to mollify the discarded ex-partner in the "affair." This involved a dramatic reversal of policy by both Washington and Beijing, calculated to produce a Soviet reaction limited to passive anxiety. The Soviet assumption had been that they alone were authorized to represent the communist bloc in the world at large, and they reacted with some pique to the accreditation of a third full player in the game; yet they quickly apprehended that their choice was between acceptance of American assurances and relegation to pariah status, and became more rather than less receptive to American offers. Prior to this opening, Soviet-American relations had been bogging down. On August 19, 1968, the United States and the USSR had agreed to announce that SALT negotiations would commence the following October, but this opening was deferred by the Czech invasion. When Nixon requested a resumption of talks on June 11, 1969, the Soviets refused to set a starting date.

At this point, the United States began to exploit the observed Soviet obsession with their China problem. In June, Nixon privately suggested to Kissinger that Washington "subtly encourage" countries being publicly urged not to establish diplomatic relations with the PRC to do so anyhow.[4] In July, the United States announced an easing of restrictions on trade and travel to China, and in August, Nixon privately asked Pakistan and Romania to open channels of communication between American and Chinese leaders.[5] On August 2–3, Nixon visited Romania—the first presidential visit to a communist state since Yalta—where he discussed with Ceausescu the need for a new Sino-American relationship.[6] Telegraphing Soviet concern about these developments, Dobrynin, in a calculated use of protocol, delivered an aide-mémoire to Nixon on the day of the Soviet commencement of border negotiations with China (October 20) that the USSR was willing to set an opening date for SALT talks, while at the same time warning against any attempt "to make profit from Soviet-Chinese relations at the Soviet Union's expense."[7] "Thus the United States, which had initially been the *demandeur* or supplicant for a summit, had reversed roles with the introduction of the China factor."[8] The Soviets apparently hoped the ongoing border talks would screen their problems with China from Washington so that SALT could proceed without any implicit U.S. threat to exploit Sino-Soviet tensions.[9]

But at their characteristically deliberate diplomatic pace, the Soviets found themselves overtaken by the rapid unfolding of Sino-American rapprochement. Four days after the stunning July 15, 1971, announcement that Kissinger had secretly traveled to China and that Nixon would accept Zhou Enlai's invitation to visit Beijing, Dobrynin inquired whether a Soviet-American summit might precede the president's trip to the PRC (previously, the Soviets had refused to commit themselves to a date for a summit, hoping to extract additional substantive concessions on West Berlin and SALT).[10] Nixon declined, but agreed to a summit immediately afterward.

Yet the Soviets were able to counter with a flanking movement to the south. The most compelling reason behind the American diplomatic demarche—probably even exceeding U.S. impatience with SALT in its immediate political importance—was to obtain the moderating influence of North Vietnam's patrons for a diminution of hostilities in South Vietnam that would permit the graceful extrication of American forces. China proved receptive, partly because, once convinced the Americans were leaving, they saw their own interests in Indochina best served by a stalemate rather than North Vietnamese hegemony.[11] The U.S. conduct of the war had sufficed to prevent the collapse of Saigon but not to defeat Hanoi, suggesting that Washington shared Beijing's interest in maintaining a balance in Indochina. The Soviets, on the other hand, took advantage of the American withdrawal plus growing Sino-Vietnamese alienation to consolidate an alliance based on mutual suspicion of the PRC. The July 1971 announcement of Nixon's forthcoming presidential visit to China was followed within a month by Soviet dispatch of heavy military equipment—T54 tanks, 130mm artillery, SA7 antiaircraft missiles—to North Vietnam by sea, in preparation for a major offensive. In the context of the Sino-Soviet dispute, the North Vietnamese had formerly equivocated, hoping to elicit support from both sides, but Beijing's perceived betrayal and their own need for advanced weaponry during the terminal phase of their civil war drew them into the Soviet embrace, yielding to a new China containment strategy.[12] There also seems to have been a causal link between Sino-American rapprochement and Soviet-Indian friendship. Again, within a month of the announcement (i.e., August 9, 1971), a twenty-year treaty of "peace, friendship and cooperation" was signed between Moscow and New Delhi. This would make it possible for Indira Gandhi to avail herself of the opportunity to dismember Pakistan, on the assumption that Moscow would deter both Beijing and Washington.[13]

This implied that Soviet and Chinese patronage of a national liberation movement was in effect mutually exclusive. China urged the Vietnamese to fight a pure "protracted people's war," stressing self-reliance and avoiding large-scale offensives. This would keep the United States bogged down in the war (reducing the pressure of American encirclement of China) and, by keeping the scale of fighting limited, reduce the incentive for Washington to escalate or expand the war. China's advice adhered to the Maoist "model" of national liberation, reaffirming the international validity of the Chinese experience. It also enabled the Chinese to opt out of a hopeless competition with the Soviet Union to supply large quantities of modern heavy weaponry. When Hanoi nonetheless adopted Giap's strategy, which called for a shift to such weapons, Soviet arms shipments increased while Chinese aid fell commensurately.[14] By 1967, Moscow had eclipsed Beijing as major supplier of military equipment to Hanoi. As Nixon noted in July 1969, "Three years ago, Red China was furnishing over 50 percent of the military equipment, the hardware, for the North Vietnamese. Now it is approximately the other way around."[15] Having only recently condemned the Paris peace talks as a "smokescreen" for capitulating to Johnson's expansion of the war, the Chinese now reversed course, seeking to induce the Vietnamese not only to negotiate but to do so in good faith. North Vietnamese Deputy Foreign Minister Nguyen Co Thach has revealed that in November 1971, when Prime Minister Pham Van Dong visited Beijing, Mao himself, in a tense meeting, urged the Vietnamese to accept a compromise.[16] Mao also rejected a North Vietnamese request that China not receive Nixon as scheduled in February 1972.[17] When the United States imposed a naval blockade and resumed bombing, China put the DRV on short rations, ensuring that the blockade had the desired effect of bringing Hanoi to the negotiating table, where it was obliged to accept a compromise settlement in the wake of the military failure of its 1972 spring offensive. Had the Chinese reopened rail lines (constricted since 1969) and allowed Soviet use of South China ports, the offensive could probably have been sustained.

Albeit compromised by their escalated arms shipments to Hanoi, even the Soviets made some accommodating diplomatic efforts on American behalf. The North Vietnamese offensive (Tet) did not commence until after Nixon's February visit to Beijing. Coming just before the Nixon-Brezhnev summit (May 1972), the offensive prompted Nixon to sharply escalate bombing attacks on the north and to mine Haiphong harbor (where Soviet ships were docked), leading Kissinger to fear cancellation of the visit. Just before Kissinger's departure for Moscow in the spring of 1972, Brezhnev assured him that Washington was being challenged not by the USSR but by those opposed to a Soviet-American summit: North Vietnam and the PRC. Moscow was not behind the Tet offensive, he claimed—Hanoi had been hoarding arms for two years. He, Brezhnev, was proceeding with the summit despite a formal Vietnamese request to cancel it. The summit was not only not canceled, but provided the occasion for the highest-level American-Soviet exchange on Vietnam hitherto. Brezhnev offered to send a high Soviet official to Hanoi to urge a "negotiated settlement" involving Vietnamese as well as American concessions, which he had previously refused to do. A month later Soviet President Nikolai Podgorny in fact went to Hanoi. Almost immediately after his visit, Hanoi began communicating to its troops that the initial phase of the invasion was over and that it was time to begin preparations for a settlement.

Again, during the crucial American–North Vietnamese negotiations during the fall and winter of 1972, both Moscow and Beijing urged Vietnam to come to terms.[18] That the Vietnamese were as dilatory as they were in doing so was due basically to their intransigence in defense of hard-won gains—a factor that transcended triangular logic. Ambassador Dobrynin told Kissinger at the end of 1971, for example, that China's cavalier attitude toward the DRV in giving only thirty-six hours' notice of Kissinger's visit to Beijing in July "had so infuriated Hanoi it had put the negotiations on ice to show that peace had to be made with it and not imposed by the great powers."[19] Yet even Hanoi was constrained to make certain concessions. In June 1973, after the

Nixon-Brezhnev meeting, Secretary General Le Duan of the Vietnamese Workers' Party (VWP) visited Moscow and Beijing; both promised economic assistance, but held back any fresh military aid. Mao advised against a military offensive, arguing that "there has to be some interval in the south, whether it be half a year, one year, or even two years. . . . The revolution in the south should be carried out in two stages. If done in one step, the United States will not accept it."[20] The VWP leadership thus agreed (at the Twenty-first Plenum of their Third CC), under conditions difficult for them, to sign a peace accord with Washington that accepted the maintenance of a regime in the south under Thieu, a proposal they had previously spurned.[21]

In Vietnam and beyond, American interests were served by stimulating a competitive suit for the pivot's favor between the two wings, thereby facilitating a better relationship with each than would otherwise have been feasible. The announcement of a forthcoming Sino-American summit in Beijing prompted the Soviets to accelerate preparations for a Soviet-American summit in Moscow. Thus they expedited negotiations resulting in the signing of the Berlin Quadripartite Agreement in July 1971, and by September had reached agreement on Measures to Reduce the Risk of Accidental Outbreak of Nuclear War. The SALT I talks were completed with relative dispatch, in preparation for signing at the May 1972 summit. Indeed, in the wake of the dramatic presidential visit to Beijing, Soviet-American agreements considerably outdistanced the progress made during the early years of Sino-American rapprochement.

Between the two wings there was an inherent conflict of interest, for each was attracted to the pivot for protection against the other wing. On the one hand, the Chinese had entertained American overtures for the express purpose of countering an immediate Soviet nuclear threat, which stood at the very least to knock them out of the game, at most to knock them out, period. On the other hand, as in the mid-1960s, a primary Soviet motive for Soviet-American détente had been to preempt the Chinese threat to their eastern flank. Thus the Americans constantly found themselves obliged to adjudicate between each side's demands for security against the other.

Vis-à-vis the USSR, with whom the United States was intensively involved in disarmament talks during this early period, this involved fending off proposals for a Soviet-American condominium against China. Thus in August 1969, a Soviet embassy official in Washington asked a middle-level State Department specialist in Soviet affairs what the U.S. reaction would be to a Soviet attack on Chinese nuclear facilities. In July 1970, when SALT negotiations had been under way for just nine months, the Soviet delegation floated a proposal for Soviet-American "joint retaliatory action" against any third nuclear power that undertook "provocative" action against one of them.[22] The United States quickly rejected the proposal, but Vladimir Semenov, leader of the Soviet delegation, warned that more would be heard of it. Indeed, Soviet overtures for anti-Chinese collusion continued to surface, in the form of: (1) the draft of an anti-Chinese treaty on preventing nuclear war (first given to Nixon in May 1972); (2) an offer of an alliance against China, made to Kissinger in early 1973; (3) frank discussion of the Chinese nuclear threat at the 1973 summit at San Clemente; (4) an offer of an anti-Chinese alliance made to Nixon in 1974 at the last summit; (5) the same offer repeated to Ford at Vladivostok; and (6) the same offer revived for Carter upon the signing of SALT II in Vienna.[23] Failing to obtain Soviet-American collusion against the PRC, the Soviets demanded that Chinese forces be taken into account in the SALT talks.[24]

The Americans, for the most part, responded negatively to these invitations, shifting from the more ambiguous stance they seem to have taken in 1963–64 to side with the weaker party, in accord with classic balance-of-power theory. Thus in September 1969, Under Secretary of State Elliot Richardson stated publicly that while the United States would not involve itself in Sino-Soviet relations, "we could not fail to be deeply concerned, however, with an escalation of this quarrel into a massive breach of international peace and security."[25] In 1971, in the wake of the dismemberment of Pakistan in the India-Pakistan War, both Nixon and Kissinger reassured the Chinese that "if their [i.e., China's] decision was to assist Pakistan, we would not be indifferent to a Soviet attack on China"—thereby manifesting a willingness to extend deterrence on behalf of a rescue operation of a shared client.[26] Washington also needed to make some accommodating response to allay Soviet insecurity, and so Article 4 of the final text of SALT I stipulates that the parties will "enter into urgent consultations" if relations between the two of them or between either side and a third party "appear to involve the risk of nuclear conflict."[27]

For their part, the Chinese did not at this time feel sufficiently secure about their American connection to make concrete proposals for joint action against the Soviets, but they manifested an intense "jealousy" about the prospect of betrayal and abandonment. Thus Mao warned the United States not to stand on the shoulders of China to reach the USSR, or to "push ill waters eastward." The Chinese were determined to avoid being "used," preferring, of course, to be users: In Zhou Enlai's revised assessment, the two superpowers were both imperialist, and contradictions between them were inherent; but American imperialism was on the defensive while Soviet "social imperialism" was on the offensive, so it was possible and necessary "to take full advantage of the contradiction between the U.S. and the USSR and to magnify it."[28]

Such double-dealing is endemic to the romantic triangular configuration, but the structural uncertainty tended to dampen, rather than stimulate, aggressive propensities. The two most antagonistic players were now inhibited by the pivot from consummating their disagreements in large-scale warfare. At the same time, the pivot made clear its intention to contract, rather than expand, its international obligations, engaging in arms limitations talks with one wing, slowly but surely withdrawing forces from the periphery of the other. Having diplomatically resolved its security dilemma in East Asia, the United States was able to withdraw from Vietnam, eliminate bases in Taiwan and Okinawa, and to shift from a two-and-a-half to a one-and-a-half war strategic planning framework—without, apparently, seriously disequilibrating the power balance in the Far East (Indochina was, to be sure, something of an exception).

In this newfound post-Vietnam "triangular peace," the entire Pacific Basin experienced explosive economic growth. This boom, initially triggered by Vietnam War-related demand, quickly underwent a transition to peacetime production in the more stable security environment, and thrived.[29] By 1981 American transpacific trade surpassed transatlantic trade for the first time, increasing by more than 200 percent within only four years. American defense expenditures, which had ranged from a low of about U.S. $23 billion in 1950 to a high of about $90 billion in 1968 (in 1970 constant dollars), declined after 1968 to a figure of $69 billion in 1973.[30] During the decade of the 1970s, the United States decreased its defense spending by more than 20 percent in real terms.[31] The U.S. Navy became a less salient force in the region, as scarce budgetary resources were shifted to Europe: by 1977, the number of service forces in the western Pacific was down to 140,000 (the lowest level since 1941); the number of general purpose ships in the Pacific Fleet fell from 503 to 206 between 1968 and 1978.[32]

China, too, was relieved of the most immediate threat to its national security. China's defense expenditures, after hovering at about U.S. $2.5 billion through 1960, turned abruptly upward in 1961 (immediately after the efflorescence of Sino-Soviet hostilities), temporarily declining during the Cultural Revolution, then steeply climbing again until 1971, after which they declined precipitously; production and procurement of military hardware in 1972–74 was about 25 percent lower than during the peak period of 1970–71.[33] In 1973, Zhou Enlai told delegates to the Tenth Party Congress: "the Soviets are making a feint to the East while attacking to the West." In 1974, Chinese officials told a visiting group of Canadian journalists: "At the moment we do not think there is a possibility of the Soviet Union launching an immediate war against us. . . . They will not dare to launch a war against China until they have control of Europe and the Middle East."[34] By 1977, both unofficially and in the domestic press, the Chinese said: "until the Soviet Union defeats the United States, the Soviet Union will not launch an attack against China."[35] The Chinese reckoned that any actual invasion would take the Soviets three weeks, and could be quickly detected by Western reconnaissance satellites (the data from which they would receive in exchange for permitting several U.S. tracking stations in Xinjiang to monitor Soviet tests).

This heightened Chinese sense of security perhaps helps to account for the marked hiatus in PRC nuclear weapons development during the 1970s. Whereas China launched its first satellite in 1970 (followed by seventeen more satellites over the next dozen years), suggesting imminent ICBM capability, the first ICBM was not launched until 1980, the first test of MIRV capability (three satellites launched by one carrier rocket) not until 1981, the first SLBM launched underwater in 1982.[36]

Even the Soviet Union, which would seem to have found cause in China's realignment for heightened security concern, seems to have slackened its armament efforts in the region somewhat after the border crisis dissipated. On the one hand, it seems clear that the Ussuri clash prompted the Soviets to build up their military forces in all categories in the Central and East Asian theaters to a level that was relatively self-sustaining, preparing for the contingency of a two-front war in Europe and Asia. The number of tactical combat aircraft increased from 200 to 1,200 by 1973, and the old SS-4 medium-range ballistic missiles (MRBMs) and SS-5 intermediate-range ballistic missiles (IRBMs) were replaced by some 120 SS-11 variable-range missiles (i.e., intermediate or intercontinental range).[37] But after a period of accelerated expansion in the immediate aftermath of the border clashes, the Soviet buildup reached a plateau until the late 1970s (Table 12.1).[38] Why? After an initial period of intensified contact in the wake of Nixon's China visit, it appeared that Sino-American relations would stabilize short of the level of cooperation that would seriously imperil Soviet security in the Far East. (The radical faction in Beijing, among other factors, was perceived

TABLE 12.1. Number of Chinese and Soviet Army Divisions
Deployed along the Sino-Soviet Border, 1970–75

Year	Chinese Divisions	Soviet Divisions
1970	47	30
1971	51	33
1972	65	44
1973	70	45
1974	75	45
1975	81	43

SOURCE: *Defense of Japan* (Tokyo: Ministry of Defense, 1976 edition), p. 13.

to act as a brake on rapprochement with Washington.) So although the USSR felt obliged to shift from a one-front to a two-front war scenario, China was not yet assumed to be a reliable partner of the United States. Moreover, it was no longer fruitful to consider preempting China's infant nuclear weapons program or to pursue a policy of intimidation, in view of apparent American willingness to include the PRC under its nuclear umbrella.

Soviet *diplomatic* efforts, however, seemed to intensify following China's defection. Beginning in early 1969, the Soviet Union proposed to create an Asian Collective Security System, evidently hoping to expand Soviet influence while displacing the receding American containment structure.[39] Brezhnev repeated the proposal in March 1972.[40] Due to the rather cool response the proposal received (only Outer Mongolia supported it), the Soviets began to emphasize that the idea of collective security must be approached in a gradual manner, perhaps by establishing a series of bilateral treaty arrangements as "building blocks" for an eventual edifice of collective security that would embrace all states on the Asian continent. Still there was little interest. Japan then proposed an alternative Pacific Basin concept in 1979–80 (under Prime Minister Masayoshi Ohira), which Soviet official media vigorously criticized. The Soviets nonetheless continued to pursue their building block strategy with great patience and even incremental success, negotiating a series of bilateral friendship treaties with countries along China's periphery, including India (1971), Iraq (1972), Afghanistan (1978), and Vietnam (1978). In February 1978, Moscow presented to Tokyo the draft of a Soviet-Japanese treaty of friendship and cooperation, evidently hoping to preempt a Sino-Japanese peace treaty. (Japan declined, put off by the intractable Soviet stance on the Northern Territories question, inter alia.) The prize windfall in Soviet efforts along these lines was Vietnam, displaying an annoyance at China's accommodation with its prime adversary that would continue to rankle throughout the decade. Relations were further aggravated by China's seizure of the Paracel Islands in January 1974. For as long as the war continued, Vietnam had an interest in promoting Sino-Soviet cooperation in order more effectively to pursue the war effort, but victory eliminated that incentive. Upon PAVN's triumph over GVN forces on April 30, 1975, the Sino-Vietnamese alliance effectively ceased to function, as symbolized by the cessation of Chinese military aid.[41] (To be sure, Vietnam no longer seemed to need such assistance, having inherited large amounts of abandoned U.S. military hardware upon Saigon's capitulation.)

Whereas consummation of the romantic triangle in 1972 ushered in an aura of live and let live—if not good will—unique in the post–World War II association of the three Asian players involved, it may have raised expectations artificially high. Relations reached a plateau, extending over five or six years, then began to unravel. There are many reasons for this, among which it is difficult to establish a clear rank order. Certainly among the most important was the incapacitation of the pivot. Watergate and the collapse of South Vietnam essentially bankrupted the domestic political base of the Nixon-Kissinger-Ford foreign policy. Crippled by the oil embargo, the U.S. economy in 1974–75 sank into its deepest political recession since the 1930s, exacerbating political difficulties. Depletion of domestic political capital made it difficult for the pivot to issue positive or negative reinforcements to the two wings, who became suspicious and alienated. As far as positive reinforcement was concerned, in 1974 and 1975 the Senate prescinded a reward already vouchsafed by attaching conditions to Soviet-American trade liberalization: the Jackson-Vanik amendment to the Trade Act withheld most-favored-nation treatment pending relaxation of emigration for Soviet Jews, and the Stevenson amendment to the Export-Import Bank bill set a $300 million limit on the amount the Soviet Union could borrow, and prevented this from being used for development projects or energy generation in Siberia. This inability to reward the Soviet Union implied a "tilt" toward China, which mitigated Soviet interest in détente. The administration of negative reinforcement was hobbled in the shadow of Vietnam by the War Powers Act of 1973, which required that the President consult with Congress before sending troops into hostilities. Moreover, defense spending as a percentage of total national budget dropped from 44 percent at the time Richard Nixon took office in 1969 to 24 percent by the time Gerald Ford left it in 1977; defense spending as a percentage of GNP fell from 8.7 percent in 1969 to 5.2 percent in

1977.[42] Thus it was widely assumed among American policy intellectuals during this period (and apparently by the Soviet leadership as well) that the international "correlation of forces" had come to favor Soviet advances.[43]

Under the circumstances, the pivot was unable to sustain a sense of forward momentum in its relation with the two wings. Talks toward SALT II made painfully slow progress during the Ford administration, with cruise missiles and Backfire (TU-22M) bombers constituting the sticking point; although an agreement seemed very close in late 1975 and early 1976, the Soviets made little effort to close the gap. Sino-American relations also deteriorated in the aftermath of Nixon's resignation in 1974 because of the continuing U.S. relationship with Taiwan, with whom total U.S. trade swelled to U.S. $4.8 billion in 1976 (while U.S.-PRC trade fell to a low point of $336 million). The romantic triangle relies for its stability on the pivot keeping both wings reasonably content, without which each will seek to collude with the other or to force the pivot to "choose sides." The Ford administration was not making rapid progress in relations with China, nor was it prepared to join the USSR against China; Sino-Soviet enmity continued, and American intercession seemed unlikely to resolve it one way or the other.

CHAPTER 13

Sino-American Marriage, 1976–1981

The 1976–81 period was one in which détente disintegrated under the strain of intensified Soviet-American competition, Sino-American friendship blossomed into marriage, and the Soviet Union was relegated to the position of "pariah." These developments reinforced one another in a case of circular causation, with Soviet-American antagonism stimulating an American search for offsetting coalition partners, and the prospect of Sino-American strategic coordination inducing the Soviets to search more aggressively for offsetting gains. The end result was not enhanced security but Sino-American disagreement over the scope of their envisaged strategic coordination and an escalating East Asian arms race.

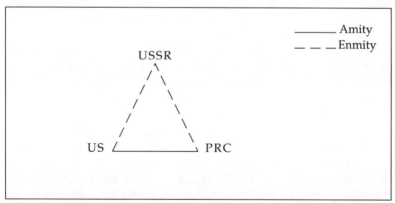

In Washington, the rise of Jimmy Carter ended the brief period of Kissingerian ideological agnosticism with an emphasis on universalizing American moral standards of "human rights."[1] This offered the prospect of regenerating a domestic consensus for international involvement around values of bicentennial nationalism at a time of post-Watergate malaise, but also placed both communist participants in the triangle (particularly the Soviets, who had after all signed the 1975 Helsinki Accord) on the rhetorical defensive. In the absence of MFN,

Soviet-American trade slackened: the slowdown in Soviet imports of Western equipment began in 1976, was accentuated in 1977–78, and in 1979 the volume of imports actually dropped, diminishing further in 1980. Probably even more profound in its impact was the policy vacillation that came to characterize the Carter foreign policy, swinging unpredictably from Brzezinski's anticommunist animus to the irenic liberalism of Cyrus Vance.

Both China and the Soviet Union seem to have equated vacillation with weakness, though they responded to it in different ways. In Moscow, the reaction seems to have been to maximize the favorable "correlation of forces" to communist advantage. It was evidently assumed that the United States would recognize incipient Soviet superiority (military, not economic, superiority was deemed ultimately decisive) and adapt rationally to this inevitable trend by yielding to Soviet demands. Thus even after SALT I and the Vladivostok agreement had recognized Soviet strategic parity with the United States, after the U.S. defeat in Vietnam, after a decade of rapid increases in Soviet defense expenditures and several years of declining U.S. defense spending, the Soviets decided in 1975 to further expand defense spending even at the cost of sharply reduced investment in the civilian economy.[2] This extra burden was willingly undertaken in order to backstop a series of increasingly bold initiatives in the Third World.

It has been suggested that the latter may have been motivated by an attempt to compensate for the "loss" of China (it is rational for a vulnerable actor to adopt an offensive posture when the balance seems to be shifting against it).[3] There is no question that China's defection spurred the Soviet arms buildup by necessitating preparations for major war in two dispersed theaters. Soviet isolation also seems to have revived Russian nationalism and reinforced an ideologically based sense of a unique historical mission. In any case, whereas until the early 1970s Soviet circumspection had yielded pride of place to the vigorous rhetoric of late Maoism in the socialist quest for revolutionary clients in the Third World, now the PRC was pursuing normalized state-to-state relations with LDC governments while the Soviets demonstrated a newly acquired capability for international power projection (bolstered by Cuban expeditionary forces) to exploit a series of targets of opportunity—as in Portuguese Africa, where the death of Salazar in 1974 (followed by the brief rise of the Portuguese Communist Party under Cunhal) created a power vacuum amid the throes of decolonization. To be sure, the Soviets had their share of problems: Soviet advisers were expelled from the Sudan (1971) and Egypt (1972), followed by the latter's reentry into the U.S. camp under Sadat in 1976; the Soviets became persona non grata in Guinea in 1975, and between 1977 and 1979 in Somalia, Iraq, and Equatorial Guinea. But these losses were more than counterbalanced by gains in Angola, Laos, and South Vietnam (1975), Ethiopia and Mozambique (1977), Afghanistan (1979–80), and Cambodia (1979).[4] These noteworthy advances coincided with a series of American humiliations, from the evacuation of Saigon in 1975 to the seizure of the embassy in Tehran in 1979; the Soviets publicly exulted in these misfortunes and sought to profit from them. Intensification of Soviet activity in the Third World coincided with a deadlock on SALT.

The Soviets also undertook major efforts to beef up their forces in the Far East, after about five years of relative stagnation. Their motives were plural: having secured their European borders via the Helsinki agreement, they could now turn eastward, moving into the vacuum left by the American withdrawal, establishing a secure power base to fend off prospective Sino-American-Japanese collusion.[5] Military technology played a role as well, particularly in the decision to shift the bulk of Soviet strategic forces to Central and East Asia.[6] The security dilemma was clear: 80 percent of Soviet energy was consumed west of the Urals and 80 percent of it was produced in the east, in this vast and richly endowed but sparsely populated (and strategically vulnerable) region.[7] (As the Soviets often pointed out, they made no territorial claims on the PRC, but the latter made rather vast claims on Soviet territory.) The Soviets calculated that expansion of Far Eastern extractive and manufacturing industries might contribute to economic development while also reducing the logistic difficulties of the military buildup.[8]

For all of these reasons, the Soviets launched an ambitious second stage of military fortification in the Far East in the late 1970s. The buildup began with a public visit by Brezhnev and Defense Minister Ustinov to the commands at Khabarovsk, Novosibirsk, and Vladivostok in April 1978. During his inspections, Brezhnev noted that the greater part of the expanded defense budget was now going to the Soviet Far East—that for the first time defense expenditures for Asia had moved ahead of those for Europe.[9] In December 1978 two new theaters of military operations (TVDs) were established east of the Urals, one in Central Asia, consisting of thirteen divisions of the Central Asian and Siberian Districts; and the more important Far Eastern Theater, comprising the thirty-nine divisions of the Transbaikal, Far Eastern, and Mongolian Districts and the Pacific Ocean Fleet— the first such consolidated regional command in this area since the Korean War. In October 1981, they established an Air Command Cen-

TABLE 13.1. Soviet Military Deployment in the Far East, 1980–83

Forces	1980	1981	1982	1983
Ground Forces				
Divisions	34	39	39	40
Troops	350,000	360,000	360,000	370,000
Naval Forces (Pacific Fleet)				
Warships	785	800	810	820
Tonnage	1,520,000	1,580,000	1,600,000	1,620,000
Air Forces	2,060	2,210	2,120	2,100
Bombers	450	450	420	440
Fighters	1,450	1,600	1,550	1,510
Patrol planes	160	160	150	150

SOURCE: *Defense of Japan* (Tokyo: Ministry of Defense, 1980, 1981, 1982, 1983 editions).

ter on Sakhalin to coordinate all air and aeronaval operations in the Far East. In a sense this reorganization formalized Soviet acknowledgment of the need for a permanent, self-sufficient, and very large military presence in the area, thereby abandoning the feasibility of the "swing" strategy of massive shifts from west to east. The two theaters would be able to fight independently of reinforcement and central command, at least during the initial stages of combat.[10] Beginning in 1978, SS-20 IRBMs (mobile, with three independently targeted warheads) began to be deployed, as well as TU-22M Backfire medium bombers (with a speed of Mach 2.5 and a range of 8,800–9,600 km, without midair refueling). In 1978 the USSR also began fortification and garrisoning of the southern Kurile Islands (alias the Japanese Northern Territories), thereby adopting the forward deployment vis-à-vis Japan they had already adopted against China in Mongolia. Japan's White Paper on Defense (see Table 13.1) estimated in 1980 that the USSR had placed a fourth of its total ground forces along the Sino-Soviet border, of which about 34 divisions (350,000 regulars) were positioned in the area from Lake Baikal to Vladivostok.[11] Moreover, the Soviets continued to bolster their position: by 1980–81 they had 46 divisions along the border (including 6 tank divisions), rising to 48 in 1982, and 52 in 1983.[12] During the same period the Pacific Fleet, headquartered in Vladivostok, increased by about a third (since the mid-1970s), becoming the second largest of the four, with some 120 submarines (25 nuclear) and 85 major surface combatants.

Opposing the Soviets were Chinese land forces generally conceded to be more numerous—according to the same sources, 70 divisions were stationed along the frontier in 1978, 64 in 1979 (the drawdown owing to China's Vietnam war), 78 in 1980–81, 74 in 1982—but far less well-equipped.[13]

Meanwhile, in the PRC, evidence of a major Soviet arms buildup and military expansion into the Third World (particularly into areas on China's periphery), combined with the perhaps unrealistically hopeful pro-Western atmosphere that accompanied the turn from Cultural Revolution to reform and Sino-American normalization, engendered a visceral anti-Soviet posture. The hitherto fairly complacent Chinese estimate of the Soviet threat gyrated upward. In June 1977 a commentator in *Renmin Ribao* declared that the Soviet Union had become the most dangerous source of world war in the present era. Reference began to be made to an alleged Soviet goal of subjecting China to a "pincers attack from north and south" and a "southern mass encirclement." In 1978, Chinese defense spending began to grow for the first time since the early 1970s, from RMB 14.9 billion in 1977 to 16.8 billion the following year, peaking at 22.3 billion in 1979 (though this may have also reflected preparation for China's "pedagogic war" against Vietnam). Chinese nuclear weapons development also seems to have accelerated after a long period of benign neglect, resulting in the test launching of its first full-range ICBM in 1980, first MIRV warhead in September 1981, first SLBM in 1982.

The PRC also intensified diplomatic efforts to build an international anti-Soviet united front, engaging in a spate of unprincipled coalition building with a number of anticommunist political actors, including Chile's Pinochet, the Greek junta, and assorted conservative or Christian Democratic parties throughout Western Europe and Latin America. In the Chinese peace treaty with Japan signed in August 1978, the PRC insisted on inserting an "antihegemony" clause, then added injury to insult by attempting to dissuade Japan from concluding deals for joint exploitation of Tyumen oil and Yakutsk gas deposits.[14] The Chinese appear to have accelerated Sino-American normalization talks in order to preempt the scheduled completion of Soviet-American negotiations on SALT II. When the January 15 date of Deng's trip leaked to the press, the Soviets dug in their heels, accusing the Americans of suddenly toughening their position on a key issue related to verification (encryption of telemetry on missile tests). The upshot was that Brezhnev's triumphal signing visit was postponed, as the United States reversed priorities to give precedence to strengthening ties with China over an early summit and SALT agreement with the Soviets. During his January 1979 visit to the United States to sign the normalization agreement, Deng Xiaoping also made every effort to place an anti-Soviet construction on Sino-American rapprochement, not only insisting on inclusion of an "antihegemony" clause but granting public interviews in which he derogated the SALT talks and called instead for a defense "alliance" between the United States, China, Japan, and Western Europe to "place curbs on the polar bear." [15]

The Americans were at first reluctant converts to China's united front against "hegemonism," still holding an interest in pursuing arms control negotiations and otherwise nurturing the dying embers of détente. The breakup of the romantic triangle and the shift to a quasi alliance with China was thus not an abrupt move but an incremental decision, formed in the light of Soviet belligerence and friendly Chinese overtures. Sino-American relations had tended to stagnate following their dramatic debut, with no further high-level interaction after Ford's visit in December 1975. When Cyrus Vance visited in August 1977, he initiated discussion of normalization to an apparently somewhat skeptical Chinese reception.

The decisive breakthrough seems to have been Zbigniew Brzezinski's May 1978 "polar bear" baiting visit, during which he assured the Chinese that the United States had "made up its mind" on the normalization issue. He also informed Chinese officials of the course of the disarmament talks, and even broached secret White House documents containing the U.S. assessment of the world military-strategic balance and the Carter administration's plans of action, giving special attention to the definition of spheres of "parallel interest." The Soviets protested strongly to news of this "leak." Following the Soviet invasion of Afghanistan in December 1979, however, ratification of SALT II became a dead letter and Soviet-American détente fell into disrepute, offering the Chinese respite from their fears of collusion and leading the Americans to adopt the more anti-Soviet Chinese reading of the triangular dynamic. In 1979 about thirty Chinese delegations of all kinds visited the United States each month, some four times more than in 1978. Defense Secretary Harold Brown visited Beijing immediately after the invasion (January 5–9, 1980), where he discussed the possibilities of an expanded "security dialogue," noting that such steps "should remind others that if they threaten the shared interests of the United States and China, we can respond with complementary actions in the field of defense as well as diplomacy." Later the same month the Defense

Department announced that Washington was now prepared to authorize the sale of "dual use" (i.e., both civilian and military) equipment to China. In June 1981, during the visit of Secretary of State Haig, the United States finally agreed to sell specific categories of lethal weapons.

All efforts at "evenhandedness" toward the two communist states soon went by the board, as the administration began granting China special concessions denied the Soviets, including MFN treatment for Chinese imports, Export-Import Bank credits (up to $2 billion through the mid-1980s), Overseas Private Investment Corporation (OPIC) insurance coverage for American investors in China—all without an explicit quid pro quo. Just before the August 1979 Mondale visit, a trade agreement was signed calling for $8–10 billion in Sino-American trade through 1985. In 1979 China was promised the sale of a special radio station equipped to receive information from Landsat-D, an American space satellite. In late 1980 an electronic intelligence gathering station was installed in Xinjiang, near the Soviet border, to replace monitoring facilities lost during the Islamic revolution in Iran.

Ironically, at just this moment of most auspicious flowering, the strategic premises of the Sino-American relationship were tried—and, it would seem, found wanting. Chinese rhetoric urging construction of a "united front against hegemonism" and American talk of shifting China's function from "implicit counterweight" to one of active strategic collaboration, did not in themselves stymie Soviet expansionism, nor did the increasing frequency of official visits and other such diplomatic signals. To have any credibility, such verbal "card playing" would have to be operationalized in concrete parallel security policies. But early attempts at policy concertment in the Third World, and particularly in Indochina, were to prove disappointing to both sides.

In the Third World, China's rightward shift tended to dim its ideological charisma, with the paradoxical upshot that the closer China moved toward the United States the less use it served for American foreign policy. Whereas the Chinese had previously been able to compensate rhetorically to some extent for their lack of material aid or global strategic outreach capabilities, the repudiation of late Maoism conducted by the Deng Xiaoping group in their effort to tarnish the escutcheon of Hua Guofeng, together with the cutback in PRC foreign aid, tended to alienate Western Maoists and to undermine the idealized image of New China in the Third World. Even China's staunchest African allies before 1975, such as Mozambique and Tanzania, shifted their support to Soviet African policies in the post-Mao period.[16] In Afghanistan, although Chinese and American interest in repulsing the Soviet invasion coincided, this proved to be a higher priority to the United States than to China.

In Indochina, China and the United States could agree on the need to contain Soviet *qua* Vietnamese expansionism, but could not agree on the best way to achieve this. Sino-Vietnamese relations plummeted after the fall of the south: China ended the last of its civilian economic aid programs in the spring of 1978 and recalled hundreds of Chinese technicians and advisers. The SRV responded by joining the CMEA, and (in November 1978) signing a military alliance with the USSR—now aimed at China rather than the United States. As Sino-Vietnamese relations soured, Beijing transferred allegiance to the Khmer Rouge (who seized power from the pro-American Lon Nol regime in 1975) and never allowed its loyalty to flag. To the United States, any link to the Khmer became politically unpalatable in the wake of the urban resettlement policies of 1975–78, which resulted in the deaths of an estimated 1.5 million Cambodians. Compounding cruelty with political stupidity, the Khmer also initiated a series of border incidents against their more powerful neighbors in early 1977, finally on Christmas Day 1978 precipitating a classic blitzkrieg by some 150,000 PAVN troops, which captured Phnom Penh and overran most of the country within a month. Deng's visit to the United States to celebrate and sign normalization documents coincided with this invasion, and he made clear in private talks with the Carter administration that China could not accept Vietnam's "wild ambitions"; Carter reserved judgment, and the Chinese seem to have construed this as tacit approval.[17] This minor tributary state had been in China's orbit since the second century B.C., and its insolence would not be tolerated. En route home, Deng stopped off in Tokyo, where his hosts imparted cautionary counsel upon learning of his plans.

The final decision to invade was made the day after Deng's return, at a February 9 meeting of the Military Affairs Commission.[18] Mobilizing some 500,000 troops and 800 aircraft, the Chinese PLA struck on February 17 in what they hoped would be a quick and devastating blow. The proximity in timing of the military thrust to the American summit meeting suggested that the Chinese were seeking to bluff the Soviets with nonexistent U.S. endorsement ("play the American card"). Deng had secured a joint press communiqué reiterating Sino-American opposition to hegemony during his visit, helping to convey the impression that China had tacit U.S. support.

Washington did use its diplomatic good offices to help contain the repercussions of the crisis: in late January, Moscow is reported to have received a private message from Washington urging the Soviet Union not to become involved in the event of Sino-Vietnamese hostilities.[19] Hoping to play down the international outcry to the invasion by putting it in perspective, Washington also called for "two withdrawals" (Vietnam from Cambodia, China from Vietnam). But the American response pales in comparison to the support rendered during the preemptive nuclear strike scare of 1969–70 or the India-Pakistan War in 1971.[20] A State Department spokesman made clear that a Soviet strike on China's northern border—the most logistically feasible military response—"would not be of direct concern to the U.S."[21] The United States avoided reaffirming strategic support for China as Beijing faced increased Soviet pressure in the wake of its incursion. U.S. naval forces were not deployed—as they had been in 1978—to counter the augmented Soviet naval presence near China during the confrontation.[22] During the (clearly threatening) Soviet military exercises along the Sino-Soviet border in March 1979, U.S. officials avoided comment. Treasury Secretary Michael Blumenthal even reportedly criticized the incursion when he visited China in February 1979; while in Washington some officials were reportedly discussing possible adoption of a new "quarantine doctrine," under which the United States would pull back from involvement in Asia and avoid entanglement in the intracommunist conflicts expected to dominate East Asia over the next several years.[23]

Although China was spared a Soviet invasion along its northern border,[24] or an embarrassing setback at the hands of the Vietnamese, the outcome must have been rather disappointing to both the Chinese and their putative patrons. To the Americans, the unilateral Chinese resort to "pedagogical war" in defense of a morally indefensible client demonstrated that the PRC could act boldly and unilaterally without much concern for American sensibilities. Like the Soviets during the Taiwan Strait embroilment in 1958, the Americans were disconcerted by a seeming Chinese predilection for the role of agent provocateur. To the Chinese, American backing for a venture in which China bore the main risk of failure was exceedingly pusillanimous, not only clouding prospects of further "joint action" but placing American extended deterrence in some question. China's interest in an anti-Soviet "alliance" faded rapidly, as first signaled during Defense Secretary Brown's visit (January 1980). By June 1980 Deng had fallen back upon urging (in an interview with a visiting delegation of American strategic theorists) the Carter administration's line of parallel American and Chinese policies toward the Soviet Union.

As for the Vietnamese, whether they learned their "lesson" remains unclear; Hanoi was obliged to redeploy more than half its frontline troops to the provinces facing the PRC, but the invasion did not produce the desired pullback of Vietnamese forces from Cambodia. China inflicted heavy casualties on the PAVN, but the PLA also suffered (an estimated 28,000 killed, 43,000 wounded in less than a month, while exacting perhaps three times that number on the enemy), losing the aura of invincibility it had gained in the otherwise analogous Indian border conflict seventeen years earlier. Financial and opportunity costs were also steep.[25] Soviet guarantees of Vietnamese security were not even discountenanced, for although it is true that Soviet troops did not intervene, the Chinese were clearly worried by the massing of Soviet firepower to the north,[26] and hence made it clear from the outset that they would not enter the Red River delta or attempt to overrun Hanoi and unseat the Vietnamese government: "We do not want a single inch of Vietnamese territory . . . all we want is a peaceful and stable border."[27] Far from becoming more deferential toward the Chinese after this chastisement, the Vietnamese remained nettlesome neighbors, and border friction has persisted. More damaging still, the Vietnamese threw themselves into the arms of their patrons, becoming increasingly dependent on Soviet aid.[28] In return, the Soviets accrued the right to conduct naval port visits, to use and enlarge naval support facilities at Cam Ranh Bay, and to use Vietnamese airfields to host long-range naval reconnaissance flights from the Soviet Far East.

For both spouses, the value of their "marriage" was due for serious reconsideration. To the Americans, the Cambodian episode, the invasion of Afghanistan, and the Soviet air and naval buildup in the western Pacific all pointed up the limits of Chinese restraint on Soviet actions. The U.S. Defense Department conducted a study in 1979 which reportedly concluded that China's armed forces were backward in terms of weaponry, could be modernized only at prodigious expense, and posed no threat to Soviet naval and air bases on the Pacific coast or to Soviet territory in Siberia.[29] The Chinese, too, had been severely disappointed in their new partners within months of the euphoria of normalization: most clearly in American military and diplomatic passivity during their handling of the Vietnam problem, but also in what they construed to be an American betrayal of their understanding on Taiwan (see the following chapter).

CHAPTER 14

Sinocentric Romantic Triangle, 1981–1985

After 1981, the PRC found it feasible to back away from its increasingly uncomfortable quasi alliance with Washington without serious risk of Soviet-American collusion. China responded favorably (with frequently emphasized reservations) to resumed Soviet overtures, gradually shifting to a more "independent" (sometimes privately referred to as "equidistant," but denied in public commentaries in favor of the vaguer term) stance between the two superpowers.[1] The strategic triangle thus reverted to its "romantic" configuration, with the significant difference that the PRC sought to occupy the "pivot," as depicted below:

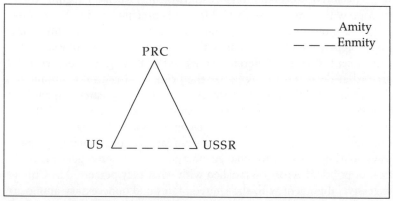

There are several likely reasons for Sino-American disenchantment and the simultaneous breakthrough in relations between Beijing and Moscow in the early 1980s. From the Soviet perspective, the prospect of détente with the United States was rapidly receding, while the newly acquired Soviet gains in the Third World were proving difficult to consolidate and a net drain on the Soviet economy.[2] At the same time, the Soviet economic slowdown and overextension in South Asia and Africa placed increasing constraint on its rearmament efforts at a time when prospects for arms control seem to have seriously diminished, prompting Brezhnev to look more favorably toward an accommodation with Beijing.[3] For the United States, the election of Reagan seemed to presage a shift from a foreign policy that pivoted on human rights to a defense of first principles *qua* "free enterprise," with an initial tendency to lump China and the Soviet Union in the same ideologically hostile camp. At the same time, Reagan brought with him a mandate for military rearmament and an optimistic nationalism that let the China "card" seem more dispensable. Taiwan, a small but intensely loyal cynosure of capitalist development, stood to benefit from this shift. The U.S. Congress passed the Taiwan Relations Act in March 1979, and arms sales to that country enjoyed a resurgence in 1980 to make up for the year's moratorium. Reagan advocated upgrading diplomatic relations with Taiwan during his successful 1980 presidential campaign, and although this controversial proposal was dropped after his inauguration, American military aid to Taiwan grew significantly, from $330 million in 1981 to $800 million in 1983.

China's increased amenability to Soviet overtures can be attributed to both domestic and foreign policy considerations. Domestically, this was a period of consolidation ("readjustment") when the regime sought to cope with some of the early difficulties precipitated by the reforms. In the ideological context of a campaign against "bourgeois liberalization," steps were taken to clarify the first principles of Chinese socialism: a central work conference convened in Beijing in February 1982 arrived at decisions to emphasize the primacy of central planning and the secondary role of market forces, and to place greater emphasis on heavy industry (which had been deemphasized since mid-1979). The pragmatic coalition assembled by Deng Xiaoping, having deposed the radicals who constituted a common threat, was beginning to splinter, as escalating pressure for change emerged from a heterogeneous coalition of political actors dissatisfied with what they perceived as China's excessive alignment with the United States and unnecessary animosity toward the USSR.[4] Deng Xiaoping had reportedly been strongly criticized in the wake of the unsatisfactory outcome of the Vietnam invasion, and came under increasing pressure over the next two years from those who considered that episode symptomatic of the folly of overreliance on the United States.[5]

Among foreign policy considerations were increasing Soviet-American polarization, which reduced the need to fear superpower collusion against PRC interests, while the vigorous Reagan rearmament program mitigated balance-of-power reasons to tilt toward Washington.

In this context Washington's continuing security relationship with Taiwan, hitherto tacitly (if reluctantly) tolerated, became less acceptable. In 1973 Mao had said: "we can do without Taiwan for the time being, and let it come after one hundred years. . . . Why is there need to be in such great haste?"[6] But the Chinese had since come to feel that time was no longer on their side. As Taiwanization proceeded on the island under auspices of democratization, they became increasingly restive. Finally, an American marriage was increasingly out of kilter with China's commitment to the Third World. At the September 1979 summit of non-aligned countries in Havana, only Pakistan rose to China's defense in the face of Castro's pairing of the United States and China as the two "arch-enemies" of the Third World. The Reagan administration's line on Central America, South Africa, and North-South issues in general would make China's American friendship an increasing embarrassment to its role of choice as a socialist developing country.

In their effort to distance themselves from Washington and strike a more evenhanded stance, the Chinese dropped their anti-Soviet polemics and began criticizing both superpowers. In December 1981, the United States was again branded "imperialist."[7] In January 1982, for example, Li Xiannian, then PRC chief of state, declared in an interview with West European journalists that Sino-Soviet differences primarily concerned state-to-state relations and not ideological issues. He said that the PRC had no preconditions for Sino-Soviet negotiations, though the border troops and the situations in Kampuchea and Afghanistan would have to be discussed, and that the United States was "always an imperialist country" with whom the PRC had no "intimate relations."[8]

By early 1983, China had again depicted the United States as a "hegemonic superpower" that represented a threat to world peace and security equal to that of the Soviet Union. China now refused to identify one superpower as more aggressive than the other.[9] An American analyst writing in 1986 concluded: "Compared with its treatment of the Soviet Union, China's public criticisms of the United States range over a broader spectrum of issues and areas, and negative media comments are more frequent."[10] The gravest threat to world peace now derived from the risk emanating from hegemonistic competition between the "two superpowers," various Chinese spokesmen contended.[11] The Third World proved rhetorically convenient in this redefinition of China's place in the world: Beijing's move away from Washington was not toward the Soviet Union, but away from both superpowers, toward the Third World. China thus withdrew support for U.S. policy in the Middle East, South Africa, and Central America, and became increasingly critical of American policy toward Nicaragua, Namibia, and other hot spots.[12]

Signs began to appear quite early of a Chinese diplomatic propensity to balance between—and extract concessions from—both superpowers. Only three months after the establishment of Sino-American relations (and less than two after China's disappointing foray against Vietnam), the Chinese Ministry of Foreign Affairs agreed without precondition to negotiate a normalization agreement with the USSR to replace the friendship treaty China was allowing to lapse (but talks were then postponed two years because of Afghanistan). The first three rounds of Sino-Soviet talks after they resumed in 1982–83 were scheduled immediately following the visits of U.S. cabinet secretaries; the seventh (October 1985) came immediately after Weinberger's visit. Arkhipov's 1984 visit was originally scheduled immediately following Reagan's trip in April. (Soviet postponement of this visit, on 24-hour notice, may have signaled their unwillingness to play this game.) Using diplomatic signals to flirt with one wing while negotiating with the other, China also seemed deliberately to combine pressure against one side with the propitiation of the other. Thus in the early 1980s China placed strong pressure on the United States for movement on the Taiwan issue, and this eventually rebounded in the January 1982 decision not to sell Taiwan the FX fighter and in the August 17, 1982, joint communiqué placing quantitative, qualitative, and eventual time limits on U.S. arms sales to Taiwan. On the other hand, China simultaneously upgraded Sino-Soviet relations by entering into vice-ministerial talks and tacitly agreeing to commence economic and cultural exchanges (in the context of continued Soviet nonaction on security issues). But with vice-ministerial talks seemingly going nowhere and American investors backing off, the Chinese began to respond more positively to U.S. initiatives and to modulate pressure on Taiwan, while intensifying pressure on Moscow over the Three Fundamental Obstacles, particularly the installation of SS-20s in Siberia.

Of course, China was not a completely unmoved mover, but had to be prepared to accommodate pressure arising from one wing or the other in order to maintain a balance. On March 5, 1983, for example, Secretary of State George Shultz, in a speech to the San Francisco World Affairs Council, for the first time publicly derogated the importance of the Chinese connection and shifted focus to the strategic importance of Japan and other traditional U.S. allies in East Asia. The thrust of his speech, itself the outcome of a concerted review of U.S. Asian policy in early 1983, was that China's role must be seen in a regional context in which others (notably Japan) also played an important part. Clearly implied was that PRC demands were becoming annoying, and that the limits had perhaps been reached in Sino-American strategic cooperation, given the basic ideological differences dividing the two countries.[13] Although Hu Yaobang reportedly argued that the United States had not been a reliable partner in any case and proposed to ignore this warning in favor of further improvement of ties with the Soviet Union and Eastern Europe, the Shultz speech seems to have given the Chinese leadership pause,[14] inducing them to arrest their anti-American tilt for the time being. Using trade, cultural exchanges, and the prospect of military collusion as positive inducements, the PRC was thus able to control the relationship by alternating between pressing the Americans on Taiwan and criticizing the Soviets on the Three Obstacles.

The premises on which China based its move to the pivot were not altogether seamless strategically, for Chinese strategic analysts continued in fact to view the Soviet Union as the major threat to Chinese security, and accordingly to prepare for the contingency of "fighting an early, major and nuclear war." From this perspective, the two wings were not really equidistant. PRC foreign policy decision makers nevertheless found it to their advantage to play a balancing act, reasoning that the Soviet threat could be satisfactorily countered through a combination of accommodating bilateral diplomacy and extended U.S. deterrence without major additional increments to their own military budget. This assumption was bolstered by the argument that the Soviet buildup was aimed at the United States rather than China, and that American forces had since the early 1980s regained sufficient strategic credibility in the Pacific Basin to deter further Soviet encroachments.

How accurate was the Chinese assessment of the balance of power? The record is fairly clear. The Soviet Union continued its East Asian arms buildup, but shifted its emphasis from ground forces to naval, air, and missile forces of increasing technological sophistication. Soviet ground forces deployed along the border have varied slightly from year to year: never "more than one million troops," as sometimes alleged by the Chinese, they ranged from fifty-two divisions (480,000 men, if at full strength) in 1978, forty divisions in 1979, forty-six in 1980 and 1981, forty-eight in 1982, back to fifty-two from 1983 to 1986.[15] The general assumption of Western analysts is that Soviet border fortifications during this period were indeed essentially defensive in function, based on a "stab in the back" scenario should Soviet-American conflict erupt. This is indicated by the fairly low density of Soviet ground forces, and the high proportion of motorized rifle (rather than tank) divisions in the Far Eastern TVD compared with the European ones.[16]

On the other hand, there had been a major augmentation of Soviet strategic, air, and naval forces, though the strategic missile forces seemed to be aimed at American or Japanese targets, with the air and naval forces deployed primarily to defend strategic weapons or for regional missions. The sparsely populated region had thus become the USSR's prime strategic nuclear launch site, providing the dispersed location of the major part of its ICBM force and about a third of its ballistic missile-launching submarines (SSBNs).[17] To protect this strategic basing area from preemptive attack, beginning in 1982–83 Soviet air forces in the Far East (now consisting of about 2,390 combat aircraft—including over 1,600 fighters and 435 bombers—or about a quarter of total Soviet air armies) were upgraded,[18] and the Pacific Fleet became the largest of its four (the others being the Northern, Baltic, and Black Sea fleets), with an estimated 840 vessels, including 90 major surface vessels and 140 submarines (half nuclear), displacing about 1.85 million tons (as of 1986).[19] One noteworthy feature of this modernization is that qualitative growth was now given high priority. The first SS-20s were employed in Asia (171, by 1986) rather than Eastern Europe, for example, and the first two Soviet aircraft carriers were first deployed in the Pacific; the Soviet Pacific submarine fleet constituted a third of the Soviets' most modern Delta-class submarines.

This massive Soviet buildup had the effect of stimulating vigorous American rearmament efforts in the northern Pacific, beginning to some extent under Carter in the late 1970s but gaining momentum following Reagan's 1980 landslide. The Reagan administration had fulminated at the outgoing Carter administration for allowing the U.S. Navy to slip to 479 ships, and pledged to increase this to 600 ships by 1988 by building 133 new vessels and refitting 16 old ones.[20] Incoming Secretary of the Navy John Lehman had pledged in 1981 to increase the Pacific Fleet in particular by one-third, and it had indeed grown to 231 warships by 1984 (from 206 in 1980), with a goal of 300 by the time the buildup ended in 1988.[21] Beginning that same year (1984), overall U.S. military spending surpassed Soviet spending, by Pentagon estimates.[22] The most visible manifestation of Pacific Fleet modernization has been the transfer of nuclear-powered aircraft carriers to the Pacific (and an American attack carrier outguns a Kiev-class ASW carrier): the *Carl Vinson* and the *Nimitz* were shifted to the Pacific in 1983 and 1987 respectively, complementing the *Enterprise*. Their offensive capability was enhanced by the deployment of conventional and nuclear-tipped Tomahawk cruise missiles. Tactical air forces in the Pacific came to include about 300 fighter, attack, and reconnaissance aircraft—a 25 percent increase over the 240 aircraft in the command a few years earlier.[23]

In quantitative terms, Soviet naval forces seemed to have gained the edge, whether measured by number of ships or in their total displacement; but the Americans were believed to have retained qualitative superiority, thanks in particular to the power of their carrier task forces, and the geostrategic advantages of open ocean access. Politically, the forces aligned with the United States far outweighed those aligned with the Soviet Union in the East Asian region.[24] Particularly during the Reagan administration (and as nondefense economic competition within the Pacific basin intensified), Washington placed increasing emphasis on burden sharing, persuading Japan to pledge responsibility for defense of the sea-lanes 1,600 kilometers to its south and east. Korea was also upgraded from a "significant interest area" to a "vital interest area," and given equal billing with Western Europe as a "first line of defense."[25]

The Soviet buildup, and the American response in kind, reflected a momentous shift in the locus of superpower competition from Europe to Asia in the early 1980s, following the shift of economic power in the same direction, creating an atmosphere of mounting tension in the region.[26] The more competitive environment was reflected in the tendency of both sides to hold military maneuvers in grander scale and to conduct them in ever closer proximity to the borders of the adversary. Thus the U.S. Navy refused to accept the Sea of Okhotsk as an exclusive Soviet domain: U.S. attack submarines began conducting routine peacetime patrols in the Sea of Okhotsk, and two aircraft carriers were provocatively deployed off Vladivostok in December 1984. Soviet attack submarines for their part come closer to U.S. naval bases and ports, sometimes covertly entering U.S. naval exercises.[27]

How did the Chinese PLA and its defense strategy respond to the changing security environment in East Asia? The Soviet air and naval buildup presented China with a problem of interpretation; for example, the more powerful Soviet fleet was officially assumed to be designed chiefly to protect Soviet strategic offensive forces and to deal with American bases and Japanese self-defense forces, but it also posed the threat of amphibious landings along the Chinese coast, making some 60 percent of the Chinese population vulnerable to a naval strike from Soviet cruise missiles fired from offshore ships. The Chinese made some

TABLE 14.1. China's Strategic Forces

Type	Number Deployed	Range (km)	Warhead
DF-5 (ICBM)	2	13,000	5 MT
DF-4/CSS-4 (ICBM)	4	10,000	2 MT
DF-3/CSS-3 (ICBM)	60	5,000	2 MT
DF-2/CSS-2 (IRBM)	50	1,800	20 MT
Xia-class sub (SSBN)	2	2,800	12 1-2 MT

effort to modernize their forces to cope with such threats. The Chinese navy is believed to have acquired four Han SSBNs, about forty-four major surface ships, and an undisclosed number of operational SLBMs (though the Chinese do not plan to rely primarily on submarine basing of their deterrent force, due to expense and poor geographical access to Soviet cities). The air force has over 4,000 fighters and 1,000 bombers and ground attack aircraft, though their vintage is from the period of Sino-Soviet "marriage" (Chinese air defense depends on the F-6, for example, a Chinese version of the MiG-19PF). Increasingly, China began to rely on its relatively low-budget nuclear strike force, by 1985–86 boasting a respectable retaliatory arsenal force of 128 or so nuclear armed missiles. The composition of this force is shown in Table 14.1.[28]

An innovative deployment strategy (including launch unit mobility, hardened storage for launchers, concealment practices, and dispersal in mountainous terrain) was designed to ensure a second strike capability, thereby providing a survivable deterrent in the event of nuclear war.[29] In addition to missiles, China had 120 H-6 bombers, with a combat radius of about 3,000 km. The use of a tactical nuclear weapon during 1982 summer maneuvers in Ningxia (unreported in the national media) suggests that Beijing assumes it can take such action against invading troops on its own soil without triggering Soviet strategic retaliation.[30]

Although the Chinese no longer anticipated an invasion using conventional forces, PLA strategy was to defend the country via "people's war under modern conditions." If attacked, the PLA would not automatically abandon territory and "lure the enemy in deep," but try to block advance through positional warfare, then go on the offensive.[31] Although it is conceded to be inadequate to rely on infantry alone and increasing interest is shown in a "combined arms" concept, the border terrain is rugged and well suited to infantry or guerrilla tactics, and any attempt to subdue the entire country with conventional forces would indeed probably bog down in an interminable people's war. But most military analysts believe China remains vulnerable to more limited strikes—into Xinjiang, say, to take out the nuclear facilities, or from Mongolia to Beijing, to capture the seat of power and annex the industrialized Northeast. China's conventional forces are in no position to repel such attacks, and a people's war would be inoperative if the enemy's intention is to destroy and then withdraw.[32] Although positional defense would require technological enhancement, the PLA seems to have been given lowest priority in Chinese modernization efforts. A 1982 U.S. Defense Department report on the Sino-Soviet balance in the Far East concluded that "China's relative low priority on military modernization means the balance will increasingly favor the Soviet Union, which steadily improves its forces there."[33] Until Tiananmen stimulated more spending for essentially nonmilitary reasons, the last significant increase in Chinese defense expenditures occurred in mid-1979, as planners allocated resources needed to cover replacement costs for equipment lost in the Vietnamese expedition.

The upshot of these trends in the triangular arms race has been to strengthen the two wings relative to the pivot, making the role of the latter increasingly tenuous. (Chinese unease about its relative strategic decline has manifested itself, inter alia, in great sensitivity about recent increases in Japanese defense spending, for fear that Japan will fill the breach left by the declining United States. That apprehension tends to drive the PRC into the arms of the USSR.) The ability of the PLA to perform its mission of national defense should the arms race eventuate in conflict would depend, first of all, on the configuration of the triangle. Should China retain the pivot in a romantic triangle, she could avoid entanglement and watch the tigers fight with relative impunity (superpower conflict might inflict some collateral damage in the eventuality of a nuclear exchange). Even if China were to confront the USSR as junior partner of the United States, it is conceivable that the Soviet Far Eastern arsenal would be too preoccupied with Japan, U.S. forward bases in the Pacific, and the American West Coast to be fully deployed against the PRC. Past experience with this configuration suggests, however, that the pariah prefers to confront the weaker partner in the marriage. In an "American" romantic triangle in which Washington remained neutral at pivot, a Sino-Soviet confrontation could be very damaging. Least desirable of all, needless to say, would be a Soviet-American condominium designed to eliminate the China factor, although this possibility has appeared remote since the early 1970s.

Thus China's strategy was to retain the pivot, and try to collude simultaneously with each of the wing players, in order to avoid contradictions that might alienate either wing. Collusion is necessary in a romantic triangle because each wing needs some reinforcement in its otherwise thankless task of deterring the other wing and cooperating with the pivot, yet it is generally the downfall of a pivot due to the difficulty of playing an evenhanded game. There are two types of security collusion in a triangle, which may be termed *benign* and *malign*. Malign collusion consists of covert cooperation with one wing against the other, as in an alliance or less formal form of military coordination. Benign collusion consists of cooperation with one wing that clearly does not threaten the other, as in various arms control and disarmament regimes. In the Sinocentric romantic triangle the PRC simultaneously engaged in malign, or escalatory, collusion with the United States, and benign, or deescalatory, collusion with the USSR, betraying a tacit Chinese estimate that the latter still represented the major threat to Chinese security. The relationship between the two superpowers remained essentially competitive (i.e., noncollusive), as is structurally appropriate to their triangular positions.

Malign collusion with the United States coincided with the objective Chinese need to respond to the Soviet arms buildup with a fiscally realistic program of weapons technology acquisition. After all, the problem of technological obsolescence was pervasive in the PLA: China had no operational surface-to-air missile system, its surface-to-surface system was primitive, it had no over-the-horizon radar or airborne warning and control system (AWACS) aircraft, its long-distance supply and communications were weak, its land-based naval air force quite limited, and so forth.[34] For security reasons, the Chinese opted once again to "lean to one side," relying exclusively on Western suppliers. This has involved bargaining, as Beijing has attempted to retain maximal freedom of action whereas Washington has attempted to make sales contingent upon guarantees that the purchases will not be used against the United States or its clients (particularly Taiwan). Washington seeks to use weapons as a lever to pry China from its position as pivot into partnership in an anti-Soviet marriage; Beijing tends to counter with overtures to Moscow, demands for concessions on Taiwan, or improved access to U.S. markets (both technology and export).

Serious negotiations concerning arms sales began in 1981, when Secretary of State Haig offered to make more U.S. weapons available with the implicit understanding that Taiwan would also retain access to the arms market. But Beijing showed little interest in such an arrangement, insisting that it would not move ahead with increased military cooperation until the Reagan administration clarified its position on Taiwan. The Americans essentially complied to this demand by canceling the sale of the FX fighter in January 1982 and agreeing to declining qualitative and quantitative limits on arms sales. In terms of access to U.S. military technology, China was upgraded in 1981 from Category Y status (to which the USSR and Eastern Europe are assigned) to Category P status (which meant that it was permitted to import more technology than the USSR or Eastern Europe but less than Western Europe), and from Category P to Category V in May 1983 (in conjunction with the visit of Commerce Secretary Baldridge), ranking it with Western Europe, Australia, New Zealand, Japan, India, most of Africa, and some Arab countries. China could now purchase a much wider variety of sophisticated dual-use technologies, with heavy emphasis on advanced electronics. Yet even after the December 1985 CoCom decision to liberalize regulations still further, eliminating over 75 percent of interagency reviews concerning Chinese technology export requests, Beijing insisted that Washington was still imposing unreasonable barriers against access. Arms purchase agreements finally began to materialize in 1984, amounting to $2 billion in that year (as compared with only $932 million in 1983) and surging even more impressively in 1985–86.[35]

Aside from weapons sales, other channels for implicitly anti-Soviet collusion became available, including consultations and exchanges of visits of military personnel. Since 1983, the two countries have exchanged virtually all their highest-ranking military leaders. In September 1983, Defense Secretary Weinberger went to China; in the summer of 1984, Navy Secretary Lehman; in January 1985, General Vessey, then chairman of the Joint Chiefs, and Admiral Crowe, then commander in chief of the Pacific (the first serving military officer to visit China since 1949); and General Gabriel, chief of staff of the Air Force, followed in October. In 1984, five Chinese military delegations were hosted by the U.S. Defense Department in addition to a number of visits by Chinese military procurement agencies.[36] Late in 1984, three separate U.S. teams visited China to consider an agreement on transfer of technology for the improved antitank TOW missile, artillery-shell manufacturing, and the (1986) $550 million avionics package. In 1986, Yang Dezhi, chief of the PLA General Staff, visited the United States, while Secretary Weinberger made a second visit to the PRC; in 1987, Yang Shangkun, vice-chairman (and acting chair) of the CCP Military Affairs Commission, visited the United States. China's recently established National Defense University began to exchange students, professors, and training materials with its American counterpart; as of 1987, there were at least fifty Chinese military personnel studying political science or international relations on American campuses, more than those studying the natural and applied sciences. In March 1982, Weinberger outlined the Reagan administration's "Defense Guidance" policy for 1984–88, foreseeing selective American military assistance to China during any Sino-Soviet conflict, in exchange for which the PLA would pin down Soviet forces on China's northern border. By the spring of 1985, Washington was using twelve listening posts on Chinese territory to monitor Soviet military developments, in return for which the United States shared satellite photographs of Soviet forces deployed along China's borders. Though the Chinese reacted adversely to the initial American proposal for a naval port visit in the spring of 1985, three ships were welcomed to Qingdao in November 1986. The Soviets responded by simulating bombing attacks on the Alaskan and Chinese coasts.[37]

With regard to both Sino-Soviet and Sino-Vietnamese relations, the U.S. administration played the same spoiler's role the PRC played vis-à-vis Soviet-American arms control negotiations in the 1960s and 1970s, expressing dismay at any new negotiating links, alarm at any sign of accord.[38] Although former president Nixon prophetically suggested as early as 1984 that Sino-Soviet rapprochement was also in the U.S. interest, President Reagan seized every opportunity during his April-May 1984 visit to try to resuscitate Deng Xiaoping's "alliance" proposal, inviting China to engage in collaboration with Washington against "Soviet hegemony" in the Third World and elsewhere. The Chinese refused to publish or broadcast those parts of his speech they deemed provocative; Moscow nonetheless postponed the scheduled visit of Vice-Premier Arkhipov.

The Soviets countered the prospect of Sino-American strategic collusion with a two-track policy of benign collusion with the PRC in a proliferating set of bilateral negotiating forums and cultural and economic exchanges (reviewed in Chapter 4), coupled with displaced competition via the pursuit of geographically extended security arrangements, consisting of a network of alliances and bases surrounding the PRC. Like the Americans, the Chinese viewed Soviet extended security arrangements as being directed against them, and demanded their disbandment. To the Soviets, these arrangements enhanced Soviet influence and prestige as well as military security, and they thus opted to ignore Chinese protests. Access to Vietnamese facilities in Cam Ranh Bay and Danang[39] enabled the Soviets to utilize warm water ports, repair and storage facilities midway between Vladivostok and the Indian Ocean, to maintain a permanent presence in the South China Sea, and more easily to conduct surveillance of the whole Chinese coastline.[40] From this vantage point the Soviet fleet could threaten crucial shipping lanes in the area, particularly should the United States lose Subic Bay and Clark Air Force Base, only 700 miles away. The base (which the Soviets deny is a base) would be highly vulnerable in the event of nuclear war, but could be useful in crises below that threshold: it contributed to the containment of China and helped intimidate other Asian countries (e.g., Japan, Thailand). Other Soviet naval facilities in the Pacific—except for Petropavlovsk (which has its own problems), and including the main base at Vladivostok—border the ocean on the Sea of Japan or the Sea of Okhotsk, where they are easily bottled up.

In return for these facilities, the Soviets unstintingly supplied the heavy equipment Vietnam required for its invasion and subsequent counterinsurgency campaign in Cambodia. Vietnam gained access to Soviet armor, artillery, APCs, and MI-24 helicopter gunships, and about 2,000 Soviet military advisers, some 400 of them deployed in Cambodia. And Vietnam became one of the USSR's main aid recipients, receiving aid in the range of $3 million daily. In the 1978–83 period, for example, Hanoi is estimated to have received about $5.7 billion, the military portion of which has been estimated from $500 million to $1 billion per year. Despite its ongoing rapprochement with the PRC, the Soviet Union promised Hanoi an increase in Soviet-Vietnamese trade by 70 percent in the 1986–90 Five-Year Plan period and to double its aid package (40 percent to be used for new projects, 60 percent on existing enterprises).[41]

The Soviets have also undertaken extended security arrangements in Northeast Asia. Since 1978, 10,000 men have been posted in the northern Kuriles, and the USSR has increased the number of its airports from three to five.[42] They have also taken pains to improve relations with North Korea, beginning in May 1984 with Kim Il Sung's first official visit to Moscow since 1961 and culminating in his 1986 state visit. Soviet headway in this courtship is indicated in the trend of economic cooperation as well as by tabulation of official visits and other diplomatic signals.[43] In response to Reagan's December 1981 decision to scrap the Carter embargo on advanced weapons sales to the South (36 F-16C/D Fighting Falcons were scheduled for phased arrival from 1986 to early 1989), Kim made the pilgrimage to Moscow in 1984 to ask for more aid. Gorbachev agreed to rescind Brezhnev's embargo on advanced weapons sales, but at a price.[44] In return, the Soviet Union got port-of-call privileges at Wonsan port on the east coast of North Korea and (reportedly) access to Nampo on the west coast, plus overflight and landing rights for Soviet aircraft.[45] Economic interdependency grew.[46]

These arrangements had direct repercussions on Chinese security, allowing Soviet aircraft to conduct reconnaissance of the Manchurian industrial heartland, Bohai Gulf and Yellow Sea areas, the North China Fleet Headquarters at Dairen, and other Chinese installations.[47] In apparent emulation of the close strategic coordination between American, Japanese, South Korean, and occasionally Chinese forces, a joint naval exercise was conducted off North Korea's northeastern coast in October 1986, and North Korean vessels made frequent calls at Soviet ports; delivery of a Soviet nuclear reactor started in October 1986. In response to the escalating Soviet-Korean security collaboration, Beijing has made some effort to improve its diplomatic relationship with Pyongyang. Thus in May 1987, Beijing rolled out the red carpet for Kim Il Sung's first visit since November 1984. China has, however, been placed at a disadvantage in this competition by its inability to match Soviet arms aid, also by its burgeoning economic relationship with South Korea.[48]

CHAPTER 15

Ménage à Trois, 1986–1990

From 1985–86 to the present, the triangle seems to have reverted to the *ménage à trois* with which it began in the early postwar period, before the dawn of the cold war. Decisive in precipitating the shift was rapprochement between the two wings, Moscow and Washington, beginning with arms control agreements (INF) and gradually including trade and cultural exchanges. Rather than leading to a polarization of Sino-Soviet relations, as in Khrushchev's thaw or Brezhnev's détente, Soviet-American rapprochement stimulated an even more rapid improvement of Sino-Soviet relations, as if the Chinese were eager not to be left out. Chinese anxieties about alienating the United States by pushing the Soviet dalliance too fast or too far were allayed by the fact that the Americans, too, began responding to Moscow's blandishments. Thus the Americans, rather than playing jilted lover in the wake of accelerated Sino-Soviet courtship, have held their tongues. The triangle returns to the earlier pattern:

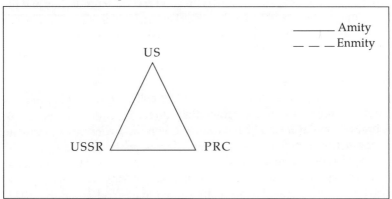

This new (and still tentative) configuration is based not solely on an attitudinal transformation, but also on reassessments of the balance of power. All three players modified their outlook on security somewhat, but Moscow and Beijing made perhaps the most substantial changes, with Washington still reserving judgment (at this writing) to see how genuine or lasting these changes are.

From 1977 through 1984, PRC security policy focused on the threat of major Soviet attack, of "an early, major and nuclear war."[1] A debate on arms reduction from 1983 through 1985 culminated however in a May-June 1985 meeting of the Military Affairs Commission, in which the leadership made a "strategic shift" to the assumption that there would be no major wars for the rest of the century. The PLA would hence shift from a strategy of immediate war preparedness to one of building a "regularized and modernized revolutionary army during a period of peace."[2] By reducing size while improving quality, the military share of the budget could be held constant in absolute terms while shrinking relative to the expanding civilian sector. Soviet military hegemony had reached its acme in the mid to late 1970s, according to this revised analysis, and then had begun its decline at the end of the decade due to the growing economic strength of Eastern Europe, frustration encountered in its Third World ventures, sharp deterioration of Soviet influence in the international communist movement, and economic stagnation.[3]

The theoretical assumption that American and Soviet forces had reached a "strategic stalemate" had by mid-1984 become authoritative doctrine. Whereas the Chinese previously anticipated war between a rising Soviet power and a declining American one, they now came to believe that the Reagan administration had reversed this decline and the two superpowers were equal or even that the United States "has begun to surpass the Soviet Union," and that this balance would remain fairly stable for some time.[4] Thus they foresaw little prospect of military conflict with the USSR, whose power was directed against other regions and strategic points. The Chinese also came to view the Soviet threat as more political than military, consisting of collusion with other nations around China's periphery rather than direct invasion. By late 1984, Chinese popular media began to play down the Soviet threat, drawing a distinction between Soviet ground forces in the Far East, still denounced as provocative, and the naval and air detachments of Soviet Far Eastern deployments, now portrayed as part of Moscow's "global strategic posture" directed against the United States and Japan. By 1985, high-level Chinese security officials were privately informing Western visiting dignitaries that they now viewed the fifty-odd Soviet ground force divisions as essentially defensive. Chinese strategists were quick to admit that the PLA would be unable to stop a major Soviet invasion or surgical strike in the next thirty to forty years, but now deemed a "people's war under modern conditions" of considerable deterrent value. Their self-confidence was buoyed by Soviet inability to defeat the *mujahideen* in Afghanistan, a nation of a mere fifteen million, who were not even trained or competently led (from the Chinese perspective). Whereas the Soviet Union remained a major security concern, planners now devoted their attention to unanticipated localized conflicts rather than full-scale invasion.[5]

This reassessment was in a sense only a rectification of the cognitive dissonance afflicting the foregoing shift to pivot, for Chinese budgetary policy was already incompatible with the prospect of "major war." Military expenditures reached their peak at 17.5 percent of the budget in 1979 (contributing to a hitherto unprecedented budget deficit), declining an average of 7 percent per annum in monetary terms thereafter: 16 percent in 1980, 15.6 percent in 1981, 10 percent in 1986, 8.8 percent in 1987, 8.2 percent in 1988. But according to figures released by the CIA in May 1988, China's real defense spending may account for only 4 percent of GNP. For defense industries had been shifted to the production of civilian consumer goods; in 1985, for example, factories under the Ordnance Ministry reportedly turned out 500,000 motorcycles, 400,000 bicycles, 200,000 cameras, and 100,000 refrigerators for civilian use. The share of civilian products produced by Chinese military industries rose from 10 percent in 1979 to 40 percent in 1985.[6] From being listed last among China's Four Modernizations, defense dropped to tenth place in Premier Li Peng's opening speech to the Seventh NPC outlining the government's economic priorities (sources said an earlier draft of Li's speech did not even mention defense); as of this writing, only two active military officers retain positions on the party Politburo.[7] These cutbacks in the army have coincided with a shift of resources to naval armament, apparently intended to protect China's growing maritime fleet (most of China's trade is transported by sea, and the "gold coast" developmental scenario and opening of Hainan presume its continued growth), perhaps even to assert Chinese claims in certain territorial disputes (e.g., the March 1988 Sino-Vietnamese clash in the Spratlys).

Is the new Chinese assessment based on realistic analysis of power shifts, or on wishful fiscal assumptions? To what extent the Soviet threat has receded remains controversial. There are two dimensions: the Soviet-American strategic equilibrium, and the Soviet threat to China and its chosen sphere of influence, the Pacific Rim. If Europe is not taken into account (where the USSR may be deemed to have suffered a major strategic setback since 1989), the Soviet-American strategic balance has remained roughly even, with perhaps a slight advantage to the United States.[8] Although the issues and outcome of the START talks are beyond the scope of this book, the successful conclusion to the INF talks may be considered a substantive beginning for formal disarmament.

As for Asia, while Soviet divisions assigned to the Far East command have remained steady at fifty-five or fifty-six, their states of readiness and modernity of equipment seem to have declined. Whereas two-thirds of these contingents were in categories one and two of readiness in 1976–77, in 1977–83 only half were in this category, and only 35 percent after 1984, indicating "skeletonization" of the units.[9] Thus while the Soviets at this writing probably still enjoy a 3:1 advantage in tanks, they probably suffer at least a 2:1 disadvantage in first-line personnel; even if they chose to bring existing units to full strength, Soviet ground forces would be at a great manpower disadvantage. The Chinese air force and navy enjoy overwhelming quantitative superiority over their better-equipped Soviet counterparts in the Asian region.[10] From 1984 to 1988, the Soviets reduced the size of their Pacific Fleet by about 20 percent (40 ships), though they have replaced most of their aging ships with modern, more capable surface warships and submarines, and deployed new bombers designed to strike U.S. ships and shore facilities. Gorbachev seems to have significantly reduced the status and resources of the Soviet Navy, as a result of budgetary stringencies and changing strategic priorities. On the one hand, the deployment of a new generation of Soviet mobile IBMs has reduced the importance of the navy to the country's nuclear deterrent; on the other, the cutback in Soviet military ventures in the Third World reduces the need for naval power projection. There seems to have been a significant cutback on naval activities beyond Soviet territorial waters: according to Australian Foreign Minister Bill Hayden, Soviet naval activity in the Pacific in 1987 was 50 percent down from 1986.[11] Some American officials disagree, alleging that Soviet retrenchment has been greatly exaggerated.[12] The trend line is perhaps not yet entirely unequivocal, but a comparison of major naval vessels in 1987 (Table 15.1), before Soviet retrenchment moves had taken effect, suggests that the United States is in a strong position.

The new Soviet approach to East Asia did not burst upon the scene *ex nihilo,* but as the culmination of a protracted series of arms reduction negotiations and actions. This process has not yet found its designated institutional forum in Asia, as it has in the West (where it sired a litter of acronyms: SALT, START, INF, MBFR), but a solid beginning has

TABLE 15.1. Major U.S. and Soviet Naval Vessels in 1987

Principal Surface Combatants	United States	USSR
Aircraft carriers	6	2
Battleships	2	0
Cruisers	18	15
Destroyers	29	16
Frigates	46	55
Submarines:		
Strategic (SSBN)	8	32
Attack (SSN)	43	90
Amphibious craft	30	21

SOURCE: Compiled by the Institute of Southeast Asian Studies, and published in *Asia-Pacific International and Strategic Studies Newsletter*, no. 6 (December 1987), p. 2.

been made, and it is not impossible to envisage the Sino-Soviet dialogue as a future locomotive of international arms control regimes. The pattern has been one of a series of tacitly reciprocal moves masquerading as unilateral concessions.

The first step was taken in May 1983, when the Chinese first cited the SS-20s as a threat to China. In apparent response, Andropov announced in an interview with *Pravda* on August 26 that any Soviet weapons removed from the European theater in connection with the INF talks would be destroyed rather than redeployed in the Far East, as originally foreseen. In the successful conclusion to the INF talks in late 1987, the Soviet Union in fact agreed to the elimination of 436 intermediate and short-range nuclear missiles stationed in the Soviet Far East, including all 180 Asian SS-20s, without any quid pro quo from China (perhaps hoping to forestall deployment of U.S. IRBMs in Alaska). True, Soviet mobile ICBMs of the SSX24 and SS-25 types stationed in Central Asia remain capable of hitting Chinese targets.

The second step in the sequence was the unilateral Chinese announcement that the PRC would reduce military troop strength. Manpower reductions began in 1982 with the demobilization of 500,000 soldiers, and continued with the June 1985 announcement of a further reduction of one million men (including 600,000 officers), consolidating China's eleven military regions into seven. Completion of this downsizing within two years reduced the total number serving in the PLA from some 4 million in 1984 to 2.95 million by 1986, enlisting a mere 0.29 percent of the Chinese population.[13] After years of boasting the world's largest standing army, the PLA now took second place (after the Soviet Union). Although not explicitly associated with Sino-Soviet rapprochement (actually different rationales have been articulated in different contexts), its benign implications were immediately recognized.[14] The Chinese also, beginning in August-September 1985, adopted the Soviet position in opposition to the Strategic Defense Initiative (which, if successfully developed by both superpowers, would render the minimal Chinese deterrent irrelevant).[15]

The next step was Gorbachev's, who proposed in his July 1986 Vladivostok speech to begin negotiations for "balanced" reductions in conventional ground force levels in the Far East, evidently hoping to draw the Chinese into another institutionalized negotiating forum analogous to the MBFR talks in Europe. For Asia as a whole, Gorbachev sought to resuscitate the old (1969) Soviet quest for a Collective Asian Security System (hitherto doomed by the refusal of either China or India to endorse it) in the new clothes of an Asian Security Conference. Despite its provenience, this new set of proposals, vague and idealistic as they were, does represent a departure in Soviet Asia policy, designed to appeal to a constituency that is not necessarily communist or even procommunist. Patterned on the highly successful (from the Soviet perspective) Helsinki process and CSCE agreement (which sanctified Soviet territorial gains in Europe since World War II in exchange for unenforceable human rights promises), such a conference would no longer be anti-Chinese. China is, in fact, invited to take part; Soviet statements refer to Chinese and Soviet proclamations renouncing first use of nuclear weapons as a preliminary model for international cooperation. (China has not explicitly supported the proposal, but has also not condemned it.) To be convened in the symbolically potent city of Hiroshima, such a conference would discuss naval reductions; withdrawal of seaborne nuclear weapons; limits on major classes of warships, submarines, and naval bases; and international agreements to restrict submarine activity in certain Pacific Ocean zones. The Indian proposal for a zone of peace in the Indian Ocean would be adopted and extended to the Pacific littoral. Thus naval and air forces in the northwestern Pacific would be frozen; the superpowers would agree to keep warships armed with nuclear missiles beyond the range of their targets; antisubmarine forces would be limited in agreed-upon zones and eliminated in others; and naval exercises would be limited.[16] The implicit target of such appeals is still the American presence in the Pacific: as the dominant air and naval power, the United States stands to lose most from such changes.[17] This was also true of Gorbachev's seven-point peace plan presented in September 1988 at Krasnoyarsk, which proposed a freeze on deployment of nuclear weapons in the Asia-

Pacific region, a Soviet withdrawal from Cam Ranh Bay in exchange for American evacuation of its Philippine bases, and so forth.

The most recent and dramatic concession in Asian arms reduction also originated from the Kremlin, this time as part of a Janus-faced package facing both East and West. In a December 1988 address to the United Nations, Gorbachev announced a massive 500,000-troop unilateral reduction of the Soviet army within two years. During a meeting with the Trilateral Commission in January 1989, Gorbachev expanded upon this pledge, promising that the defense budget would be cut by 14.2 percent and the production of weapons and military equipment by 19.5 percent during the same period. Western eyes tended to focus on the withdrawal of Soviet forces (more than 50,000 troops and 5,300 tanks) from East Germany, Czechoslovakia, and Hungary, which has proceeded apace.[18] This was promptly followed by announcements by several Warsaw Pact members that they would reduce defense expenditures by 10-17 percent, which immediately anticipated the mass upheaval leading to the collapse of communist regimes in those countries and the fall of the iron curtain. Yet the largest proportion of the announced cuts would affect Asia not Europe, with 40 percent of the cuts coming from the slightly more than a quarter of all Soviet forces stationed east of the Urals. As Gorbachev made clear in subsequent remarks, and as Shevardnadze underscored during his February 2–4, 1989, visit to China, 120,000 of the 200,000 troops to be removed from this vast region would come from the Soviet Far East, including twelve divisions of ground forces, eleven air force regiments, and sixteen warships from the Soviet Pacific Fleet. "We are prepared to work for withdrawal, on terms to be agreed with China, of [all] military units and armaments from border areas leaving only personnel required for performing routine borderguard duties," Gorbachev announced.[19] The promised Soviet force reductions[20] include six tank divisions from Eastern Europe (four from the GDR, one from Czechoslovakia, and one from Hungary) and a total of 10,300 tanks (5,300 from Eastern Europe and 5,000 to be "liquidated," with others converted to tractors and training vehicles). Reductions would include artillery (8,500 total) and aircraft (800 total), with parts of planes to be used as spares; ground support equipment would be "redistributed." The personnel reductions (500,000 total) would include 240,000 from European USSR, 60,000 from the south, and 200,000 from the east. In Mongolia, three of the four ground force divisions would be withdrawn, and air forces would be eliminated.

The pattern of these cutbacks calls for reconsideration of the geopolitical logic of arms reduction. Heretofore one of the factors inhibiting Western acceptance of Sino-Soviet border troop reductions has been the assumption that Soviet troops demobilized in the east would be redeployed in the west (a *compensatory* model). From recent developments, however, it would seem that a *correlative* model might be more applicable, according to which military reductions in the south or east correlate with arms reduction in the west, for essentially identical reasons (budget, labor shortages).

Corresponding to this ecumenical Soviet approach to the Pacific Rim, there has been a sea change in Soviet rhetoric vis-à-vis the Third World, from the encouragement of "national liberation" among impoverished new states to cooperation with geopolitically important "young states traveling the capitalist road," such as ASEAN, India, Indonesia, South Korea, Mexico, and Brazil. This approach is part of Gorbachev's "new political thinking" (*novoe myshlenie*), with its emphasis on "common human values" rather than class interests as the ideological basis for foreign policy. It abstractly bespeaks an impatience with economically backward client states lacking popular legitimacy who trade on ideological sympathy for unlimited Soviet aid, and a corresponding eagerness to reorient Soviet foreign policy from a military-strategic to an economic-diplomatic calculus. According to the traditional Marxist-Leninist classification, there were only three categories of countries in the world—socialist, capitalist, and developing (Third World)—and no such category as NICs. With most such newly industrialized countries the USSR in fact had no diplomatic relations. Besides acknowledging their ascendancy, Gorbachev announced in his political report to the February Party Congress: "Today, too, we are more firmly convinced that promoting revolution from the outside, and even more so by military means, is futile and inadmissable." The Soviets already during the terminal phase of Brezhnev's reign were finding the pursuit of revolution in the Third World very costly, even with Cuban support. Given the most optimal revolutionary outcome, the new client proved to be economically exiguous, while neighboring countries turned to the West for security assistance, leading to an increased U.S. presence and the potential for superpower confrontation. With Soviet encouragement, both Najibullah and Heng Samrin regimes have thus adopted united front strategies, attempting to broaden their social bases, describing themselves as "national democratic" governments, and postponing the transition to full socialism.

A no less impressive breakthrough in Sino-Soviet relations during this period is essential resolution of the problem posed by the Soviet quest for extended deterrence, which Chinese strategists took to be a strategy to surround and contain the PRC. Although the Chinese indicated a certain flexibility as early as April 1985, when Deng Xiaoping announced that "[the USSR] can still maintain its relations with Vietnam and can still obtain bases provided by Vietnam"[21] (so long as the Vietnamese withdraw their troops from Cambodia), and in another context hinting that progress on even one of the Three Obstacles might be enough to get the ball rolling, China's conceptualization of the Three Fundamental Obstacles entailed that real ground would have to be ceded by the Soviets. The Soviets made at least a modest beginning in Gorbachev's Vladivostok speech in July 1986, which touched upon each of the obstacles, making substantive concessions on two of them.

First, apparently assuming this obstacle to be least salient in Chinese eyes, Gorbachev made a transparently token gesture regarding Afghanistan, announcing the withdrawal of six regiments whose absence would not affect combat effectiveness and in any case involved less than 7 percent of Soviet units. Although he referred to Afghanistan as a "bleeding wound" in early 1986, Gorbachev at this phase still hoped to prevail militarily, having sent in one of the Soviet Army's top commanders, General Mikhail Zaitsev, and authorized the bombing of supply lines in Pakistan.

Second, Gorbachev indicated that the USSR had been "discussing" with Mongolia (MCP First Secretary Jambyn Batmonh was in Moscow at the time) the withdrawal of a "considerable" portion of the five Soviet divisions estimated to be stationed there. Since the speech, the Soviets have specified their intention to withdraw one motorized rifle division initially, or one-fifth of their contingent (10,000 to 20,000 troops); this withdrawal was duly implemented in April–June 1987. As for the Sino-Soviet border, Gorbachev publicly offered to accept the thalweg as the riverine demarcation line.

Third, as to Indochina, Gorbachev had least to offer, merely suggesting that the PRC and DRV should iron out their differences in bilateral talks. But whereas previous Soviet negotiators had refused even to discuss "sovereign third parties" with China,[22] the Soviets also agreed, beginning at the ninth round of vice-ministerial talks in October 1986, to discuss "all issues" directly with the PRC (to the visible discomfiture of Hanoi).

The Chinese response to the Vladivostok proposals was basically positive—acknowledging that some new points had been made—but reserved. Deliberately drawing attention to the problem area on which the Soviets had offered least, Deng Xiaoping offered in a September 2 television interview with American journalist Mike Wallace to travel "anywhere" in the Soviet Union for a summit if the Cambodian problem could be solved.[23] This seemed to imply an escalation from the earlier position pleading for movement anywhere to a harder line staking all on one "main obstacle," the Soviets plaintively noted, accusing the Chinese of "bait and switch" tactics.[24] Yet not only did the Soviets make no substantive concessions on Indochina, but shortly after Vladivostok Vietnam received an increase in Soviet aid, effectively doubling the rate from the prior level of U.S. $1.1 billion per year to the equivalent of $14.5 billion (9 billion rubles) over the next five-year plan period (1986–90).[25] Moreover, it must be conceded that the Chinese responded readily enough to concrete Soviet concessions when they were offered. Take Outer Mongolia: since January 1986, Beijing and Ulan Bator have signed a civil-aviation agreement, a long-term trade protocol, and a consular treaty—coincidentally facilitating U.S. recognition for the Mongolian People's Republic.[26] The Soviets responded in December 1988 by promising to withdraw three-fourths of their remaining troops within two years, following up in March 1989 with an announcement of the withdrawal of all but one of the remaining divisions in Outer Mongolia plus all Soviet air forces, to be withdrawn during 1989 and 1990 (withdrawal began the day Gorbachev arrived in Beijing). The MPR promptly announced it would reduce its armed forces from 25,000 to 13,000 soldiers, deactivating two of its four motor rifle divisions and eighteen aircraft from its air force, also demobilizing some 200,000 reservists and cutting the defense budget by 11 percent.[27]

With regard to the Indochina quagmire, where China was the main supplier to the tripartite resistance coalition in Cambodia as well as the principal guarantor of Thai security, the PRC steadfastly refused to talk with Hanoi until all Vietnamese troops were withdrawn. While refusing to abrogate aid commitments, the Soviets seem to have put some pressure on the Vietnamese: on April 15, 1988, Rogachev told Thai Foreign Minister Siddhi Savetsila that the USSR's having withdrawn its troops from Afghanistan set an example for other regional conflicts, such as Cambodia's. Despite a persisting cleavage between the PRC and other Western opponents of the Vietnamese-aligned Cambodian regime concerning the future role of the Khmer Rouge, the Chinese eventually agreed to an "external solution" leaving the internal composition of the Cambodian regime in abeyance while focusing on the removal of Vietnamese forces: 50,000 troops were withdrawn by the end of the year, with a timetable for evacuation of the remaining 50,000 by the end of the following year (actually achieved ahead of schedule, by September 1989). In August 1986 Beijing surprised observers by welcoming a Lao bid for normalizing relations with China, even though Moscow finances a major part of that country's five-year plan and all of its modern armaments, and there are thought to be more than 2,000 Soviet advisers in Laos. Continuing disagreement over the domestic balance among fractions within Cambodia has nonetheless led China to keep the pressure on, maintaining some 400,000 troops (thirty divisions) in intermittently belligerent status along the Sino-Vietnamese border (and forcing Hanoi to reinforce border guard defenses with 500,000 mainforce troops, or half its regular army). Meanwhile Sino-Soviet normalization has neutralized Soviet backing for Vietnam.[28] It is interesting that when Chinese and Vietnamese ships clashed over the disputed Spratlys in March 1988, the Soviets made no gesture in support of Hanoi. In fact, the Soviets have been withdrawing their forces from Cam Ranh Bay over the past several years, in line with an overall reduction in overseas commitments; Shevardnadze told a delegation of U.S. senators in Moscow in early 1990 that there would soon be no Soviet military forces in Asia beyond that country's own borders.[29] In Afghanistan, where captured weapons with Chinese markings point to a major Chinese effort in support of the *mujahideen* resistance, the Soviets made no significant offer and the Chinese no reciprocal concessions. The PRC was essentially left out of eventual UN settlement of this issue.[30]

Superficial comparison of these three cases (the Sino-Soviet and Mongolian border, Indochina, and Afghanistan) indicates that Chinese demands, albeit insistent, were limited strictly to the security dimension, and as such negotiable. The Chinese adopted a two-track policy, consisting on the one track of benign collusion with the USSR combined with relentless pressure for concessions on Soviet extended security policies. On the second track, the Chinese have shifted from their previous policy of refusing to have anything to do with the client state to a carrot-and-stick policy designed to induce the client to shift to more conciliatory policies. If the client has made what China considers a significant concession, China can "reward" the client with normalization and bilateral exchanges (as in the case of Mongolia); if not, China can "get tough" while simultaneously threatening to "buy off" the patron in Sino-Soviet talks (as in the case of Vietnam).[31] As a communist party-state, the PRC can have no objection to the maintenance of a socialist system in Cambodia or Afghanistan, nor to continuing indigenous guerrilla movements, nor even to the maintenance of patron-client ties with the USSR; only the presence of Soviet troops and military facilities is objectionable. Given the Soviet wish to extricate themselves from a series of costly and embarrassing embroilments and reallocate resources to domestic priorities,[32] the Chinese stance facilitates matters by removing the threat of rival patronage for indigenous "revolutionary" or "national liberation" forces (as in the 1960s). And, at this writing, settlement terms for both Cambodia and Afghanistan leave an embattled socialist regime precariously in place, still dependent on Soviet material assistance.

China's more flexible attitude toward Soviet extended security policy places the objects of that policy—North Korea, Vietnam, Outer Mongolia, Afghanistan, India—in a geopolitical force-field in which their own options are constrained. During the Sino-Soviet dispute, an amicable relationship with the Soviet Union implied a hostile relationship with China, and vice versa. In the context of Sino-Soviet détente, it becomes possible to have simultaneous good relationships with both—or alternatively, to be bereft of patronage by their mutual agreement. In most cases this set of relationships has not been integrated into the politics of the "great" power triangle, because Washington has perceived no interest in establishing independent contact with the smaller communist client states. Washington seems to have been inhibited from overtures to Pyongyang by its sensitivity to South Korean amour propre, from overtures to Hanoi by Chinese sensibilities.[33] Each socialist client thus enters into a subordinate triangle consisting of the client's relationship to two rival patrons, Beijing and Moscow. Sino-Soviet rapprochement can be problematic to the client insofar as it reduces the tension through which it can extort payoffs from its two patrons. Thus it is in the interest of client states to exacerbate tension between their two patrons— though they do not in fact have much leverage to do so.

Since 1989, as Sino-Soviet tension has dissipated and triangular relations have moved toward a *ménage*, the North Korean regime, for example, has felt itself increasingly isolated. In an interview in late 1988, Soviet commentator Aleksandr Bovin gave his personal opinion that there were two independent sovereign states on the Korean peninsula, which should enjoy "cross-recognition." This signaled a major shift, and beginning in February 1989 the East European regimes proceeded one after another to recognize Seoul, even though this prompted Pyongyang to break off relations. When Moscow established diplomatic relations in September 1990, however, Pyongyang could not easily cut off its major trade partner and weapons supplier. China might have been expected to follow suit, were it not for Tiananmen; still, the "close as lips and teeth" relationship has remained largely symbolic, as Beijing continued to ply far more trade with South Korea than with the North. Seeing the drift of things, Pyongyang initiated negotiations with Tokyo, just as Seoul opened a trade office in Beijing. Having been deprived of radical options by the Sino-Soviet thaw, North Korea may be forced to launch its own reform program, or at least to maintain a moderate and low-key foreign policy posture.

The smaller Asian countries in the Western orbit, on the other hand, have an interest in greater Sino-Soviet amity, as this also reduces the competitive incentive for East-West polarization. In Taiwan, for example, China's shift to a more pro-Soviet posture quiets fears of a U.S. sellout and may improve chances for arms transfer or coproduction of weapons arrangements. Meanwhile, Western ostracism of Beijing after Tiananmen created an investment and trade vacuum into which Taiwanese businessmen have hastened to move. For Japan and the East Asian NICs, if Sino-Soviet rapprochement can be achieved without antagonizing the United States (i.e., moving toward a "marriage"), that would make U.S. security guarantees less imperative while opening up the prospect of profitable, conflict-free commerce with all three powers. Commercially considered, a *ménage* is the best of all possible worlds.

The United States has been relatively slow to join the Pacific disarmament regime, seeing in it a threat to its hitherto secure regional hegemony. The seeming irrelevance of a high level of military preparedness in the face of a declining threat and the attractions of a "peace dividend" have made themselves manifest, however, and by early 1990 U.S. defense officials were considering options for reducing American forces in the Pacific. Current plans call for withdrawal over 1990–93 of up to 15,000 of the total 120,000 American soldiers in East Asia, larger local financial contributions from Japan, abandonment of the Philippine bases by the end of the century, and a skeletonization of the contingent in South Korea.[34]

Although the *ménage* presumes positive relations among all three participants, the jealousy factor persists, due to the high stakes involved and the lethal weaponry in play—as well as the historical awareness that the triangle may also take other forms. There are two ways to handle jealousy: the first is to succumb to it, choose a desired "mate" and attempt to annihilate one's rival; the second is to employ what psychoanalysts term the "defense mechanisms" of repression and denial. Survival of the *ménage* is premised on each player's exclusive resort to the second technique. The result is a pattern in which each player repeatedly asserts its absolutely evenhanded stance and denies the existence of a triangle. Beijing was first to recognize this, when shifting away from the U.S. embrace in the early 1980s to the position of pivot, amid recurrent assurances that "Improvement of Sino-Soviet relations will not impair relations between China and the United States, and it will be in the interests of world peace." [35] For several years the Americans refused to accept this (e.g., during Reagan's 1984 state visit), maintaining a crusade against Moscow while trying to revive the dying embers of the Sino-American romance of the late 1970s. But the Reagan administration conducted a review of its China policy in the wake of Gorbachev's Vladivostok speech, at which point the question was raised: what could Washington actually *do* to head off Sino-Soviet rapprochement? Some suggested making further concessions to Beijing on Taiwan. After careful consideration, the administration decided not to change existing U.S. policy: nothing more could be done. [36] This conclusion was publicly signaled by Secretary of State Shultz during his July 1988 visit to Beijing, when he told Chinese officials that Sino-Soviet normalization was "a prospect that can be welcomed." [37] "We've passed the day in the U.S.-China relationship where anyone talks about 'playing a card,'" echoed Bush during his February 1989 visit. [38] Moscow has likewise suppressed indications of "jealousy," now publicly attesting understanding of China's defense ties with the United States. [39] Disclaiming any interest in collusion, Shevardnadze in 1988 noted that in the past, "it was assumed that improvements in relations between two sides invariably resulted in political damage to a third side. . . . The times of such 'political geometry' are gone and never to return." [40]

From such statements it is possible, reading between the lines, to induce that each player is still quite insecure about the relationship between the other two. Moreover, there are reasons to expect this insecurity to continue or even possibly to increase. A *ménage* assumes an evenhandedness among all three that has not yet been achieved, and even as trends among the powers continue to move in that direction certain risks and costs are exposed. China is engaged in "benign" collusion with the USSR and "malign" collusion with the United States. This makes sense in terms of PRC security needs but also gives rise to certain paradoxes. Aside from the fact that Sino-Soviet benign collusion reduces Chinese defenses vis-à-vis its gravest security risk, the two collusions are in tension, for benign Sino-Soviet collusion belies the premise on which malign Sino-American collusion is based. One possible solution would be to "balance" the two collusions by entering into malign collusion with the USSR as well (that is, purchasing weapons from both sides, as India has begun to do). The Chinese PLA still relies rather heavily on Soviet-designed equipment and military literature, and Soviet security aid could thus make a positive contribution to Chinese modernization.[41] Already amid preparations for the Gorbachev visit the two agreed to exchange military visits, including such symbolic gestures of friendship as naval port calls.[42] In late 1990 reports were emanating from Beijing that the Soviets might beef up the Chinese arsenal with a sale of naval hardware and one of their hottest supersonic fighters, the Sukhoi SU-27. How far can such triangular cooperation proceed on sensitive security matters without arousing the jealousy of third parties?

Despite (because of?) recent improvements in Sino-Soviet relations, Sino-American malign collusion has also increased in the context of the *ménage*. Washington has invested heavily in building a broad strategic relationship with China. Right up till June 1989 there had been a steady stream of high-level defense exchanges between the two countries of the kind one normally associates with great power allies.[43] The two cornerstones on which the relationship was built are: (1) Chinese air and naval modernization, designed to counter Soviet air and naval modernization since the late 1970s, and (2) intelligence gathering. The United States has been assisting China with a variety of defense and dual-use technology, including missiles and artillery-shell technology, sophisticated sonars, radars, ASW torpedoes, and ship-borne air defense systems. The relatively modest early military sales (amounting to about $43 million by 1985) paved the way for two blockbuster deals negotiated in 1986, providing for the Chinese manufacture of advanced 155mm artillery shells, and for the sale of avionics to upgrade China's F-8 fighters to all-weather capability. These agreements brought China into the upper echelons of U.S. weapons clients, ranking second only to Saudi Arabia among weapons recipients in fiscal year 1987. As for intelligence gathering, China is host to U.S. listening posts in Xinjiang, which replaced those lost in Iran in 1980. China also cooperates in monitoring Soviet nuclear tests.

This strategic relationship is far from invulnerable, however. Despite the ongoing secularization of Chinese Marxism, differing ideologies and value systems sometimes still come into play. The crushing of the democracy demonstrations at Tiananmen in June 1989 caused a furor that has interrupted military sales and cooperation, for example, although cooperation with intelligence gathering has apparently not been affected. There is also the question that once plagued Sino-Soviet military cooperation: will the client's enhanced military capabilities be used in the patron's interests? The danger is now less that Beijing should shift its strategic throw-weight to Moscow than that it may pursue its own interests more aggressively. In 1990 the military budget was increased in percentage terms for the first time in a decade, by some 15 percent, and it is conceivable that the greater emphasis on strong centralized authority may presage a higher future prioritization of the military.[44] China is already a formidable regional power, with the third largest tank corps in the world, an air force many times larger than other regional air forces, and a growing navy. It might be assumed that higher military spending represents only a political payoff, an insurance policy against future domestic instability. But there are indications of an interest in the use of military power in pursuit of more conventional foreign policy objectives. Since 1989 the PLA has fundamentally revised its force doctrine, called "people's war," from a defensive strategy to an offensive one, the key element of which is called "local war," founded on the premise that China would be the aggressor in warfare conducted within limited space, time, and means for limited objectives. To this end China's military has been training rapid-deployment forces, called Fist Battalions, since 1988. Organized around a core of attack helicopters, these units are designed for a ten-hour response time. In October 1990, six hundred paratroopers conducted a mock attack on an island in the South China Sea, according to *Jiefangjun Bao*. Long-range naval air force bombers conducted exercises in the Pacific for the first time in 1986, and the air force is believed to have acquired in-flight refueling technology for its fighters. A more assertively nationalistic foreign policy may be consonant with a regime of domestic suppression.[45]

China is at this writing still in the throes of a succession crisis that will determine, among other things, its future strategic direction. If we assume that the eventual successor leadership should rediscover an interest in reform, China may in due course come to prefer a "positive" balance (i.e., *benign* collusion with both wings), as a way of reducing military outlays while shifting resources to modernization.[46] Further steps toward Sino-Soviet collusion might be expected to follow, now that the Three Obstacles have been essentially removed: Chinese accession to a nonaggression or non-use-of-force treaty, or agreement on confidence-building measures along the border. But even benign collusion is not necessarily cost-free. Cooperation on such confidence-building measures would tend to sanction and add international legitimacy to a Soviet (or Russian) bid to gain influence in Asia, arousing American (and Japanese) misgivings. Already, getting friendly with China has helped the Soviets shed their image of an overarmed polar bear looming on the horizon, and may facilitate an improvement in relations with such hitherto diehard anti-Soviet Chinese clients as Pakistan or Thailand. Will an apparently peace-loving Soviet Union/Russia primarily concerned with economic modernization rather than military arms races prove less of a threat to Western interests in Asia, or merely a threat of a different sort? American defense analysts and decision makers are apt, by professional habit, to hope for the former but prepare for the latter contingency.

CHAPTER 16

The End of the Strategic Triangle?

In Part III, in order to reduce politics among the powers to its essentials and thereby facilitate exploration of its structural logic, the "strategic triangle" has been conceptualized as an abstract "game" with three players. Chapters 9 through 15 have investigated the historical evolution of the relationship empirically, in order to see how well game and political reality coincide. What generalizations may now be inferred from this analysis? Does the game in any sense explain the politics?

To place the strategic triangle in context, it would be an overstatement to deem it the axis on which the globe has always rotated. Europe has traditionally been regarded as the cockpit of the international system; Berlin and Eastern Europe have continued to generate world-scale crises in the postwar era, as have the Middle East and Central America. Although there was a triangular dimension to the "loss" of China in the late 1940s, the triangle first became an entity in international consciousness (a "triangle for itself") in the 1960s, coinciding with the dawning Chinese awareness of their distinct national interests and security needs, and the acknowledgment of Chinese autonomy by the two superpowers. The triangle played probably its most weighty international role in the 1970s, perhaps fading somewhat in significance in the 1980s; thus Chinese nuclear forces were not factored into the START or INF talks (although the Soviets advocated their inclusion). Still, two major semiconventional land wars have sucked the three players into the Asian vortex since World War II, and the brink of nuclear war was approached on both of these occasions and on several others. With Asia's emergence in the last two decades as the world's most dynamic engine of economic growth, thereby promising to mediate both East-West and North-South tensions, the strategic disposition of the world's largest and most populous continent has acquired added significance. The strategic salience of both China and the Soviet Union has expanded within the region during this period, while industrialization and trade have enhanced U.S. economic interests there. Even those issue areas not directly impinging on the triangle are often found to be indirectly implicated, such as nuclear proliferation or strategic disarmament talks. If not necessarily the fulcrum of international politics, the strategic triangle is a nodal point of crucial and growing importance.

Four different triangular configurations exhaust the logically conceivable options. We have tagged these the *ménage à trois,* romantic triangle, stable marriage, and unit-veto triangles (listed in order of positive relationships in the triangle). From a systemic perspective, the *ménage à trois* is an optimal configuration, providing equal security to each participant at minimal cost. But during the time span under review, it has been relatively evanescent and is often dismissed as unrealistic. The unit-veto triangle, a Hobbesian *omnium contra omnes,* multiplies sources of uncertainty, enhancing frustration and danger to all participants (particularly when each has an assured second-strike capability) while offering minimal positive reinforcements. Empirical investigation of the only period when it pertained (the 1960s) confirms this negative assessment: Moscow and Beijing were constantly at each other's throats, yet each also engaged in contests with Washington (Cuba, Vietnam, Berlin, and so forth).

This leaves us with the marriage and the romantic triangle. To judge from its longevity, marriage might be deemed the more stable of these configurations: the romantic triangle has been relatively unstable, emerging amid tension only to "regress" to some new form of marriage. And yet from a systemic perspective, marriage seems relatively conducive to polarization and conflict: an intensified arms race, hyperactive compensatory behavior on the part of the cornered pariah, and displaced competition in third countries. This seems to hold true regardless of the actors involved—witness the exchange of roles from 1949–59 to 1959–69, and again in 1976–81; in each case the pariah— first the United States, then the PRC, then the USSR—engaged in hyperactive compensatory behavior, contributing to an arms race and ultimately to some form of conflict among the three, either directly or via proxies.[1] The romantic triangle, on the other hand, albeit perhaps more tenuously balanced, seems relatively conducive to declining defense expenditures and the resolution of conflict, sometimes to even more positive steps to improve relations. The differing propensities of the two configurations flow from their structure: while marriage is conducive to relentless polarization between couple and pariah (i.e., irresolvable given the nuclear standoff), in the romantic triangle the pivot has an interest in mediating between the two opposing wings and modulating tension. Moreover, each wing's determination to subdue the opposing wing tends to be mitigated by mixed hope and fear regarding the unpredictable "swing" role of the pivot.[2]

Does the game explain the politics? Do the players play by the rules? That is, do they act "rationally," according to the logic of their position in the triangle? Not entirely: there are certain constraints on their freedom of alignment and elective affinities. The two chief constraints on freedom of alignment are security and ideology: on the one hand, it is difficult to align with a spouse posing a major security threat; on the other, it is illegitimate to align with one embracing antithetical ideological values. Both of these constraints coincide with regard to the Soviet-American relationship, making it very difficult to form a stable coalition. There has never been a Soviet-American condominium, despite occasional overtures, and the achievements of détente (motivated in part by joint suspicions of the PRC) remain politically controversial. The Sino-American marriage was also fleeting, possibly the briefest geopolitical match in the postwar era. The Sino-Soviet marriage has actually had the longest endurance record, though in retrospect the relationship seems to have been more strained than appeared at the time. The Sino-Soviet relationship is essentially one of ideological affinity, but since the advent of a Chinese nuclear capability, and particularly since the Sino-Soviet border clash with all its accoutrements (nuclear blackmail, international encirclement and counterencirclement), the Soviet Union is perceived by China to pose its greatest security risk, while China is perceived by the Soviet Union to pose a worrisome if not necessarily fatal threat to its rear. Thus ideological affinity was counterbalanced by opposing geopolitical security interests. The Sino-American relationship is not at present perceived to threaten the security of either, but it is deemed ideologically illegitimate, even in the light of the post-Mao redefinition of Marxism–Leninism–Mao Zedong Thought that accompanies the reforms. For these reasons, any "tight" marriage of the sort that obtained in the 1950s can probably be ruled out for any of the three players for the foreseeable future. But if ideology and geopolitical security interests place certain broad constraints, or create certain elective affinities, in alliance behavior, these have over time been shown to be rather weak. The triangle has constantly shifted from one configuration to another, defying either ideological or geopolitical "logic."

And so what if the players do not play by the rules? The truism is widely accepted that the international system is essentially anarchic, with no supranational actor empowered to impose penalties for violation of rules. Thus when any player violates the rules, the other two players are realistically induced to compensate, and the game undergoes transformation to a new configuration. The rules of the game are of analytical utility, permitting us to distinguish between normal play and deviant play, and thereby making the system contingently predictable. If the rules are followed ("normal" play), a given triangular configuration will remain stable; if the rules are violated ("deviant" play), it is likely to transform into a different configuration, as each player reorients itself in order better to survive and enhance its interests within the new climate of expectations. The reason for recurrent configuration shifts has typically been a player's dissatisfaction in a particular configuration, leading to an attempt to "break out." Thus in the 1950s, China opted to break out from the role of (junior) partner in a "marriage"; in the mid-1970s, the Soviet Union chose to break out from the role of (relatively neglected) wing in a romantic triangle. A fully developed model of triangular politics would also contain rules of transformation, predicting within each configuration precisely which violation would lead to which new configuration. At this stage, however, only a few hypotheses and tentative generalizations may be ventured.

An actor may violate the rules either to take advantage of perceived opportunities to cheat or because the present situation poses intolerable risks or burdens. Each triangular configuration places a different mix of temptations and strains on each actor to violate the rules. In a marriage, for example, the two spouses are in a position of relative security and the pariah in a position of relative insecurity; the latter will have strongest inducement to deviate from his role. The most tempting deviation would be compensatory self-strengthening—either through new coalitional arrangements or greater investment in arms—in an effort to "knock out" one spouse (rationally, the weakest); alternatively, the pariah may pursue diplomatic efforts to seduce one spouse into marriage and push the other into pariahdom. These two tactics may, of course, be pursued simultaneously, as the Soviet Union pursued détente with the West in the 1960s while attempting to ostracize China or even knock it out of the game. The United States as a pariah in the 1950s was in such a dominant strategic position that it was able to rely primarily on self-strengthening efforts, investing relatively heavily in military armaments and constructing an international alliance network. But recent disclosures indicate that the United States also pursued a rationally differentiated strategy toward the marriage, responding positively to Khrushchev's overtures for collusion while taking a hard line toward more radical Maoist policies. To the extent that the pariah relies on self-strengthening efforts, this configuration is conducive to an arms race and competitive coalition building. The greatest fear of each spouse must be that the other will defect to the pariah. This apprehension is exacerbated if there is a hierarchical order among the spouses, which tends to enhance the desire of a disgruntled subordinate to defect. Defection is a deviant move which transforms the marriage into a new configuration: either a realigned marriage (if the pariah succeeds in seducing the estranged spouse), or, if no new marriage is consummated, a romantic or unit-veto triangle. The only configuration that can be safely foreclosed in the wake of a defection is a *ménage à trois*.

In a romantic triangle, the pivot is in a position of relative structural advantage, but no player is as severely deprived as the pariah in a marriage, so the inducement to cheat is not as strong. The pivot role is the most delicate one to play, with its requirement of being closer to each wing than that wing is to the other wing; the pivot must be perceived by each wing to be fairer than the other wing and even fairer than itself. The role of each wing is to contend with the opposing wing and try to collude with the pivot. In order for the pivot to maintain a balance, it must convince each wing that its collusion with the other is not "malign"; at the same time, however, in order for the pivot to invoke discipline against deviance by either wing it must be able to augment its own strength via collaboration with the opposing wing.[3] If the pivot is perceived to be engaged in malign collusion, the excluded wing almost necessarily gravitates into pariahdom. The disintegration of the American romantic triangle in the mid-1970s calls for further empirical investigation, but seems to have involved both an American "tilt" to the Chinese wing and disequilibrating Soviet gains in the Third World (with Vietnamese and Cuban collaboration), motivated either by (premature) compensation for Sino-American collusion or simple opportunism.[4]

The addition of "extended" security arrangements (e.g., the American base and alliance network, the Soviet external and internal blocs and would-be Collective Security System or All-Asia Forum, China's "united front against hegemonism") seems to complicate triangular dynamics by involving new, autonomous actors without basically altering any of the rules.[5] Each player has an interest in making such arrangements (insofar as resources and power-projection capabilities permit), and each player has a corresponding incentive to force rival players to divest themselves of such augmentations. The tactics employed may be expected to vary, from courtship to punitive war against the client, but in any case the client is treated only as proxy; that is, the internal arrangements and policies of the client are not at issue, only the military presence of the patron. Thus triangular dynamics are extended and perhaps complicated, but not essentially modified. Yet the opportunities and risks to the clients may vary according to the triangular configuration; an adequate investigation of these links remains for future research.

In the case of one actor's deviance the romantic triangle has a propensity to break down to either a marriage or a *ménage à trois,* depending essentially on how much insecurity between the other two is generated by its collapse. The first (Nixon-Kissinger) triangle degenerated into Sino-American marriage amid high anxiety about Soviet behavior, while the second (Sinocentric) triangle shifted to a *ménage* when China's opening to the Soviet Union resulted not in marriage but in a reprise of Soviet-American détente. In either case, the pivot, who was most advantageously situated in the foregoing configuration, remains in a good position, but the shift to a *ménage* marginally reduces the pivot's security while enhancing that of both wings. Yet the pivot may accede to this if overall threat perception is relatively low, because it may result in greater security for all players and hence in a more stable configuration (also because the pivot's control is limited).

The triangle may be characterized in its latest configuration as an emergent *ménage.* It is "emergent" because the configuration is still mixed with residues from its immediate predecessor. There are still occasional indications, for example, of continuing rivalry between the two superpowers, as well as Chinese efforts to play pivot. Yet already some of the new configuration's advantages have become manifest. Aside from removing impediments to commerce and growth in the Pacific, an emergent *ménage* offers low-risk opportunities for relief from heavy military burdens to exhausted superpowers eager to resuscitate declining civilian economies. This configuration is inherently conducive to arms control and disarmament in the sense that while benign collusion is stabilizing, malign collusion is inherently destabilizing, given the secrecy ("jealousy") and menace inherent in security policy. As noted above, the *ménage* thus opens a window of opportunity to resolve a series of world problems hitherto inextricable due to their embroilment in triangular rivalries.

To be sure, certain drawbacks of the *ménage* are also likely to become manifest over time. Clearing the Third World of pointless embroilment in the intrigues of the great powers may also expose the developing countries to a phase of benign neglect, and leave former clients dangling. It is even conceivable, given the willingness of the major powers to sell weaponry to developing countries in order to keep their own arms industries operating efficiently during an era of effective arms control among the powers, that various forms of communal, sectarian, and other internecine violence may erupt in the Third World. Lacking a clear and present danger against which to coordinate security arrangements deprives the triangle of a clear *raison d'être*. There is relatively scant historical basis for establishing rules of the game, and the absence (or ubiquity) of jealousy implies a game without leverage or relative structural advantage for any player or set of players. There is also less basis for leadership in such a configuration, making likely a resort to what communists refer to domestically as "collective leadership," historically associated with rift, vacillation, and deadlock. Although the net benefits to all three participants in terms of available trade, technocultural, and disarmament regimes outweigh those of any easily arranged alternative, a *ménage* seems likely to require skillful and sensitive diplomacy to coordinate activities around a common strategic agenda. Multilateral sensitivity will be required: *every* actor a pivot. Lacking such diplomatic savoir faire, the triangle will tend to disintegrate into anomic multipolarity. Past experience suggests, however, that this would be only an interlude leading back to a more structured configuration—probably either marriage or romantic triangle.

It has been suggested that the Gorbachev-Deng summit marks the "end" of the triangle, and in a sense this is perhaps so. After all, if the triangle is "strategic," it is essentially concerned with security, and if no one threatens anyone else within the triangle, the configuration might be thought to become functionally irrelevant. Such a consummation is devoutly to be wished, but cannot realistically be assumed by prudent security analysts or policy planners. More easily conceivable is that the strategic triangle may temporarily recede from "for itself" to "in itself" status. The relative military capabilities of the three players have not disappeared, but merely become for the time being inconvenient to use, because of the higher stakes industrialization has introduced to the game, the establishment of mutually credible nuclear deterrents, and the self-defeating outcome of competition in the Third World.

Though this is quite speculative, we might hypothesize that the triangle becomes most visible ("for itself") during periods of crisis, when the national security of one or more players is at stake and the logical alternatives present themselves with stark clarity. During a protracted period without crisis, triangular considerations tend to fade from view, defense expenditures appear a thankless burden, and the variables of political economy—trade barriers and balances, GNP growth rates, the international division of labor, product cycles, scientific development—become relevant criteria for the international allocation of prestige. This by no means implies a death of ideology or end of conflict, but these now manifest themselves and are weighed in terms of the relevant currency of the age—GNP growth rates, productivity, trade balances, and so forth. Assuming a sustained avoidance of security crises—perhaps a generous assumption—the triangle undergoes what we might call a "disappearing act": not only do strategic factors give way to the variables of political economy, the triangular powers themselves cede hegemony to militarily less significant merchant nations, such as Japan and the East Asian NIEs.

Yet it is worth bearing in mind that this is only an "act": so long as military capabilities are retained, the strategic triangle still exists, albeit visible only to strategic analysts and planners. The rules of the game also remain logically valid, whether the triangle is "for itself" or only "in itself." There is an ever-present temptation for an actor with well-developed military capabilities to use them to advance its interests, particularly if its civilian economy is not functioning satisfactorily. The transformation of the post-cold war "new world order" since the August 1990 invasion of Kuwait demonstrates how suddenly strategic considerations can reassert themselves.

PART IV

CONCLUSIONS

The purpose of the foregoing has been to bring the reader up to date on the most recent developments in Sino-Soviet relations, but also to go beyond the dispute that has preoccupied us for the past three decades and try to rethink the possibilities implicit in the relationship. It is true that the relationship has been strained longer than it has been friendly, but this is also true of Franco-German relations; that a long border need not imply continual discord is illustrated by modern Canadian-American relations. Relations have already improved quite dramatically over the past decade. The question is: how much can they continue to do so?

This study seeks an explanation for conflict and cooperation, and for the frequent transition from one to the other, in patterns of economic development, the search for national identity, and the struggle for international power and security. Hardly unique in finding that the vicissitudes in the relationship cannot be accounted for by any single variable, it is relatively distinctive in seeking to analyze these in terms of three different perspectives. Such a "prismatic" approach permits greater depth and breadth in tracing the implications of the relationship, bringing into focus for example the close connection between Sino-Soviet relations and Chinese relations with the international communist movement, the Third World, and the United States; the relationship between domestic economic development and foreign policy can also be explored. Each perspective has an inherent logic that can be fully understood only if isolated and pursued systematically. Although no single perspective is sufficient to explain the Protean vicissitudes of the relationship, each has a useful contribution to make.

Our task is now one of synthesis, of putting the puzzle back together. A second question customarily addressed at this point is that of the future: where does the relationship go from here? Let us first review the most recent developments since the achievement of "normalization" in May 1989, then turn to a consideration of the future, based on the three analytical perspectives developed in the preceding chapters.

257

Speculations About the Future

The implications of Sino-Soviet normalization flow not only from the carefully patterned diplomatic and material exchanges that culminated in the May 1989 Beijing summit, but from the overall context of that event, both planned and fortuitous. As it happened, the meeting coincided with other epochal events. While the summit proceeded more or less as planned and was deemed a success by both parties, these events placed it in a quite different framework from what had been originally intended. Particularly portentous were two occurrences, which were also causally interrelated. The first was the student-led Chinese democracy movement at Tiananmen, which climaxed in a brutal crackdown by PLA troops on the night of June 3–4, leaving at least several hundred demonstrators dead.[1] The second is the breaching of the Berlin Wall, in the wake of similar such demonstrations aggravated by a mass exodus of East Germans to the West, resulting in the de facto fall of the iron curtain in Eastern Europe.

These two events symptomize a systemic crisis of legitimacy for international socialism, as a result of its failure to achieve either revolution in the industrialized countries theoretically most eligible for revolution, or transition to the communist utopia in those countries where communist parties had seized power prematurely.[2] This legitimacy crisis was so acute, or the party-states' control mechanisms had fallen into such disrepair, that mass insurrections could no longer be prevented by mere manipulation of symbols. The responses of the Chinese and East German party authorities to these mass upheavals illustrate the two logically alternative ways of dealing with them. The CCP opted (after half-hearted and inconclusive efforts at negotiation) to use lethal force to crush the protests, the East German SED chose to make significant concessions, including a purge of Honecker's hard-line leadership on October 17 and an opening of the wall on November 9. When similar crises struck other socialist polities later in the fall and winter of 1989–90, local authorities would select from this two-policy repertoire. Thus the Hungarians, Poles, Czechoslovaks, and Bulgarians all opted for the East German "model"; only the Romanian Communist Party under Ceausescu opted for the Chinese response (albeit unsuccessfully).

The reason this particular array of alternatives presented itself is simple: Although East European developments have their own causal chain, the Chinese event occurred first (Gorbachev was himself a bystander at the Tiananmen protests), and when other communist parties were subsequently challenged by their own citizenry, they defined themselves in terms of whether or not to resort to the "Chinese solution." It was not unusual for the leadership to split over this issue—as, for example, in East Germany, where Honecker left explicit instructions to crack down hard on demonstrators in Leipzig, only to be countermanded by an insurgent Politburo majority led by Egon Krenz. Once the leadership split, the outcome depended on whether the conservatives could command the necessary power to enforce their preferred decision. The CCP leadership had also split concerning the invocation of martial law on May 20, but in this case the conservative majority was able to command the necessary force to purge the Zhao Ziyang contingent and crush popular dissent. The East European regimes could not command a reliable domestic instrument of political violence. In the crunch, their legitimacy proved to be essentially derivative. Ultimately decisive in determining the outcome was therefore not the indigenous party leadership, but Soviet patronage. And as matters unfolded, the Soviet leadership adopted what Gerasimov (spokesman for Foreign Minister Shevardnadze) facetiously referred to as a "Sinatra doctrine": "Let them do it their way." This "doctrine" had been formulated as early as 1987 (see Chapter 6) and oft reiterated, but not until the crisis erupted in the fall of 1989 was it possible to tell whether it would supersede the Brezhnev Doctrine in practice.

Gorbachev not only refrained from intervening militarily in support of the beleaguered regimes, but warned incumbent conservatives of the need for reform and otherwise conveyed sympathy for the protesters' demands. Reportedly one major factor in his decision was his distaste for the "Chinese solution," based partly on his own peripheral involvement in that event. Gorbachev's visit to Beijing on May 15–18 was enthusiastically hailed by the democracy demonstrators (though they blocked him from the Square). Indeed, his arrival seemed to revive the flagging protest movement, either because of his reputation as a forthright reformer (in contrast to Deng's more equivocal stance) or due to the international media attention he attracted—giving protesters the opportunity to grab the spotlight. In their preparations for the summit, the Soviet side had seemed eager to inflate its significance, the Chinese more interested in playing it down. Thus Beijing sought to deflect any suggestion of ideological kinship with the Soviet Union during this period, cut the size of Gorbachev's entourage from 1,000 to 300, held the reception to "moderate scale," stipulated that greetings be limited to shaking hands rather than embracing, and rejected the Soviet proposal to issue a "joint communiqué" on the normalization of relations. No agreements or breakthroughs on major issues were announced at the meeting's conclusion. Gorbachev diplomatically held his tongue concerning the protests that disrupted his visit, and even after the massacre said nothing publicly that might be construed as criticism.[3] Yet he seems to have been moved by the demonstrators, or at least alerted to the political payoff available to a politician able to deal more flexibly with masses aroused by reformist aspirations. His initial reaction came in Bonn, some ten days after the crackdown, when he said that he regretted "some aspects of what has happened" in China; during his visit he had received letters from the demonstrating students, and many of their concerns seemed legitimate. Several conservative East European regimes on the other hand expressed forthright support for the CCP's Draconian measures: the GDR on June 12, Bulgaria June 19, Czechoslovakia June 20.[4] So far as Sino-Soviet relations are concerned, the atmospherics reversed after the crackdown, with the Chinese seeking to play up the visit's significance (to twit the West, for decrying human rights abuses and imposing economic sanctions) and the Soviets playing it down.[5] Messages to the Soviet leadership became unusually fulsome and warm.

Sino-Soviet relations since the summit may be divided into two stages. In the first stage, from June to October 1989, the Soviet Union seemed likely to reap windfall profits from Beijing's indignant response to Western sanctions. While Western trade and investment slumped amid Chinese tirades against "Western imperialism," "peaceful evolution," "monopoly capitalist circles," and so forth for having incited the disturbances, Sino-Soviet trade turnover expanded to 2.4 billion rubles (U.S. $3.95 billion) for the year. And while Western sanctions were mild and temporary, and channels in fact remained opened for unofficial (and secret) visits, no socialist country imposed sanctions of any kind. Gorbachev rebuffed Sakharov when this renowned dissident called for a statement in the Supreme Soviet condemning the June 4 violence.

During the second stage, from October 1989 through March 1990, relations frayed in the light of Chinese criticisms—never public, but widely circulated within the CCP—of Gorbachev for "deviating from the path of socialism," by promoting reforms that exposed the bloc to the forces of "peaceful evolution." The CCP leadership was particularly disturbed by the fall of the Bucharest regime and execution of the Ceausescus in early December, and convened a series of Politburo meetings in which Deng, Li Peng, and Jiang Zemin vied in denouncing Gorbachev and even predicting his imminent political demise.[6] How the CCP could logically have expected the CPSU to react differently to the East European upheavals is moot, inasmuch as its own criticism of the Brezhnev

Doctrine and the whole notion of "socialist hegemonism" had contributed in no small measure to the evolution of a more latitudinarian intrabloc policy. The point, of course, is that Gorbachev's contrasting reaction to a situation roughly analogous to Tiananmen amounted to a subtle repudiation of the crackdown. China was no less susceptible to the demonstration effect of emancipation in Eastern Europe than the Baltic republics or Outer Mongolia, making Gorbachev's survival hazardous to the political health of the hard-line Beijing regime.

Which option will prove politically correct remains to be seen. Certainly the CCP's hard line incurred at least temporary economic costs in terms of international trade, tourism, loans, and investment, which the USSR has successfully avoided. But the Soviet Union has yet to profit from a massive influx of Western aid or investment, and the international component of either nation's economy is still too marginal for this to be decisive. The Soviet soft line seems to have enhanced the international reputation of Gorbachev's "new thinking," but not without cost: from a strictly military perspective the loss of Eastern Europe and reunification of Germany exacerbates the security risk in the West, and the departure of these countries from the Soviet orbit has had a mischievous effect on the minority Soviet republics, enticing a number of them to take steps toward secession.

Economically we have a balance of losses: the Chinese seem to have reduced (but not yet eliminated) the rate of inflation, but only by so drastically slowing their economy that unemployment and stagnation may come to represent a greater political threat than inflation. The Soviet economy, ensnared in the toils of "partial reform," has gone into a tailspin culminating in zero or even negative growth in 1989–91.[7] Neither country is moving aggressively ahead in economic reform at this point; indeed, China has taken several steps backward since June 1989 (while denying it). And although political reform seems to have gained considerable momentum in the Soviet Union (in rather stark contrast to the PRC), its future is clouded by the prospect of disintegration and the lack of any palpable economic payoff or consensus on how to achieve one in the foreseeable future.

The immediate impact of this divergence on Sino-Soviet relations has been at least mildly adverse: as in 1956, relations seemed to go into a downward spiral amid Chinese feelings of ideological betrayal. As in the 1950s, disagreement over Soviet custody of Eastern Europe proved an early sore point, bringing to the surface an old Chinese ambivalence about the relative priority of independence versus conformity; as in the 1950s, the Chinese began by advocating looser reins, only to urge a severe lashing when the horse threatens to bolt. If Tiananmen is the future of reform, Gorbachev wants nothing to do with it; if Eastern Europe and Lithuania are the ultimate destination of reform, the CCP would rather bail out. Each alternative represents the other's worst nightmare.

Yet over the longer term the current contretemps may loom less large. Neither country is possessed by the dogmatic self-assurance they shared in the 1950s and 1960s, and uncertainty may impart greater tolerance. Thus although the Chinese have criticized the Soviet "subversion of socialism," Jiang Zemin repeated in December 1989 that "While China cannot but show concern over the development of the situation in socialist countries, it will not interfere in the internal affairs." [8] Notwithstanding the repudiation of the leading role of the communist party by the East European former satellites, followed by elections in many of them in which the communist party dwindled to minority status, Beijing retained amicable relations with all—perhaps inspired by fear that they would otherwise recognize Taiwan, as they had just recognized South Korea (they covet new investment). But this is also logical: Any criticism of the Soviets or the East Europeans would violate the principle of noninterference in the domestic affairs of other countries that China uses to disqualify foreign condemnation of Tiananmen. This principle, once deemed incompatible with proletarian internationalism, is now at the heart of Gorbachev's "new political thinking," and has been adhered to in Eastern Europe as well despite tumultuous change there. Even countries like Poland and Hungary uphold the principle of noninterference despite their harsh critique of the bloodshed in Beijing.

Both the PRC and the USSR are now more preoccupied with economic prosperity than with ideological verities or security concerns, placing a premium on cooperation. Thus when Li Peng visited Moscow in April 1990, the first visit of a Chinese premier since 1961, he seems to have had a strained (marred by protests, like the summit) but on the whole successful trip. Again refusing to sign a joint communiqué, and emphasizing that the Soviet model of economic and political change did not apply to China, he nonetheless signed a ten-year agreement on economic and scientific cooperation focusing on the high-tech proficiency that both countries need—in nuclear energy and outer space, fuel and power industries, and environmental protection. Agreements were also signed for a long-term Soviet credit for China to build two power engineering facilities, in return for $735 million in short-term Chinese credits to provide Soviet consumers with textiles and light industrial products.[9] Trade continues to flourish (see Figure 3), and the first meeting

FIGURE 3. Chinese Trade with the Soviet Union, the United States, and Japan 1989–1990.

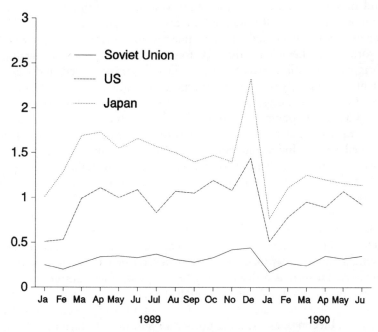

SOURCE: *China Statistics Monthly* No. 9 (December 1989): p. 62, No. 5 (August 1990): p. 64.

of military experts was held in November 1989 in Moscow to discuss mutual border force reductions, each side well aware of the advantages of cooperation.[10] It is true that Tiananmen and Eastern Europe have momentarily impeded their convergence as well as placing obstacles in the way of further reform, but the damage may be remediable.

Thus the future relationship of the two countries hangs in the balance together with their domestic developmental prospects. To help sort out these prospects, we return to the analytical perspectives developed in previous chapters.

Three Standpoints

The conceptualization of national identity adopted here assumes that a new nation-state requires an international reference group with which it can identify in learning how to comport itself in the international system. The PRC was somewhat unusual in having not one but two international reference groups, one of which served as an ideological and developmental model, the other as a model of unfair victimization and motivational resource base for "continuous revolution." The former helped to strengthen the regime's legitimacy; the latter provided a forum and clientele for the PRC to exercise international leadership. Originally no split between reference groups was perceived, and China identified intensely with both, arranging them into a hierarchical order that fit revolutionary stage theory (i.e., today's Third World would, via revolution, "graduate" into tomorrow's bloc). But China's preceptoral role was co-opted in the mid-1950s by the Soviet Union and (to a more limited extent) India, inducing China to redefine its role and its following in increasingly exclusive terms. The domestic failures of the late 1950s also came into play, leading the Maoist leadership to infer that revolutionary purity was incompatible with material satisfaction ("goulash"), and that virtue coincided with self-abnegation. Embracing a relatively extreme form of revolutionary asceticism, the nation pursued growth through very high rates of capital accumulation and frozen living standards, reproaching those who consumed a higher share of the material surplus as backsliding "revisionists." This austere identity could be accepted only under a high degree of social constraint that stultified other necessary aspects of development (e.g., education, science, and technology), leading post-Mao reformers to turn their backs on radical Maoism in favor of a more tolerant attitude toward intellectual diversity and mass consumption. Yet the tendency to identify with the developed Western democracies that had realized the highest living standards—to believe that the moon is not only brighter but rounder in the West—was also considered dangerous, tending to fuel discontent with the political status quo. Identification with liberal bourgeois democracies was thus repressed, most recently (and emphatically) at Tiananmen. Since then China has been seeking alternative reference groups, with a noticeable proclivity for "old friends."

Identification with the developing countries was far less threatening from the perspective of the political-cultural demonstration effect, and few Third World countries have criticized China for human rights abuses. Thus there has been a strenuous effort to improve relations with the Third World in the aftermath of Tiananmen. Li Peng made his first official visit after Tiananmen to Nepal, Bangladesh, and Pakistan. President Yang Shangkun visited Egypt and other Arabic countries in his first official visit after the crackdown, and toured Latin America in 1990. China has even taken a more flexible stance toward Third

World countries with which it has no formal diplomatic relations, such as Israel (in 1990 China opened a tourism office in Tel Aviv, and Israel opened an "academic liaison office" in Beijing). The Thai prime minister made an official visit in 1989, and Indonesia finally reestablished formal diplomatic ties in June 1990, opening the way to diplomatic links with Singapore.[11] Yet whether this represents anything more than an "any port in a storm" panic reaction to Beijing's ostracism from the West remains to be seen. Identification with the developing countries is in a sense inauthentic, for these nations represent China's past, not "models" of its future. Reciprocal admiration has also tended to cool somewhat since the 1970s, partly due to a decline in PRC aid, partly because of China's rather self-serving use of this identity to compete for markets, tariff exemption, and aid.

We have noted that Chinese identification with the communist bloc countries has revived since the recent advent of reform, though there is no clear notion of what socialism is any more, and the only joint project that unites them is the transformation of a Leninist organizational apparatus they have all grown more or less dissatisfied with. Amid this confusion the anxieties brought to a focus by Tiananmen seem to have reopened the geopolitical cleft of the 1960s between European and Asian communism, in which ideological leanings tend to coincide with geography. China might, in its earlier, reform incarnation, have been expected to follow the East Europeans in establishing diplomatic relations with South Korea, for example, or at least the Soviet Union in exchanging consular offices with Seoul (now upgraded to formal recognition as well). In the wake of Tiananmen, it is Sino–North Korean relations that have grown closer. When Kim Il Sung made a secret visit to China in the fall of 1989, Deng Xiaoping himself reportedly met him at the train station. While vociferously denying that China is a conceivable reference point, Vietnam has also taken a more conservative position since Nguyen Van Linh's experiments with economic reform (doi moi), launched at the Sixth CPV Congress in 1986, precipitated a bout of inflation.[12] Even the nonruling Asian communist parties (e.g., the Nepalese Communist Party, the Communist Party of India-Marxist) take an ideological position substantially to the left of their European compatriots.[13]

The ideological position of the nonruling communist parties in Asian democracies may be pushed to the left of the spectrum by the relatively socialist orientation of their mainstream electoral competitors, the class divisions in their societies, and their backward economies, but the geopolitical cleavage between relatively "revisionist" ruling parties in Europe and more orthodox parties in Asia may be somewhat more artificial. Many of the Asia ruling parties are afflicted with a "gerontocratic overhang," consisting of revered veteran revolutionaries with a diehard commitment to first-generation values. In Korea, Kim Il Sung has achieved perhaps the longest incumbency of any ruler in the twentieth century, having insured himself against a coup via the world's most overblown "personality cult" and by selecting a weak and unpopular heir apparent (his son, Kim Jong Il). In the PRC and the SRV, the senior veterans have officially retired, but their political influence remains potent, enabling them to enjoy power without responsibility. Like the erstwhile Sino-Soviet rift, the geopolitical split between Asia and Europe may hence be the temporary artifact of prolonged generational succession in the Asian parties.

What does the national identity perspective suggest about the future of Sino-Soviet relations? Inasmuch as that perspective is derived from psychoanalysis and developmental psychology, it seems legitimate for heuristic purposes to extrapolate hypotheses from the study of the individual to the study of the group—with the proviso, to be sure, that these will require empirical testing in their new context. A country's quest for national identity (in this case the PRC's) might be seen to follow a path roughly analogous to that of a maturing individual, beginning with a "childhood" of intense, unquestioning identification with a selected reference group, followed by an "adolescence" of no less intense ambivalence, when the new nation spurns chosen reference groups for having "betrayed" the ideals they once stood for and resolves that only the new nation itself can fully realize its own identity. This *Sturm und Drang* is eventually superseded by "maturity," entailing acceptance of the need to compromise with given realities and to adhere to conventional limits, with less reliance on external reference groups and greater confidence in a now more fully integrated sense of identity. Assuming that Reform China has reached "maturity," as many of the features of post-Mao foreign policy would lead one to assume, what can we infer from this model about the future of Sino-Soviet relations? These relations should become increasingly rational and based on the coordination of mutual national interests rather than on transcendental conceptions of class, ideology, or bloc foreign policy. In the context of growing pragmatism and rational self-interest, both of China's reference groups will tend to fade in significance (or be manipulated cynically on behalf of instrumental needs). Members of both groups will be treated with symbolic deference but declining intimacy.

Even if this sort of freehand extrapolation from individual to collective entities is dismissed, the empirical study of national identity affords certain broad negative generalizations about China's future vis-à-vis the Soviet Union. First, some sort of international crusade, based on a misplaced or exaggerated identification with external reference groups (e.g., Aryans, the international working class), can probably be ruled out. This much can be inferred from political experience with other such cases. This would mean specifically that a reconstitution of a joint policy-making Sino-Soviet alliance, or some regrouping of radical regimes in the Third World as a basis for pooling foreign policy efforts, is probably not in the cards.

Second, certain developmental propensities become more likely than others. Once established, a national identity may be expected to crystalize expectations for the future, as material and ideal interests become attached to given patterns of identification. Given our assumption that China has undergone a process of maturation this would normally have a stabilizing effect, and indeed we have already drawn attention to recent regime efforts to bolster commitment to old reference groups. However, in view of the unprecedented changes that have swept the communist "bloc" and (to only slightly lesser degree) the Third World, China finds itself adrift without accustomed international bearings, amid an incipient domestic succession crisis. Thus, whereas at this moment the country's identity seems secure, China may be sitting on another national identity crisis, of which Tiananmen was the first but not the last manifestation.

Third, the claim to Taiwan and other irredenta has been firmly incorporated into the national identity and will not be "outgrown" in the process of maturation, but persist like a scar; it is even conceivable that the regime may resort to violence over such issues (cf. the March 1988 clash over the Spratlys), even though this might be considered irrational on a means-end calculus. Of course, there are different ways that this identity might be achieved, ranging from centralized dictatorship to a loose confederation or common market. But this is not necessarily to say that these irredentist claims are valid or will *ever* be realized, only that they will remain a nagging presence. Thanks to Soviet flexibility on the border issue and the progressive withdrawal of troops from Outer Mongolia, irredentist claims now mar only the Sino-American relationship (the Sino-Indian dispute also lingers, but there India is the aggrieved party).

In security terms the geopolitical region of greater East Asia may be characterized as a triangle among three major powers, which may logically assume one of four conceivable configurations. And the triangle has in due course run the gamut, from *ménage* through various forms of marriage, romantic triangle, and unit-veto system. Although every configuration but the unit-veto system has at least one beneficiary, some configurations rank above others in terms of the collective goods they allocate to the three players. If the three players act in their own rational long-term interests and learn from their experience with the various available prior configurations, those configurations that allocate fewest collective goods are less likely to recur or to be sustained, while those that allocate the most collective goods are more likely to do so. In this light, guarded optimism is perhaps warranted that the present *ménage* may sustain itself longer than one might otherwise anticipate in view of its relatively anomic political structure.

The *ménage* presupposes the suspension or balancing of strategic threats among the three players, and the triangle may hence be expected to remain in its current configuration until one player opts to threaten another, either directly or indirectly (via proxy), singly or in concert with a third. All three players are currently burdened by relatively heavy, chronic budget deficits, and concerned about economic competition from other countries with lighter defense burdens, in the context of which the likelihood of military attack or even a military buildup to threaten such an attack can perhaps be discounted for the foreseeable future. There is still the possibility of confrontation resulting from the escalation of proxy conflict, as in Korea, Vietnam, or Cambodia, but the chances of negotiating such contradictions are better in a *ménage* than in a unit-veto triangle, marriage, or a romantic triangle. This configuration is generally conducive to arms control and disarmament regimes, which may conceivably even replace the arms race as a means of adjusting the military balance within the triangle. Should one player refuse to join an arms control regime, this would provide an inducement, other things remaining equal, for the other two players to join in marriage in order to nullify the strategic advantage that would otherwise accrue to the holdout.

If the present *ménage* should nonetheless phase out, either because of perceived threat or the quest for enhanced security through combination, relapse to a previous configuration is predictable. Which one? The abstract logic of the triangle provides few clues. Caplow, whose analysis of this logic has been outstanding, places heavy emphasis on the power factor in predicting the shape of the configuration; thus in a 3–2–1 distribution of power, he would predict a marriage between 2 and 1 against 3. Any other combination would not enhance 3's capability to prevail over the third player any more than 3 would have acting alone, reducing its incentive to "pay" much for it.[14] This logic may help to explain the shift to the Sino-Soviet marriage in 1949–50, but otherwise does not take us very far, for the power ratio among members of our triangle has remained roughly constant throughout the postwar era (United States = 3, Soviet Union = 2, China = 1), yet the triangle has exhausted every conceivable permutation. If we modify this logic to take into account perceptions of strength and projections of growth curves, it takes us further, permitting us to hypothesize that relatively conspicuous growth in power by any actor can contribute to the collapse of a given configuration.[15] Yet this modification, aside from depriving the relative power explanation of its hard precision, cannot explain China's 1959 defection from the Sino-Soviet marriage for a strategically irrational opposition to both superpowers, nor can it explain the romantic triangle, which seems based less on relative power than on the manipulation of mutual hostility. Since China acquired a "hard" (survivable) second-strike nuclear capability in the late 1960s, the three actors may be deemed roughly equal in their strategic deterrent capabilities, and they have also become more equal in conventional military power; thus the relevance of the power factor is further mitigated.

The strategic triangle has not yet been developed to the point where it affords clear and certain predictions of the sequence of configurations. Our analysis has hence focused less on abstract necessity than on a political analysis of the actors in the foregoing configuration—not only their objective power, but their perceptions of relative power and future potential in the context of quite variable ideologies and national ambitions. Based on such an analysis, if the current *ménage* disintegrates, the triangle seems likely to evolve in one of three conceivable directions.

(1) The post-Tiananmen ostracism of China, plus the post-cold war cordiality between the two superpowers, raises the prospect of condominium, or Soviet-American marriage, based partly on a value consensus on democracy and *perestroika*, partly on a pooling of super power to govern the "new world order."[16] This possibility is contingent on three factors. First, the continuation of progress in strategic disarmament; otherwise, the structural importance of these two enormous nuclear arsenals facing each other will sow distrust. Second, the irrationality of China, in allowing itself to gravitate to the position of pariah opposing two superior adversaries. China needs a certain level of hostility toward the outside world to rationalize domestic repression, but seems aware of the folly of needlessly isolating itself, and has made skilled use of the Gulf crisis to divest itself of remaining international sanctions. Third,

the tenability of Soviet-American marriage depends on Soviet ability to derive tangible advantage from its opening to the West, either in the form of direct aid and investment (which has not been forthcoming), or in the form of a model of market capitalism and democracy that can regenerate a stricken Soviet economy. Thus far, the opening has entailed only losses, as many Soviets perceive it, and the model has not proved readily adaptable or useful.

(2) A Moscow-centered romantic triangle is possible, in view of recent improvements in Soviet-American relations, and a certain deterioration in Sino-American relations, over such issues as trade and human rights. It is true that for a short period in 1989 Moscow appeared to have better relations with Beijing and Washington than these two had with each other. Yet this contingency would assume Chinese and American strategic irrationality. There is no great conflict of interest between these two powers, beyond certain ideological differences, and both seem aware of the stupidity of allowing their differences to be exacerbated to the point where they could be manipulated by a *tertius gaudens*.

(3) A reconstituted Sino-Soviet marriage is conceivable if their economies should both go into such a decline that combination was deemed necessary to offset the threat to each of a more dynamic U.S. economic and military threat. It is true that both China and the Soviet Union experienced recessions of varying magnitude at the end of the 1980s. Yet the U.S. economy has also had its difficulties, and long-term growth rates seem unlikely to enhance American superiority significantly. At this writing, although the *ménage* has been buffeted by increasing strain, it does not yet appear likely to give way to one of these alternative configurations.

The developmental perspective used in Part I focused on the general theory of convergence. Perhaps unsurprisingly, it seems most effective in making sense of the periods of Sino-Soviet cooperation, and least effective in explaining why cooperation was interrupted. In 1950–60 and in the 1980s, a neofunctional logic was effective in fusing the two countries together. Although the Chinese later complained that the terms of the exchange were to their disadvantage, they seem to have been the net beneficiaries of the arrangement in material terms. Thus the interruption of the relationship is not really explicable in economic-developmental terms, so far as we could determine. Although the two systems could both survive the truncation of trade and other forms of exchange and even launch diverging patterns of economic development, neither realized any tangible advantage from doing so. There are contrariwise mutual benefits in economic cooperation; while these have been plausibly deprecated in view of various environmental and infrastructural difficulties, the potential has never been fully explored, due to political obstacles now largely removed, and may bear more fruit than expected.

Both the Soviet Union and China have, however, experienced a crisis of confidence in system legitimacy in the last several years, and both have invested in "reform" as a way of rectifying systemic economic inadequacies, though this has expressed itself in different forms. There are two types of reform: economic reform, consisting of some combination of marketization and privatization; and political reform, consisting of some form of democratization plus civil rights. Most communist regimes have adopted one or the other type of reform, but not many have adopted both. The choices the leading systems have made at this writing (and needless to say, all are still very much in flux) sort themselves out as illustrated below. (The German Democratic Republic is excluded from this comparison because it is not a separate state but a portion of a state, now dissolved into the Federal Republic.)

Economic Reform

		Yes	No
Political Reform	Yes	Hungary Poland Czechoslovakia	USSR
	No	PRC SRV	Cuba North Korea

The PRC and the USSR are at this point at obverse quadrants—the former having made considerable progress in economic reform but very little in political reform, the latter having forged ahead politically while remaining in the doldrums in economic reform. While in theory this constitutes a complementary relationship, in fact it has engendered a certain amount of tension that occasionally threatens to derail their convergence. If socioeconomic convergence is conducive to politically amicable relations, the differences between the two systems should ideally be reduced if Sino-Soviet relations are to continue to improve. This might be done in several different ways. The options are depicted in the contingency table.

Bilateral Implications of Socialist Reform

	USSR		PRC	
	Political Reform	Economic Reform	Political Reform	Economic Reform
1	yes	yes	yes	yes
2	yes	no	yes	yes
3	no	yes	yes	yes
4	no	no	yes	yes
5	yes	yes	yes	no
6	yes	no	yes	no
7	no	yes	yes	no
8	no	no	yes	no
9	yes	yes	no	yes
10	yes	no	no	yes
11	no	yes	no	yes
12	no	no	no	yes
13	yes	yes	no	no
14	yes	no	no	no
15	no	yes	no	no
16	no	no	no	no

All told, there are no fewer than sixteen logically conceivable combinations. The status quo (row 10) —in which the Soviet Union is engaged in political but not economic reform, while China pursues economic but not political reform—can be dismissed from discussion, not because it is not possible but because it is not an option but a fact. Seven other options (rows 3, 5, 6, 7, 8, 11, and 15) can be eliminated based on the premise that a *complete* transformation by either actor (in the case of China, for example, from "yes" on economic reform and "no" on political reform to "no" on economic reform and "yes" on political reform) is just not credible.[17] This leaves us with eight credible options, which may be grouped into four categories: positive convergence, divergence, negative convergence, and asymmetrical mixes.

First, there is one positive scenario (row 1), in which both China and the Soviet Union consummate the reform process, with China moving toward political reform, perhaps under a successor generation of leadership, while the Soviet Union makes a breakthrough to successful economic reform. The two systems face different obstacles on their way to completion. For the Soviet Union, the introduction of market reforms and privatization to a complex industrialized economy that has been socialized to operate according to central planning for more than a generation must be assumed to be far more complex than China's quasi marketization of the relatively primitive agricultural and service sectors of its economy. For the Chinese, the task of political democratization will also prove very difficult in the context of one of the world's oldest and proudest authoritarian political traditions, which lacks alternative political organizations capable of holding the nation together should the CCP collapse or splinter, has a tendency toward factionalism that greatly complicates attempts at formal organization, and also has anarchic tendencies that impede the institutionalization of mass participation. Perhaps one reason for the diverging pattern that reform has taken in the two systems is that each has postponed until last the aspect of reform that is most difficult for that system. If the two should nonetheless succeed in reforming while somehow still maintaining their socialist identity, the impact on the world could be enormous. Relations between them might then be expected to prosper greatly, based not only on trade complementarity but on the sharing of different experiences in realizing a common vision. Relations with the West might also be expected to improve, as functional economic relations are supplemented by continuing convergence and reciprocal learning between socialist and laissez-faire systems.

Second, there are two possibilities (one for each country) of divergent development (rows 4 and 13): one system reduces the strain of partial reform by completing the reform process, while the other resolves that tension by reverting to orthodoxy. Which one would do which is very difficult to predict at this stage: over the past several years, the two countries have alternated in their apparent propensity to complete reform. Should only one succeed in doing so, that system is likely to move to the forefront of what remains of the international communist movement, perhaps even give it new life. Divergent development, however, seems likely to exacerbate tension between the reformist and the antireformist system.

Third, there is the distinct prospect of negative convergence (row 16), in which both systems repudiate reform and regress to some form of centrally planned dictatorship. For the Soviet Union, this might involve a Politburo coup with the support of the military and the KGB (whose dissatisfaction with the consequences of reform has been palpable for some time); or it might simply involve a declaration of martial law by the incumbent leadership. The prodemocracy forces in the Soviet Union have always been politically cautious, the legislative organs are still manipulable by the executive, and if a crackdown should occur—say, in Lithuania—an "inner emigration" seems more likely than massive protests. The Soviet army is still the largest in the world, and there is little question that it could make short work of any conceivable domestic resistance (true, at the cost of temporarily damaged popularity abroad). For the PRC, regression would involve return to a command economy. There have already been some tendencies in this direction since June 1989, in the form of the strengthening of the central planning apparatus, subsidization of the state-owned sector, and a crackdown on private enterprise, via intensified tax collection along with the selective withholding of credit.[18] Should there be simultaneous regression, involving economic retrenchment in China and political reaction in the Soviet Union (an outcome that Chinese conservatives would welcome, to judge from their wishful thinking about the fall of Gorbachev), this would still offer certain undeniable advantages: socialism would again have a clearly definable content, old organizational loyalties and constituencies would be properly rewarded (instead of allowing wealth and power to pass into the hands of the former "class enemy"), and it might even be possible to revive some form of bloc foreign policy.

Yet there are serious obstacles in the way of this solution. First, of course, it would forfeit the good will that the communist world has gained among uncommitted forces in the more economically advanced countries of the Third World, and portend a shift back to the support of the more severely deprived (hence more revolutionary) countries in the so-called Fourth World—who would make claims on depleted socialist budgets for both developmental aid and security assistance. Second, whether in China or the Soviet Union, the conservatives seem devoid of ideas on how to resuscitate the vitality of the centrally planned economy. Both systems experienced the problem of gradually declining rates of growth before launching their varied experiments with reform, and neither has discovered any effective alternative way of coping with this. To return to central planning at the cost of a drop of several percentage points in GNP growth rate would amount to an admission of defeat, giving rise to a legitimacy crisis that could be kept under control only through heftily increased expenditures on military and domestic security forces. This would be likely to revive the cold war and the arms race with the West, further escalating such expenditures.

Finally, there are four asymmetrically mixed scenarios (rows 2, 9, 12, and 14) in which one system either completes or disavows reform while the other remains locked in partial reform. If we assume that the system that has committed itself one way or the other is likely to exert pressure on the other to do likewise, these mixes may be divided into two subtypes: positive momentum mixes (rows 2 and 9), in which one country is fully committed to reform while the other is engaged only in political (or economic) reform (but not both); and negative momentum mixes (rows 12 and 14), in which one system forswears reform while the other remains partly reformed. The assumption is that other things being equal, momentum will be set by the preponderant direction of movement, an assumption that seems consistent with the fact that both are in the same reference group. But all other things may not be equal: if economic reform in the partly reformed system should prove conspicuously successful, for example, that system might be expected to exert magnetism on the antireform system.

These asymmetrical mixes beg the whole question of the relationship between political and economic reform. This question is complex, and remains to be more thoroughly investigated empirically. The Chinese reformers and Soviet reformers alike contended that political reform was a prerequisite for meaningful economic reform, but others have countered that political reform can only make economic reform impossible: such unpopular but necessary measures as price reform, they argue, require strong authority. Only after economic reform has been given a certain forward momentum can political reform be initiated. Yet successful economic reform does not necessarily lead to political reform. The New Economic System in East Germany, for example, was so successful from 1963 to 1970 that Honecker could afford to put an end to it in 1970; and the success of the Chinese reform movement in 1979–89 enabled conservatives to focus criticism on its failings and argue that it was unnecessary to proceed further.

Based on our comparison of the reform experience in China and the Soviet Union, we would propose the following chain of contingencies. On the one hand, economic reform is a necessary condition for political reform, in the sense that the latter will eventually be compromised by an unsatisfactory economic performance. This is the dilemma now faced by the Soviet leadership. On the other hand, political reform is also a necessary condition for economic reform in the sense that without it, an unreconstructed leadership will tend to rescind reforms and retreat to familiar nostrums whenever the situation becomes painful. This is currently the case in the PRC. Communist elites seem to adopt economic reforms if they think they will raise GNP or per capita income, and to adopt political reforms if economic reforms fail. If economic reforms succeed, on the other hand, they are likely to generate mass demands for political reform, which communist elites are likely to greet more warily. If economic reforms fail in the context of elite-sponsored political reforms, the latter are apt to be rescinded. The progress of economic reform is constrained by its inherent difficulty plus bureaucratic resistance; the progress of political reform is impeded by elite vested interests and by the lack of institutionalized alternatives to the status quo.

In view of the complexity and mutually frustrating character of this set of contingencies, there are two economic programs that will bear close scrutiny over the next several years. One is the attempt at radical price and property reform now sweeping Eastern Europe, most notably Poland. The other is China's recentralization and reaffirmation of revolutionary values in the context of economic retrenchment. Should both policies succeed in regenerating a respectable growth rate without excessive inflation and other dislocations, the cleavage between Asian and European communism may be expected to widen further. But if one approach succeeds while the other fails, the former may well define the future of international communism. Should both fail or achieve only indifferent success, the picture is likely to remain clouded for some time to come.

This "conclusion" has deliberately avoided any single-factor explanation or univocal forecast. In view of the great flux currently prevailing in the communist world, there is in fact an unusually wide array of options available to the people living in those systems, and to ignore these possibilities for the sake of intellectual closure represents neither good science nor political insight. It seems the better part of valor at the current juncture to try to define the situation as clearly as possible, and to map out the logical consequences of the various alternatives that flow from it, rather than trying artificially to foreclose options that are still realistically possible.

All things considered, it seems more likely than not that Sino-Soviet relations will continue to improve for the foreseeable future. This likelihood may be enhanced by the prospect of socioeconomic convergence or troubled by divergence, but the relationship also has an intrinsic value aside from its symbolic utility in bolstering domestic legitimacy by facilitating identification with a common reference group. Certainly if the two should come to see one another as threatening vital national security interests, relations could nosedive, but both seem to have realized the futility of an indefinite arms race along their common border, and the advantages of investing that money elsewhere. The intrinsic value of the relationship has to do with economic growth, particularly in regions that tend to suffer neglect without cooperation, and the practical reciprocal benefits each can contribute to that effort. These benefits were spelled out earlier and need not be recapitulated.

It seems plausible to assume that the exhaustion of the dispute after nearly three decades of wrangling involved a learning process. If so, that should reduce the probability that conflict will be regenerated, at least by those issues that precipitated it in the past that in retrospect appear specious or intractable. How continued Sino-Soviet détente affects relations with the United States will depend very much on the way it occurs. Positive convergence offers the rosiest prospect, of course, and negative convergence the bleakest, while divergence will tempt Washington with another marriage.

Notes

Introduction

1. L. M. Karakhan was the acting commissar for foreign affairs under the new Soviet regime, whose declaration the Soviets subsequently reconstrued as a basis for negotiation only. For the text of the Karakhan Declaration, see Allen S. Whiting, *Soviet Policies in China, 1917–1924* (New York: Columbia University Press, 1954), pp. 269–71. See also Dennis J. Doolin, *Territorial Claims in the Sino-Soviet Conflict* (Stanford: Hoover Institution, 1965), pp. 14–16.

2. The pretext at the time was that the USSR was establishing only a temporary protectorate. Thus Soviet Foreign Minister Grigorii Zinoviev said in 1925 that "Outer Mongolia would return to China when the Chinese will have liberated themselves from their oppressors." David J. Dallin, *Soviet Foreign Policy After Stalin* (Philadelphia: J. P. Lippincott, 1961), p. 75. Thus when Mao enunciated the same expectation in 1936, this was not necessarily an act of insubordinate nationalism. See Klaus Mehnert, *Peking to Moscow* (New York: Mentor Books, 1964), p. 264.

3. Mao, in an interview with Edgar Snow on July 23, 1936, as quoted in Stuart Schram, ed., *The Political Thought of Mao Tse-tung* (New York: Praeger, 1963), p. 286. One should of course bear in mind that Mao was speaking to an American reporter; this interview was not included in the official Beijing version of Mao's *Selected Works* (Beijing: Foreign Languages Press, 1965–77).

4. Mao Zedong, *Lun Xin Jieduan*, as quoted in Schram, *Political Thought*, p. 114. The term "Sinicization of Marxism" was removed from the official version of the *Selected Works*.

5. Liu Shao-ch'i, *On the Party* (Peking: Foreign Languages Press, 1951), pp. 8, 29.

6. I am deliberately exempting from this survey the voluminous and quite perceptive literature on interparty relations in the 1930s and 1940s (e.g., Whiting, Brandt, Thornton). The dynamics of the relationship between party-state and party is quite different from that between sovereign nation-states.

7. G. F. Hudson, Richard Lowenthal, and Roderick MacFarquhar, eds., *The Sino-Soviet Dispute* (London: The China Quarterly, 1961); Donald Zagoria, *The Sino-Soviet Conflict, 1956–1961* (Princeton: Princeton University Press, 1962); William E. Griffith, *The Sino-Soviet Rift* (Cambridge, Mass.: MIT Press, 1964); and John Gittings, *Survey of the Sino-Soviet Dispute: A Commentary* (London: Oxford University Press, 1968).

8. I owe this insight to Eric Harwit.

9. Richard Lowenthal, "Diplomacy and Revolution: The Dialectics of a Dispute," in Hudson et al., eds., *Sino-Soviet Dispute*, pp. 9–34.

10. Harrison E. Salisbury, *War Between Russia and China* (New York: W. W. Norton, 1969).

11. Ibid., p. 51.

12. See Doolin, *Territorial Claims*; also Tai-Sung An, *The Sino-Soviet Territorial Dispute* (New York: Westminster Press, 1973).

13. Donald Zagoria, *Vietnam Triangle: Moscow, Peking, Hanoi* (New York: Pegasus, 1967). Uri Ra'anan, "Peking's Foreign Policy 'Debate,' 1965–1966," in Tang Tsou, ed., *China in Crisis*, vol. 2: *China's Policies in Asia and America's Alternatives* (Chicago: University of Chicago Press, 1968), pp. 23–71. Harold Hinton, *The Bear at the Gate: Chinese Policy-Making Under Soviet Pressure* (Washington, D.C.: American Enterprise Institute for Public Policy Research, 1971); Hinton, *The Sino-Soviet Confrontation: Implications for the Future* (New York: Crane, Russak, 1976). Kenneth Lieberthal, *Sino-Soviet Conflict in the 1970s: Its Evolution and Implications for the Strategic Triangle* (Santa Monica: Rand Corporation, 1978). Harry Harding and Melvin Gurtov, *The Purge of Lo Jui-ch'ing: The Politics of Chinese Strategic Planning* (Santa Monica: Rand Corporation, 1971). Melvin Gurtov and Byong-Moo Hwang, *China Under Threat: The Politics of Strategy and Diplomacy* (Baltimore: Johns Hopkins University Press, 1980). Also see Michael Yahuda, "Kremlinology and the Chinese Strategic Debate, 1965–66," *China Quarterly*, no. 49 (January–March 1972), pp. 32–75.

14. See Andrew J. Nathan, "A Factionalism Model for CCP Politics," *China Quarterly*, no. 53 (January–March 1973), p. 44 et passim; and Tang Tsou's critique in *The Cultural Revolution and Post-Mao Reforms: A Historical Perspective* (Chicago: University of Chicago Press, 1986), pp. 95–112.

15. Zagoria first coined the geometrical metaphor in his March 1965 congressional testimony, in which he defined the "triangle" as a pattern in which "change in the relationship of any two of the powers unavoidably affects the third." As cited in Gordon H. Chang, *Friends and Enemies: The United States, China, and the Soviet Union, 1948–1972* (Stanford: Stanford University Press, 1990), pp. 265–66. Other pioneers include Michel Tatu, *Le triangle Washington-Moscou-Pékin et les deus Europe(s)* (Paris: Casterman, 1972); and Thomas Gottlieb, *Chinese Foreign Policy Factionalism and the Origins of the Strategic Triangle* (Santa Monica: Rand Corporation, 1977); for further citations on this topic, see Part III.

16. Robert Scalapino, "Containment and Countercontainment: The Current Stage of Sino-Soviet Relations," in Douglas Stuart and William Tow, eds., *China, the Soviet Union, and the West* (Boulder: Westview, 1982), pp. 173 et passim.

17. See Zagoria, *Vietnam Triangle*; also Chin O. Chung, *P'yongyang Between Peking and Moscow: North Korea's Involvement in the Sino-Soviet Dispute, 1958–75* (Tuscaloosa: University of Alabama Press, 1978).

18. See, for example, Robert G. Sutter, *Chinese Foreign Policy: Developments After Mao* (New York: Praeger, 1986).

19. There are but two other extensive reconsiderations of the relationship that take us beyond the Brezhnev era, and each is quite worth while: Thomas G. Hart, *Sino-Soviet Relations: Reexamining the Prospects for Normalization* (Aldershot: Gower, 1987); and Harvey Nelsen, *Power and Insecurity: Beijing, Moscow, and Washington, 1949–1988* (Boulder: Lynne Rienner, 1989). Hart and Nelsen do not, however, attempt all that I undertake to do here (for better or for worse), nor do they encompass normalization.

20. See, for example, *New York Times*, October 13, 1985, p. E2. Listed in descending rank order of priority (from the Chinese perspective), the Three Obstacles are (or were): (1) Soviet aid to the Democratic Republic of Vietnam (DRV) in its efforts to crush the Khmer Rouge guerrilla forces and their non-communist confederates and thereby subjugate Kampuchea; (2) Soviet military fortifications along China's northern borders, and along the Outer Mongolian border with China; and (3) Soviet troops fighting *mujahideen* guerrilla resistance forces in Afghanistan.

21. Graham T. Allison, *Essence of Decision: Explaining the Cuban Missile Crisis* (Boston: Little, Brown, 1971); see also G. T. Allison and Peter Szanton, *Remaking Foreign Policy: The Organizational Connection* (New York: Basic Books, 1976).

Part I. Development and Détente

1. See Alfred G. Meyer, "Theories of Convergence," in Chalmers Johnson, ed., *Change in Communist Systems* (Stanford: Stanford University Press, 1970), pp. 313–42; also Zbigniew Brzezinski and Samuel Huntington, *Political Power USA/USSR* (New York: Viking Press, 1964); John H. Kautsky, *Communism and the Politics of Development: Persistent Myths and Changing Behavior* (New York: John Wiley, 1968); and Peter C. Ludz, *The Changing Party Elite in East Germany* (Cambridge: MIT Press, 1972).

2. The political implications of détente have been examined in Hisahiko Okazaki, *A Japanese View of Detente* (Lexington: D. C. Heath, 1974).

1. Socialist Dependency

1. The notion of dependent development under socialism has been perhaps most fully developed in Dennis Ray, "Chinese Perceptions of Social Imperialism and Economic Dependency: The Impact of Soviet Aid," *Stanford Journal of International Studies* 10 (Spring 1975): 36–83.

2. *Zhongguo Tongxun She* (Hong Kong), May 15, 1989, in *FBIS–China*, May 15, 1989, p. 22.

3. "Oppose the Bourgeois Ideology in the Party" (August 12, 1953), as trans. in Michael Y. M. Kau and John K. Leung, eds., *The Writings of Mao Zedong, 1949–1976* (Armonk, N.Y.: M. E. Sharpe, 1987), vol. 1, *September 1949–*

December 1955, p. 331. And again: "We mustn't list our Chinese comrades as equals of Marx, Engels, Lenin, and Stalin. The relationship is one of teacher to pupil and ought to be such." "The Atomic Bomb Cannot Scare the Chinese People" (January 28, 1955), ibid., p. 371. As late as February 1957, one year after the Twentieth Party Congress, Mao said: "In order to turn China into an industrial country, we must learn conscientiously from the advanced experience of the Soviet Union. The Soviet Union has been building socialism for forty years and its experience is very valuable to us. Let us ask: who designed and equipped so many important factories for us? Was it the United States? Or Britain? No, neither the one nor the other. Only the Soviet Union was willing to do so, because it is a socialist country and our ally." Mao, *Selected Works*, 5:420.

4. "Mao's Speech to 7,000 Cadres" (January 30, 1962), as trans. in Stuart Schram, ed., *Chairman Mao Talks to the People: Talks and Letters, 1956–1971* (New York: Random House, 1976), p. 178.

5. See *Mao Zedong Sixiang Wansui* [Long Live Mao Zedong Thought] (Hong Kong: n.p., 1969), p. 432; hereafter *Wansui* (1969).

6. Schram, *Chairman Mao Talks*, p. 191.

7. C. P. FitzGerald, *Changing Directions of Chinese Foreign Policy* (Melbourne: Australian Institute of International Affairs, 1971), pp. 8–9. (A second lasting advantage of the Chinese intervention was the ability to exert greater influence on North Korean politics, in part by playing on Kim's gratitude—but in part also because Chinese troops remained in North Korea long after the armistice.)

8. *Renmin Ribao* [People's Daily], December 4, 1953.

9. Jacques Levesque, *Le conflit sino-sovietique et l'Europe de l'Est: Ses incidences sur les conflits soviéto-polonais et soviéto-roumain* (Montréal: Les Presses de l'Université de Montréal, 1970), p. 24.

10. Carl Riskin, *China's Political Economy: The Quest for Development Since 1949* (New York: Oxford University Press, 1987), pp. 74–75.

11. Georges Sokoloff and Françoise Lemoine, *China and the U.S.S.R.: Limits to Trade with the West* (Paris: Atlantic Institute for International Affairs, 1982), p. 41.

12. See Chin Ssu-k'ai, *Communist China's Relations with the Soviet Union, 1949–1957* (Kowloon: Union Research Service, 1961).

13. "Sino-Soviet Economic Relations," in G. F. Hudson et al., eds., *Sino-Soviet Dispute*, p. 37.

14. *The First Five-Year Plan* (Peking: Foreign Languages Press, 1956), p. 38.

15. Roy Medvedev, *China and the Superpowers* (Oxford and New York: Basil Blackwell, 1986), p. 27.

16. Lawrence Freedman, "Sino-Soviet Economic and Technological Factors," in Douglas Stuart and William Tow, eds., *China, the Soviet Union, and the West* (Boulder: Westview, 1982), p. 80.

17. It was in connection with this project that Chinese scientists trained and worked at the Joint Institute for Nuclear Research in Dubna. *Foreign Broadcast*

Information Service (hereafter *FBIS*) Daily Report, Soviet Union, February 4, 1981, p. B2; as cited in Leo Orleans, "The Soviet Union's Evolving Perceptions of China's Science and Technology," paper presented at the Fifteenth Sino-American Conference on Mainland China, June 8–14, 1986, Taipei, Taiwan, pp. 9, 39.

18. Hans Heyman, "Acquisition and Diffusion of Technology in China," in Joint Economic Committee of Congress, *China: A Reassessment of the Economy* (Washington, D.C.: Government Printing Office, 1975), p. 678.

19. L. V. Filatov, *Ekonomicheskaia otsenka nauchno-tekhnicheskoi pomoshchi Sovetskogo Soiuza Kitaiu, 1949–1966* (Moscow: Nauka, 1980), as quoted in Orleans, "The Soviet Union's Evolving Perceptions," pp. 13–14.

20. O. Vladimirov, "The Question of Soviet-Chinese Economic Relations in 1952–1966," *Voprosy Istorii* [Problems of History], no. 6, 1969, quoted in *Chinese Economic Studies* 8–9 (Fall 1969): 8.

21. M. Suslov, "On the Struggle of the CPSU for the Solidarity of the International Communist Movement" (Report of the Central Committee, February 1964), as trans. in *Current Digest of the Soviet Press*, April 29, 1964, p. 3; Vladimirov, "The Question," p. 9; Leo Orleans, *Professional Manpower and Education in Communist China* (Washington, D.C.: Government Printing Office, 1960), p. 117.

22. See Leo A. Orleans, "Soviet Influence on China's Higher Education," in Ruth Hayhoe and Marianne Bastid, eds., *China's Education and the Industrialized World: Studies in Cultural Transfer* (Armonk: M. E. Sharpe, 1987), p. 189, n. 16.

23. Ibid., p. 189, n. 17.

24. S. G. Yurkov, "Fifty Years of Soviet-Chinese Relations," *Far Eastern Affairs*, no. 2, 1974, p. 54; as cited in Yung-hwan Jo and Ying-hsien Pi, *Russia Versus China and What Next?* (Lanham, Md.: University Press of America, 1980).

25. Suslov, "On the Struggle," p. 3; *Renmin Ribao*, October 4, 1959, as cited in Orleans, *Professional Manpower*, p. 115; also Medvedev, *China and the Superpowers*, p. 27.

26. Zoia A. Muromtseva, *Problemy industrializatsii Kitaiskoi Narodnoi Respubliki* [Problems of Industrialization in the People's Republic of China] (Moscow: Nauka, 1971), p. 121; as cited in Orleans, "The Soviet Union's Evolving Perceptions" (see note 17 above).

27. Medvedev, *China and the Superpowers*, p. 223.

28. Orleans, *Professional Manpower*, p. 116.

29. Vladimirov, "The Question," p. 8. According to Chinese sources, some 5,000 Chinese students were sent out of the country for study in 1950–55, rising to 14,000 by 1959, plus about 7,000 teachers. Orleans, *Professional Manpower*, p. 79.

30. Orleans, "The Soviet Union's Evolving Perceptions," p. 11.

31. Orleans, "Soviet Influence," p. 188, n. 13.

32. See *Women Kan Sixiang Gaizao yu Gaodeng Jiaoyu Gongzuo* [Our Observation of Thought Reform and Higher Education Work], in *Wenhui Bao* (Shanghai), May 20, 1959; also "Jiaoyu yu Jiede Jiaotiaozhuyi" [Dogmatism in Education], *Jiao Shi Bao* (Beijing), May 28, 1957. As quoted in Tony Kuangsheng Liao, "Antiforeignism and Chinese Communism in Mao Zedong's Era," unpublished paper, Chinese University of Hong Kong, 1987.

33. "The Reply of the Central Committee of the Communist Party of China to the CPSU's Letter" (February 29, 1964), in *Renmin Ribao*, May 9, 1964.

34. By 1964, free world trade was 67 percent of China's total trade, rising from a low point of 25 percent during the American blockade in the early 1950s. Although Sino-Soviet trade certainly dwindled in the 1960s and 1970s, formal trade agreements or their equivalent were signed each year throughout the dispute.

35. David Floyd, *Mao Against Khrushchev* (New York: Praeger, 1963), p. 12. There is no contemporaneous evidential foundation for these rumors, which may have arisen only subsequently, in the wake of more generous Soviet awards to other clients. See Mao's interview with a Soviet reporter in January 1950, in *Jianguo yilai Mao Zedong wenxuan, 1949.9–1950.12* [Selected Mao Zedong Documents Since the Founding of the PRC, September 1949–December 1950] (Beijing: Zhongyang Wenxian Chubanshe, July 1987).

36. New China News Agency, June 18, 1957, quoted in *New York Times*, June 24, 1957, p. 1.

37. Kang Chao and Feng-hwa Mah, "A Study of the Rouble-Yuan Exchange Rate," *China Quarterly*, no. 17 (January–March 1964), p. 193.

38. Joseph Camilleri, *Chinese Foreign Policy: The Maoist Era and Its Aftermath* (Oxford: M. Robertson, 1980), pp. 52–53.

39. Griffith, *Sino-Soviet Rift*, pp. 233–34.

40. Robert F. Dernberger, "The Foreign Trade and Capital Movements of Communist China" (Ph.D. dissertation, Harvard University, 1965), as quoted in Dernberger, "Economic Development and Modernization in Contemporary China: The Attempt to Limit Dependence on the Transfer of Modern Industrial Technology from Abroad and to Control Its Corruption of the Maoist Social Revolution," in Frederic J. Fleron, Jr., ed., *Technology and Communist Culture: The Socio-Cultural Impact of Technology Under Socialism* (New York: Praeger, 1977), pp. 261–62.

41. Geoffrey Jukes, *The Soviet Union in Asia* (Berkeley: University of California Press, 1973), p. 269.

42. Medvedev claims that the economic efficiency of capital investment was higher during the Soviet tutelage than during subsequent industrialization, pointing out that the time required to pay for large and medium projects built during the First FYP was only 3.5 years on the average whereas not one of the similar projects built in the 1970s had yet been paid for by 1980. He seems not to have taken into account the shorter loan period tolerated by the Soviets. Medvedev, *China and the Superpowers*, p. 205–6.

43. Nelsen, *Power and Insecurity*, p. 45.

44. *Peking Review*, no. 1, 1959, p. 12; Adam Ulam, *Expansion and Coexistence: Soviet Foreign Policy, 1917–73* (New York: Praeger, 1974), p. 621.

45. Klochko's revealing discussions with then Soviet ambassador Chervonenko and other high officials in Beijing on the eve of his evacuation indicated that the brunt of the disagreement concerned foreign affairs—the handling of India, worsening Chinese relations with Indonesia, needless exacerbation of relations with Yugoslavia and excessive friendship for Albania, contradictions in Chinese perceptions of the American threat. Generally, it was felt that China was trying to take over leadership of the world revolution. Mikhail A. Klochko, *Soviet Scientist in Red China* (New York: Praeger, 1964), pp. 188–90.

2. Divergent Development

1. Bruce Reynolds, "China in the International Economy," in Harry Harding, ed., *China's Foreign Relations in the 1980s* (New Haven: Yale University Press, 1984), pp. 71–107.

2. Mao Zedong, "Reading Notes on the Soviet Text *Political Economy*," in Mao, *A Critique of Soviet Economics* (New York: Monthly Review Press, 1977), p. 122.

3. As Tan Zhenlin observed at the time, the destruction of the Stalin myth by Khrushchev opened up new theoretical possibilities throughout the communist world. *Guanyu Tan Zhenlin Wentide Chubu Conghe Cailiao* [A Preliminary Synthesis of Material on the case of Tan Zhenlin], March 17, 1967, p. 22; as cited in Roderick MacFarquhar, *The Origins of the Cultural Revolution*, vol. 2: *The Great Leap Forward, 1958–1960* (New York: Columbia University Press, 1983), p. 39, n. 38.

4. Mao, "On the Ten Major Relationships" (April 25, 1956), in *Selected Works*, 5:284–308, at p. 285.

5. Ibid.

6. "Resolution of the Eighth National Congress of the Communist Party of China," in *Eighth National Congress of the Communist Party of China* (Peking: Foreign Languages Press, 1956), vol. I (Documents), p. 116.

7. "On Khrushchev's Phoney Communism and Its Historical Lessons for the World. Comment IX on the Open Letter of the Central Committee of the CPSU," in *Peking Review*, no. 29 (July 17, 1964), pp. 7–28.

8. "True, the productive forces, practice, and economic base generally play the principal and decisive role; whoever denies this is not a materialist. But it must also be admitted that in certain conditions, such aspects as the relations of production, theory, and the superstructure in turn manifest themselves in the principal and decisive role. . . . When the superstructure (politics, culture, etc.) obstructs the development of the economic base, political and cultural changes become principal and decisive." Mao, *Selected Works*, 1:336; as quoted in Tang Tsou, *The Cultural Revolution and Post-Mao Reforms*, pp. 112–13.

9. The latter, a hybrid of the "mass line" with "criticism and criticism" (hitherto confined to the small group context, as in the work unit or party branch), had its heyday during the Great Proletarian Cultural Revolution. See my "Mass Line and 'Mass Criticism' in China: An Analysis of the Fall of Liu Shao-ch'i," *Asian Survey* 13, no. 8 (August 1973): 772–92.

10. Mao, *A Critique*, pp. 53, 90–91, 80, 87.

11. Mao, "Talks at Chengdu: The Pattern of Development" (March 20, 1958), in Schram, ed., *Chairman Mao Talks*, p. 105.

12. Mao, "Speech at the Group Leaders' Forum of the Enlarged Meeting of the Military Affairs Commission," as trans. in Schram, ed., *Chairman Mao Talks*, p. 129.

13. Mao's comments at the Zhengdu Conference (March 1958) are compiled in *Wansui* (1969), and translated in *Issues and Studies*, November 1973, pp. 95–98.

14. Riskin, *China's Political Economy*, pp. 82–83.

15. Gross procurement of grain in 1959–60 reached the remarkable level of 67.49 million tons, which was 32 percent higher than the 1958–59 amount, based on an output of 170 million tons, which was 15 percent *below* that of 1958. Net procurement thus rose from 15.9 percent of output in 1958–59 to 28 percent in 1959–60. See Kenneth Walker, *Food Grain Procurement and Consumption in China* (Cambridge: Cambridge University Press, 1984), p. 149.

16. Riskin, *China's Political Economy*, pp. 83–84.

17. Todor Zhivkov, Bulgarian Communist Party first secretary, declared that "Bulgaria will make a great leap forward in which every year will be equivalent to several years of development," and fifteen Bulgarian collective farms were merged into a larger unit called a "commune." *Rabotnichesko Delo*, November 14, 1958; *Zemedelsko Zname*, November 12, 1958.

18. Hemen Ray, *China and Eastern Europe* (New Delhi: Radiant, 1988), pp. 31–34.

19. In May 1957, Khrushchev called for overtaking the United States in per capita production of meat, butter, and milk "in the near future." In his keynote address to the Supreme Soviet the following November, he promised to overtake the United States "within the next 15 years" in the output of "important products." MacFarquhar, *Origins*, 2:16. The Soviet Union would overtake the United States economically by 1970 and attain communism "in the main" by 1980, according to the 1961 Party Program. Martin Crouch, *Revolution and Evolution: Gorbachev and Soviet Politics* (New York: Philip Allan, 1989), p. 44.

20. *Xinhua Banyue Kan*, no. 1 (1958), p. 2; in MacFarquhar, *Origins*, 2:17, n. 64.

21. See Crouch, *Revolution and Evolution*, p. 44; see also Jerome Gillison, *The Soviet Image of Utopia* (Baltimore: Johns Hopkins University Press, 1975), pp. 6–7.

22. MacFarquhar, *Origins*, 2:48.

23. As quoted in Yang Junshi, *Xiandaihua yu Zhongguo Gongchanzhuyi* [Modernization and Chinese Communism] (Hong Kong: Chinese University Press, 1987), p. 83.

24. *Pravda* and *Izvestiia*, October 19, 1961, as trans. in *Current Digest of the Soviet Press*, vol. 13, no. 44 (October 20, 1961), p. 9; as quoted in Gillison, *Soviet Image*, pp. 6–7.

25. MacFarquhar, *Origins*, 2:226.

26. Barry Richman, *Industrial Society in Communist China* (New York: Random House, 1969), p. 613.

27. The famine is examined in Thomas P. Bernstein, "Stalinism, Famine, and Chinese Peasants: Grain Procurements During the Great Leap Forward," *Theory and Society* 13, no. 3 (May 1984): 339–77. The tragedy was so severe that the average death rate rose from 11 per thousand in 1957 to 17 per thousand in 1958–61, while the birth rate declined from 34 per thousand in 1957 to 23 per thousand in 1958–61. See Judith Banister, "Population Policy and Trends in China, 1978–83," *China Quarterly*, no. 100 (December 1984), pp. 717–41.

28. See Lowell Dittmer, *China's Continuous Revolution* (Berkeley: University of California Press, 1987).

29. Riskin, *China's Political Economy*, p. 181.

3. Convergence and Its Complications

1. The polemics of the early 1960s have been perhaps more thoroughly analyzed than any other facet of the relationship, making radical abridgment possible here.

2. Richard Wich, *Sino-Soviet Crisis Politics: A Study of Political Change and Communication* (Cambridge: Council on East Asian Studies, Harvard University, 1980) p. 65; as quoted in Nelsen, *Power and Insecurity*, pp. 83–84.

3. See *Beijing Review*, no. 16, 1974, pp. 6–11.

4. To complete the analogy, the Second World plays the role of the petty and national bourgeoisie and the CCP's other coalition partners in the revolutionary United Front.

5. Thus Chinese social scientists pointed out that the combined GNP of the superpowers as a percentage of world GNP declined from 39.9 percent in 1970 to 34.2 percent in 1980 and was projected to fall to 30 percent in 1990. By contrast, the combined GNP of Western Europe, Japan, and the Third World as a percentage of world GNP rose from 47.3 percent in 1970 to 53.5 percent in 1980 and was projected to rise to 57 percent by 1990. (Most of this growth is, however, accounted for by expansion in the Second rather than the Third World.) Xing Xhugang, Li Yunhua, and Liu Yingna, "Soviet-U.S. Balance of Power and Its Impact on the International Situation in the 1990s," *Guoji Wenti Yanjiu* [Journal of International Affairs], no. 1, 1983, p. 31. The authors derive these figures from a Western source for which they give no specific reference.

6. Editorial Department, "Chairman Mao's Theory of the Differentiation of the Three Worlds Is a Major Contribution to Marxism-Leninism," *Renmin Ribao*, November 1, 1977.

7. Cf. *Wenyi Baijia*, no. 2, 1979, pp. 254–56. The revelation that most Chinese Soviet specialists now considered the USSR to be socialist reportedly angered Deng, who was concerned lest it scare off investors and otherwise jeopardize China's budding relationship with the West.

8. *Renmin Ribao*, April 2, 1980. Yet the issue remained sensitive. Deng Xiaoping denied in 1981 that the USSR was socialist, and as late as the fall of 1983 a Canadian scholar was told by a Chinese academic counterpart, "The USSR is not socialist, but I don't believe it is capitalist either." Jacques Levesque, "Les 'trois obstacles' dans un monde changeant," *Le Monde diplomatique* 31, no. 361 (April 1984): 1, 6–7.

9. According to Wu Zhan, deputy director, Institute of American Studies, Chinese Academy of Social Science, in an oral presentation at the Institute of International Studies, University of California, Berkeley, March 16, 1989.

10. During Vice-Premier Arkhipov's December 1984 visit, the honorific was restored in Peng Zhen's welcoming speech.

11. A broad united front could not deter the two superpowers from exploiting regional disputes and expanding their influence, it was felt, and in any case most countries in the Second and Third Worlds were too involved with one or the other superpower to be interested in participating in such a united front. Third World countries were interested in establishing a new international economic order (NIEO), entailing at least passive cooperation by the First World, while developed countries in the Second World hoped for progress in détente and arms control; they had to rely on the American nuclear umbrella, and did not wish to provoke the USSR.

12. See Nina P. Halpern, "Learning from Abroad: Chinese Views of the East European Economic Experience, January 1977–June 1981," *Modern China* 2, no. 1 (January 1985): 77–111. Chinese interest in the Hungarian reforms has continued, omitting news of the indifferent success of the Hungarian economy in the last few years. See Yi Han, "Advancing in the Course of Reform: Hungary's Political Restructuring," *Renmin Ribao*, August 22, 1986, as trans. in *FBIS–China*, August 28, 1986, pp. H2–H3; Lu Shuxi, "Reform Is a Global Phenomenon," *Guangming Ribao* (Beijing), October 21, 1986, p. 2, and Dong Fusheng, "Theoreticians in Yugoslavia, Romania, Poland, and Hungary Explore Questions of Socialist Theory," *Renmin Ribao*, August 1, 1986, p. 7. These later reports have become bolder in suggesting the implications for Chinese reforms than Halpern found in the earlier literature.

13. Thus one article argues that China's plan to quadruple national income by the year 2000 can be facilitated by studying the Soviet economic model and strengthening Sino-Soviet economic ties. The USSR offers a stable market, in contrast with those in the West that are volatile and infringed by protectionism. *Shijie Jingji Daobao* [World Economic Herald] (Shanghai), August 19, 1985, in *FBIS–China*, September 10, 1985, p. A1.

14. As of 1986, there were more than twenty specialized journals in the social sciences and humanities on the Soviet Union and about forty others that regularly carried articles on that country. But in early 1985, American library collections had access to only one Chinese journal on the Soviet Union; all the rest were classified. According to China's National Periodical Index, by 1983 approximately 2,000 articles per year in the social sciences, including translations, were focused on the Soviet Union; but most of these, too, were classified. Cf. Gilbert Rozman, *The Chinese Debate About Soviet Socialism, 1978–1985* (Princeton: Princeton University Press, 1987).

15. Ibid.; see also Rozman's "China's Soviet-Watchers in the 1980s: A New Era in Scholarship," *World Politics* 37, no. 4 (July 1985): 435–74.

16. For example, Fang Xuan writes in 1986 that "the reform process in the political, economic, cultural and educational fields in Soviet society is rather noticeable," attributing the alleged reversal of the decline in growth over the previous ten years to the reforms. Fang Xuan, "The Soviet Reform Process," *Renmin Ribao*, July 26, 1986, p. 7. Among other publicly accessible accounts (which seem to echo the themes in the *neibu* materials), see Li Nan, "Waves of Reform Are Sweeping Across the Soviet Union and Eastern Europe," *Liaowang Overseas Edition* (Hong Kong), no. 43 (October 27, 1986), pp. 30–31; Zhou Xiangguang, "Scoring Initial Results, Progressing with Difficulty: Changes Brought by Reform in the Soviet Union Over the Past Year," *Renmin Ribao*, December 25, 1986, p. 6; Tang Xiuzhe, "Political Reform Indispensable for Transforming Soviet Society, Says Soviet Scholar" [interview with Georgii Shaknazarov, chairman of the Soviet Association of Political Science], *Xinhua* (Beijing), March 8, 1987, in *FBIS–China*, March 9, 1987, p. C3; and Lu Nanquan, "The CPSU XXVII Congress Gives Green Light for Economic Reform," *Shijie Jingji* [World Economy] (Beijing), no. 6, 1986, pp. 64–68.

17. Rozman, *Chinese Debate*, and "China's Soviet-Watchers"; see also Guocang Huan, "Sino-Soviet Relations to the Year 2000" (Washington, D.C.: Atlantic Council, Occasional Paper, 1986).

18. See *Shijie Jingji*, no. 2, 1987, pp. 21–22; *Jingji Ribao*, March 7, 1987; *Banyue Tan*, no. 1, 1987, p. 33.

19. For example, see Vladimir Shlapentokh, *Soviet Ideologies in the Period of Glasnost* (New York: Praeger, 1988), p. 131.

20. Reports on the Soviet thaw in culture and the arts started appearing in the Chinese press in the spring of 1986. See, for example, *Shijie Jingji Daobao*, May 12, May 19, July 28, 1986; *Renmin Ribao*, March 6, August 12, 26, September 10, and December 6, 25, 1986; *Shijie Zhishi* [World Knowledge] (Beijing), no. 18, 1986, p. 12; and *Guangming Ribao*, February 3, 1987.

21. *Renmin Ribao*, July 26, 1986; *Shijie Zhishi*, no. 20, 1986, p. 10; *Shijie Jingji*, no. 2, 1987, pp. 21–23. Another Chinese writer agrees that "the extremely important experience of the USSR and Eastern European countries consists in that a reform of the economic structure cannot be carried out in isolation; it must be closely linked with a reform of the political structure." *Lilun Xinxi Bao*, February 23, 1987, as quoted in O. Artemyeva, "The Chinese Press

on the Socio-Political Impact of *Perestroika* in the USSR," *Far Eastern Affairs*, no. 2, 1988, pp. 61–72.

22. Zhang Xu, for example, calls attention to three areas where the Soviet "record could be borrowed and studied in China." The first is in the use of legislation for the "deepening" of the reforms, such as in the drafting of thirty-eight fundamental laws in eight fields. The second is in "enhancing the role of the working masses in the reforms." Third is the focus on "making cost-accounting the pivot of the experiments with the greater independence of enterprises." *Lilun Xinxi Bao*, February 23, 1987; see also Zheng Hongqing's article in *Hongqi*, no. 22, 1986, p. 12.

23. See Lowell Dittmer, "China in 1986: Domestic Politics," in John Major and Anthony Kane, eds., *China Briefing, 1987* (Boulder: Westview, 1987), pp. 1–27.

24. See the series of editorials in *Kommunist*, nos. 12 of 1973, 1974, 1975, and 1977; as cited in Chi Su, "China and the Soviet Union: 'Principled, Salutary, and Tempered' Management of Conflict," in Samuel S. Kim, ed., *China and the World: Chinese Foreign Policy in the Post-Mao Era* (Boulder: Westview, 1984), pp. 135–61.

25. Owing to logistical problems, the sample covers the period January–June 1983 and every month of all other years except 1985, which includes January through February and June through August. The count is based on *Letopis' Zhurnal'nykh Statei*, a comprehensive index of Soviet periodical and newspaper articles. I am indebted to Dr. Yong-chool Ha in this context for his translations and research assistance.

Press Coverage of the PRC (number of articles)

Subject	1980	1981	1982	1983	1984	1985
Foreign Policy	123	118	31	1	15	2
Military	12	6	2	0	2	1
Political	34	63	11	0	0	1
Cultural	17	16	1	1	2	2
Economic	13	38	4	3	3	1
Total	199	241	49	5	22	7

26. This literature is generally consistent with the popular press, but based on a more complex and comprehensive rationale. According to one of the more perceptive students of Soviet China-watchers, this literature provides the intellectual underpinning for policy. Chi Su, "Soviet China-Watchers' Influence on Soviet China Policy," *Journal of Northeast Asian Studies*, 2, no. 4 (December 1983): 26–27; see also his article "U.S.-China Relations: Soviet Views and Policies," *Asian Survey* 23, no. 5 (May 1983): 566. The political significance of theoretical rationales has been demonstrated repeatedly. For example, the first Soviet venture into the Third World in the late 1950s and early 1960s was legitimated by Khrushchev's theory of "peaceful transition" to socialism

under a "revolutionary democratic" leadership which was expected to launch a "revolution from above." Following the disappointing sequel of the downfalls of Nasser, Sukarno, Nkrumah, et al., a new theory of the international dictatorship of the proletariat was introduced in 1975, which saw little prospect for installing a scientific socialist system in a developing country without external involvement. This doctrinal innovation in turn inaugurated the phase of socialist revolutions aided by Soviet arms transfers and proxy forces in Angola, Ethiopia, Afghanistan, et al.

27. R. Ia. Matiaev and V. P. Stepanov, "Nekotorye tendentsii razvitiia KPK," *Problemy Dal'nego Vostoka* [Problems of the Far East] (hereafter *PDV*), no. 1, 1982, pp. 46–58.

28. Thus the 1980 yearbook of the Institute on the World Labor Movement cautioned against interpreting internal changes in China as de-Maoization, insisting that such views have "no serious foundation," and that recent developments in China do not constitute a "return to a socialist policy . . . but on the contrary, a further strengthening of the military-bureaucratic dictatorship created during the life of Mao Zedong." Institut Obshchestvennykh Nauk, *Problemy Kommunisticheskogo Dvizheniia* (Moscow: Mysl', 1981), p. 248.

29. See G. Nikolaev, in *Pravda*, May 26, 1980.

30. To my knowledge, the first important Soviet official to speak out on behalf of the Chinese reforms was Fedor Burlatsky, who noted as early as 1978 that the Chinese had made "certain advances," including a reendorsement of the platform of the Eighth Party Congress, and presented a sophisticated analysis of the alternative foreign and domestic policies available to the PRC and the likely consequences of each. F. Burlatsky, "Nasledniki Mao," *Novyi Mir*, no. 9, 1978, as trans. in *JPRS–Soviet Union*, no. 72443. The China scholar and foreign policy official Mikhail Kapitsa, writing under the pseudonym M. S. Uraintsev, delivered a report to the Second United States Conference of Sinologists in Moscow on January 25–27, 1982, suggesting that important changes were taking place in Chinese domestic and foreign policies. M. S. Uraintsev, "Soviet-Chinese Relations: Problems and Prospects," *PDV*, no. 2, 1982. The influential *Izvestiia* commentator (and former Khrushchev speechwriter) Aleksandr Bovin was sent by the Soviet leadership to China in late February 1983, and he returned with largely optimistic impressions, though nothing appeared in print. *New York Times*, March 20, 1983.

31. See B. Barakhta, in *Pravda*, March 20, 1981.

32. *Izvestiia*, April 16, May 21, 1984.

33. Gilbert Rozman, "Moscow's China-Watchers in the Post-Mao Era: The Response to a Changing China," *China Quarterly*, no. 94 (June 1983); also see Rozman, *Mirror for Socialism: Soviet Criticisms of China* (Princeton: Princeton University Press, 1985).

34. See Carsten Herrmann-Pillath, *Die chinesische Wirtschaftsreform im Spiegel sowjetischer Darstellungen, 1979–1986* (Cologne: Berichte des Bundesinstituts für ostwissenschaftliche und internationale Studien, no. 42, 1986),

p. 14, n. 19; also Gail Warshofsky Lapidus, "Changing Soviet Perspectives and Policies in Northeast Asia," in Robert Scalapino and Qimao Chen, eds., *Pacific-Asian Issues: American and Chinese Views* (Berkeley: Institute of East Asian Studies, 1986), pp. 93–111.

35. Thus discussions of the Maoist "personality cult" become an elaborate metaphor for a critique of Stalinism. One cannot but be struck by the similarities between the criticisms that Kosygin's (aborted) 1965 reform generated and the subsequent Soviet critique of the far more ambitious reforms launched in China under Deng Xiaoping. Soviet construals also seem to reflect presuppositions based on how their own system operates: not for a moment is the Chinese claim taken seriously that reform initiatives (such as the production responsibility system) percolated up from the masses, for example; the decisions were assumed to have been made by the Politburo, and usually for political-strategic (rather than economic) reasons.

36. See B. Barakhta, in *Pravda*, August 5, 1984.

37. *Pravda*, June 14, 1986.

38. Cf. *Pravda*, October 25, 1984.

39. See M. Iakovlev, in *Izvestiia*, January 10, 1982.

40. M. Iakovlev, in *Izvestiia*, March 5, 1982.

41. I. N. Korkunov, "Sotsial'no-ekonomicheskie problemy kitaiskoi derevni," *PDV*, no. 2, 1982, p. 60.

42. Z. Marmtsev, "Modernization of Agriculture in the PRC: The Question of Capital Investment," *Far Eastern Affairs*, no. 2, 1985, pp. 95–105.

43. V. N. Remyga, "Kharakhter izmenii v sisteme upravleniia narodnym khoziaistvom KNR," *PDV*, no. 4, 1980, pp. 95, 101; also S. V. Stepanov and V. Ia. Portiakov, "Aktual'nye problemy khoziaistvennogo razvitiia ekonomiki Kitaia," in *PDV*, no. 2, 1985, p. 80.

44. B. Barakhta, in *Pravda*, August 5, 1984; also August 5, 1985.

45. A. S. Murguzin, "Sotsial'no-ekonomicheskaia kharakhteristika kitaiskogo krest'ianstva," in *PDV*, no. 4, 1984, pp. 59–75.

46. G. Nikolaev, in *Trud*, December 8, 1981.

47. S. Liudin, in *Trud*, June 9, 1980.

48. A. Ostrovsky, "The Working Class of China as a Productive Force of Society," *Far Eastern Affairs*, no. 2, 1984, pp. 75–85.

49. G. Nikolaev, in *Trud*, December 8, 1981.

50. G. Nikolaev, in *Izvestiia*, December 8, 1981.

51. Cf. *PDV*, no. 3, 1979, p. 23.

52. B. Barakhta, in *Pravda*, June 25, 1982.

53. It has also been reliably reported that in 1985 an office was established within the Central Committee of the CPSU specifically for the observation of the Chinese reform program. Herrmann-Pillath, *Wirtschaftsreform*, p. 14, n. 19.

54. S. Kuznetsov, in *Trud*, December 12, 1985.

55. See S. V. Stepanov and V. Ia. Portiakov, "Shestaia piatiletka KNR: Itogi i problemy," *PDV*, no. 2, 1986, p. 79.

56. A. M. Kruglov, "Mel'koe promyshlennoe proizvodstvo KNR," *PDV*, no. 4, 1984, pp. 79 ff.

57. For example, cf. *Literaturnaia Gazeta*, June 6, 1986, p. 14, as cited in Marshall Goldman and Merle Goldman, "Soviet and Chinese Economic Reform," in *America and the World, 1987/88* (New York: Pergamon Press, 1988), pp. 551–74.

58. *Literaturnaia Gazeta*, June 22, 1986, p. 14; as quoted in Marshall I. Goldman, *Gorbachev's Challenge: Economic Reform in the Age of High Technology* (New York: W. W. Norton, 1987), pp. 196–98. Burlatsky, a former Khrushchev speechwriter, had previously used China as a sort of polemical shooting gallery to warn his compatriots of the perils of neo-Stalinism. See his *Mao Tse-tung: An Ideological and Psychological Portrait*, trans. David Skvirsky (Moscow: Progress Pub., 1980).

59. Cf. *Pravda*, April 11, 1986; also *Pravda*, May 25, 1986.

60. V. Portyakov and S. Stepanov, "China's Special Economic Zones," *Far Eastern Affairs*, no. 2, 1986, p. 36.

61. *Pravda*, June 14, 1986. The Soviets thus take notice (in *Pravda*, May 7, 1986) of the publication of a complete Chinese edition of the works of Marx and Engels; the reminiscences of former victims of the Cultural Revolution are also prominently featured in reviews (e.g., *Pravda*, May 7, 1986).

62. *Pravda*, July 11, 1985; March 16 and April 15, 1986.

63. The March 29, 1986, issue of *Pravda* gives a comprehensive summary of Zhao Ziyang's position on disarmament; also see *Pravda* of April 16, April 26, May 17, and June 4, 1986.

64. See Heinz Timmermann, "The Communist Party of the Soviet Union's Reassessment of International Social Democracy: Dimensions and Trends," *Journal of Communist Studies 5*, no. 2 (June 1989): 173–85.

65. A survey conducted by USIA in Moscow in 1983–84 revealed a considerable diminution of the sense of threat from the PRC that had been noted in a comparable survey conducted in 1980–81. The 1983–84 survey continued to find deep suspicion of the Chinese among an overwhelming majority of respondents, however, with three-fourths estimated to believe that Soviet interests conflicted with those of the PRC. By contrast, only a third felt that Soviet and American interests inherently conflicted. Richard Dobson, *Soviet Elite Attitudes and Perceptions: Foreign Affairs* (Washington, D.C.: Office of Research, USIA, February 1985).

66. The Institute for World Economy of the Academy of Sciences (currently led by academician Oleg Bogomolov) comprises perhaps the largest institution for the study of Eastern Europe in the world (though they also have a section devoted to the study of China). Within the Committee for Cooperation in the Area of Planning (within the Council of Ministers) is a standing work group to evaluate reform experiments in economic and social areas; the USSR is also involved in the institutions of Comecon, which monitors (in the course of regulating) the East European systems. Yet although East European experience with reform antedates that of the Chinese by several decades, the Soviets never seem

to have taken it too seriously. Why? There are essentially two types of East European reform: "plan-compatible reform" exemplified by Honecker's East Germany or Czechoslovakia after Dubček; and structural reform, exemplified by Hungary and Yugoslavia. The former has been relatively successful in terms of economically measurable improvements, but failed to excite the Soviet reform constituency (and in any event was politically defunct by the fall of 1989). The structural reform model has greater political appeal but has been economically unsuccessful since the second oil shock in the late 1970s: Hungary has had zero economic growth from 1985 through 1987, an inflation rate of 7–8 percent per annum, and an adverse trade balance; Yugoslavia had a 200 percent inflation rate and a foreign debt of U.S. $21 billion. *New York Times*, September 6, 1987.

67. The magnitude of these two countries (viz., 1.1 billion and 280 million inhabitants, on 9.6 million and 22.4 million square kilometers, respectively) provides large internal markets and resource bases, ensuring an economic self-sufficiency unmatched by smaller powers (not one of the East European countries is as large as any Chinese province). Neither has had systemic experience with a market economy, as have most of the East European states. Michael Kaser, " 'One Economy, Two Systems': Parallels Between Soviet and Chinese Reform," *International Affairs* 63, no. 3 (Summer 1987): 395–413.

68. Paul M. Johnson, *Redesigning the Communist Economy: The Politics of Economic Reform in Eastern Europe* (Boulder: East European Monographs, 1989), p. 214.

69. Grigorii Kahnin and Vasilii Seliunin have suggested that there was hardly any economic growth during the first half of the 1980s. Aleksandr Zaichenko has argued that the Soviet Union ranks about fiftieth or sixtieth in the world in terms of consumption. Anders Aslund, "Soviet and Chinese Reforms," *The World Today* 45, no. 11 (November 1989): 188–91; see also *New York Times*, April 24, 1990, p. 1. Aslund points out, however, that the perception that the country faced economic crisis did not exist in 1985, and had to be created by reform economists under *glasnost'*.

70. Some other noteworthy indicators: agricultural productivity has not grown, either absolutely or relative to that of the United States. Industrial growth was lower throughout the 1970s than in the preceding decade; output actually declined in 1980 and averaged less than 1 percent in 1979–81. Factor productivity in the economy as a whole essentially stagnated in the 1970s, compared with a gain of 11 percent in the 1970s. See Daniel L. Bond and Herbert S. Levine, "The Soviet Domestic Economy in the 1980s," in Helmut Sonnenfeldt, ed., *Soviet Politics in the 1980s* (Boulder: Westview, 1985), pp. 3–23.

71. See Richard Kaufmann et al., in *Soviet Economy* 1, no. 1 (1984), for a detailed discussion of the evidence surrounding the downward revision of CIA estimates of Soviet defense spending.

72. Don Oberdorfer reviewed recent intelligence estimates in the *Washington Post*, March 27, 1987, p. 431. Ryzhkov's "Report on the Basic Guidelines

of Economic and Social Development for 1986–90," including the period up to the year 2000, foresees doubling national income and industrial production by that time. The Twelfth Five-Year Plan calls for an average annual growth rate in national income of 4.1 percent (compared with 3.1 percent in 1981–85), and industrial production to grow by 25 percent over the five-year period. Annual average farm production (in perhaps the least realistic projection) is to increase by 14.4 percent over the previous five years. However, the most recent reports indicate that the growth rate, after spurting in 1986, slipped well below target in 1987 and 1988, amounting to only about 1.5 percent both years. See "The Soviet Economy in 1988: Gorbachev Changes Course," a report by the CIA and DIA to the Subcommittee on National Security Economics of the Joint Economic Committee, April 14, 1989.

73. Anders Aslund, a Swedish specialist on the Soviet economy, estimates that real GNP fell by 4–5 percent in 1989 and would fall by 8–10 percent in 1990. *New York Times*, March 13, 1990. Grigorii Kahnin has shown that material production changed from a growth rate of 3 percent in 1986 to a decline of 4.5 percent in 1989, while the budget deficit rose from 4 percent of GNP in 1985 to more than 9 percent in 1989 (conservatively estimated). Aurel Braun and Richard B. Day, "Gorbachevian Contradictions," *Problems of Communism*, 39, no. 3 (May–June 1990): 36–51.

74. China's national product growth rate over the two decades 1955–57 to 1975–77 averaged only 5.1 percent per year, or less than 5 percent if the more realistic prices of the late 1970s are used to measure national product (China's relative prices in the 1950s were skewed in favor of industry and against agriculture). Since Mao's death, China's rate of capital formation has fallen slightly, but the growth rate in national product in the nine years between 1977 and 1985 has been among the highest in the world, averaging over 8 percent per year. Real national income per capita grew by an average of 4 percent per annum in 1952–82 and by 6.8 percent in 1979–84. Productivity growth may be assumed to account for much of the change, according to recent estimates. Dwight H. Perkins, *China: Asia's Next Economic Giant?* (Seattle: University of Washington Press, 1986), pp. 9–10.

75. If Chinese defense spending is only 6 percent of GNP in 2010 (in 1988 it was 8 percent), it will be more than 50 percent of the Soviet estimated spending, compared with less than 20 percent in 1988. See Commission on Integrated Long-Term Strategy, *Sources of Change in the Future Security Environment* (Washington, D.C.: The Pentagon, April 1989).

76. Although China's urban economy remains dominated by the 94,000 state-owned enterprises (as of 1985), which produced 70 percent of industrial output that year, an August 1988 survey indicated that 17 percent of the 6,000 "major" state enterprises were still unprofitable, losing U.S. $1 billion in the first six months of that year. By mid-1991, 38 percent were losing money. *New York Times*, September 18, 1991, pp. C1, C16.

77. *Izvestiia*, June 1, 1985, p. 3; *Pravda*, October 25, 1984, p. 5; see also

Tat'iana Zaslavskaia, *A Voice of Reform*, ed. Murray Yanowitch (Armonk: M. E. Sharpe, 1989).

78. The brigade contract system was one of the few experiments authorized in the New Agricultural Program of 1982. Based on Zaslavskaia's results in Altai, the May 1982 CC Plenum decided to extend the experiment to all collective farms. But the state farms refused to participate, and the bureaucracy was unenthusiastic. Goldman, *Gorbachev's Challenge*, p. 59; see also Alec Nove, "Soviet Agriculture: Problems and Prospects," in David Dyker, ed., *The Soviet Union Under Gorbachev: Prospects for Reform* (London: Croom Helm, 1987), pp. 91–106.

79. *New York Times*, March 16, 17, 1989.

80. Although the 1986 grain crop (at 210 million tons) compared favorably with the 180 million ton average of 1981–85, Soviet agricultural productivity declined over the next several years.

81. Certainly a reform of tenurial arrangements is important, but without concurrent reform of pricing, markets, and the supply of consumer goods it seems unlikely to have much impact. Karen M. Brooks, "Soviet Agriculture's Halting Reform," *Problems of Communism*, 39, no. 2 (March–April 1990): 29–42.

82. See Padma Desai, *Perestroika in Perspective: The Design and Dilemmas of Soviet Reform* (Princeton: Princeton University Press, 1989), pp. 57–58.

83. Alexander II's emancipation of the serfs in 1861 allotted land to the peasants but required them to pay the dues of redemption and transferred land not to individual households but to the *mir* (community). Not until Stolypin's reforms in 1908 were all outstanding dues abolished and peasants allowed to buy and sell land, or to leave the *mir*.

84. For every hectare of tilled land the USSR has roughly twenty times fewer agricultural workers than China, but several times more capital input.

85. A 1987 poll of Soviet farm specialists reported by Vorobyev indicated that only 10 percent would unconditionally accept to work a farm under the contract system. A later poll of collective farm chairmen from the same source revealed that 30 percent would be willing to take up such a contract. Yu. Vorobyev, "Ob Arende–Otkrovenno," *Pravda*, April 18, 1989, p. 2, as cited in Frederic Pryor, "When Is Collectivization Reversible?" unpublished paper presented to the Comparative Study of Communist Societies Seminar, University of California, Berkeley, February 1990. G. I. Shmelev, "Sotsial'no ekonomicheskii potensial semeinogo podiada," *Sotsiologicheskie Issledovaniia*, April 1985, pp. 16–20; as quoted in Goldman, *Gorbachev's Challenge*, p. 190; see also Goldman and Goldman, "Soviet and Chinese Economic Reform," pp. 557–74. But such poll findings cannot be taken as definitive. Speculative in nature, they typically elicit majority support for "undecided." Early polls conducted in China on the production responsibility system detected a similarly high level of reserve, which declined quickly once the system established itself.

86. Between 1978 and 1988, China's private sector grew spectacularly, from 180,000 to 20 million units. *New York Times*, November 11, 1988, p. A7. This

fell to 19.3 million in 1989, a drop of 16.44 percent from 1988, but climbed back to 20.24 million in 1990. Between 1985 and 1988 the number of private enterprises doubled (from 3 to 6 million), increasing its share of national industrial output from 1.85 percent to 4.35 percent (4.8 percent by 1990). China's collectively owned industries, employing about 15 percent of China's labor force but representing some 30 percent of total industrial output, grew by about 30 percent in 1985, 16.7 percent in 1986, and an estimated 36 percent in 1987.

87. Whereas state budgetary allocations had accounted for 90 percent of all capital-construction investment in 1957 and 83 percent in 1978, by 1984 the state budget's share of investment had fallen to 54.4 percent, dropping further (to 40–45 percent) in 1985. This was partly a consequence of the budgetary autonomy granted the collective and state sectors, but also of the rapid growth of the private and collective sectors.

88. *Renmin Ribao*, May 11, 1985.

89. *Renmin Ribao*, April 11, 1987. By 1990 the number of free markets had reached 72,130, according to the State Administration for Industry and Commerce. Associated Press, December 14, 1990.

90. Central planning via material balances by 1988 involved only about 20 percent of industrial gross production, and the enterprises concerned have the opportunity to dispose of overplan production independently. The administrative relationship between central authorities and enterprises has become increasingly indirect: the fiscal relationship has shifted to a differentiated tax system.

91. The percentage of investment in economic construction funneled through the state budget shrank from 76.6 percent to 31.6 percent over the past decade, while the percentage derived from bank credit rose from 23.4 percent to 63.4 percent. Liu Guoguang, "A Sweet and Sour Decade," *Beijing Review*, January 2–8, 1989, pp. 22–28.

92. Inflation in 1986–87 reportedly reduced living standards for a fifth of China's 200 million urban dwellers. *New York Times*, September 6, 1987, p. E2.

93. Associated Press (AP), December 14, 1990. This would, to be sure, represent a rate of growth considerably below that of the previous five years.

94. In a major policy speech in mid-1985 to a private meeting of high-level East European economic planners, Gorbachev pronounced himself opposed to such reforms as had been introduced in Yugoslavia or the PRC. "Many of you see the solution to your problems in resorting to market mechanisms in place of direct planning," he said. "Some of you look at the market as a lifesaver for your economies. But comrades, you should not think about lifesavers but about the ship. And the ship is socialism!"

95. See Goldman, *Gorbachev's Challenge*.

96. See Philip Hanson, "The Economy," in Martin McCauley, ed., *The Soviet Union Under Gorbachev* (London: Macmillan, 1987), pp. 97–118.

97. "Osnovnye polozheniia korennoi perestroiki upravleniia ekonomikoi,"

Pravda, June 27, 1987; as cited in Ed A. Hewett, *Reforming the Soviet Economy: Equality Versus Efficiency* (Washington, D.C.: Brookings Institution, 1988), p. 325.

98. *Izvestiia*, January 21, 1989.

99. Not until March 1990 was a new ownership law pushed through the Supreme Soviet that, while avoiding the words "private property," included leeway for individuals to own small businesses, and for big companies to be sold to workers in the form of stock. *New York Times*, May 13, 1990, p. 13.

100. David Lane, "The Societal Dimension," in Curtis Keeble, ed., *The Soviet State: The Domestic Roots of Soviet Foreign Policy* (London: Royal Institute of International Affairs, 1985), pp. 25–42. In the 1970s, the total Soviet labor force was 155 million, which represented an increase of 24 million over the previous decade; in the 1980s, the labor force will have increased by only 8 million. On the other hand, the number of retired workers is slated to increase: there are about 37 million at present, and this number will swell to 80 million by the end of this century. The rate of population growth is now two and a half times as great in Central Asia as in the Slavic republics.

101. China's total trade with the rest of the world has quadrupled from U.S. $20.6 billion in 1978 to $82.7 billion in 1987; as a percentage of GDP exports have risen from an average of 2.62 percent in 1950–76 to 5 percent in 1980, to 8.31 percent in 1982–84, to 16.85 percent in 1987. Whereas average GDP growth in 1982–84 was 10.6 percent, the rate of growth for total trade was 18.7 percent; by 1987, China's trade dependency ratio (exports plus imports as a proportion of GDP) was around 30 percent. He Xinhao, "Exploit the Role of Foreign Trade and Accelerate the Rate of China's Economic Development," *Guoji Maoyi* [International Trade], no. 5, 1982, as trans. in *Chinese Economic Studies* 16, no. 4 (Summer 1983): 37–50; *Far Eastern Economic Review* (hereafter *FEER*), August 29, 1989, p. 51.

102. As soon as joint ventures were approved in China, there was immediate response. In 1980 there were two joint ventures and one wholly owned foreign enterprise; by 1989 China had approved a cumulative total of 21,781 foreign investment projects valued at U.S. $33.7 billion, of which $15.4 billion had actually been invested. In addition, China has established 277 enterprises outside China. There are also 130 wholly owned foreign enterprises in China. *Beijing Review*, July 6, 1987, p. 23; and April 10, 1987, p. 20; *International Trade Tribune* (Beijing Institute of International Trade), no. 2, 1989, p. 1.

103. *Washington Post Weekly Edition* 6, no. 32 (June 12–18, 1989): 6. There was a substantial drop in new investment after Tiananmen (43 percent down in October–December 1989, followed by a 42 percent decline in the first quarter of 1990). But there was no wave of divestment, and by the end of 1990 China was enjoying a resurgence of direct foreign investment. Shen Xiaofang, "A Decade of Direct Foreign Investment in China," *Problems of Communism* 39, no. 2 (March–April 1990): 61–74; *Business Week*, December 23, 1990.

104. *Renmin Ribao*, June 16, 1988.

105. Samuel S. Kim, "Chinese World Policy in Transition," *World Policy*

Journal, Spring 1984, pp. 603–33. Thus in 1986 China paid U.S. $6.5 million into the United Nations and received back $27.7 million from the UN Development Program in technical assistance and $1.2 billion from the World Bank in loans and credits. In 1982 China contributed $300,000 (0.23 percent of the total) to the United Nations Fund for Population Activities (UNFPA), receiving in return $11 million in aid. At the same time, China criticizes the industrialized countries for inadequate magnanimity.

106. When A. W. Clausen visited China in May 1983, he indicated that the Bank had already provided loans and aid amounting to U.S. $870 million, and would give $2.4 billion in loans in 1984 and 1985 for the construction of twenty projects in agriculture, energy, education, industry, and communications. In 1986, China received another $1.2 billion from the World Bank to help fund ten projects, and it was anticipated that loans given to China during the Seventh Five-Year Plan period (1986–90) will double or triple the amount given in the previous five years.

107. Chen Huijun, "Moscow Opens Its Economic Doors," *Beijing Review* 32, no. 20 (May 15–21, 1989): 15–18. The Soviets have also shown greater interest in the UN Economic and Social Commission for Asia and the Pacific, sending Minister of Foreign Trade Boris Aristov to ESCAP's April 1987 meeting in Bangkok, for example. Stephen M. Young, "Gorbachev's Asian Policy: Balancing the New and the Old," *Asian Survey* 28, no. 3 (March 1988): 317–40. By September 1991 the Soviet Union had been granted associate membership in the IMF.

108. *New York Times*, April 15, 1990, p. 13; *Financial Post*, April 19, 1990.

109. Chen, "Moscow Opens," pp. 16–17.

110. See David Dyker, "Soviet Industry in the International Context," and Alan H. Smith, "International Trade and Resources," in Dyker, ed., *Soviet Union*, pp. 75–91 and 106–25, respectively.

111. The Soviets under Gorbachev have opened the doors as never before, letting out Jews, Armenians, and Germans at a rate of some 200,000 per year (as of 1989).

112. According to CIA figures (sometimes criticized as being too conservative), as cited in *New York Times*, May 13, 1990. As of 1990, the country had a debt service ratio of 25 percent. *Toronto Globe and Mail*, March 13, 1990; *New York Times*, March 16, 1990; *Christian Science Monitor*, October 15, 1991, p.1.

113. At least one of its original coauthors (Charles A. Vanik, now a trade lawyer) has manifested a change of heart concerning the Jackson-Vanik amendment, urging bestowal of MFN treatment to Gorbachev's USSR. *New York Times*, May 5, 1989, p. A5. President Bush endorsed this recommendation at the 1989 Malta summit, and Jackson-Vanik was accordingly rescinded in June of 1991.

114. To alleviate the impact of energy price rises in the 1970s, the USSR agreed to provide oil and gas to CMEA members at a price that would only gradually catch up with the prices other countries were paying on the world

market. Eastern Europe is thus estimated to have received an implicit Soviet subsidy amounting to U.S. $5.8 billion in 1974–78, about $11.6 billion in 1979, $17.8 billion in 1980, and $18.7 billion in 1981. But the average subsidy for 1982–84 is estimated to have dropped to $12.1 billion, reaching $10–11 billion in 1984. Michael Marrese and Jan Vanous, *Implicit Subsidies and Non-Market Benefits in Soviet Trade with Eastern Europe* (Berkeley: University of California Press, 1982). Although some economists consider these estimates excessive, there is no disagreement about either the existence of Soviet subsidies in the 1970s or their decline in the 1980s.

115. By the late 1970s, most East European countries were devoting between 25–45 percent of their export earnings to debt service.

116. *Christian Science Monitor*, January 9, 1989, p. 4; Kent M. Wiedemann, "China in the Vanguard of a New Socialism," *Asian Survey* 26, no. 7 (July 1986): 774–92.

117. See Stephen White, "The USSR Supreme Soviet: A Developmental Perspective," and William A. Welsh, "The Status of Research on Representative Institutions in Eastern Europe," in Daniel Nelson and Stephen White, eds., *Communist Legislatures in Comparative Perspective* (Albany: State University of New York Press, 1982), pp. 247–74 and 257–308, respectively.

118. Standing Committees, not unlike the various functionally specialized committees in the U.S. Congress, typically engage in at least three activities: (1) periodic investigations of the acts of government ministries; (2) monitoring the implementation of parliamentary acts by the state bureaucracy on a continuous basis; and (3) participating in the drafting of legislation.

119. Quantitative evidence shows that Gorbachev precipitated more personnel turnover from March 1985 to August 1988 than his three preceding incumbents during their combined tenures. See Jyiki Iivonen, "Gorbachev's Personnel Policy," in R. J. Hill and J. A. Dellenbrant, *Gorbachev and Perestroika: Towards a New Society?* (Aldershot: Edward Elgar, 1989), pp. 171–94.

120. Crouch, *Revolution and Evolution*, p. 65.

121. See Thomas Remington, "A Socialist Pluralism of Opinions: *Glasnost'* and Policy-Making Under Gorbachev," *Russian Review* 48, no. 3 (July 1989): 271–305.

122. See Seweryn Bialer, "The Changing Soviet Political System: The Nineteenth Party Conference and After," in Bialer, ed., *Politics, Society, and Nationality Inside Gorbachev's Russia* (Boulder: Westview, 1989), pp. 193–241; see also *Christian Science Monitor*, August 1, 1988, p. 9; *New York Times*, March 9, 1989, p. 1.

123. See Dittmer, *China's Continuous Revolution*.

124. This verdict may seem overly harsh in the light of the posthumous critique of Stalinism. Yet Khrushchev's critique remained at a personal level, derogating Stalin as an individual but failing to take on the system he built; and that criticism was discontinued under Brezhnev.

125. A measure of ideological tolerance was further signaled by the publica-

tion in 1988 of the early writings of Chen Duxiu, expelled from the party in 1929 and subsequent founder of the Chinese Trotskyist movement.

126. For example, cf. L. Viskresenskii, "En socialistik marknod," *Nyheter fran Sovjetunionen*, February 1987, pp. 46–47.

127. *New York Times*, February 19, 1988, p. 1.

128. Tat'iana Zaslavskaia, "Doklad o neobkhodimosti bolee uglublennogo izucheniia v SSSR sotsial'nogo mekhanizma razvitiia ekonomiki," *Materiali samizdata*, as cited in Robert F. Miller, "Doctrinal and Ideological Issues of Reform in Socialist Systems," *Soviet Studies* 91, no. 3 (July 1989): 430–49.

129. See Zaslavskaia, "Social Justice and the Human Factor in Economic Development," and "Urgent Problems in the Theory of Economic Sociology," as trans. in *A Voice of Reform*, pp. 85–103 and 123–40.

130. Remarks at the Center for Slavic and East European Studies, University of California at Berkeley, February 1990.

4. Building Functional Bridges

1. C. G. Jacobsen, *Sino-Soviet Relations Since Mao: The Chairman's Legacy* (New York: Praeger, 1981), p. 89.

2. In a speech in Tashkent on March 24, Brezhnev made a major policy statement to pave the way for the second resumption of talks. Four points in this declaration were noteworthy:

(1) We did not deny and do not now [deny] the existence of a socialist system in China [*sic*]—although China's fusion with the imperialists' policy in the world arena is, of course, at variance with the interests of socialism. (2) We have never supported and do not now support in any form the so-called concept of two Chinas. . . . (3) We are also ready to discuss the question of possible measures to strengthen mutual trust in the area of the Soviet-Chinese frontier. (4) We are prepared to come to terms, without any preconditions, on measures acceptable to both sides to improve Soviet-Chinese relations on the basis of mutual respect for each other's interests, noninterference in each other's affairs and mutual benefit—certainly, not to the detriment of third countries.

Pravda, March 25, 1982. Brezhnev reaffirmed his proposals in a speech in Baku on September 26, whereupon the Soviet press halted all polemical attacks on the PRC.

3. That is, increasing from an estimated U.S. $2.6 billion in 1986 to $5–6 billion by 1990. *Guoji Maoyi*, no. 10, 1985, pp. 14–15.

4. Lu Zejian, "Observing Sino-Soviet Relations on the Eve of the Summit," *Guang Jiao Jing*, 199 (April 16, 1989), pp. 12–16.

5. The previous organization was Eurocentric (Australia and New Zealand, for example, were grouped with England, Ireland, and Canada in the Second European Department as English-speaking Commonwealth countries) and otherwise obsolete (the First Far Eastern Department handled China, Mongolia, and North Korea, because all three were treaty allies of the USSR at the time). Under the reorganization, East Asia is divided into three departments,

each of which has been upgraded to a directorate. The First Far Eastern Department, to be called the Directorate of Socialist Countries in Asia, will include the PRC, Mongolia, and North Korea, plus the Indochinese states. The Southeast Asian Department will include the five ASEAN countries with which the USSR has diplomatic relations, plus Brunei. The third department, to be called the Directorate for Pacific Cooperation, will group Japan with Australia, New Zealand, and other South Pacific countries with which the USSR has diplomatic relations. In addition, separate departments may be created to deal with general problems of Soviet foreign policy, such as the Third World, the nonaligned movement, and disarmament and arms control.

6. A considerable number of Soviet-trained cadres have risen in the party and government hierarchy, at least fifteen of them holding key ministerial posts on the State Council. Most prominent of these is Li Peng himself, Zhou Enlai's foster son, who studied at the Moscow Power Institute from 1948 to 1955; and Jiang Zemin, who replaced Zhao Ziyang as party general secretary in June 1989. Those who are national councillors and head a key ministry or commission are Li Peng, Li Tieying, Song Jian, Zou Jiahua, and Li Guixian. Others include Zou Jinmeng, Qian Qichen (for many years China's leading authority on Soviet affairs, foreign minister since 1988), and Ding Henggao, a protege of Deng Xiaoping recently named minister in charge of National Defense Industry and the Science Commission. Soviet-trained CCP Politburo members include Li Peng, Jiang Zemin, Li Tieying, Yang Shangkun (also permanent secretary of the Military Affairs Commission), and Ding Guangen (alternate member).

7. See David Michael Lampton, "China's Limited Accommodation with the USSR: Coalition Politics," *AEI Foreign Policy and Defense Review* 6, no. 3 (August 1986): 26–35.

8. Rajan Menon and Daniel Abele, "Security Dimensions of Soviet Territorial Disputes with China and Japan," *Journal of Northeast Asian Studies* 8, no. 1 (Spring 1989): 3–20. Cooperation on energy projects that harness these two rivers encourages high hopes: Chinese economists believe China's industrial northeast could ease at least 20 percent of its power shortfall through closer integration with Siberian energy sources. Gary Klintworth, *China's Modernization: The Strategic Implications for the Asian-Pacific Region* (Canberra: AGPS Press, 1989), pp. 62–69.

9. *New York Times*, December 4, 1988.

10. This aspect appeared particularly attractive to the Chinese in the mid-1980s. In late 1984 and early 1985, China's foreign exchange reserves plunged by 30 percent. In the January–July 1985 period, Beijing reported a cumulative trade deficit of U.S. $7.89 billion. Since that time, the PRC has been able to rectify its trade imbalance with the United States for at least the time being, though it continues to have difficulties with Japan and some other countries.

11. Moscow Radio Peace and Progress in Mandarin to China, December 25, 1984, in *FBIS–USSR*, December 28, 1984, p. 82.

12. "Given the present situation, where Western powers are taking steps to

strengthen protectionism in foreign trade, and where China's exports come under numerous restrictions and barriers, we should consider the issues related to market policies, bearing in mind the growth of trade and economic ties with the Soviet Union and East European countries. This will ensure a reliable external market for our country." *Shijie Jingji Daobao*, August 19, 1985.

13. Kasuyuki Kinbara, "The Economic Dimension of Soviet Policy," in Gerald Segal, ed., *The Soviet Union in East Asia: Predicaments of Power* (London: Heinemann, 1983), pp. 102–28. Soviet advisers and specialists would probably be considerably cheaper for Beijing to hire than Western or Japanese personnel.

14. *FBIS–China*, October 20, 1987, pp. 1–2.

15. Deborah Diamond-Kim, "Partners in Austerity," *China Business Review*, May–June 1987, p. 15.

16. *South China Morning Post* (hereafter *SCMP*), April 3, 1989, pp. 1, 6.

17. *China Daily*, May 13, 1989, p. 2. In contrast, by the end of 1989, the United States, as the leading foreign investor, had invested some $4 billion, in more than four hundred joint ventures.

18. In 1987, total Soviet trade with Asia, including India, was only U.S. $12.8 billion (U.S. trade with the region in 1988 totaled $280 billion). Soviet trade has hitherto tended to focus on a few allies, with whom the relationship is quite lopsided, due to Western embargoes against several of the smaller Asian socialist countries. North Korean and Vietnamese imports from the USSR constitute 40 percent of their total imports, while their exports to the USSR amount to about a third of their total exports. Ed A. Hewett and Herbert S. Levine, "The Soviet Union's Economic Relations in Asia," in Donald Zagoria, ed., *Soviet Policy in East Asia* (New Haven: Yale University Press, 1982), p. 202, n. 34.

19. It is estimated that 82 percent of the total hydroelectric potential of the USSR is east of the Urals, 75 percent of the coal reserves in the A+B+C1 class and as much as 93 percent of geological reserves, and 81 percent of natural gas reserves in the A+B+C1 class. See Yong Chi Kim, "Soviet Economic Policy Toward East Asia," and Theodore Shabad, "Siberian Development and Soviet Policy in East Asia," in J. K. Park and J. M. Ma, eds., *The Soviet Union and East Asia in the 1980s* (Boulder: Westview, 1983), pp. 264–77 and 250–64, respectively; also Sidney Bearman, "Soviet Policy Toward East Asia," in Douglas Stuart, *Security Within the Pacific Rim* (Aldershot: Gow Publishing Co., 1987), pp. 9–22; and Allen Whiting, *Siberian Development and East Asia: Threat or Promise?* (Stanford: Stanford University Press, 1981), p. 44.

20. Crouch, *Revolution and Evolution*, p. 187.

21. Li Changjiu, "The Soviet Union Accelerates the Development of Siberia and the Soviet Far East," *Renmin Ribao*, November 6, 1985, p. 7.

22. *Pravda*, July 24, 1987.

23. As quoted in Peter Ellingsen, "Vladivostok To Be Used as Test for Economic Glasnost," *The Age*, October 3, 1988, p. 8.

24. *Christian Science Monitor*, September 15, 1989, pp. 1–2.

25. *New York Times,* February 5, 1989.

26. See Leslie Dienes, *Soviet Asia: Economic Development and National Policy Choices* (Boulder: Westview, 1987).

27. Jochen Bethkenhagen, *Die Rolle Asiens in der sowjetischen Aussenwirtschaftspolitik* (Cologne: Berichte des Bundesinstituts für ostwissenschaftliche und internationale Studien, no. 48, 1986).

28. *FBIS–China,* April 14, 1989, p. 3; May 17, 1989, pp. 35–36.

29. Lu Zejian, "Observing," pp. 12–16. China indicated during Foreign Economic Minister Konstantin Katushev's visit to Beijing in March 1990 that it wants trade on a hard-currency basis. The Soviets agreed, in a January 1991 directive placing all of their intra-bloc trade on that basis. *FEER,* April 26, 1990, pp. 12–13.

30. *FBIS–China,* January 12, 1988, pp. 6–8.

31. Despite Mao's objections, some 200,000 Chinese workers worked in Siberia in the 1950s. Diamond-Kim, "Partners," p. 15.

32. Qian Hong, "Nation Looks to Work Overseas for Construction Jobless," *China Daily Business Weekly,* January 22, 1989; *Christian Science Monitor,* February 9, 1989, p. 4; *SCMP,* January 18, 1990.

5. Parellel Development

1. *Christian Science Monitor,* February 7, 1989, p. 1.

Part II. China's Search for a National Identity

1. The concept of identity is derived from the post-Freudian phase of psychoanalysis, specifically the work of Erik Erikson. See, for example, Erik H. Erikson, "Ego Development and Historical Change," *Psychoanalytic Study of the Child* 2 (1946): 359–96; and *Childhood and Society* (New York: W. W. Norton, 1963, 2d ed.).

2. In its earliest incarnation, the term "national identity" tended to refer to the relationship between mass public and political regime, like the concept of "political culture" as used by (say) David Easton. Thus Pye refers to the "political identity crisis" that occurs "when a community finds that what it once unquestionably accepted as the physical and psychological definitions of its collective self are no longer acceptable under new historic conditions." Lucian Pye, "Identity and the Political Culture," in Leonard Binder et al., *Crises and Sequences in Political Development* (Princeton: Princeton University Press, 1971), pp. 101–35. See also Peter Du Preez, *The Politics of Identity: Ideology and the Human Image* (Oxford: Basil Blackwell, 1980), and Kenneth R. Hoover, *A Politics of Identity: Liberation and the Natural Community* (Urbana: University of Illinois Press, 1975).

3. See Lowell Dittmer, "Political Culture and Political Symbolism: Toward a Theoretical Synthesis," *World Politics* 29, no. 4 (July 1977): 552–84.

4. See Andrew J. Weigert, J. Smith Teitge, and Dennis W. Teitge, *Society*

and Identity: Toward a Sociological Psychology (Cambridge and New York: Cambridge University Press, 1986).

5. Erikson, "Ego Development," pp. 359–96.

6. See George Herbert Mead, *Mind, Self, and Society* (Chicago: University of Chicago Press, 1934), pp. 337 et passim.

7. Helen Merrell Lynd, *On Shame and the Search for Identity* (New York: Science Editions, 1965), pp. 210–58; see also Erikson, *Young Man Luther: A Study in Psychoanalysis and History* (New York: W. W. Norton, 1962).

8. See Yehezkel Dror, *Crazy States: A Counterconventional Strategic Problem* (Lexington, Mass.: D. C. Heath, 1971). The principal example of the "crazy state" for Dror appears to be Nazi Germany.

9. See C. P. FitzGerald, *The Chinese View of Their Place in the World* (London: Oxford University Press, 1965).

10. Pye has argued to the contrary that China, almost unique among developing countries, never experienced an identity crisis. Because of their ancient imperial tradition, the Chinese, according to Pye, have always had a secure sense of identity; the major crisis in the context of Chinese modernization has not been identity, but rather authority. Lucian Pye, *The Spirit of Chinese Politics: A Psychocultural Study of Political Development* (Cambridge, Mass.: MIT Press, 1968). This is true if national identity is defined in terms of the cultural tradition and political experience of a people *qua* citizenry, but not if it pertains to the nation-state as a collective entity. Emerging from a tradition as a multiethnic empire built on a shared culture and lacking the properties of a modern nation-state, China had considerable difficulty adapting to the post-Westphalian international system it encountered in the eighteenth and nineteenth centuries. More recently, Pye seems to have shifted his position: "China's identity problem, which is at the core of its legitimacy difficulties, is manifestly obvious, but few in China dare give voice to it." Pye, *The Mandarin and the Cadre: China's Political Cultures* (Ann Arbor: Center for Chinese Studies, University of Michigan, 1988), p. 167.

11. A negative identity is one that the actor has been explicitly warned against becoming, but embraces because positive identities are impossible to realize—such as the parson's daughter who becomes a nightclub floozy because being her father's daughter is too hard. Although Erikson seems to consider the negative identity pathological or at least problematic, it may also contribute to creative transformation, as in "Black is beautiful."

6. China and the International Communist Movement

1. "On Nationalism and Internationalism," in *The Collected Works of Liu Shao-ch'i* (Hong Kong: Union Research Institute, 1969). Though written in 1948, Liu's article was not published until 1949.

2. Robert Conquest, *Power and Policy in the USSR: The Struggle for Stalin's Succession, 1945–1960* (New York: Harper and Row, 1967), pp. 202–3.

3. During Khrushchev's October 1954 visit to Beijing, he said: "The victory

of the Chinese people's revolution is the most outstanding event in world history since the great October socialist revolution." *Renmin Ribao*, October 3, 1954. This signified that the PRC should rank second in the bloc. As Molotov put it, in a February 1955 foreign policy report to the Supreme Soviet, "There has been formed in the world a socialist and democratic camp headed by the Soviet Union, or to be more exact, headed by the Soviet Union and the People's Republic of China." He described China as "co-leader" of the bloc, with "co-responsibility for its internal cohesion and external aims." *Renmin Ribao*, February 10, 1955; *Pravda*, February 15, 1955.

4. "Better Fewer, but Better," in V. I. Lenin, *Selected Works* (New York: International Publishers, 1943), 9:400.

5. Strobe Talbott, ed., *Khrushchev Remembers: The Last Testament* (Boston: Little, Brown, 1974), pp. 250–51.

6. Cf. Paul Keal, *Unspoken Rules and Superpower Dominance* (London: Macmillan, 1983).

7. See Parris Chang, "Research Notes on the Changing Loci of Decision in the CCP," *China Quarterly*, no. 44 (October–December 1970), pp. 169–95.

8. This type of mimeses was perhaps not exclusively one-way. Thus Medvedev states that "it is clear that it was certainty of firm support from Peking that prompted Molotov, Malenkov, Kaganovich and their supporters to come out against Khrushchev in June 1957." Medvedev, *China and the Superpowers*, p. 30.

9. Cf. "On Historical Experience Concerning the Dictatorship of the Proletariat," *Renmin Ribao*, April 5, 1956, as trans. in *Current Background*, no. 403 (July 25, 1956), p. 1.

10. According to a 1985 interview with a member of the Institute of Soviet and Eastern European Studies of the Chinese Academy of Social Sciences in Beijing.

11. "It seems that Poland and China understand one another very well, for some time, without knowing it," Mao said to Ochab. "The Poles are good company for us, and we welcome them." Flora Lewis, *A Case History of Hope* (New York: Doubleday, 1965), pp. 183–84; as quoted in Levesque, *Conflit*, p. 30.

12. K. S. Karol, *Visa pour la Pologne* (Paris: Gallimard, 1958), p. 37. The PRC published the full text of Gomulka's speech to the Eighth Plenum of the PUWP as an expression of Chinese support for the Polish road to socialism. *Renmin Ribao*, November 1, 1956.

13. *Renmin Ribao*, November 21, 1956; as quoted in Zbigniew Brzezinski, *The Soviet Bloc: Unity and Conflict* (New York: Praeger, 1961, rev. ed.), pp. 277, 502.

14. G. V. Astafiev, A. M. Dubinski, et al., *The PRC's Foreign Policy and International Relations, 1949–1973*, 2 vols. (Moscow: Mysl', 1974), 1:64. Indeed, the Chinese press did not at first refer to the rebels as counterrevolutionaries (merely as rioters), and did not blame the rising on Western instigation.

Nor did it carry any report on the actions of the Soviet forces, except the announcement of the Hungarian defense minister that they would be withdrawn by October 31.

15. *China and the Soviet Union*, compiled by Peter Jones and Sian Kevill (New York: Facts on File, 1985), p. 8.

16. Levesque, *Conflit*, pp. 45–47. On November 3, *Renmin Ribao* gave a full account of the Hungarian incident in an editorial, accusing the Nagy government of "leaning to the imperialist side and betraying the national interests of Hungary by scrapping the Warsaw Pact." The following day, the paper urged the Hungarian people to "defend socialism and defeat the insurrection of counterrevolutionaries." On November 5, in an editorial entitled "Celebrate the Great Victory of the Hungarian People," the paper emphasized the correctness of the Soviet decision to suppress the uprising.

17. See Ray, *China and Eastern Europe*, pp. 6–31.

18. These events have been most fully described by Roderick MacFarquhar, in *The Origins of the Cultural Revolution*, vol. 1: *Contradictions Among the People, 1956–1957* (London: Oxford University Press, 1974).

19. It was during the Hundred Flowers movement that the first criticisms of the Soviet model publicly emerged. General Long Yun, vice-chairman of the National Defense Council, said that since China was fighting in Korea for the sake of socialism, it was unfair to have to shoulder the burden of all its war expenditures; although the Soviets granted a loan, it had to be paid back in a relatively short period of only ten years plus interest. Moreover, during the Soviet occupation of Manchuria at the close of World War II, the Soviets had dismantled and removed to the USSR large quantities of machinery and industrial equipment, without indemnification. *Dagong Bao* (Tianjing), July 14, 1957. Others complained about having to learn everything from the Soviet Union, calling this dogmatism. *Harbin Ribac* (Harbin), August 13, 1957. Anti-Soviet utterances reported by the Chinese press during the Hundred Flowers were made in all parts of the country, but particularly in Manchuria.

20. In the spring of 1957, the temporary rehabilitation of Stalin reached its zenith. An article in late March stated: "Great credit is due to Stalin for what he has done for our Party, the working class and the international workers' movement. . . . Marxism does not deny the role of outstanding personalities in history, nor does it deny the role of the leaders of the working people in leading the revolutionary liberation movement and in building a society." "Why the Cult of the Individual Is Against the Spirit of Marxism-Leninism," *Pravda*, March 28, 1957. The resolutions adopted by the CPSU Central Committee and published in *Pravda* on July 2 gave an even higher appraisal of Stalin's contributions, holding (with the Chinese) that Stalin had more merits than faults.

21. In December, opposition to dogmatism and opposition to revisionism were accorded the same priority: "While we are strengthening the opposition to dogmatism, we must simultaneously firmly oppose revisionism." *Renmin Ribao*, December 29, 1956; as quoted in Yang Junshi, *Xiandaihua yu Zhong-*

guo Gongchanzhuyi, p. 150, n. 4. Then at a propaganda work conference in March 1957, it was decided that "In the current situation, revisionism is even more dangerous than dogmatism." Mao Zedong, in Ding Wang, ed., *Mao Zedong Xuanji Buyi* [Supplement to Mao Zedong's Selected Works] (Hong Kong: Ming Bao Monthly Pub., 1971), 3 (1949–59): 140. The same accent is visible in Mao's essay, "On the Correct Handling of Contradictions Among the People," published three months later.

22. Quoted by Hoxha in Jon Halliday, ed., *The Artful Albanian: Memoirs of Enver Hoxha* (London: Chatto and Windus, 1986), p. 215. Mao insisted that the phrase "The socialist camp is headed by the USSR" be included in the conference declaration, but Khrushchev caviled at the term "head." Khrushchev later revealed in conversation that it was not at his initiative that the leading role of the CPSU was explicitly set forth in the declaration. *Pravda*, July 12, 1958; *New York Times*, June 15, July 15, 1958.

23. As quoted in Levesque, *Conflit*, p. 26. The fortieth anniversary conference, which included representatives of the ruling parties of all thirteen socialist countries (excluding only Yugoslavia), was one of the last to meet under relatively normal circumstances. Khrushchev displayed great cordiality toward the Chinese delegation, whose support he needed to consolidate his own still precarious ascendancy. The Chinese delegation, under the leadership of Mao himself, enthusiastically championed Soviet primacy, grateful as they were for Khrushchev's promises of strategic military assistance. The final declaration incorporated significant concessions on which the CCP had insisted in a compromise formulation that both reaffirmed the principle of peaceful coexistence and the possibility of "nonpeaceful" transition to socialism, and condemned both "revisionism" and "dogmatism."

24. See the polemic, *In Refutation of Modern Revisionism* (Beijing: Foreign Languages Press, 1958), p. 45. A more critical attitude toward Gomulka became evident immediately after the Hungarian crackdown. "The fundamental problem with some East European countries is that they have not done a good job of waging class struggle and left so many counterrevolutionaries at large," Mao declared in November 1956. Mao, *Selected Works*, 5:341–47.

25. Participants have later reported that Mao's pro-Moscow role in 1957 particularly annoyed the Polish Workers' Party and the Italian Communist Party. See P. Ingrao (PCI Standing Committee member), "Mao a Mosca nel 1957," *Rinàscita* (Rome), no. 37, September 17, 1976, pp. 10 ff.; as cited in Heinz Timmermann, *Peking's 'eurokommunistische' Wende: Zur Wiedereinschaltung der Kommunistische Partei Chinas in das internationale kommunistische Parteiensystem* (Cologne: Berichte des Bundesinstituts für ostwissenschaftliche und internationale Studien, no. 25, 1983).

26. Incidentally, the Great Leap also had repercussions in Eastern Europe, particularly Bulgaria, which conducted some Maoist-inspired experiments in agriculture. See Nissan Oren, *Revolution Administered: Agrarianism and Communism in Bulgaria* (Baltimore: Johns Hopkins University Press, 1973).

27. See Walter Lafeber, *America, Russia, and the Cold War, 1945–1980* (New York: Wiley and Sons, 1980), p. 37.

28. See Christer Joensson, *Superpower: Comparing American and Soviet Foreign Policy* (New York: St. Martin's Press, 1987).

29. Robin Edmonds, *Soviet Foreign Policy, 1962–1973: The Paradox of Super Power* (London: Oxford University Press, 1975), p. 17.

30. Ray, *China and Eastern Europe*, p. 51.

31. *China and the Soviet Union*, p. 48.

32. On the eve of the Moscow Conference, thirty-nine of the eighty-eight communist parties in the world were pro-Soviet, five pro-Chinese, thirty split, and fourteen independent or neutral, according to U.S. government calculations. "The World's Communist Parties," *Time*, June 13, 1969, p. 28.

33. Jo and Pi, *Russia Versus China*, p. 63.

34. Andrzej Korbonski, "CMEA, Economic Integration, and *Perestroika,* 1949–1989," *Studies in Comparative Communism* 23, no. 1 (Spring 1990): 47–73.

35. Zdenek Kavan, "Gorbachev and the World—the Political Side," in Dyker, ed., *Soviet Union*, pp. 164–204.

36. Levesque, *Conflit*, p. 105.

37. Cf. Albert Hirschman's analysis of the power of the threat of boycott, in his *Exit, Voice and Loyalty: Responses to Decline in Firms, Organizations, and States* (Cambridge: Harvard University Press, 1970).

38. Ray, *China and Eastern Europe*, pp. 73–76.

39. Kevin Devlin, "Schism and Secession," *Survey*, January 1965, p. 38; and "Lonely Revolutionaries: The Pro-Chinese Groups of Western Europe," Radio Free Europe Report, February 25, 1970, as quoted in Barbara Barnouin, "Dissonant Voice in International Communism," in H. Kapur, ed., *The End of an Isolation: China After Mao* (Dordrecht: Martinus Nijhoff, 1985), p. 213.

40. The resolution of World War II boundary issues (between West Germany and the USSR and Poland in 1970, between West and East Germany in 1973) lowered the threat of German revanchism. In 1969, the Soviets linked Chinese and German territorial aggression, and the Bulgarians and even the East Germans invoked the threat of Naziism by referring to an alleged Bonn-Beijing axis. By 1972, the West Germans were disappearing from such nightmare scenarios. Jeffrey Simon, *Cohesion and Dissension in Eastern Europe: Six Crises* (New York: Praeger, 1983), p. 126.

41. Raymond L. Garthoff, *Detente and Confrontation: American-Soviet Relations from Nixon to Reagan* (Washington, D.C.: Brookings, 1985), p. 200. Thus Zhou Enlai assured Romania of Chinese support, and the PRC halted polemics with Yugoslavia immediately after the invasion. It is even conceivable that Soviet consideration for their vulnerable Chinese flank inhibited them in moving against Bucharest.

42. Military intervention in Czechoslovakia forced the Romanians to recognize that it was the WTO that posed the principal threat to their independence.

They denounced the use of force against a fraternal ally, adopted the Yugoslav policy of territorial defense, developed a credible Patriotic Guard, and broadened economic, political, and military ties with the West, the PRC, and the nonaligned Third World. Simon, *Cohesion and Dissension*, p. 222.

43. The Sino-Albanian romance ended in the summer of 1978, when Hua Guofeng arrested the Gang of Four, rehabilitated Deng Xiaoping, and invited Cyrus Vance to China. On July 7, *Zeri i Popullit* launched an attack on the "three-world theory" as "anti-Leninist" and "pseudo-imperialist." The Albanians blamed China for proposing that the socialist camp had disappeared and for putting itself and Albania in an indiscriminate Third World, alongside Mobutu's Zaire and Pinochet's Chile, and for erasing all "class differences" among states. See Elez Biberaj, *Albania and China: A Study of an Unequal Alliance* (Boulder: Westview, 1986), pp. 95–96, 126–38.

44. Richard Nixon went to Romania on August 2–3, 1969, in the first visit to a communist state since Roosevelt met at Yalta in 1945, where he discussed with Ceausescu the need for a new Sino-American relationship. The Romanians conveyed this message to Beijing. In his October 26, 1970, meeting with Ceausescu in Washington, Nixon proposed an exchange of high-level representatives short of the reestablishment of diplomatic relations, and this message was relayed to Beijing in a visit by Vice-premier Corneliu Bogdan. Zhou Enlai responded with a message to Nixon to the effect that the PRC was prepared to receive a special envoy in Beijing and that in view of Nixon's pioneering visits to Bucharest in 1969 and Belgrade in 1970, Nixon himself would be welcome in Beijing. Romania was the only Warsaw Pact member to react favorably to Nixon's July 15, 1971, public acceptance of Zhou's invitation.

45. Jacques Levesque, "Les 'trois obstacles' dans un monde changeant," *Le Monde diplomatique* 31, no. 361 (April 1984): 1, 6–7.

46. *Renmin Ribao*, May 7, 1987, p. 4; as cited in Chi Su, "Sino-Soviet Relations in the 1980s: From Confrontation to Conciliation," in Samuel Kim, ed., *China and the World*, 2d ed. (Boulder: Westview, 1989), p. 115.

47. Constitution of the Communist Party of China, adopted by the Twelfth National Congress (September 1982), "Principles Governing Relations with Foreign Communist Parties," *Beijing Review*, no. 17, 1983.

48. Deng Xiaoping, "An Important Principle for Handling Relations Among Fraternal Parties" (May 31, 1982), *Beijing Review*, May 22, 1983, p. 15.

49. Dong Fusheng, "Theoreticians in Yugoslavia, Romania, Poland, and Hungary Explore Questions of Socialist Theory," *Renmin Ribao*, August 1, 1986, p. 7.

50. Radio Beijing, June 25, 1986.

51. *Xinhua*, November 1978; as cited in Barnouin, "Dissonant Voice."

52. Pierre-Antoine Donnet, Hong Kong AFP, October 17, 1986, as reprinted in *FBIS–China*, October 17, 1986, p. C1.

53. The PCI remains the most advanced in this regard, although the CCP is not far behind. One of the theses adopted at its Seventeenth Party Congress in

April 1986 states that the PCI sees itself "as a part neither of a given ideological camp nor of an organized movement on a European or global level."

54. Timmermann, *Peking's 'eurokommunistische' Wende*, pp. 41–43; see also Timmermann, *The Decline of the World Communist Movement* (Boulder: Westview, 1987), p. 109.

55. *The Times* (London), April 11, 1987; *New York Times*, November 5, 1987, pp. 1, 6. Speaking in Prague on April 10, Gorbachev said: "We are far from appealing to every socialist country to copy us. Every socialist country has its specific features and fraternal parties determine their political line with a view to their national conditions."

56. Gavriil Popov, in *Moscow News*, no. 4 (January 24, 1988), p. 4; as cited in Gail W. Lapidus, "The Making of Russia's China Policy: Domestic/Foreign Linkages in Sino-Soviet Relations," unpublished paper, University of California, Berkeley, 1989.

57. *New York Times*, March 19, 1988, p. 1. Although this would certainly seem to nullify the Brezhnev Doctrine, it is worth noting that a similar document was issued in 1955, just one year before Soviet troops crushed the Hungarian uprising.

58. *New York Times*, November 1, 1988.

59. *Pravda*, May 20, 1987.

60. That is, by claiming that no communist party has the universally correct "line," the CCP implicitly endorses a pluralistic conception of doctrine at odds with its claim to exclusive domestic ideological and political hegemony. Moreover, by broadening the ambit of bloc relations to include democratic socialist as well as communist parties, the CCP risks including alternative models for political reform. "Our Party will continue to strengthen its friendly relations with socialist parties and social democratic parties in various countries," as one wary article put it. "However, we cannot deny the principled differences between the Communist Party and the Social Democratic Party in the ideological field and between scientific socialism and 'democratic socialism.' " Educational Work Department of Beijing Municipal CPC Committee, "Who Represents the Mainstream and Direction of the Socialist Movement? Analyzing and Commenting on 'Democratic Socialism,' " *Guangming Ribao*, April 21, 1987, p. 3.

7. China and the Third World

1. Liu Shao-ch'i, *On the Party* (Beijing: Foreign Languages Press, 1951), p. 31.

2. Mao Zedong interview with Anna Louise Strong, as quoted in Zagoria, *Sino-Soviet Conflict*, pp. 25 ff.

3. *Xinhua*, November 23, 1949; see also Robert C. North, "Two Revolutionary Models: Russian and Chinese," in A. Doak Barnett, ed., *Communist Strategies in Asia* (London: Pall Mall Press, 1963).

4. At the CPI's Second Congress, Ranadive remarked without Soviet ap-

proval on the "international significance" of the Chinese revolution. Throughout 1948, reports and articles appeared in *People's Age* (the central CPI organ) hailing the victories of the CCP and predicting that "the final victory of the Chinese revolution will decisively shift the balance of forces in favor of the fighting people of Asia against the imperialist-bourgeois axis." *People's Age*, September 9, October 12, November 11, December 5, 1948, as cited in Hemen Ray, *The Sino-Soviet Conflict Over India* (New Delhi: Abhinav Pub., 1986), pp. 7–8.

5. Ranadive was chosen to deliver the first public repudiation of Mao, calling him a "heretic" and "deviator" from "Marxist, Leninist, and Stalinist teachings" and emphasizing (in a 35,000-word article in the CPI's theoretical journal) the validity of the "experience of the Russian revolution" for other communist parties. *The Communist* 2, no. 4 (June–July 1949): 9–89; Barnouin, "Dissonant Voice," pp. 202–33.

6. David Allen Mayers, *Cracking the Monolith: U.S. Policy Against the Sino-Soviet Alliance, 1949–1955* (Baton Rouge: Louisiana State University Press, 1986), p. 117.

7. Nelsen, *Power and Insecurity*, p. 10.

8. Strobe Talbott, ed., *Khrushchev Remembers* (Boston: Little, Brown, 1970), p. 462. Khrushchev's account was constructed retrospectively, but circumstantial evidence confirms his version of Soviet mistrust preceding the break. A Chinese informant recounted that Khrushchev had asked Adenauer during a state visit in the early 1950s what he should do about his Chinese threat, implying that he hoped the Germans might in some way help offset the PRC.

9. In late 1945–early 1946, the CPSU and other communist parties still praised nationalist movements and their leaders in Asia, advocating a united front "from above." Evgenii Varga was a leading exponent of this viewpoint. But it came under attack in 1947, when Zhdanov, in his speech to the inaugural session of the Cominform, called for a more aggressive policy in the colonies consistent with his world strategy of struggle between "two camps," repudiating bourgeois nationalism. The attitude toward the newly independent states thus became one of nonrecognition and subversion. Roger E. Kanet, "The Soviet Union and the Colonial Question, 1917–1953," in R. E. Kanet, ed., *The Soviet Union and the Developing Nations* (Baltimore: Johns Hopkins University Press, 1974), pp. 1–26.

10. Mao Zedong, "Talk with the American Correspondent Anna Louise Strong" (August 1946), *Selected Works* (Beijing: Foreign Languages Press, 1967), 4:98.

11. Kuo-kang Shao, "Chou En-lai's Diplomatic Approach to Nonaligned States in Asia: 1953–60," *China Quarterly*, no. 78 (June 1979), p. 324.

12. During the mid-1970s, the Vietnamese charged that Zhou had sacrificed their interests at Geneva by agreeing to the neutrality of the Laotian and Cambodian royal governments, inter alia. Ronald C. Keith, *The Diplomacy of Zhou Enlai* (New York: Macmillan, 1989), p. 69.

13. Roger Kanet, "Soviet Attitudes Toward Developing Nations Since Stalin," in Kanet, ed., *Soviet Union and Developing Nations*, pp. 27–51.

14. Keith, *Zhou Enlai*, p. 98.

15. *Renmin Ribao*, March 11, 1955. (Yet his support may have been nominal, for when Molotov was purged on charges of antiparty activities in April 1957, one of his alleged crimes was his opposition to peaceful coexistence.)

16. *Rnmin Ribao*, February 18, 1956, as quoted in Chin Szu-k'ai, *Communist China's Relations with the Soviet Union, 1949–1957* (Kowloon: Union Research Institute, 1961).

17. Talbott, ed., *Khrushchev Remembers: The Last Testament*, p. 254.

18. See V. Solodnovikov and V. Boslovisky, *Non-Capitalist Development: An Historical Outline* (Moscow: Progress, 1975); also Y. Zhukov et al., *The Third World: Problems and Prospects* (Moscow: Progress, 1970).

19. Edmonds, *Soviet Foreign Policy*, p. 12.

20. Robert O. Freedman, *Economic Warfare in the Communist Bloc: A Study of Soviet Economic Pressure Against Yugoslavia, Albania, and Communist China* (New York: Praeger, 1970), pp. 119, 139.

21. Thomas W. Wolfe, *Soviet Power and Europe, 1945–70* (Baltimore: Johns Hopkins University Press, 1970), p. 130.

22. *Renmin Ribao*, February 28, 1958.

23. On July 19, 1958, Khrushchev proposed that the Soviet Union, United States, Great Britain, France, and India meet to discuss "removing threats to peace." Beijing's reaction was quite hostile, viewing this as a Soviet attempt to annoint India the leader of the Asian and African countries. After his visit to Beijing later that summer, Khrushchev dropped the proposal. *Pravda*, July 20, 1958; for the Chinese reaction see *Renmin Ribao*, August 4, 1958.

24. Lin Biao, "Long Live the Victory of People's War," *Renmin Ribao*, September 2, 1965; trans. in *Peking Review*, September 3, 1965, pp. 9–30.

25. *Pravda*, June 22, 1960. The Soviet assumption at the time was that the United States would not tolerate the loss of a strategic spot anywhere on the globe without putting up a fight, utilizing local incidents to realize global strategies in a nuclear exchange. Writing Eisenhower in 1957, Premier Bulganin conveyed the impression that the polarization of the world had virtually precluded the possibility of limited hostilities anywhere. "Poslanie Predsedatelia Soveta Ministrov SSSR, N. A. Bulganina, Prezidentu Soedinnenykh Shtatov Ameriki, Duaitu D. Eizenkhauery," *Pravda*, December 12, 1957, as cited in John Yin, *Sino-Soviet Dialogue on the Problem of War* (The Hague: Martinus Nijhoff, 1971), pp. 135–40. Khrushchev expressed the same idea in talks with the British Labour Party in October 1957. Interviewed by a group of Brazilian journalists, he said that in the present epoch "small wars" could not remain small for long and would ultimately involve other nations and even coalitions of nations. *Mezhdunarodnye Zhizn'* [International Life], 12 (December 1957), p. 6, as cited in Yin, *Sino-Soviet Dialogue*, pp. 138–39.

26. Moscow was initially less willing to concede the necessity for violent

transition to socialism because this would have stultified its own peace policy. But in the face of Chinese pressure (and apparent success in some cases), Khrushchev was ultimately persuaded to relent. At the Twenty-second CPSU Congress in early 1961, he said that national liberation wars were just and ought to be supported by the bloc, endorsing such struggles in Algeria, Vietnam, West Irian, and the Congo. Later, after coming to the brink of war with the United States over Cuba in the fall of 1962, he reverted again to a more prudential policy. Under Brezhnev, the Soviets of course became major backers of guerrilla wars in Vietnam and elsewhere. Although it is difficult to generalize in view of such tactical vicissitudes, it would seem that (1) the Soviets have always been less rhetorically exuberant than the Chinese in their endorsement of national liberation wars; (2) the Soviets have also been more wary of any direct confrontation with the United States.

27. See Harry Harding, "China's Changing Roles in the Contemporary World," in Harding, ed., *China's Foreign Relations in the 1980s* (New Haven: Yale University Press, 1984), pp. 181–93.

28. Lillian Craig Harris, *China's Foreign Policy Toward the Third World* (New York: Praeger, 1985), pp. 30–40.

29. Marie-Luise Naeth, *Strategie und Taktik der chinesischen Aussenpolitik* (Hannover: Niedersaechsischen Landeszentrale für politische Bildung, 1978).

30. The recognition of the PRC took place in three phases. During the first phase, in 1970–71, China established diplomatic relations with nineteen countries, only four of which were from the West (Canada, Iceland, Italy, Austria), the other fifteen of which were with developing countries. During the second phase, in 1972–73, those nations that had withheld recognition out of deference to the United States, now taking their cue from the Nixon visit and Chinese entry into the UN, established relations with the PRC. Twenty were in this group, including the United Kingdom (which upgraded relations to the ambassadorial level, having recognized the PRC in 1950), West Germany, Japan, Australia, New Zealand—most of them anticommunist. During the third phase, in 1974–76, an additional seven states, all of them staunchly anticommunist, recognized the PRC, including Malaysia, Thailand, Brazil, and the Philippines. Finally, in January 1979, the United States formally established ties.

31. *Peking Review*, no. 47, 1971; also no. 26, 1972, p. 3.

32. Trans. in Franz Schurmann and Orville Schell, eds., *China Readings*, vol. 3: *Communist China* (Middlesex: Penguin, 1967), p. 368.

33. *Renmin Ribao*, January 21, 1964; trans. in *Peking Review*, no. 4 (January 24), 1964, p. 7.

34. *Renmin Ribao*, September 1, 3, 1986, as quoted in *Beijing Review*, no. 37, 1986, pp. 10–11.

35. Deng's speech is translated in *Peking Review*, Special Supplement to no. 15 (April 12), 1974.

36. The Chinese scenario is that the strong will progressively decay while the weak correspondingly grow stronger, resulting in an emerging multipolarity.

Thus they argue that the 1970s mark the beginning of a shift in the balance of economic power from the First to the Second and Third Worlds.

37. Sutter, *Chinese Foreign Policy*, p. 46.

38. The American delegation, placed in an awkward position by public announcement of Nixon's forthcoming trip to China, opted for the first time not to define China's admission to the UN as an "important question," as a result of which the issue could be decided on the basis of a simple majority, rather than a two-thirds majority vote. Thus when the draft Albanian resolution was introduced to award all of "China's" rights to the PRC and exclude the KMT regime, the most strenuous U.S. efforts to defeat it proved of no avail.

39. Detailed analyses of China's General Assembly voting record during its first decade in the UN shows that its positions were more favorable to the Third World than to the West, though it seems to have had little impact in the UN program area. See Trong R. Chai, "Chinese Policy Toward the Third World and the Superpowers in the UN General Assembly, 1971–1977: A Voting Analysis," *International Organization* 33, no. 3 (Summer 1979): 392; see also Samuel Kim, *China, the United Nations, and World Order* (Princeton: Princeton University Press, 1979), pp. 280, 329–30, 402. In 1983, China voted against the United States almost 80 percent of the time; in 1989, China voted with the United States 11.1 percent of the time (contrasted with 98.4 percent agreement with the Soviet Union), just below Burkina Faso. But China's alignment with the Third World is by no means automatic. For example, China continued its friendship with the Augusto Pinochet regime in Chile, seeing the relationship as strategically and economically useful, and refused to join Third World–sponsored resolutions at the UN condemning the Pinochet regime's violation of human rights, despite considerable criticism.

40. See Gerald Chan, *China and International Organization: Participation in Non-Governmental Organizations Since 1971* (Hong Kong: Oxford University Press, 1989).

41. Robert L. Worden, "International Organizations: China's Third World Policy in Practice," in Lillian Craig Harris and Robert Worden, eds., *China and the Third World: Champion or Challenger?* (Dover, Mass.: Auburn House, 1986), pp. 75–100.

42. Robert Manning, "The Third World Looks at China," in Harris and Worden, eds., *China and the Third World*, pp. 139–56, at p. 154.

43. Bruce Reynolds, "China in the International Economy," in Harding, ed., *China's Foreign Relations*, pp. 93–104. China has nonetheless consistently supported the Third World position on Law of the Sea matters, championing the 200-nautical mile territorial sea for reasons of solidarity as well as in order to protect its own wealthy coastal area.

44. Although the PRC cannot compete in the market for sophisticated weaponry, it does produce an extensive line of conventional arms, and Chinese arms sales are up several times over what they were in 1980. The Congressional Research Service estimates that China sold U.S. $5.3 billion worth of arms be-

tween 1983 and 1986; exports of "aerospace products" reached $2.1 billion in 1989, an increase of 60 percent over 1988. While the top three sold far more—the USSR almost $60 billion worth, the United States $25.5 billion, and France $16.5 billion during this period—the rapidity of China's emergence in this market is striking, representing a 167 percent increase in sales over the previous three-year period. And future prospects are bright, particularly in view of the superpower breakthrough from arms control to disarmament: the recently concluded INF talks have given the PRC a monopoly on the production of ballistic missiles with ranges from 300 to 3,000 miles. The Chinese estimate that arms sales bring in more money (about $1.34 billion per year) than the Chinese military spends on arms (the best foreign exchange earners are the missiles). China's sales policy seems to be relatively indiscriminate, oriented around earning foreign exchange rather than promoting any particular ideological cause; see, for example, the lucrative recent sale of arms to both Iran and Iraq. (Between 1980 and 1987 nearly 70 percent of China's exports went to these two belligerents, delivering nearly a third of the weapons in value that Iran imported from abroad, and about 10 percent of Iraq's arms imports—all running athwart Beijing's declared policy of promoting a negotiated settlement.) When it was discovered in 1988 that China had sold CSS-2 (1,600-mile range) IRBMs to Saudi Arabia, the U.S. exerted pressure to discontinue such sales; but Western leverage has diminished in the wake of Tiananmen. A diplomatically isolated PRC increasingly holds the key to arms proliferation. See Wei-chin Lee, "The Birth of a Salesman: China as Arms Supplier," *Journal of Asian Studies* 6, no. 4 (Winter 1987–88): 32–47; Harry Gelber, "China's New Economic and Strategic Uncertainties and the Security Prospects," *Asian Survey* 30, no. 7 (July 1990): 646–68; *FEER*, September 22, 1988, p. 42.

45. The total number of Chinese experts and workers sent abroad under such contracts increased from about 18,000 in 1979–81 to 31,000 in 1983, to 59,000 by the end of 1985. From 1979 through 1985, the total value of labor service contracts was U.S. $5.1 billion. Samuel S. Kim, *The Third World in Chinese World Policy* (Princeton: Center of International Studies, Woodrow Wilson School, January 1989), pp. 37–39.

46. *Liaowang* [Outlook], no. 12, 1986, pp. 30–31.

47. See Carol Lee Hamrin, "Domestic Components of China's Evolving Three Worlds Theory," in Harris and Worden, eds., *China and the Third World*, pp. 34–53.

48. In this connection, Chinese writings about Third World schemes for economic redistribution have begun to assume a more critical tone. "Factors such as failed policies and improper management can be held responsible to varying degrees in particular countries," writes one author. "It is not practical to blame the North for all the South's troubles, though exploitation is truly a root cause of the situation." Tong Dalin and Liu Ji, "North-South Cooperation for Mutual Prosperity," *Beijing Review*, no. 26 (July 1, 1986), p. 19; as quoted in Samuel S. Kim, "China and the Third World," in Kim, ed., *China and the World*, 2d ed. (1989).

49. Levesque, "Les 'trois obstacles,' " p. 6; Qi Yan, "New Trends in Cuba's Foreign Relations," *Shijie Zhishi*, no. 9 (May 1, 1985), pp. 7–8, in *FBIS–China*, May 15, 1985, p. J1.

50. Lawrence Freedman, *The West and the Modernization of China* (London: Royal Institute of International Affairs, Chatham House, 1979), p. 19.

51. See Pye, *Spirit of Chinese Politics*. Pye enjoys satirizing and to some extent even mocking Chinese feelings of righteous indignation. Still, it seems inescapable that such feelings do play a prominent role in the makeup of the modern Chinese national identity.

52. I owe this point to Susanne Hoeber Rudolph, in a very perceptive commentary.

53. Commentator article in *Liaowang*, January 8, 1990.

8. Realizing National Identity

1. For an interesting theoretical extension of the concept of "bandwagoning" (which does not, however, inform my use of the term here), see Avery Goldstein, "A Theory of Politics in the People's Republic of China: Structural Constraints on Political Behavior and Outcomes, 1949–1978," Ph.D. dissertation, Political Science Department, University of California at Berkeley, 1985.

2. The official repudiation of the doctrine of "Continuing the Revolution under the Dictatorship of the Proletariat" was a lengthy and contentious process, culminating in the resolution on party history adopted by the Sixth Plenum of the Eleventh CC on June 27, 1981. *Resolution on CPC History* (Beijing: Foreign Languages Press, 1981).

3. *Renmin Ribao*, November 1, 1977, as quoted in Michael Yahuda, *China's Role in World Affairs* (New York: St. Martin's, 1978), p. 242.

Part III. The Strategic Triangle

1. Although this rather primitive formalization does make some claim to originality, it did not emerge *ex nihilo*, but derives from a series of penetrating analyses. Among the first (and best) such discussions is Michel Tatu, *The Great Power Triangle: Washington-Moscow-Peking* (Paris: Atlantic Institute, 1970), which discussed the options open to the United States at that time with remarkable prescience. See also Thomas Gottlieb, *Chinese Foreign Policy Factionalism and the Origins of the Strategic Triangle* (Santa Monica: Rand R-1902-NA, 1977); Roger Glenn Brown, "Chinese Politics and American Policy: A New Look at the Triangle," *Foreign Policy*, no. 23 (Summer 1976), pp. 3–23; Michael Pillsbury, "U.S.-Chinese Military Ties?" *Foreign Policy*, no. 20 (Autumn 1975), and "Future Sino-American Security Ties: The View from Tokyo, Moscow and Peking," *International Security* 1 (Spring 1977): 142; Banning Garrett, "China Policy and the Strategic Triangle," in Kenneth A. Oye et al., eds., *Eagle Entangled: U.S. Foreign Policy in a Complex World* (London and New York: Longman, 1979), pp. 228–64; William E. Griffith, ed., *The*

World and the Great-Power Triangles (Cambridge, Mass.: MIT Press, 1975); and Raju G. C. Thomas, ed., *The Great-Power Triangle and Asian Security* (Lexington, Mass.: D. C. Heath, 1983). Other contributions to this voluminous literature will be cited in the course of this section.

2. See, for example, John Franklin Copper, *China's Global Role: An Analysis of Peking's National Power Capabilities in the Context of an Evolving International System* (Stanford: Hoover Institution Press, 1980).

3. This seems to be the position of Michael Ng-Quinn, "International Systemic Constraints on Chinese Foreign Policy," in Samuel Kim, ed., *Chinese Foreign Policy in the 1980s* (Boulder: Westview, 1984); see also Jonathan Pollack, *China's Potential as a World Power* (Santa Monica: Rand, Paper 6524, July 1980).

4. As one advocate of this position puts it, "China is unique. Although it is not an advanced industrialized state, it possesses a nuclear-weapons capability and a massive military machine. While its ability to influence politics and military balances in Africa and Latin America is negligible, China's foreign and defense policies clearly affect the regions of Asia and Europe. Nearly every Asian state must consider China's military posture. China, for instance, could tilt the military balance between India and Pakistan, between North and South Korea, or between Vietnam and its Southeast Asian neighbors. . . . Thus the size and central location of China make almost every Asian state take note of Beijing's military posture. Similarly, China's military power may affect the Euro-strategic military balance between NATO and the Warsaw Pact countries." Raju G. C. Thomas, "Introduction," p. 3, in Thomas, ed., *Great-Power Triangle*, pp. 1–21.

5. The recently concluded INF talks have already given the PRC an effective monopoly on ballistic missiles with ranges from 300 to 3,000 miles, as pointed out earlier. Should the START talks succeed in cutting each of the superpowers' nuclear warheads by 50 percent and placing a ceiling of 1,600 on launchers, the ratio between total number of Chinese strategic launchers and that of either superpower would rise to 17 percent, from less than 1 percent two decades ago. See Laird, *Christian Science Monitor*, August 1, 1988, p. 13.

6. Freedman, *The West and the Modernization of China*, p. 4.

7. Perhaps even less than this: according to recent statistics revealed by Soviet economists, the United States has consistently overestimated the Soviet economy (and concomitantly underestimated Soviet military spending). Viktor Belkin, Oleg Bogomolov, Iurii Dikhonov, and other academicians at an April 1990 conference estimated the real per capital Soviet GDP at 25 to 40 percent that of the United States, probably closer to the former. Soviet military spending may account for as much as 20 to 25 percent of that. *New York Times*, April 24, 1990.

8. See John Wilson Lewis and Litai Xue, *China Builds the Bomb* (Stanford: Stanford University Press, 1988), p. 2. The combined British and French nuclear forces had 215 launchers as of 1988.

9. Thomas, *Great-Power Triangle*, p. 3.

10. Anne Gilks and Gerald Segal, *China and the Arms Trade* (London: Croom Helm, 1985), pp. 19–24.

11. See Ralph N. Clough, *Chinese Elites: World View and Perceptions of the U.S.* (Washington, D.C.: USICA Office of Research, 1982). Deng Xiaoping asserted in his 1974 speech to the United Nations that "China is not a superpower nor will she ever seek to be one." The Chinese term for "superpower" (*chaojidaguo*), like the term "hegemony" (*bachuan*), connotes power politics *qua* international bullying, as traditionally juxtaposed to "the princely way" (*wangchuan*) of leadership by moral example.

12. Foreign Minister Huang Hua told UN Secretary-General Perez de Cuellar in late August 1982, "China will never cling to any superpower. China will never play the 'U.S. card' against the Soviet Union, nor the 'Soviet card' against the United States. We will also not allow anyone to play the 'China card.'" *Xinhua*, August 29, 1982, in *FBIS–China*, August 30, 1982, p. A2.

13. Huan Xiang, "Viewing Wuhan's Development and Prospects from [the perspective of] the International Political and Economic Situation," *Shijie Jingji Daobao* (Shanghai), July 9, 1984. Huan stated that the Pacific, not the Atlantic, contained the most important countries in current world affairs, and also noted that there was only one world market, and that China was a part of it.

14. Sometimes, perhaps, an exaggerated notion. When Prince Sihanouk in early 1982 told his Chinese host, "Today the United States needs China, not China the United States," Deng Xiaoping replied: "We have said this often." *Liaowang*, no. 3 (1982), p. 3. The deputy editor-in-chief of *Xinhua* wrote in 1981: "This means that the United States will continue to need China to tie down the million Soviet soldiers in the north, and the several hundred thousand Vietnamese soldiers in the south. And it will need to coordinate with China on Afghanistan and Kampuchea in support of these people's resistance and of ASEAN's effort against the Soviet and Vietnamese threat. The United States will also need to coordinate with China on any and all steps that may bear on global strategic situations." Mu Guangren, "The Current U.S. Policy Toward China," *Banyue Tan*, no. 16, 1981, p. 53. On the other hand, somewhat later Deng told a visiting Japanese delegation: "People in the world are talking about the great triangle in the international situation. To be frank with you, our angle has very weak power. . . . When China gets developed, the peaceful power constraining war will greatly increase." Deng, "Reconstructing China's Special Socialism," in *Selected Works* (Beijing: Foreign Languages Press, 1986 ed.), p. 95.

15. Of all the warning messages ever addressed by nuclear states to their adversaries, more have been addressed to China than to any other nation. China was threatened with nuclear war on at least five occasions: (1) On November 30, 1950, Truman called a press conference to announce he was considering a nuclear bombardment of China. The resultant outcry cooled such thoughts. (2) When the Korean armistice negotiations stalled, Eisenhower indicated that nuclear weapons might be used: "In order to compel the Chinese Communists

to an armistice, it was obvious that if we were to go over to a major offensive the war would have to be expanded outside of Korea—with strikes against the supporting Chinese air force in Manchuria, a blockade of the Chinese coast. . . . Finally, to keep the attack from becoming overly costly, it was clear that we would have to use atomic weapons. . . . we dropped the word, discreetly, of our intention." Dwight David Eisenhower, *Mandate for Change, 1953–1956: The White House Years* (Garden City, N.Y.: Doubleday, 1963), 1:178–81. (3) During the 1954–55 Taiwan Strait crisis, Dulles threatened the use of tactical nuclear weapons: "At no other time in the cold war did the U.S. come so close to unleashing a preventive war." Stephen E. Ambrose, *Rise to Globalism: American Foreign Policy, 1938–1970* (Hammondsworth: Penguin, 1973), p. 224. (4) In the Jinmen (Quemoy) crisis of 1958, Eisenhower again threatened to use nuclear weapons. (5) Following the Ussuri clashes, the Soviets threatened nuclear attack. See P. R. Chari, "China's Nuclear Posture: An Evaluation," *Asian Survey* 18, no. 8 (August 1978): 817–29; also Ken Coates, *China and the Bomb* (Nottingham: Spokesman, 1986), pp. 12, 14–19.

16. The system was later aborted, as Nixon's opening to China made it seem increasingly irrelevant.

17. Banning N. Garrett and Bonnie Glaser, *War and Peace: The Views from Moscow and Beijing* (Berkeley: Institute of International Studies, Policy Paper no. 20, 1984).

18. The average growth rate of the Asian Pacific region in 1988 was 8 percent, much higher than the world average of 3.8 percent. The stellar performers included Singapore, 11.1 percent; Thailand, 10.5 percent; Malaysia, 7.4 percent; Philippines, 6.4 percent; Indonesia, 3.8 percent; and China, 8.5 percent.

19. By the year 2000, the GNP of the Asia-Pacific region may surpass that of the United States and EEC countries, according to Under Secretary of State Michael Armacost, in a speech to the American-Japanese Society in New York, summer 1988.

20. Allison, *Essence of Decision* (see Introduction, above, note 21). The term "rational" is taken here to refer to self-interested calculation that is intersubjectively (or internationally) comprehensible in some sort of means-ends schema, not necessarily to a lack of emotional involvement in the pursuit.

21. Taken from the classic romantic triangle, in which two (usually male) suitors vie for the favor of the same love object, such as King Arthur and Sir Lancelot in quest of Queen Guinevere, King Mark and Tristan in pursuit of Isolde, and so forth.

22. Taken from Morton Kaplan's "unit veto system," in *System and Process in International Politics* (New York: John Wiley, 1957), pp. 50–52.

9. Ménage à Trois, 1945–1949

1. Service was impressed during his discussions with CCP leaders with the "depth and conviction of a desire for American friendship and cooperation

with China." On March 13, 1945, Mao told him: "America is not only the most suitable country to assist the economic development of China, she is also the only country fully able to participate. For all these reasons, there must not be any conflict, estrangement, or misunderstanding between the Chinese people and America." John Stewart Service, *The Amerasia Papers: Some Problems in the History of U.S.-China Relations* (Berkeley: China Research Monograph, 1971), p. 175. See also John W. Garver, *Chinese-Soviet Relations, 1937–1945: The Diplomacy of Chinese Nationalism* (New York: Oxford University Press, 1988), p. 254 et passim.

2. Joseph Esherick, ed., *Lost Chance in China: The World War II Despatches of John Stewart Service* (New York: Random House, 1974), pp. 306–8, 315–16.

3. Ibid., p. 295.

4. Quoted in Allen Whiting, "Foreign Policy of Communist China," in Roy C. Macridis, ed., *Foreign Policy in World Politics* (Englewood Cliffs, N.J.: Prentice-Hall, 1972), p. 312.

5. Service reported (in his March 23, 1945, report on the Soviet presence in Yanan) the presence of three Soviets, whereas there were actually five at the time, and they were working much more closely with the CCP leadership than Service was told. Service was kept ignorant of the presence of a Soviet liaison officer named Vladimirov, a Soviet radio transmitter at Yanan, and the visit of a Soviet aircraft in October 1943. Peter Vladimirov, *The Vladimirov Diaries: Yanan, China, 1942–1945* (New York: Doubleday, 1975), p. 161.

6. Whenever actively engaging in talks with the Americans, Mao also intensified his communication with Moscow. In November 1944, after his discussions with Roosevelt's personal representative, Patrick Hurley, Mao requested that Vladimirov radio Moscow with Mao's interpretation of the talks. Shortly after Hurley left Yanan, Mao sent another cable describing the great strengths and good prospects of the CCP. Vladimirov's interpretation was that Mao wished to play on the American fear of the USSR to induce the United States to pry the CCP away from Moscow's embrace, without jeopardizing Soviet favor. Ibid., p. 230.

7. Werner Link, *The East-West Conflict: The Organization of International Relations in the Twentieth Century* (Dover, N.H.: Berg, 1986), p. 57.

8. See Steven M. Goldstein, "Chinese Communist Policy Toward the United States: Opportunities and Constraints, 1944–1950," in Dorothy Borg and Waldo Heinrichs, eds., *Uncertain Years: Chinese American Relations, 1947–1950* (New York: Columbia University Press, 1980), pp. 235–79.

9. Michael H. Hunt, "Mao and the United States: The Making of a Chinese Foreign Policy, November 1948–June 1950," in Borg and Heinrichs, eds., *Uncertain Years*, pp. 185–234; Edwin W. Martin, *Divided Counsel: The Anglo-American Response to Communist Victory in China* (Lexington: University Press of Kentucky, 1986), pp. 14–16 et passim.

10. Vladimir Dedijer, *The Battle that Stalin Lost: Memoirs of Yugoslavia,*

1948–1953 (New York: Viking Press, 1971), p. 68; see also Milovan Djilas, *Conversations with Stalin* (New York: Harcourt, Brace and World, 1962), p. 182.

11. Schram, ed., *Chairman Mao Talks*, p. 191. To be sure, Mao does not seem to have taken this advice too seriously; "we did not do what he said," he adds.

12. Medvedev, *China and the Superpowers*, p. 46.

13. See "Industrialization of China Bogs Down in Russian Relations," *Christian Science Monitor*, March 25, 1953, p. 8, as quoted in Robert R. Simmons, *The Strained Alliance: Peking, Pyongyang, Moscow and the Politics of the Korean Civil War* (New York: Free Press, 1975), p. 55, n. 29. Of course, the possibility cannot be precluded that Stalin was intentionally misleading the American envoy about Soviet intentions.

14. C. P. FitzGerald, *Revolution in China* (London: Cresset Press, 1952), p. 164; see also Djilas, *Conversations with Stalin*, p. 182, for Stalin's advice to the CCP at the end of World War II to form a coalition government with the KMT (perhaps with the Czechoslovak model of "peaceful" revolutionary takeover in view).

15. In the Yalta accords, the USSR was given Dairen, Port Arthur, and the corridor for a railway through Manchuria in return for Soviet entry into the war against Japan. See Marc S. Gallicchio, *The Cold War Begins in Asia: American East Asian Policy and the Fall of the Japanese Empire* (New York: Columbia University Press, 1988), pp. 2–3.

16. Allen Whiting and General Sheng Shih-ts'ai, *Sinkiang: Pawn or Pivot* (East Lansing: Michigan State University Press, 1958), pp. 117–18. So cordial were Soviet relations with the KMT regime at this time that when the Red Army occupied the Nationalist capital of Nanjing (in April 1949), only the Soviet ambassador among foreign diplomats accompanied the Nationalists in their flight to Guangzhou.

17. Alvin Z. Rubinstein, *Soviet Foreign Policy Since World War II: Imperial and Global* (Cambridge, Mass.: Winthrop Publishers, 1981), pp. 60–61.

18. On May 31, Michael Keon, an Australian correspondent, relayed to Colonel David Barrett, an American assistant military attaché, a message from Zhou Enlai to the American and British governments, which alleged that the CCP leadership was divided between a pro-Soviet wing under Liu Shaoqi and a pro-American wing under Zhou; the latter advocated early establishment of relations with the United States, which alone could help China economically. A victory for Zhou's wing would mean that the PRC would not always follow Moscow's foreign policy dictates but would exercise a moderating influence. For excerpts, see Robert M. Blum, "Secret Cable from Peking," *San Francisco Chronicle*, September 27, 1978, p. F1, also *San Francisco Examiner and Chronicle*, August 13, 1978; as quoted in Gurtov and Hwang, *China Under Threat*, p. 35. The Americans took the message to be authentic, but interpreted it as a plea for economic assistance made with the full knowledge of the party apparatus (and perhaps the approval of Moscow). The American response, that

the United States wanted to maintain good relations with China but that these should be based on "mutual understanding, respect and cooperation, on reciprocity as well as equality," was never delivered, albeit not for want of trying. Then on June 15, scarcely two weeks after receipt of Zhou's overture, Mao made a speech to the Preparatory Committee of the CCP in which he announced China's intention to align with the Soviet Union; Barrett recommended under the circumstances that the American response be forgone.

19. Liu Shaoqi, "On Internationalism and Nationalism," *Jiefano Ribao* (Shanghai), June 6, 1949.

20. *China Digest* (Hong Kong), April 19, 1949, p. 2, as quoted in Partha S. Ghosh, *Sino-Soviet Relations: United States Perceptions and Policy Responses, 1949–1959* (New Delhi: Uppal, 1981), p. 48.

21. U.S. Department of State, *United States Relations with China with Special Reference to the Period 1944–1949* [The China White Paper] (Washington, D.C.: Government Printing Office, 1949), Annex 120, pp. 720–29. Mao's "lean to one side" position was foreshadowed as early as early 1947 in a speech by Lu Dingyi.

22. Mao Zedong, "On the People's Democratic Dictatorship" (June 30, 1949), *Selected Works*, 4:417. See also the interpretation published in a foreign ministry organ: Zhang Mingyang, "Why Must We Lean to One Side," *Shijie Zhishi*, August 5, 1949, as translated in *Chinese Press Survey*, August 11, 1949, pp. 106–7.

23. Mao, *Selected Works*, 4:370–71.

24. Chen Minshu Memorandum, in *Foreign Relations of the United States*, 1949, 8:773–74.

25. As quoted in Robert Scalapino, "In Quest of National Interest: The Foreign Policy of the PRC," in Yu-ming Shaw, ed., *Power and Policy in the PRC* (Boulder: Westview, 1985), pp. 111–41.

26. Yu-ming Shaw, "John Leighton Stuart and U.S.-Chinese Communist Rapprochement in 1949: Was There Another 'Lost Chance in China'?" *China Quarterly*, no. 89 (March 1982), pp. 74–97. Although Shaw's editorial bias is evident, his documentary corroboration of this point seems solid enough.

27. The public defense of the "perimeter" was articulated in Dean Acheson's speech to the National Press Club, Washington, D.C., January 12, 1950. See John Lewis Gaddis, "The Strategic Perspective: The Rise and Fall of the 'Defense Perimeter Concept,' 1947–1951," in Borg and Heinrichs, eds., *Uncertain Years*, pp. 61–119.

28. U.S. policy during the Truman administration was defined by a paper issued under Dean Acheson's imprimatur in 1949 entitled "U.S. Policy Toward China," quoted in Chang, *Friends and Enemies*, p. 80.

29. Nancy Bernkopf Tucker, *Patterns in the Dust: Chinese-American Relations and the Recognition Controversy, 1949–1950* (New York: Columbia University Press, 1983); see also Beverly Hooper, *China Stands Up: The End of the Western Presence in China, 1948–1950* (London: Allen and Unwin, 1986).

30. After the U.S. National Security Council indicated in October 1949 that

the United States would not provide military support for Hong Kong in the event of a Chinese military assault, the British felt obliged to reach some sort of accommodation. Mayers, *Cracking the Monolith*, p. 56.

31. He did so in the course of Liu Shaoqi's second visit in May 1949. Shi Zhe, "I Accompanied Chairman Mao," *Far Eastern Affairs*, no. 2 (1989), pp. 125–33.

32. According to two members of the U.S. embassy staff in Moscow, in a telegraph from the embassy to the State Department, as cited in Martin, *Divided Counsel*, p. 117.

33. Medvedev, *China and the Superpowers*, p. 22.

34. Talbott, ed., *Khrushchev Remembers: The Last Testament*, p. 240.

35. Salisbury, *War Between Russia and China*, pp. 106–7. Khrushchev seems to have projected the intensity of later clashes into incipient indications of divergence, thereby rationalizing his own responsibility for the split.

36. Russell Spurr, *Enter the Dragon: China's Undeclared War Against the U.S. in Korea, 1950–51* (New York: Newmarket, 1988), p. 59.

37. Schram, ed., *Chairman Mao Talks*, p. 191. The possibility of Chinese defection à la Tito was widely bruited about. The Yugoslavs discussed it, as we have seen above, and U.S. State Department intelligence freely speculated about it. "Titoism and the Theory of 'Colonial' Revolution as Applied to China," U.S. State Department, Office of Intelligence and Research (OIR), report 4845, February 20, 1949; "Communist China: Satellite or Junior Partner of the USSR?" Office of Strategic Services, Research and Analysis report 5681-5, January 1952; as cited in Keith, *The Diplomacy of Zhou Enlai*, p. 38.

38. See *Wansui* (1969), p. 432.

39. Shi Zhe, "I Accompanied," pp. 125–33; see also N. Federenko, "The Stalin-Mao Summit in Moscow," *Far Eastern Affairs*, no. 2, 1989, pp. 134–48.

10. Sino-Soviet Marriage, 1950–1960

1. Zagoria, *Sino-Soviet Conflict*, p. 20.

2. Mao Zedong, "Telegram to the Communist Party of the United States" (October 6, 1949), as trans. in Michael Ying-mao Kau and John K. Leung, *The Writings of Mao Zedong, 1949–1976* (Armonk: M. E. Sharpe, 1986), vol. 1, *September 1949–December 1955*, p. 98.

3. See, for example, Simmons, *The Strained Alliance*, who argues that the timing served Soviet interests by forestalling such events as the "liberation" of Taiwan and UN recognition of the PRC.

4. Considering that the Soviets were still boycotting the UN Security Council when the attack took place (and thus not in a position to veto the American resolution calling on North Korea to withdraw), Stalin seems to have been as surprised by the timing of the North Korean attack as Truman was. The reasons for the invasion, and for its precise timing, have been extensively researched, and the results all attribute the decision to events on the peninsula. Some scholars have emphasized factional conflict within the North Korean Workers' Party;

for example, Simmons notes the rivalry between Kim and Pak, and speculates about alleged provocation from Syngman Rhee in the South. Hiroshi Sakurai has attributed the timing to a desire to preempt land reform in the South; see his paper, "Why Did the Korean War 'Break Out' on June 25, 1950? A Summary of a New Hypothesis," Berkeley, Institute of East Asian Studies, May 1983.

5. Mark A. Ryan, *Chinese Attitudes Toward Nuclear Weapons: China and the U.S. During the Korean War* (Armonk: M. E. Sharpe, 1989), p. 24; Spurr, *Enter the Dragon*, p. 51.

6. As first suggested in Allen Whiting's pathbreaking study, *China Crosses the Yalu* (New York: Macmillan, 1960).

7. I wish to thank Jonathan Pollack for this information.

8. Huang Hua, "Report on the World Situation" (July 30, 1977), as trans. in *Issues and Studies*, January 1978, p. 113. Later, when it became clear that the Western response to the invasion would remain localized, Stalin expressed warm gratitude for the Chinese intervention.

9. Gurtov and Hwang, *China Under Threat*, pp. 54–55.

10. Richard K. Betts, *Nuclear Blackmail and Nuclear Balance* (Washington, D.C.: Brookings Institution Press, 1987), p. 37.

11. According to Sherman Adams: "Talking one day with Eisenhower about the events that led up finally to the truce in Korea, I asked him what it was that brought the Communists into line. 'Danger of an atomic war,' he said without hesitation. 'We told them we could not hold a limited war any longer if the Communists welshed on any truce. They didn't want a full-scale war or an atomic attack.'" Daniel Ellsberg, "Call to Mutiny," in Ellsberg, *Endpapers One* (Nottingham: Spokesman, 1981), p. 20. So the threat was in any event decisive in American eyes. The Chinese denied being intimidated by threats of an "atomic attack," dismissing this as a "paper tiger," though it is noteworthy that they now accepted certain American demands they had originally rejected, including American insistence on voluntary prisoner repatriation. Lewis and Xue, *China Builds the Bomb*, pp. 14–16. This may, however, have been due to other considerations: Stalin died in early March, and by the end of the month the PRC manifested its first sign of compromise.

12. See Chang, *Friends and Enemies*, pp. 81–88.

13. Memorandum to the Chairman of the Joint Chiefs of Staff, from Rear Admiral Edwin Layton, Deputy Director for Intelligence, June 1955, in Declassified Government Documents. The authoritative NSC 68, written by Paul Nitze (who became head of the Policy Planning Staff after the resignation of George Kennan in late 1949) also insisted that power reposed in "two centers," dismissing the possibility that China might take an independent position. Chang, *Friends and Enemies*, pp. 75–80.

14. Central Intelligence Agency, "The Tenth Anniversary Celebration of the People's Republic of China," September 1, 1959, Eisenhower Library, WHO OSANSA, NSC, Briefing Notes, box 5, as cited in Chang, *Friends and Enemies*, p. 212, n. 18.

15. Mao Zedong, "Zai chuan guo gong shang lian erh jie yi ce weiyuanhui

bufen daibiao zuotanhui shang de zhishi" (December 8, 1956) [Directive to a forum of a part of the delegates to the first plenum of the second national congress of industrial and commercial associations], *Mao Zedong Sixiang Wan Sui!* (Hong Kong: n.p., 1969), p. 63.

16. Gerald Segal, *The Great Power Triangle* (New York: St. Martin's, 1982), p. 43.

17. Coates, *China and the Bomb*, p. 17.

18. *Pravda*, September 2, 1964.

19. *New Age*, November 15, 1959, pp. 1, 16. The Chinese response, anticipating their territorial dispute with the USSR, was: "Who says that a socialist country may only defend its densely populated areas but not its sparsely populated areas? The population density of the area in the eastern sector of the Sino-Indian border is roughly the same as that of the Turkmen Republic of the Soviet Union." *Xinhua*, November 2, 1963.

20. According to a recently discovered interview with Anna Louise Strong, during his October 1959 visit to Beijing to celebrate National Day following the Camp David meetings, Khrushchev spoke on behalf of Indian territorial demands, arguing that if China would yield some insignificant "frozen waste where nobody lives," they might "win Nehru to fight imperialism." Mao refused. Tracy B. Strong and Helene Keyssar, "Anna Louise Strong: Three Interviews with Chairman Mao Zedong," *China Quarterly*, no. 103 (September 1985), pp. 489–510. Upon his return to Moscow, Khrushchev dispatched N. A. Mukhitdinov to India to apprise Nehru of his talks with Chinese leaders on the border dispute and assure him of Soviet support. *Pravda*, November 1, 1959; as quoted in Ray, *Sino-Soviet Conflict Over India*, pp. 70–80.

21. The Soviets had sold some MiG-21s to China but had not given production rights and associated technology. Although the first Soviet warplanes did not reach India until February 11, 1963, well after hostilities had terminated (China announced a unilateral ceasefire and withdrawal of troops on November 21, 1962), the Soviet-Indian agreement rankled in Beijing. University Publications of America, Special Studies Series, *The Soviet Union, 1980–82 Supplement*, reel 3, frame 190, from *The Military and Security Dimensions of Soviet-Indian Relations* (Strategic Studies Research Memorandum, Strategic Studies Institute, U.S. Army War College, June 1980).

22. Ray, *Sino-Soviet Conflict Over India*, p. 83.

23. Eisenhower, *Mandate for Change*, pp. 476–77; Chang, *Friends and Enemies*, pp. 126–27.

24. Lewis and Xue, *China Builds the Bomb*, pp. 35–39.

25. *Renmin Ribao*, May 12, 1957; Camilleri, *Chinese Foreign Policy*, pp. 50–51.

26. Whereas intelligence estimates at the time assumed that this implied a Chinese threat to Taiwan, subsequent revelations suggest that Mao's objectives were limited to recovery of the offshore islands, thereby demoralizing Nationalist forces on Taiwan and driving a wedge between Washington and Taipei. See

Allen S. Whiting, "New Light on Mao: Quemoy 1958: Mao's Miscalculations," *China Quarterly*, no. 62 (June 1975), pp. 263–70.

27. This assistance included the dispatch of fighters to escort Nationalist cargo planes airdropping supplies to Jinmen, the completion of missile sites on Taiwan, and the reinforcement of the Seventh Fleet to include six aircraft carriers, three cruisers, forty destroyers, a submarine division, and twenty other support vessels. The United States also expedited the shipment of artillery, aircraft, and special weaponry, such as the Sidewinder air-to-air missiles, to the Nationalists. Nationalist garrisons were provided with new 8-inch cannon capable of firing nuclear shells. Chang, *Friends and Enemies*, p. 185.

28. *New York Times*, September 5, 1958; the president also indicated that tactical ("battlefield") nuclear weapons might be used in this defense. Eisenhower, *Mandate for Change*, p. 464.

29. *Collected Documents of Sino-American Relations* (Beijing: The World Knowledge Publishing House, 1960), vol. 2, part 2, p. 2699, as quoted in He Di, "The Evolution of the People's Republic of China's Policy Toward the Off-shore Islands (Quemoy, Matsu)," unpublished paper presented at the Center for Chinese Studies Regional Seminar, October 31, 1987, University of California, Berkeley.

30. See Paul Y. Hammond, *The Cold War Years: American Foreign Policy Since 1945* (New York: Harcourt, Brace and World, 1969), pp. 120–21. Yet Soviet commitments of extended deterrence were taken seriously in Washington; Gurtov and Hwang conclude that "Mao was not betrayed by the U.S.S.R." Gurtov and Hwang, *China Under Threat*, p. 92.

31. According to Mao's interview with Strong, Khrushchev announced upon his arrival in Beijing in 1959 that he brought "good news," that he had "found a way to solve the problem of Taiwan." His proposal was that "Taiwan should be handled in the same way that Lenin handled the Far Eastern Republic." (The latter was a short-lived creation by Lenin, which temporarily gave nominal autonomy to local authorities; after resistance to the CPSU was crushed in the context of the civil war, the Republic voluntarily rejoined the USSR.) Mao retorted that the Far Eastern Republic had been set up by Lenin and was then controlled by the CPSU; did Khrushchev imagine that Taiwan was controlled by the CCP? Khrushchev then demanded that China release certain American agents who had parachuted into northeastern China during and after the Korean War, because he had promised Eisenhower that he would intercede on their behalf. "That would be rather difficult," Mao tartly replied. "You know, we have laws in this country." Strong and Keyssar, "Anna Louise Strong," pp. 489–510.

32. Nathan Leites has alluded to the Bolshevik determination not to respond to provocation as a fundamental tenet of the Politburo's "operational code." Cf. Leites, *A Study of Bolshevism* (Glencoe, Ill.: Free Press, 1953).

33. Quoted in Lafeber, *America, Russia and the Cold War*, p. 176.

34. Chang alludes to American references to the Chinese as "hysterical,"

"irrational," and "fanatical" as indications of racist stereotypy. *Friends and Enemies*, p. 173 et passim.

35. Wang Bingnan, *Zhongmei huitan jiunian huigu* [Looking Back on Nine Years of Sino-American Talks] (Beijing, 1985), p. 69; as cited in Chang, *Friends and Enemies*, pp. 186–87.

36. MacFarquhar, *Origins of the Cultural Revolution*, 1:96–97.

37. Under Article IV, both countries were obliged to "consult each other in regard to all important international problems affecting their common interests." That the Chinese failed to do so in this case is suggested by O. B. Borisov and B. T. Koloskov, *Sovetsko-Kitaiskie otnosheniia, 1945–1970* (Moscow: Mysl', 1972), pp. 171–73; see also Astafiev et al., *The PRC's Foreign Policy*, 1:237. Mao's account confirms that he and Khrushchev did not discuss the forthcoming bombardment. Mao Zedong, *Miscellany of Mao Zedong Thought (1949–1968)* (Washington, D.C.: JPRS 61269-1, -2, 1974), 1:135.

38. Borisov and Koloskov, *Sovetsko-Kitaiskie otnosheniia*, p. 81.

39. Chang, *Friends and Enemies*, pp. 186–90.

40. See *Renmin Ribao*, December 22, 1957, which omitted from its summary Khrushchev's proposals to abandon nuclear confrontation and not to change the status quo by force, but indicated Chinese rejection of these proposals. The first Bulganin letter (January 1956) proposing a Soviet-American friendship treaty had contended, to Chinese consternation, that there were no territorial disputes between the two powers that might lead to confrontation. *Renmin Ribao*, January 30, 1956.

41. N. Federenko, "Khrushchev's Visit to Beijing," *Far Eastern Affairs*, no. 2, 1990, pp. 213–24.

42. See joint editorial, *Renmin Ribao* and *Hongqi*, September 6, 1963.

43. This was not the first time Mao had limned this worst-case postnuclear scenario. In early 1955, shortly after the U.S. Congress had adopted the "Formosa Resolution" which authorized President Eisenhower to employ U.S. armed forces to protect the security of Taiwan and the offshore islands, he said: "The atomic hoax of the United States cannot scare the Chinese people. We have a population of 600 million, and a territory of 9.6 million square kilometers. . . . If the United States were to launch a third world war, then even if it were to last for eight or ten years, the result would be that the ruling classes in the United States, in England, and in those other countries that were their accomplices would be completely swept away, and most places in the world would become countries led by Communist Parties." Mao, "The Atom Bomb Cannot Scare the Chinese People" (January 28, 1955), trans. in Kau and Leung, *Writings*, 1:516–17.

44. He Di, "The Evolution of the PRC's Policy Toward the Offshore Islands (Quemoy, Matsu)" (see n. 29 above).

45. Andrei Gromyko, *Pamiatnoe* (Moscow: Politizdat, 1988), 2 vols.; see also *New York Times*, February 22, 1988, pp. 1, 6.

46. Mao, "Be Activists in Promoting the Revolution" (October 9, 1957), as trans. in *Selected Works*, 5:495.

47. In 1954, Malenkov took the position (departing from Stalin) that nuclear war would mean the destruction of the world. Khrushchev opposed him, arguing that communism would survive a nuclear war while capitalism would not—that nuclear war was winnable. In 1955 China embraced the Soviet position. Peter J. Gordon, "The Politics of Implementing China's Nuclear Strategy, Part 1: 1949–1965," *Journal of Northeast Asian Studies*, Spring 1989, pp. 39–56.

48. Medvedev, *China and the Superpowers*, p. 30.

49. Talbott, ed., *Khrushchev Remembers: The Last Testament*, p. 258.

50. *Mainichi Shimbun* (Tokyo), January 26, 1972.

51. Talbott, ed., *Khrushchev Remembers: The Last Testament*, pp. 261–62.

52. As quoted in Li Jingjie, "Sino-Soviet Relations and Their Future Prospects," unpublished paper presented to the Faculty Seminar for Comparative Study of Communist Societies, University of California, Berkeley, 1986, my translation, p. 6. Mr. Li is at this writing a member of the Institute of Soviet and Eastern European Studies of the Chinese Academy of Social Sciences in Beijing.

53. Mao Zedong, "Speech of September 24, 1962," trans. in *Chinese Law and Government* 1, no. 4 (Winter 1968–69): 88.

54. See Harold P. Ford, "Modern Weapons and the Sino-Soviet Estrangement," *China Quarterly*, no. 18 (April–June 1964), p. 162.

55. See the *Renmin Ribao* and *Hongqi* joint editorial, September 6, 1963.

56. Sophia Peterson, *Sino-Soviet-American Relations: Conflict, Communications and Mutual Threat* (Denver: Graduate School of International Studies, University of Denver, monograph no. 16, 1979), pp. 3–16.

57. M. S. Uraintsev [pseud.], "Sovetsko-kitaiskie otnosheniia: Problemy i perspektivy," *PDV*, no. 2, 1982, p. 15.

58. See L. Dittmer, "Mao and the Politics of Revolutionary Mortality," *Asian Survey* 27, no. 3 (March 1987): 316–40.

59. The U.S. National Security Council had concluded in early 1956 that the United States had achieved a preemptive nuclear-attack (first strike) capability against the USSR, and that situation was not immediately altered by the Soviet launching of Sputnik and the first ICBM in 1957. University Publications of America, Research Collections, *Documents of the National Security Council, 1947–77*, NSC 5602, February 1956, microfilm reel 4. Soviet strategic superiority was shown to be illusory in 1961 by the first American intelligence satellites (which replaced the risky U-2 flights). It was in order to regain Soviet strategic superiority that Khrushchev launched his daring bid to deploy SS-4s in Cuba, resulting in the October 1962 Soviet-American confrontation.

60. Khrushchev began boasting of Soviet missile capabilities after the fortieth anniversary celebrations; in 1959 he claimed that one factory was capable of producing 250 ICBMs annually. John Prados, *The Soviet Estimate: U.S. Intelligence and Russian Military Strength* (New York: Dial Press, 1982), p. 77. In 1958 and 1959, these bluffs inflated the official U.S. "national intelligence estimates" of Soviet strategic forces, fostering the "missile gap" rhetoric of the 1960 election and the subsequent Kennedy decision to outproduce the USSR.

61. One knowledgeable observer concludes from available evidence that a

"sufficient" Soviet strike capability came into being between 1962 and 1966. Walter Slocombe, *The Political Implications of Strategic Parity* (London: Institute for Strategic Studies, 1971). Another maintains that the change did not occur before 1965. Schlesinger (at that time defense secretary) said in early 1974 that the period in which the United States retained close to a disarming capability against the USSR prevailed through the late 1960s—and that both sides realized this. Link, *East-West Conflict*, p. 82.

11. Unit-Veto Triangle, 1959–1969

1. See Gerald Segal, *The Great Power Triangle* (New York: St. Martin's Press, 1982).

2. State of the Union Address, 1963.

3. News Conference of November 28, 1962, in *Department of State Bulletin*, December 17, 1962, p. 915.

4. See, for example, the intelligence memorandum to the President of November 18, 1964, which predicted: "The principal threat to world peace and Western security in the foreseeable future will almost certainly be Communist China. . . . Politically its prestige among colored peoples as the most powerful and successful colored nation will prosper, and it will use that prestige and the disproportionate share of its resources to extend its influence and create maximum disorder in Asia and Africa." The author foresaw a "shift of the center of containment from Europe to the Far East," possibly necessitating the disengagement of forces from Western Europe and concentration on "wars of liberation." Memorandum for the President, November 18, 1964, in Declassified Government Documents, 1975, p. 212B. For a relevant academic analysis of the impact of Chinese endorsement of Third World insurgencies, see Peter Van Ness, *Revolution and Chinese Foreign Policy: Peking's Support for Wars of National Liberation* (Berkeley: University of California Press, 1970).

5. Liu Shaoqi reportedly said in 1962: "Since we are preoccupied with our own cares, how can we afford simultaneously to provoke U.S. imperialism and Soviet revisionism, and aid the struggle of the revolutionary peoples of the world?" Nonetheless, in 1966–69 China dispatched some fifty to sixty thousand Chinese to Vietnam to repair roads, bridges, and perform other services; Soviet and Chinese material shipments were of roughly equal quantity and significance during this period.

6. This was most acutely felt in Vietnam, where the Johnson administration was soliciting cooperation to induce the North Vietnamese to negotiate. In January 1965 the United States expressed its hope that the USSR would exert its influence to persuade the North Vietnamese government to stop supporting the Viet Cong and to call off the attacks on South Vietnamese cities, and the Soviet Union indeed passed these demands on to North Vietnam, but to no avail. On February 16, 1965, the Soviets proposed to China and North Vietnam that an international conference on Indochina be held in France; the Chinese

denounced the proposal. Through the end of the 1960s, the Chinese abetted Hanoi rhetorically and diplomatically in its hard line while soft-pedaling military assistance, turning Vietnam into a symbol of its own high valuation of militant self-reliance (a form of support Hanoi came to appreciate less and less).

7. See Nie Rongzhen, *Nie Rongzhen Huiyi Lu* [Reflections of Nie Rongzhen] (Beijing: Zhanshi, 1983), 2 vols.

8. Ibid.

9. *Peking Review*, no. 34 (August 25), 1956, p. 21; as cited in Nelsen, *Power and Insecurity*, p. 23.

10. Altogether no less than 129 Chinese students and scientists returned to China after the repatriation agreement was signed in Geneva in September 1955. Other prominent American-trained scientists who contributed to this project included Chen Nengkuan, Guo Yonghuai, Zhu Guangya, and Wang Ganchang. See Lewis and Xue, *China Builds the Bomb*, pp. 50, 147.

11. See Nobuo Miyamoto, "Basic Structure of the Sino-Soviet Conflict and Its Prospect: Nexus of the US-USSR-China 'Nuclear' Dimension and Great Power Nationalism of the USSR and China," unpublished paper, Woodrow Wilson Center, Smithsonian Institution, Washington, D.C., May 1986; see also Agatha S. Y. Wong-Fraser, "China's Nuclear Deterrent," *Current History*, 80, no. 467 (September 1981): 245–76.

12. As quoted in Richard Nixon, *Memoirs* (New York: Grosset and Dunlap, 1978), p. 557.

13. This deterrent extended only to Siberia and Central Asia (they made numerous successful MRBM tests up to 800 miles), but that would include Vladivostok, Tashkent, or Khabarovsk.

14. Link, *East-West Conflict*, p. 115.

15. Chang, *Friends and Enemies*, p. 249.

16. Larry Wu-tai Chin, a CIA analyst, kept the PRC closely apprised of relevant political developments for some thirty years prior to his discovery and arrest in 1985. *New York Times*, January 6, 1986.

17. H. R. Haldeman, *The Ends of Power* (New York: Times Books, 1978), p. 90; see also McGeorge Bundy, *Danger and Survival: Choices About the Bomb in the First Fifty Years* (New York: Random House, 1988), p. 532.

18. See Franz Schurmann, *The Logic of World Power: An Inquiry into the Origins, Currents, and Contradictions of World Politics* (New York: Pantheon, 1974), p. 388.

19. "Possibilities of Greater Militancy by the Chinese Communists" (July 31, 1963), NSC Letter, Memorandum for the Record, on a meeting at the State Department including McGeorge Bundy, Dean Rusk, and Robert McNamara. LBJ Library, declassified September 14, 1977.

20. See Richard C. Thornton, "Strategic Change and the American Foreign Policy: Perceptions of the Sino-Soviet Conflict," in Ilpyong J. Kim, ed., *The Strategic Triangle: China, the United States and the Soviet Union* (New York: Paragon House, 1987), pp. 48–71.

21. See Wich, *Sino-Soviet Crisis Politics* (see above, Chapter 3, n. 2).

22. An article in *Renmin Ribao* in March 1963 for the first time designated the Chinese-Russian treaties of Aigun (1858), Peking (1860) and Ili (1881) as having been "unequal."

23. Conversation at a reception of Messrs. Sasaki Kozo, Kuroda Hisao, Hososaka Kanemitsu, et al., of the Socialist Party of Japan (July 10, 1964), in *Wansui* (1969), pp. 540–41 (my translation).

24. R. Judson Mitchell, *Ideology of a Superpower: Contemporary Soviet Doctrine and International Relations* (Stanford: Hoover Institution Press, 1982), p. 38.

25. By the fall of 1967 more than half of the PLA's main force units (twenty of thirty-five army corps) had been diverted from national defense to domestic pacification. Richard Thornton, *Soviet Asian Strategy in the Brezhnev Era and Beyond* (Washington, D.C.: Washington Institute for Values in Public Policy, 1985), p. 9.

26. Gurtov and Hwang, *China Under Threat*, p. 234. This hypothesis is supported, in addition to internal evidence, by the similarity of this pattern of coercive diplomacy to Chinese behavior in India in 1962 and Vietnam in 1979 (which in turn may have been patterned after traditional punitive expeditions under the empire). See Allen Whiting, *The Chinese Calculus of Deterrence: India and Indochina* (Ann Arbor: University of Michigan Press, 1975).

27. Arkady N. Shevchenko, *Breaking with Moscow* (New York: Knopf, 1985), pp. 164–65.

28. Victor Louis, "Will Soviet Rockets Czech-mate China?" *London Evening News*, September 16, 1969, as cited in *FBIS*, September 19, 1969, pp. A11–A12. Louis was also the source of a story the following month in the American press warning that "Russian nuclear installations stand aimed at the Chinese nuclear facilities"; China's vast size was no reason to withhold the benefits of the Brezhnev Doctrine from the Chinese people. See the *Washington Post*, October 8, 1969; as cited in Coates, *China and the Bomb*, p. 27.

29. Shevchenko, *Breaking*, p. 165.

30. Marvin and Bernard Kalb, *Kissinger* (New York: Dell, 1975), pp. 259–60.

31. Lo Ping, "Spy Wars Between the Soviet Union and China, U.S. and China," *Zheng Ming*, no. 106 (August 1, 1986).

32. Jacobsen, *Sino-Soviet Relations Since Mao*, p. 54.

33. According to an oral presentation by Zbigniew Brzezinski, in a seminar given at Harvard University in September 1972. I am grateful to Jacques Levesque for this report. It should be noted that the Chinese have always denied that they submitted to Soviet nuclear blackmail, or even that Kosygin made such a threat. The Chinese announcement following the impromptu Zhou-Kosygin airport "summit" explicitly indicated that China would not be intimidated by threats of nuclear war, specifically warning against strikes on nuclear facilities. By giving this subject such prominent attention, however, the Chinese indicated

that it was of serious concern and implied (by so vehemently denying it) that the threat might have influenced them to agree to negotiate.

34. Halliday, ed., *The Artful Albanian*, p. 276.

35. See M. and B. Kalb, *Kissinger*, pp. 259–60; Haldeman, *Ends of Power*, p. 89; Coral Bell, *The Diplomacy of Detente: The Kissinger Era* (New York: St. Martin's Press, 1977), pp. 15–16. According to Bell, the Soviet signals that they were contemplating a preventive war, perhaps including nuclear strikes, "were so deliberate, clumsy and obvious that it is difficult not to believe that they were stage thunder, a Russian effort to frighten the Chinese decision-makers into a more compliant attitude. The signals included, for instance, letters to communist parties in the West that seemed to be asking for advance approval of a strike against China. . . . The Russians apparently offered, via the military attachés in Washington and Moscow, at least a clear hint if not an actual bid for American acquiescence or collusion in such a strike. They were firmly snubbed by the American policy-makers concerned, and knowledge of the bid and the snub were, naturally, conveyed to the Chinese government" (p. 16).

36. David Armstrong, "The Soviet Union," in Gerald Segal and William Tow, eds., *Chinese Defense Policy* (Urbana: University of Illinois Press, 1984), pp. 180–96.

37. Haldeman, *Ends of Power*, p. 90.

38. O. Borisov, "Who Is Preventing Normalization?" *Izvestiia*, May 16, 1974. The Chinese rejected all of these overtures, pointing to a contradiction between Soviet peace rhetoric and Soviet arms escalation and refusing to negotiate under duress.

39. Paul H. B. Godwin, "Changing Concepts of Doctrine, Strategy and Operations in the Chinese People's Liberation Army, 1978–87," *China Quarterly*, no. 112 (December 1987), pp. 572–91.

40. Barry Naughton, "The Third Front: Defence Industrialization in the Chinese Interior," *China Quarterly*, no. 115 (September 1988), pp. 351–86.

12. Romantic Triangle, 1969–1976

1. Henry Kissinger, *White House Years* (Boston: Little, Brown, 1979), p. 165.

2. Ibid., p. 712.

3. Ibid., pp. 191–92, 765. For a persuasive critique of Nixon's and Kissinger's lack of evenhandedness toward the two wings, see Garthoff, *Detente and Confrontation*, pp. 219–39.

4. Kissinger, *White House Years*, p. 179.

5. Ibid., pp. 179–82.

6. Jeffrey Simon, *Cohesion and Dissension in Eastern Europe: Six Crises* (New York: Praeger, 1983).

7. Nixon, *Memoirs*, p. 405.

8. Garthoff, *Detente and Confrontation*, p. 95.

9. Dan L. Strode, "Arms Control and Sino-Soviet Relations," *Orbis* 28, no. 1 (Spring 1984): 163–89.

10. Kissinger, *White House Years*, p. 836.

11. The United States began withdrawing troops from the Asian Pacific region in 1969, and by 1973 had withdrawn 600,000 men, reducing its troop strength by two-thirds. Troop strength in Vietnam dropped from 535,000 men in 1968 to a mere 25,000 in 1973. Leszek Buszynski, *Soviet Foreign Policy and Southeast Asia* (London: Croom Helm, 1986), p. 47.

12. The problem originated following Johnson's landslide victory in the 1964 presidential election, when U.S. escalation prompted Hanoi to call for bloc assistance, in turn leading the Soviet Union to demand Chinese cooperation in such assistance in the name of international class solidarity. In an exchange of secret letters in the spring of 1965, the Soviets demanded: (1) that China grant an "air corridor" through which a massive Soviet airlift could be mounted in defense of North Vietnam, and (2) that China cede a base in Yunnan adjacent to Vietnam, where hundreds of Soviet military personnel could be stationed to support the Vietnamese war effort. *The Observer* (London), November 24, 1965; as cited in Harry Gelman, *The Soviet Far East Buildup and Soviet Risk-Taking Against China* (Santa Monica: Rand Corporation, August 1982). The Chinese accused the Soviets of seeking to exploit the escalating conflict to infringe upon Chinese sovereignty. After duly considering the proposal, on November 11, 1965, Beijing made known its decision: China refused to cooperate in limited joint action, announcing that the conflict with the Soviet Union had acquired the character of an irreconcilable class struggle. See the *Hongqi–Renmin Ribao* joint editorial, "Rejection of the Talk of the New Leaders of the CPSU about 'Joint Action,'" as translated in *Peking Review*, no. 23 (November), 1965. While spurning this sort of coordination, Mao did permit Soviet aid to Vietnam to transit his country, and also sent Chinese aid. Between 1965 and 1968, the Chinese rail corridor was the principal supply route for the Vietnamese war effort. Soviet and Chinese materiel shipments were of roughly equal quantity and size. Thornton, *Soviet Asian Strategy*, p. 12.

13. Thornton, *Soviet Asian Strategy*, pp. 34 ff.

14. Anne Gilks, "The Breakdown of the Sino-Vietnamese Alliance, 1970–1979" (Ph.D. dissertation draft, London, 1988).

15. *Background Information Relating to Southeast Asia and Vietnam*, U.S. Senate Committee on Foreign Relations, June 1970 (Washington, D.C.: Government Printing Office, 1970), p. 315. This is confirmed by the Vietnamese themselves, who complained: "In 1968, when discussing aid to Vietnam for 1969, the Chinese rulers reduced their aid by more than 20 percent compared with 1968." Socialist Republic of Vietnam Foreign Ministry, *White Book on Relations with China*, trans. in FE/242/A3/1, as cited in Gilks, "Breakdown." The drawdown may be partly explained by Vietnam's preference for more advanced Soviet weapons, but after the bombing halt in 1968 the PRC also withdrew some 50,000 troops, mostly engineer and construction battalions, who had been stationed in Vietnam since the spring of 1966.

16. Seymour M. Hersh, *The Price of Power: Kissinger in the Nixon White House* (New York: Summit, 1983), p. 442.

17. Ibid. Hersh interviewed Nguyen Co Thach (who had been present with Pham Van Dong in Beijing) during a visit to Hanoi in 1979.

18. Garthoff, *Detente and Confrontation*, pp. 258–59.

19. Kissinger, *White House Years*, p. 1043.

20. The Socialist Republic of Vietnam (SRV) Ministry of Foreign Affairs, *The Truth of Vietnam-China Relations Over the Last 30 Years* (Hanoi, 1979), as translated in *FBIS*, October 19, 1979, p. 26.

21. Levesque, *Le Conflit*, pp. 117–18. It is true that Hanoi then conquered South Vietnam with impunity in 1975, but this occurred only after Nixon had resigned amid the Watergate scandal (August 1974) and Congress adopted legislation interdicting all bombing in Indochina. Under these low-risk conditions both the USSR and the PRC were willing to provide Vietnam with the military assistance needed for the *coup de grâce*. See Tetsusaburo Kimura, *The Vietnamese Economy, 1975–86: Reforms and International Relations* (Tokyo: Institute of Developing Economies, 1989), pp. 64–103.

22. John Newhouse, *Cold Dawn: The Story of SALT* (New York: Holt, Rinehart and Winston, 1973), p. 188–89; Gerard Smith, *Doubletalk: The Story of SALT I* (New York: Doubleday, 1980), p. 106.

23. Norman D. Levin and Jonathan D. Pollack, "Managing the Strategic Triangle," Rand Note N-2125 (April 1984); Shevchenko, *Breaking*, pp. 165–68.

24. General Iurii Lebedev stated that the Soviet Union wanted Chinese forces taken into account in both SALT I and II. *FBIS* (Soviet Union), July 25, 1983, as cited in Strode, "Arms Control."

25. Kissinger, *White House Years*, p. 184.

26. Ibid., pp. 183, 910. On October 14, 1976, Victor Louis again published an article in the *London Evening News* and *France Soir* expressing the hope that reasonable men should now come to the fore in China, but warning that Soviet patience was "limited," and that the USSR might do something "irreversible" if the PRC did not make some conciliatory gesture within the next month. Secretary of State Kissinger took the occasion to warn the USSR publicly that the United States would take "an extremely dim view of a military attack or even military pressure" on China. Statement on CBS news program, "Face the Nation," October 24, 1976, as transcribed in *Department of State Bulletin*, November 15, 1976. *Pravda* responded with a denunciation of Kissinger's "clumsy intervention" and denied that the Soviet Union had ever "entertained designs" on China. *Pravda*, October 27, 1976.

27. Steven I. Levine, "China and the United States," in Samuel Kim, ed., *China and the World* (Boulder: Westview, 1984), pp. 113–35.

28. See Zhou Enlai's report on the international situation at a senior cadres' meeting in December 1971, as translated in *Issues and Studies*, January 1972, pp. 116–17; also "The Great Victory of Chairman Mao's Revolutionary Diplomatic Line," Confidential Reference Material on Education on the Situation, no. 43, for Distribution to Companies and Above (April 4, 1973), as trans. in

Issues and Studies, June 1974, pp. 99–108, and July 1974, pp. 94–105.

29. Just as the Korean War boosted Japan's industrial capacity, the Vietnam War propelled the East Asian NICs toward an export capability that would eventually challenge the American economic hegemony in the Pacific. All of the large South Korean construction firms, for example, that outbid U.S. contractors in the Middle East in the 1970s, started out by building U.S. bases in Vietnam. See L. Jones and Il Sakong, *Government, Business and Entrepreneurship in Economic Development: The Korean Case* (Cambridge, Mass.: Harvard University Press, 1980), p. 357. Thailand and the Philippines received foreign exchange from U.S. procurement and war-related business, and other Asian electronic and clothing companies that later became major exporters to the United States traced their origins to the Vietnam War. Peter Hayes, Lyuba Zarsky, and Walden Bello, *American Lake: Nuclear Peril in the Pacific* (New York: Penguin, 1986), p. 110.

30. Richard K. Ashley, *The Political Economy of War and Peace: The Sino-Soviet-American Triangle and the Modern Security Problematique* (New York: Nichols, 1980), pp. 135–36.

31. *Annual Report to the Congress for Fiscal Year 1985* (Washington, D.C.: U.S. Department of Finance, 1984), pp. 19–26.

32. Hayes et al., *American Lake*, pp. 158–62. This drawdown was rationalized at the time in terms of ship modernization, but was in fact part of a general post-Vietnam demobilization.

33. Sydney H. Jammes, "The Chinese Defense Burden, 1965–74," in *China: A Reassessment of the Economy*, a compendium of papers submitted to the Joint Economic Committee, Congress of the United States (Washington, D.C.: Government Printing Office, 1975), pp. 459–66.

34. Cited in F. Christopher Chyba, "U.S. Military-Support Equipment Sales to the PRC," *Asian Survey*, April 1981, pp. 469–84.

35. Ibid., p. 467.

36. Zhang Aiqing, "Several Questions Concerning Modernization of National Defense," *Hongqi*, no. 5 (March 1), 1983, pp. 21–24.

37. Garthoff, *Detente and Confrontation*, p. 243.

38. In the two years following the March 1969 clash, the Soviet Union increased its deployment in the Far Eastern Military District from 30 to 47–52 divisions consisting of about 750,000 troops (and the cost of maintaining forces in the border region was estimated to be three times that of comparable forces west of the Urals). These forces were backed by some 450 bombers, 2,000 combat aircraft, 35–40 percent of the Soviet ICBM force, and 20 percent of Soviet air defense systems.

39. The original proposal for a collective security system, attributed to Brezhnev, was published in *Izvestiia* on May 28, 1969, in a commentator article by Vikentii Matveyev. Included as important members in the proposal were Pakistan, Afghanistan, Burma, Singapore, and Cambodia. Brezhnev first personally mentioned the proposal in June 1969. In a Radio Moscow broadcast of

August 17, 1969, it was indicated that "India, Pakistan, and Afghanistan would form the nucleus of the system, which would eventually embrace all countries from the Middle East to Japan." Though not specifically excluded, the PRC was not mentioned in any of these announcements.

40. See L. I. Brezhnev, *Leninskim Kursom* (Moscow: Politizdat, 1970), 2:413; 3:494; and 4:253–54, 329.

41. By the end of the war, 75 percent of all military assistance to Vietnam came from the USSR, 10 percent from Eastern Europe, and 15 percent from China. After the fall of Saigon, Beijing halted all military aid to Hanoi. Thus during the 1980s the portion provided by the USSR increased to 97 percent. Douglas Pike, *Vietnam and the Soviet Union: Anatomy of an Alliance* (Boulder: Westview, 1987), p. 196.

42. Based on figures in U.S. Bureau of the Budget, *Statistical Abstract of the United States, 1979* (Washington, D.C.: Government Printing Office, 1979), pp. 364, 435.

43. Mitchell, *Ideology of a Superpower*, pp. 1–21 et passim.

13. Sino-American Marriage, 1976–1981

1. Neither Nixon nor Kissinger, in public or in private, denounced Soviet repression or claimed the superiority of American values. They simply indicated that arms control, trade benefits, and other rewards would not be forthcoming unless domestic opposition in the United States was held in check, presupposing amenable behavior on the part of the prospective beneficiary. Dimitri K. Simes, "Can the West Affect Soviet Thinking?" in Sonnenfeldt, ed., *Soviet Policies in the 1980s*, pp. 161–71.

2. In 1975, it was decided to reduce investment growth from 41 percent in the Ninth Five-Year Plan to 26 percent in the Tenth, in an effort to shield defense from the full impact of diminished economic growth. Myron Rush, "Impact and Implications of Soviet Defense Spending," in Sonnenfeldt, ed., *Soviet Policies in the 1980s*, pp. 131–47.

3. For example, Edwardian England sought to "contain" the rise of Wilhelminian Germany through a series of alliances with the United States (1901), Japan (1902), France (1904), and Russia (1907). But this only encouraged the Kaiser in his determination to break the "encirclement" by force. See also Barry R. Posen, *The Sources of Military Doctrine: France, Britain, and Germany Between the World Wars* (Ithaca: Cornell University Press, 1984), pp. 69–73.

4. Sokoloff and Lemoine, *China and the U.S.S.R.*, pp. 17–24.

5. See Young Rae Kim, "The Soviet Union's Shifting Policy Toward East Asia: Its Major Determinants and Future Prospect," in Park and Ha, eds., *The Soviet Union and East Asia*, pp. 136–63.

6. The advent at about this time of a very-long-range submarine launched ballistic missile, or SLBM (the SS-N-8, later the SS-N-18) made it possible for

the first time for Soviet ballistic missile submarines (SSBNs) to target U.S. cities without leaving "bastion areas" (i.e., partly sheltered bodies of water adjoining the Soviet Union, such as the Barents Sea in the Northwest, or the Sea of Okhotsk in the Far East). This necessitated naval reinforcement in order to deny Seventh Fleet access in time of war and to guarantee Soviet egress, and gave added strategic importance to the surrounding land areas—the Kola Peninsula in the Northwest, the Soviet Primorsky province, Kamchatka, and the Kurile chain in the Far East.

7. Lawrence Freedman, "The Military Dimension of Soviet Policy," in Segal, ed., *The Soviet Union in East Asia*, pp. 88–101.

8. Thus by 1980, the eastern part of the country was estimated to be producing 32 percent of total Soviet output of tanks, 40 percent of the planes, a quarter of the warships and a quantity of missiles; with the construction of additional refineries, Soviet mechanized forces also had ample energy supplies within easy reach. *Beijing Review*, no. 19, 1981, p. 12.

9. Jaap van Ginneken, *Indochina gendaishi* [The Conflict between China, Vietnam, and Cambodia], trans. by Y. Yamada and Y. Yoshiaki (Tokyo: Rengo-shuppan, 1988), p. 92.

10. Gerald Segal, "Arms Control and Sino-Soviet Relations," in Segal, ed., *Arms Control in Asia* (London: Macmillan, 1987), pp. 43–66.

11. *Defense of Japan* (Tokyo: Ministry of Defense, 1980).

12. *The Military Balance* (London: Institute of International Strategic Studies, 1980 to 1983 eds.). There is an important qualification to this apparent escalation in ground force division strength. Troop strength began to be "skeletonized" during this period; by 1981, many of the divisions had shrunk to "category three" status, denoting less than half the full manpower complement. Estimates of total troop strength ranged from 450,000 to 530,000 throughout the 1980s. Nelsen, *Power and Insecurity*, pp. 111.

13. Whereas the Soviet military budget had averaged $140 to $160 billion (in 1980 U.S. constant dollars) throughout the 1970s (civilian capital investment was deliberately held down in the Tenth Soviet Five-Year Plan in order to shield defense from the full impact of reduced economic growth), China's military budget was estimated at U.S. $30 to $40 billion annually, and much of their hardware was hence increasingly obsolescent. Robert S. Wang, "China's Evolving Strategic Doctrine," *Asian Survey* 24, no. 10 (October 1984): 997–1012.

14. Morris Rothenberg, *Whither China: The View from the Kremlin* (Miami: Center for Advanced International Studies, University of Miami, 1977), p. 223.

15. Garthoff, *Detente and Confrontation*, p. 619; *Time*, February 5, 1979, p. 34; *Xinhua*, January 31, 1979, as trans. in *FBIS–China*, February 1, 1979, pp. A7–A8. Deng made his unprecedented proposal for an "alliance" in an interview with Robert Novak (*Look*, February 19, 1979).

16. Jacobsen, *Sino-Soviet Relations Since Mao*, p. 93.

17. Zbigniew Brzezinski, *Power and Principle: Memoirs of the National*

Security Adviser, 1977–1981 (New York: Farrar, Straus, Giroux, 1983), pp. 409–10.

18. That Deng Xiaoping was personally pivotal in the Chinese decision to intervene is made clear in Brzezinski's memoirs. See Brzezinski, *Power and Principle*, pp. 409–10.

19. Reuters (Moscow), January 1979.

20. On the latter, see Garthoff's scathing commentary in *Detente and Confrontation*, p. 264.

21. *Christian Science Monitor*, February 29, 1979.

22. The Soviet Pacific Fleet positioned twenty surface warships and several submarines off the Chinese coast in order to warn China to limit its invasion. Hayes et al., *American Lake*, p. 317. This flotilla became the nucleus of the Soviet naval buildup at Cam Ranh Bay. Robert C. Dabling, "Sino-Soviet Tensions and China's Military Modernization," in Larry Wortzel, ed., *China's Military Modernization: International Implications* (New York: Greenwood, 1988), pp. 119–33.

23. Cf. the Richard Burt report in *New York Times*, March 15, 1979, as cited in Sutter, *Chinese Foreign Policy*, p. 90.

24. As the Chinese anticipated, the Soviets provoked a number of small incidents along the border to make a show of strength but did not mobilize massive troops, and China did not need to use its regular army to deal with them but only its semimilitary "production and construction corps." Cheng Hsiang, "Relations Along the Sino-Soviet Border—Impressions from Xinjiang (Part I)," in *Wen Wei Bo* (Hong Kong), October 7, 1985, p. 2.

25. Finance Minister Wang Bingqian estimated that the war had added RMB 2.04 billion to the 1979 military budget. *Xin Wan Bao* (Hong Kong), March 7, 1979. Taking bureaucratically hidden costs into account, Jencks estimates total expenses at RMB 5 to 10 billion. Harlan Jencks, "Lessons of a 'Lesson': China-Vietnam, 1979," in Robert E. Harkavy and Stephanie G. Neuman, eds., *The Lessons of Recent Wars in the Third World* (Lexington, Mass.: Lexington Books, 1987).

26. See Gelman, *The Soviet Far East Buildup*, pp. 95–105.

27. Chinese Vice-Premier Wang Zhen, as cited by Nayan Chanda, *FEER*, March 9, 1979, p. 14.

28. Moscow launched an airlift of military supplies during the incursion, including a large number of fighter aircraft (e.g., MiG-21s), none of which were used in the war. In early March, Soviet intelligence-gathering task force vessels began to arrive at the harbor in Danang; on March 27, a small fleet of one cruiser, one frigate, and a minesweeper became the first Russian ships to anchor at Cam Ranh Bay since April 1905. Chinese fears of "encirclement" had become self-fulfilling.

29. *New York Times*, January 4, 1980.

14. Sinocentric Romantic Triangle, 1981–1985

1. Notes from the editors, "China's Independent Diplomacy," *Beijing Review*, no. 22, 1983, p. 15; it was explicitly stated that "China is partial to neither side" in *Shijie Zhishi's* year-end wrap-up for 1983, "New Year's Chat on the International Situation in 1984." *Zhongguo Xinwen She* (Beijing), January 1, 1984, as trans. in *FBIS–PRC*, January 3, 1984, p. A1. According to *Yomiuri Shimbun*, the Japanese Foreign Ministry obtained a Chinese confidential document stating clearly that Beijing desired an equidistant diplomacy between Washington and Moscow. See *Chung-yang jih-pao* [Central Daily News] (Taipei), December 1, 1982, p. 5.

2. According to 1988 figures, Vietnam costs the Soviet Union more than U.S. $3.5 billion per annum; Cuba over $4.9 billion; Angola, Mozambique, and Ethiopia a total of more than $3 billion; and Nicaragua nearly $1 billion. Altogether, recent Soviet acquisitions cost the USSR over $35 million a day. Richard Nixon, "Dealing with Gorbachev," *New York Times Magazine*, March 13, 1988, pp. 26–30, 66–67, 78–79.

3. During the last year of his life, Brezhnev seems to have been on the defensive regarding his arms control policy; Dmitrii Ustinov described arguments critical of his approach in a lengthy defense of it in *Pravda*, July 12, 1982. Critics apparently suggested that Brezhnev's arms control initiatives were an inadequate response to Reagan's rearmament policies. Since Brezhnev's arms control initiatives were having little impact, and since he did not wish to increase defense spending substantially, China was a logical counter to the American threat. See Brezhnev's speech before the military high command in late October 1982, in which he defends Soviet defense policy and reaches out to the PRC.

4. Cf. Dorothy Solinger, "The Fifth National People's Congress and the Process of Policy Making: Reform, Readjustment, and the Opposition," *Asian Survey* 22, no. 12 (December 1982).

5. Harris, *China's Foreign Policy*, p. 30.

6. Henry Kissinger, *Years of Upheaval* (Boston: Little, Brown, 1982), pp. 60–63, 691–92.

7. Cf. BBC, *SWB/FE*, no. 6930/A1/2.

8. *L'Unità*, January 8, 1982, as trans. in *FBIS–China*, January 9, 1982, pp. G1–G2.

9. See John Garver, "China's Response to the Strategic Defense Initiative," *Asian Survey* 26, no. 11 (November 1986): 1220–40.

10. Sarah-Ann Smith, "China's Third World Policy as a Counterpoint to the First and Second Worlds," in Harris and Worden, *China and the Third World*, pp. 53–75.

11. For example, Zhao Ziyang took this position during his visit to North Korea in December 1981, as did Huang Hua during his visit to Nigeria and Ghana in November.

12. For example, whereas only a few years before, Beijing had accused Washington of flabbiness in the face of Soviet aggression in the Third World, the Chinese now accused the Americans of heavy-handedness—for example, toward Nicaragua (with whom Beijing exchanged ambassadors in 1986). S. Mirov, "China's Policy Towards Developing Countries: New Trends," *Far Eastern Affairs*, no. 2, 1988, pp. 34–49.

13. Secretary of State George Shultz, "The United States and East Asia: Partnership for the Future," *Current Policy*, U.S. Department of State, no. 459 (March 5, 1983). According to reliable reports, it was Caspar Weinberger who initiated the Japan-first strategy.

14. For one indication of this concern, see the article by the influential Shanghai American specialist Zhang Jialin, "The New Romanticism in the Reagan Administration's Asian Policy: Illusion and Reality," *Asian Survey* 24, no. 10 (October 1984): 997–1012, wherein Zhang responds critically, even indignantly, to the Shultz speech.

15. According to the International Institute of Strategic Studies (London), in yearbooks issued at the relevant dates.

16. Michael McGwire, *Military Objectives in Soviet Foreign Policy* (Washington, D.C.: Brookings Institution, 1987), pp. 161–82.

17. The Far Eastern TVD now includes at least 13 of the country's 22 operational ICBM bases, housing about 650 SS-18 and SS-11 missiles. The Soviet Union also deploys about a third of its SSBN force from bases in the Soviet Far East. Two Yankee-class nuclear submarines, carrying SS-N-6 ballistic missiles with a range of 3,000 km, are normally sailing the Pacific. Twelve Delta-class submarines, which carry SS-N-8 ballistic missiles capable of hitting targets 9,000 km away, stay in port or venture into the Japan or Okhotsk seas. About nine old Golf II- and Hotel II-class ballistic submarines are also sailing the Pacific, with 1,200-km range SS-N-5 ballistic missiles, probably aimed at theater targets. In addition to these ballistic missile submarines, the Soviet Pacific Fleet deploys a fleet of 90-odd diesel-powered submarines which fire antiship nuclear cruise missiles and torpedoes, probably intended to attack U.S. carrier task forces. In this array, the ballistic missiles of the Delta-class submarines are assumed to be targeted on the United States; the targets of the Yankee SSBNs and Golf SSBs lie within the theater, including U.S. military installations. McGwire, *Military Objectives*, pp. 161–82; also Hayes et al., *American Lake*, pp. 317 ff.

18. For example, subsonic TU-16 Badgers were replaced with 85 (as of 1986) Mach 2.5 TU-22M Backfire bombers, and MiG-17 fighters were replaced first with MiG-21s, then with MiG-23/27 Floggers, SU-24 Fencys, and MiG-31 Foxhounds.

19. These included Kiev-class ASW carriers, Kirov-class nuclear missiles, Kira-class missile cruisers, and Sovremennyi-class missile destroyers. The Pacific Fleet was believed to be growing at a rate of about eleven surface vessels and submarines per year, and looks forward to acquiring its first nuclear-powered

aircraft carrier in the early 1990s. Zainuddin A. Bahari, "The Political and Military Dimensions of Security in the Western Pacific Region," in Philip M. Chen, ed., *The Pacific Challenge and Euro-Asiatic Relations* (Taipei: Asia and the World Institute, 1985), pp. 87–101.

20. Thus the number of carriers should increase from 12 in 1980 to 15 in 1990, the number of nuclear-powered attack submarines from 74 in 1981 to 117 in 1989, and so forth.

21. Hayes et al., *American Lake*, pp. 158–62.

22. Peter Grier, in *Christian Science Monitor*, February 26, 1986.

23. Reinhard Drifte, "Arms Control and the Superpower Balance in East Asia," in Segal, ed., *Arms Control in Asia*, pp. 18–43.

24. William T. Tow, "Nuclear Security Problems in the Far East," *Asian Pacific Community*, no. 19 (Winter 1983), pp. 52–72.

25. Hayes et al., *American Lake*, p. 116.

26. See Wang Baoqin's article in *Shijie Zhishi*, no. 21, 1984; and Yang Jiefa, "Center of Gravity of U.S. Overseas Economic Interests Shifting Toward Asia," *Guoji Wenti Yanjiu* [International Studies], no. 3, 1984.

27. Drifte, "Arms Control," p. 23.

28. *The Military Balance, 1985–1986* (London: The IISS, 1986), pp. 111–13. The DF-4s have a target range covering all of the Soviet Union and the west coast of the United States. The DF-3s can target most of the Soviet Far East from launchpads well inside China. Harlan Jencks, "The People's Republic of China's Nuclear Strategy," unpublished working paper, Naval Postgraduate School (Monterey, Calif., March 3, 1987), p. 20 et passim. For a more comprehensive picture, see Chong-pin Lin, *China's Nuclear Weapons Strategy: Tradition Within Evolution* (Lexington: D. C. Heath, 1988), pp. 44, 98.

29. See Monte R. Bullard, *China's Political-Military Evolution: The Party and the Military in the PRC, 1960–1984* (Boulder: Westview, 1985), pp. 21–23.

30. Low-yield test explosions (under 20 KT) of tactical nuclear weapons began in the mid-1970s and have continued sporadically, and by the mid-1980s the PLA had nuclear mines, rockets, and artillery as well as bombs. Two outspoken articles were published as early as 1979–80 advocating deployment of tactical nuclear weapons and their use in defending against invasion: See Xu Baoshan's article in *Jiefangjun Bao* [Liberation Army Daily], September 16, 1979, p. 3, as trans. in *Current Background*, no. 88 (June 4, 1980), pp. 97–99; and Chen Maoyuan, "Three Generations of Nuclear Weapons," *Zhongguo Qingnian Bao* [China Youth News], June 24, 1980, p. 4, as trans. in *FBIS–China*, February 7, 1980, pp. L3–L4; also see Lin, *China's Nuclear*, p. 98.

31. Ellis Joffe, "'People's War Under Modern Conditions': A Doctrine of Modern War," *China Quarterly*, no. 112 (December 1987), pp. 555–72.

32. See Henry B. Gass, *Sino-American Security Relations: Expectations and Realities* (Washington, D.C.: National Defense University Press, 1984).

33. *Foreign Report*, December 2, 1982, as quoted in David Armstrong, "The

Soviet Union," in Segal and Tow, eds., *Chinese Defense Policy*, pp. 180–96.

34. See Donald Hugh McMillen, "Chinese Perspectives," in Segal, ed., *The Soviet Union in East Asia*, pp. 168–95.

35. Nayan Chanda, "Superpower Triangle," *FEER*, April 4, 1985, pp. 17–19. Over the protest of Taiwan and ASEAN, twenty-four Sikorsky helicopters were sold in the fall of 1984, followed approximately one year later by plans and equipment for an artillery shell manufacturing plant (a contract worth some $30 million). Then in January 1986, the administration agreed on terms for the sale of $550 million worth of aviation electronics gear to provide improved fire control and navigation devices for 50 F-B fighters, upgrading them to all-weather capability—the largest sale of military equipment since diplomatic contacts were first established in 1972.

36. Including Chinese Defense Minister Zhang Aiping, who visited the United States in June.

37. *Atlanta Constitution*, November 6, 1986, p. 28.

38. U.S. officials warned China that closer economic and technological ties with the Soviet Union might pose problems for U.S. technology transfer to China, and expressed surprise at any sign of a softened posture toward international issues such as Afghanistan or Cambodia. Thus the establishment of a joint scientific and technological commission with the Soviet Union, announced during Arkhipov's visit in December 1984, was said to complicate transfer of dual use technology to China. American officials expressed disappointment that China remained silent during the fifth anniversary of the Soviet invasion of Afghanistan. They also conveyed the concern of ASEAN countries when China did not "teach Vietnam a second lesson" (as they had warned they might) after Hanoi's forces overran the Khmer resistance bases along the Thai border in the dry season offensive of 1985. Chanda, "Superpower Triangle," *FEER*, April 4, 1985, pp. 17–19.

39. At last notice, these included a squadron of MiG-23s, which in turn provide air defense for eight TU-95/Bear-D reconnaissance and TU-142/Bear-F ASW aircraft at Danang (which maintain surveillance of China's southern coasts, as well as the large submarine force based in the South China Sea). There were also some sixteen TU-16 Badgers at the Cam Ranh Airfield, "the only Russian strike aircraft deployed anywhere in the world beyond Soviet borders," ten with cruise missile strike capability; with the use of refueling facilities, these may reach targets as far away as Australia. *Armed Forces Journal*, April 1984, pp. 38–40. The Soviets also reportedly established from four to six missile bases, as well as air force and logistics bases in Hanoi, Hue, Haiphong, Ho Chi Minh City, and Vientiane. Cam Ranh Bay boasts the most extensive port facilities outside home waters, plus electronic surveillance and telecommunication stations to help monitor U.S. naval movements in the area. By 1982, some fifteen ships were calling at Cam Ranh Bay each year; three years later that figure had increased to between twenty-five and thirty vessels at any given time, including six to eight surface combatants and about five submarines.

40. Donald S. Zagoria, "China and the Superpowers: Recent Trends in the Strategic Triangle," unpublished paper delivered at the conference "China in a New Era," Manila, The Philippines, August 25, 1987.

41. Although the USSR promised to increase assistance, it has for some time been pressing for an improvement on past Vietnamese performance in using aid. Ligachev led the Soviet delegation to the Vietnamese Party Congress in December 1986, and said pointedly that it was important to "ensure that each economic and social project built in Vietnam with Soviet assistance would be made operational on time, produce the greatest returns, and facilitate a speedy resolution to the problems facing Vietnam." But at a press conference afterward he announced that Soviet economic assistance to Vietnam would double under the current Five-Year Plan (1986–90) to $2,500 million per year. At a special conference on Vietnam convened by the CPSU Central Committee in Moscow on January 5, 1987, Soviet party and government leaders examined economic and scientific cooperation with Vietnam in depth and agreed on the need for a "creative rethinking" of past practice and an "innovative approach" to the solution of problems.

42. Land-based cruise missiles (SSC-1s), with nuclear warheads, have been deployed in Etorofu Island, bringing the Chitose base in Hokkaido and the F-16 fighters deployed at Misawa, not to mention East China metropolitan areas, into range of surveillance or fire. In 1986 the Soviets deployed 30-km range atomic guns to the south of Sakhalin, to prevent U.S. and Japanese fleets from blockading the Soya-Kaikyo Straits in case of war.

43. See Suk Ryul Yu, "Soviet-North Korean Relations and Security in the Korean Peninsula," unpublished paper presented to the Korea-U.S. Conference on Northeast Asia Security, convened at the Institute for Sino-Soviet Studies, George Washington University, Washington, D.C., December 2–3, 1986.

44. Recent reports indicate that North Korea has been supplied by the Soviet Union with forty-seven M-2 helicopter gunships, some fifty MiG-23E Flogger fighters, some SU-25 close-support jets, thirty SA-3 surface-to-air missiles, plus several 270-km range SCUD-B battlefield missiles. Beginning in 1988, they also received advanced MiG-29s.

45. *FEER*, September 26, 1985, p. 56; and June 26, 1986, pp. 45–46; *Christian Science Monitor*, May 21, 1987, pp. 9–10.

46. In 1980, the USSR accounted for 22 percent of North Korea's imports and 26 percent of its exports. By 1985, these figures had jumped to 47 percent and 37 percent, respectively. *FEER*, June 18, 1987, p. 82; see also Byung-Joon Ahn, "South Korean-Soviet Relations: Issues and Prospects," *Korea and World Affairs* 14, no. 4 (Winter 1990): 671–704.

47. According to Hu Yaobang, in the first half of 1986 the Soviets overflew Chinese territory thirty times. Lo Ping, "Notes on a Northern Journey: Spy Wars Between Soviet Union and China, United States and China," *Zheng Ming*, no. 106 (August 1, 1986). Until 1985 Soviet overflights were southbound only, but beginning that year Soviet aircraft based at Cam Ranh Bay have been permitted to overfly North Korea on their northbound journey.

48. As of 1987, indirect and covert trade together was estimated at $2.5 billion, considerably exceeding the level of trade with North Korea. *Asiaweek*, February 5, 1988, p. 47.

15. *Ménage à Trois,* 1986–1990

1. Bao Shixiu, "Modern PLA Advance Along the Road to Peace," *China Daily*, July 30, 1987; as cited in Tai Ming Cheung, "Disarmament and Development in China: The Relationship Between National Defense and Economic Development," *Asian Survey* 28, no. 7 (July 1988): 757–75.

2. Godwin, "Changing Concepts," p. 572.

3. In 1983, Soviet and American military forces were roughly equal, according to Chinese analysts, but American power was declining while Soviet power was steadily rising. For example, see Xing Shugang, Liu Yunhua, and Liu Yinghua, "Changing Balance of Soviet and United States Power," *Journal of International Studies*, no. 1, 1983, as trans. in *Beijing Review*, no. 14 (May 9), 1983, pp. 14–19, 26. Within two years, this verdict had changed: with Reagan's accession China saw a "new American ascendancy" over the Soviet Union. See *Beijing Review* 28, no. 24 (June 17, 1985), and 28, no. 31 (August 27, 1985).

4. Li Dai, "The Impact of Economic Crisis on International Relations," *Beijing Review*, no. 22 (May 30), 1983, p. 15; Shi Wuqing, "Superpowers Reach Military Balance," *Beijing Review*, no. 3 (January 21), 1985, pp. 14–15; and no. 4 (January 28), 1985, pp. 25–27.

5. See Zhang Qunsheng, Liang Hunan, and Yan Xiaoyin, "A Study of Local War Theory," trans. in *FBIS–China*, September 23, 1986, p. K5.

6. Rosita Dellios, *Modern Chinese Defense Strategy: Present Developments, Future Directions* (New York: St. Martin's, 1990), p. 51; U.S. Arms Control and Disarmament Agency, *World Military Expenditures and Arms Transfers* (Washington, D.C.: Government Printing Office, 1985), p. 58.

7. The two are Yang Shangkun, state president and general secretary of the Military Affairs Commission, and Defense Minister Qin Jiwei.

8. In 1981, the United States had roughly 10,900 strategic nuclear warheads that could hit Soviet targets, while the Soviet Union had 7,500 strategic weapons with which they could hit U.S. targets. By 1988, the Americans had 13,200 strategic weapons that could hit the Soviet Union while the Soviets had 10,800 weapons that could hit the United States. *New York Times*, November 11, 1988, p. A7.

9. Soviet divisions have three categories of combat readiness: category one units are fully manned and ready to roll on twenty-four hours' notice; category two divisions are 50-75 percent manned and need a month to get ready; category three units are only 20 percent manned and require two months to become combat ready. The recategorization in question represents a cutback of 80,000 to 90,000 troops. *FEER*, June 2, 1988, pp. 34–35.

10. The Soviets reportedly have some 270,000 troops deployed to deal with any Chinese threat, with some 820 aircraft and 8,100 tanks. A further 326,000

troops are deployed in the Soviet Far East to cope with any threat from the United States and Japan. The Chinese have thirteen group armies, with an estimated 650,000 frontline troops and an unknown number of combat aircraft and tanks along the Soviet border, in addition to reserves and local units. *FEER*, April 26, 1990, pp. 12–13; see also Dellios, *Modern Chinese Defense Strategy*, p. 57.

11. *FEER*, August 4, 1988, pp. 28–29; *New York Times*, March 11, 1989. Marshal Sergei Akhromeyev, chief of the Soviet armed forces, said during a July 1988 American visit that the Soviet navy had scaled back the size and scope of its maneuvers as part of its new defensive-oriented military doctrine. His host, Admiral William Crowe, chairman of the U.S. Joint Chiefs of Staff, confirmed that the Soviets have cut down the number of naval exercises far from home. *Christian Science Monitor*, August 1, 1988 editorial. *Soviet Military Power*, a U.S. Defense Department publication, confirmed in 1989 that Soviet naval activity outside home waters had dropped by 15 percent, with further cutbacks expected. *New York Times*, November 17, 1989.

12. In a speech to the Washington World Affairs Council in July 1988, Assistant Secretary of Defense Richard Armitage said that 40 vessels had been *added* to the Pacific Fleet since 1984, bringing the total to 860 vessels, and that the Soviets remain North Korea's main arms suppliers, now including top-of-the-line MiG-29s. *FEER*, August 4, 1988, pp. 28–29.

13. See the IISS, *The Military Balance*, 1986–87 edition. Counting all active, reserve, and paramilitary forces, about 25 million Chinese have military service obligations, amounting to 2.4 percent of the population. *Jane's Defense Weekly*, November 1, 1986, p. 1023.

14. A senior Soviet official familiar with Soviet Asian policy commented, "Of course, the Chinese gave other reasons, but they took this step only when they were convinced that the Soviet Union poses no threat to them." Don Oberdorfer, in the *Washington Post*, April 15, 1987, pp. A25, A30.

15. "Star Wars Must Be Avoided—Deng," *Beijing Review*, no. 32 (August 12), 1985, p. 6; see also the interview with Deng in *Liaowang*, no. 37 (September 16), 1985, as trans. in *FBIS–China*, September 30, 1985, p. K2.

16. *Christian Science Monitor*, December 18, 1989.

17. Thus although Gorbachev supports nuclear-free zones in the Korean peninsula and Southeast Asia and calls for the withdrawal of foreign bases and troops from the region, the Sea of Okhotsk and other key regions for Soviet naval operations are excluded. The proposal to establish zones free from anti-sub weapons would help create a safe haven for Soviet SSBNs in the Sea of Okhotsk and the Sea of Japan. Restrictions of the movement of nuclear air and naval forces within range of either superpower's coast would facilitate creation of a Soviet defensive naval buffer zone in the Far East, curtailing American patrol activities without affecting Soviet nuclear forces.

18. By August 1989, three of the six tank divisions scheduled for withdrawal had departed. More than half the 5,300 tanks had been removed, and about

half the manpower reductions achieved. State Department analysts have concluded that Soviet military spending declined from 15–17 percent of GNP in 1988 to 14–16 percent in 1989. The net result may be a decrease in the aggregate combat power of Soviet forces in Eastern Europe by as much as 20–25 percent. *New York Times*, November 17, 1989.

19. *The Economist*, February 4, 1989, pp. 11–12; *Jane's Defense Weekly*, March 25, 1989, p. 523; *FEER*, May 25, 1989, pp. 12–16; *FEER*, February 16, 1989, pp. 10–11.

20. From "The Soviet Economy in 1988," p. 16, as cited above, Chapter 3, n. 72.

21. Beijing Domestic Television Service, April 17, 1985, as transcribed in *FBIS–China*, April 18, 1985, p. G1. In an interview at around the same time, Huan Xiang, former chargé d'affaires to Great Britain and subsequent director of the International Relations Research Center of the State Council, said: "If Vietnam stops invading Kampuchea and withdraws its troops from Kampuchea, then the threat to us from Danang and Cam Ranh Bay is possibly reduced. Under these circumstances if the Soviet Union wishes to keep its bases in these two places, they can be tolerated." Interview published in Hong Kong's *Wenhui Pao*, June 22, 1985.

22. See Donald Zagoria, "The Moscow-Beijing Detente," *Foreign Affairs*, Spring 1983, pp. 853–73.

23. *FEER*, November 13, 1986, pp. 32–41. Deng actually first expressed interest in a meeting with Gorbachev as early as 1985. In an October meeting with Ceausescu, who was visiting Beijing, Deng asked the latter to pass on a message to Gorbachev proposing a meeting, contingent upon Soviet pressure on Vietnam to withdraw from Cambodia. The Soviet response was noncommittal. *Yomiuri Shimbun*, March 28, 1986, p. 5.

24. Based on "authoritative leaks" from both the Chinese and Soviet delegations, the Beijing correspondent of the Italian Communist Party newspaper was able to piece together a relatively clear picture of what took place during the ninth session of the Sino-Soviet normalization talks, immediately following Gorbachev's speech. The Soviets objected to the abrupt Chinese focus on Cambodia: "In that case, you do not really want to reach an agreement but only to slow down the process of normalization. You have said that you want gestures on one or two of the obstacles in order to speed up normalization. Well, you have had Gorbachev's speech at Vladivostok. Now, instead of discussing those proposals, you say that the Cambodian issue must be settled first. At this point, how can we be sure that, even if we agreed to a compromise on that, you would not then bring up a fourth obstacle?" Sigmund Ginzberg, "How Negotiations Stalled on Cambodia," *L'Unità*, October 15, 1986; as quoted in Kevin Devlin, "How the Sino-Soviet Talks Went: *L'Unità* Revelations," in Radio Free Europe Background Report/157 (Eastern Europe), November 4, 1986.

25. Dellios, *Modern Chinese Defense Strategy*, pp. 108 ff.

26. The first long-term Sino-Mongolian trade agreement, effective from 1986

to 1990, was signed in April 1986; Beijing-Ulan Bator flights resumed in June after a nineteen-year suspension. "Some Developments in Sino-Mongolian Relations," *Wen Wei Bo* (Hong Kong), August 11, 1986, p. 2; as trans. in *South China Morning Post* (Hong Kong), August 12, 1986, p. 10; also see Elizabeth E. Green, "China and Mongolia: Recurring Trends and Prospects for Change," *Asian Survey* 26, no. 12 (December 1986): 1337–64.

27. *Jane's Defense Weekly*, April 1, 1989, p. 544; *FEER*, March 23, 1989, p. 9.

28. Dellios, *Modern Chinese Defense Strategy*, pp. 162–63. Actually, Vietnam's growing isolation within what is left of the bloc is only partly due to effective Chinese diplomacy and partly to the economic logic of reform, which tends to orient socialism away from ideological goals and toward budgetary accountability. Thus since 1985 the Soviet bloc countries have drastically curtailed their assistance to Hanoi while also insisting that Vietnam balance its trade with its socialist allies. The Soviet Union, which has historically provided some 90 percent of the country's fuel and steel and 80 percent of its fertilizer and cotton at subsidized prices, cut supplies as much as 50 percent in 1989; the Soviet 1991–95 Five-Year Plan cuts aid by at least half. *FEER*, January 4, 1990, pp. 6–7; *New York Times*, February 17, 1991, p. F12.

29. According to U.S. Defense Department sources, as of early January 1990 there were still fourteen TU-16 Badger bombers, a squadron of fourteen MiG-23 fighters, several Bear ASW/recon aircraft, and an average of fifteen to twenty warships and support vessels at the base. More recent reports indicate that all the MiGs and about half the TU-16s have been withdrawn. *FEER*, February 1, 1990, pp. 8–9.

30. Chinese weapons were available in large quantities, and often seemed to be preferred to heavier, more expensive Western equipment; not until the summer of 1986, when Stinger antiaircraft missiles began reaching rebel hands, did American aid begin to play a crucial role. On January 30, 1985, the Central Committee of the People's Democratic Party of Afghanistan in Kabul wrote a letter to the CCP Central Committee protesting Chinese weapons supply and guerrilla training camps in Xinjiang province, even alleging that several hundred Chinese instructors were engaged in training *mujahideen* in Pakistan. *FEER*, February 14, 1985, pp. 24–26.

31. Whether the patron has been "bought off" is of course inherently uncertain, a matter of reading diplomatic tea leaves and subtle protocol indicators. Since Gorbachev's 1986 visit, Soviet support for India is thus perceived (by Indians) to have declined, for instance, while Sino-Soviet relations are perceived to have prospered. The Indians apprehended that the Chinese would use this to toughen their stance against India; to counter such a possibility, Rajiv Gandhi in December 1988 undertook his own trip to Beijing (the first by an Indian prime minister in thirty-four years). New Delhi is also somewhat nonplused by Soviet-American rapprochement; nonalignment loses its raison d'être when polarization gives way to superpower consultation.

32. Western analysts estimated that Moscow was in 1986 spending up to U.S. $13 million a day in Cuba, $12 million more in Afghanistan, $8 million a day in Vietnam, and $3 million a day in Ethiopia. While the United States, too, spends generously on its favored friends (e.g., $10 million a day in Israel, $6.3 million a day in Egypt, $655,000 a day in the Philippines), the U.S. economy is nearly twice as big as the Soviet economy. Cf. *Christian Science Monitor*, February 18, 1986, p. 40.

33. This may be in flux, however. A U.S.-North Korean talk was held in Beijing in February 1989, with Seoul's encouragement; Hanoi has also been eager to resume a dialogue with the United States, and if Vietnam satisfactorily terminates its Cambodian involvement, Beijing may drop its objections.

34. The Bush administration plans to pull out three of five air bases from South Korea, bringing home 5,000 to 6,000 troops by 1993 and shifting to a "supporting role" for the ROK government. The United States will also withdraw almost 6,000 troops from Japan, while asking the latter to double its annual contribution to the maintenance of U.S. forces. Withdrawal from the Philippines has been projected by the end of the century. *San Francisco Examiner*, February 25, 1990.

35. Stated by Li Peng in an interview with Associated Press on September 17, 1988. The Chinese have been very aware of the "jealousy" factor, however, expressing concern for example about the impact on Sino-American relations of closer Soviet-American ties. They also seem at times to play on the jealousy: the Chinese hosted three U.S. warships in port calls to Shanghai the *day after* the Gorbachev visit to that city, for example (in the original schedule, the two events were to coincide!).

36. Martin Lasater, *U.S. Policy Toward China's Reunification* (Washington, D.C.: The Heritage Foundation, 1988), p. 5.

37. *Oakland Tribune*, July 15, 1988. Shultz also publicly thanked both Moscow and Beijing for instilling moderation in the North Koreans. There were fears that Pyongyang would disrupt the Olympic Games.

38. *New York Times*, February 26, 1989, p. 1.

39. Thus Gorbachev, in calling for a Sino-Soviet summit meeting in his January 1988 interview with the Chinese journal *Liaowang*, explicitly stated that neither Chinese nor Soviet relations with the United States should affect the two nations' bilateral relations.

40. *New York Times*, December 1, 1988.

41. Some 70–90 percent of the foreign literature in a Chinese military library is Soviet, most of it dating from the 1950s. Russian was recently introduced into the Chinese military academy system as a "key" foreign language.

42. *Christian Science Monitor*, February 6, 1989, p. 3. Military-to-military talks resumed in April 1988, resulting in a "confidence-building" agreement in principle to reduce border troops, which was signed at the summit. Soviet military officials visited Chinese military facilities in February 1990, establishing the first direct military contacts in three decades. Major General Song Wen-

zhong, senior Chinese officer in charge of foreign military relations at China's defense ministry, visited Moscow in early April to pave the way for more military exchanges, including academic contacts. This is expected to eventuate in reciprocal visits by defense ministers. *FEER*, April 26, 1990, pp. 12–13.

43. Thus the Chinese warship *Zheng He* made a port call to Pearl Harbor in April 1989 (the first by a PLA warship to a U.S. port), reciprocated the following month by a three-ship naval squadron in Shanghai, following Gorbachev's visit.

44. An article by Li Yuansheng in *Military Economic Research*, a Chinese military magazine generally restricted to the PLA and the CCP, has called for an increase in defense spending over the next decade from the 1990 figure of U.S. $6.16 billion to $15.5 billion. This would mean an increase of 150 percent in a budget that grew only 30 percent between 1980 and 1989. Associated Press (Hong Kong), December 12, 1990.

45. Gelber, "China's New Economic and Strategic Uncertainties and the Security Prospects," pp. 646–68.

46. Of course, some minimal level of weapons purchases would still be necessary, though these might be multilateralized. There is already evidence that China is moving in that direction. Israel, for example, with whom China has no diplomatic relations, has become a significant source of weapons supply. See Yossi Melman and Dan Raviv, in *Washington Post*, November 30, 1986.

16. The End of the Strategic Triangle?

1. The case is perhaps weakest during the first marriage, when the two spouses might be said to have engaged in simple aggression, in Korea and elsewhere. However, the "revisionist" argument is useful insofar as it indicates how the Sino-Soviet alliance did contribute to American paranoia, politically expressed in anticommunism of considerable bipartisan solidarity, fiscally prodigious rearmament efforts, and the energetic construction of an international containment structure—as well as the threat to respond with "instant and massive [nuclear] retaliation" to even subnuclear provocations.

2. This appears to contradict Kenneth Waltz, *The Spread of Nuclear Weapons: More May Be Better* (London: International Institute for Strategic Studies, 1981), who posits the greater stability of a bipolar arrangement. See also his *Theory of International Politics* (Reading, Mass.: Addison-Wesley, 1979).

3. See Lowell Dittmer, "The Strategic Triangle: An Elementary Game-Theoretical Analysis," *World Politics* 33, no. 4 (July 1981): 510–11.

4. A moment's reflection on the *Zeitgeist* suggests the reasons: the United States was evacuating Vietnam (and would henceforth be crippled by a "Vietnam complex"); the 1973 oil boycott threatened to bring capitalist economies to their knees (the Soviets had their own ample supplies); Watergate humbled Nixon; the Soviets had achieved strategic parity by 1969, and for the first time had the capability to project conventional forces globally. The "correlation of forces" seemed clearly in their favor. See Mitchell, *Ideology of a Superpower*.

5. Vietnam may to some extent be an exception. The Viet Minh may be viewed as a product of the Sino-Soviet marriage in the 1950s, which weathered the 1960s split by shifting to the position of pivot in a small romantic triangle (in which the PRC and USSR were opposing wings). The advent of the romantic triangle in 1971–72 began to undermine the Sino-Vietnamese relationship, however, while the short-lived Sino-American engagement made it altogether untenable. The small triangle dissolved, and Vietnam became a Soviet client: China discontinued all aid in 1975, unilaterally withdrew advisers in 1978, and attacked Vietnam in 1979.

Part IV. Conclusions

1. The Tiananmen incident took place in Beijing and received international news coverage. Though this was certainly the focus of the movement, it was nationwide in scope, and developments in other parts of the country were less adequately covered. Internal Chinese news reports indicate that during the month of June, every province was busy restoring social order: all the major cities reported arrests, university disorders, and the ban of illegal organizations. Guangzhou, Shanghai, Changchun, Wuhan, and Hangzhou even reported road and railway blockades posing serious threats to their economies. *China DB Index*, June 1989.

2. See Zbigniew Brzezinski, *The Grand Failure: The Birth and Death of Communism in the Twentieth Century* (New York: Scribners, 1989).

3. One Soviet article (in *Pravda*, June 8) went so far as to express "understanding" for the actions taken by the Chinese authorities.

4. East Germany, Czechoslovakia, and Romania were particularly effusive in congratulating the PRC after the crackdown; Ceausescu even went so far as to visit Beijing in early July 1989.

5. John W. Garver, "The 'New Type' of Sino-Soviet Relations," *Asian Survey* 29, no. 12 (December 1989): 1136–53.

6. The Chinese were particularly shocked by the army's role in the overthrow of Ceausescu; they postponed the lifting of martial law and intensified PLA study sessions designed to reinforce loyalty among the troops. Criticisms of Gorbachev did not abate until February, when the latter strengthened his position at a Central Committee plenum.

7. The state's internal debt at the beginning of 1990 was 40 billion rubles— or more than 40 percent of GNP. The share of the budget deficit in the GNP increased from 6.9 percent in 1987 to 9.9 percent in 1989. W. M. Smirnov, "Political Reforms and Economic Changes in the Soviet Union," *Korea and World Affairs* 24, no. 3 (Fall 1990): 452.

8. *Hong Kong Standard*, December 12, 1989.

9. *New York Times*, April 25 and 26, 1990; *Christian Science Monitor*, October 15, 1991.

10. TASS, July 30, 1989, in *FBIS–SU*, no. 145 (July 31), pp. 24–25.

11. This intensified diplomatic activity may be in competition with Taiwan,

which in 1988–89 established diplomatic relations with Grenada, Belize, and Liberia. Taiwan is also rumored to be entertaining the idea of establishing some kind of direct trade relations with Moscow and even Pyongyang.

12. *VNA* (Hanoi, June 7, 1989), in *FBIS–SEA*, no. 109 (June 8, 1989), p. 64. Inflation in Vietnam reached 15 percent per month in 1988 and the first half of 1989. At the 1989 CC Plenum this triggered a harsh evaluation of the ideological situation, a political comeback for senior Politburo members who had retired at the Sixth Congress, and a suspension of further political reform.

13. *New York Times*, June 16, 1990.

14. Theodore Caplow, *Two Against One: Coalitions in Triads* (Englewood Cliffs, N.J.: Prentice-Hall, 1968), p. 23.

15. The clearest case is the collapse of the Nixon-Brezhnev-Mao triangle in the late 1970s, because of the perceived growth of the USSR to a position of strategic parity or even temporary superiority (the "window of opportunity" thesis), which was so threatening to the other two actors that they combined in wedlock. The dissolution of this marriage a few years hence can likewise be attributed to Chinese and Soviet perceptions that growth of U.S. strategic capabilities under the Reagan arms buildup reduced the danger of Soviet "hegemonism."

16. The 1990–91 Gulf crisis is instructive. The Soviet Union made no active contribution to the coalition assembled by the United States to discipline Iraq. But it voted for the UN resolution (China abstained), while its active opposition in support of Iraq would have made effective sanctions or punitive war impossible.

17. This premise can be defended by two arguments. First, such a complete transformation is unrealistically ambitious. Second, it would make no sense: we may assume that imbalance causes strain, creating pressure for either all reform or all antireform, not a shift from one form of imbalance to its opposite.

18. As a result of these economic and political pressures, the number of private enterprises and the people employed by them declined by 15 percent and 15.7 percent, respectively, in the first half of 1989—the first time since the inauguration of the reforms that there has been any decline. In September 1989 it was ruled that private entrepreneurs could not join the CCP. Since early 1990 the retrenchment seems to have eased somewhat in the face of a precipitous decline in production.

Selected Bibliography

Frequently Cited Periodicals

Beijing Review, previously *Peking Review* (Beijing).
Christian Science Monitor (Boston).
Defense of Japan. Tokyo: Ministry of Defense, annual yearbook.
Far Eastern Economic Review [abbreviated *FEER*] (Hong Kong).
Foreign Broadcast Information Service, Daily Report, People's Republic of China [abbreviated *FBIS–China*].
Foreign Broadcast Information Service, Daily Report, Soviet Union [abbreviated *FBIS–USSR*].
Guang Jiao Jing [Wide Angle] (Hong Kong).
Hongqi [Red Flag] (Beijing).
Izvestiia [News] (Moscow).
Jiushi Niandai [The Nineties], previously *Qishi Niandai* (Hong Kong).
The Military Balance London: International Institute for Strategic Studies, annual yearbook.
New York Times (New York).
Pravda [Truth] (Moscow).
Problemy Dal'nego Vostoka [Problems of the Far East; also published in English as *Far Eastern Affairs*] (Moscow).
Renmin Ribao [People's Daily] (Beijing).
Shijie Jingji Daobao [World Economic Herald] (Shanghai).
Shijie Zhishi [World Knowledge] (Beijing).
Washington Post (Washington, D.C.).
Xinhua (New China News Agency).
Zheng Ming [Contending] (Hong Kong).

Books and Monographs

Allison, Graham T. *Essence of Decision: Explaining the Cuban Missile Crisis.* Boston: Little, Brown, 1971.
Ambrose, Stephen E. *Rise to Globalism: American Foreign Policy, 1938–1970.* Hammondsworth: Penguin, 1973.
An, Tai-Sung. *The Sino-Soviet Territorial Dispute.* New York: Westminster Press, 1973.
Ashley, Richard K. *The Political Economy of War and Peace: The Sino-Soviet-*

American Triangle and the Modern Security Problematique. New York: Nichols, 1980.

Astafiev, G. V., A. M. Dubinski, et al. 2 vols. *The PRC's Foreign Policy and International Relations, 1949–1973.* Moscow: Mysl', 1974.

Background Information Relating to Southeast Asia and Vietnam. U.S. Senate Committee on Foreign Relations, June 1970. Washington, D.C.: Government Printing Office, 1970.

Bell, Coral. *The Diplomacy of Detente: The Kissinger Era.* New York: St. Martin's Press, 1977.

Bethkenhagen, Jochen. *Die Rolle Asiens in der sowjetischen Aussenwirtschaftspolitik.* Cologne: Berichte des Bundesinstituts für ostwissenschaftliche und internationale Studien, no. 48, 1986.

Bialer, Seweryn, ed. *Politics, Society, and Nationality Inside Gorbachev's Russia.* Boulder: Westview, 1989.

Biberaj, Elez. *Albania and China: A Study of an Unequal Alliance.* Boulder: Westview, 1986.

Binder, Leonard, et al. *Crises and Sequences in Political Development.* Princeton: Princeton University Press, 1971.

Borg, Dorothy, and Waldo Heinrichs, eds. *Uncertain Years: Chinese-American Relations, 1947–1950.* New York: Columbia University Press, 1980.

Brezhnev, L. I. *Leninskim Kursom.* Moscow: Politizdat, 1970.

Brzezinski, Zbigniew. *The Grand Failure: The Birth and Death of Communism in the Twentieth Century.* New York: Charles Scribner's Sons, 1989.

———. *Power and Principle: Memoirs of the National Security Adviser, 1977–1981.* New York: Farrar, Straus, Giroux, 1983.

———. *The Soviet Bloc: Unity and Conflict.* New York: Praeger, 1961.

Bullard, Monte R. *China's Political-Military Evolution: The Party and the Military in the PRC, 1960–1984.* Boulder: Westview, 1985.

Burlatsky, Fedor. *Mao Tse-tung: An Ideological and Psychological Portrait.* Trans. David Skvirsky. Moscow: Progress Publishers, 1980.

Buszynski, Leszek. *Soviet Foreign Policy and Southeast Asia.* London: Croom Helm, 1986.

Camilleri, Joseph. *Chinese Foreign Policy: The Maoist Era and Its Aftermath.* Oxford: M. Robertson, 1980.

Caplow, Theodore. *Two Against One: Coalitions in Triads.* Englewood Cliffs, N.J.: Prentice-Hall, 1968.

Chan, Gerald. *China and International Organization: Participation in Non-Governmental Organizations Since 1971.* Hong Kong: Oxford University Press, 1989.

Chang, Gordon H. *Friends and Enemies: The United States, China, and the Soviet Union, 1948–1972.* Stanford, Calif.: Stanford University Press, 1990.

Chin Szu-k'ai. *Communist China's Relations with the Soviet Union, 1949–1957.* Kowloon: Union Research Institute, 1961.

Clough, Ralph N. *Chinese Elites: World View and Perceptions of the U.S.*

Washington, D.C.: United States Information and Communications Agency Office of Research, 1982.

Coates, Ken. *China and the Bomb*. Nottingham, England: Spokesman Press, 1986.

Commission on Integrated Long-Term Strategy. *Sources of Change in the Future Security Environment*. Washington, D.C.: The Pentagon, April 1989.

Copper, John Franklin, *China's Global Role: An Analysis of Peking's National Power Capabilities in the Context of an Evolving International System*. Stanford: Hoover Institution Press, 1980.

Crouch, Martin. *Revolution and Evolution: Gorbachev and Soviet Politics*. New York: Philip Allan, 1989.

Dallin, David J. *Soviet Foreign Policy After Stalin*. Philadelphia: J. P. Lippincott, 1961.

Dellios, Rosita. *Modern Chinese Defense Strategy: Present Developments, Future Directions*. New York: St. Martin's Press, 1990.

Deng Xiaoping. *Selected Works*. Beijing: Foreign Languages Press, 1986.

Dernberger, Robert F. "The Foreign Trade and Capital Movements of Communist China." Ph.D. dissertation, Harvard University, Department of Economics, 1965.

Desai, Padma. *Perestroika in Perspective: The Design and Dilemmas of Soviet Reform*. Princeton: Princeton University Press, 1989.

Dienes, Leslie. *Soviet Asia: Economic Development and National Policy Choices*. Boulder: Westview, 1987.

Ding Wang, ed., *Mao Zedong Xuanji Buyi* [Supplement to the Selected Works of Mao Zedong], vol. 3. Hong Kong: Ming Bao Monthly Pub., 1971.

Dittmer, Lowell. *China's Continuous Revolution: The Post-Liberation Epoch, 1949–1981*. Berkeley: University of California Press, 1987.

Djilas, Milovan. *Conversations with Stalin*. New York: Harcourt, Brace and World, 1962.

Doolin, Dennis J. *Territorial Claims in the Sino-Soviet Conflict*. Stanford: Hoover Institution, 1965.

Dror, Yehezkel. *Crazy States: A Counterconventional Strategic Problem*. Lexington, Mass.: D. C. Heath, 1971.

Du Preez, Peter. *The Politics of Identity: Ideology and the Human Image*. Oxford: Basil Blackwell, 1980.

Dyker, David, ed. *The Soviet Union Under Gorbachev: Prospects for Reform*. London: Croom Helm, 1987.

Edmonds, Robin. *Soviet Foreign Policy, 1962–1973: The Paradox of Super Power*. London: Oxford University Press, 1975.

Eisenhower, Dwight D. *Mandate for Change, 1953–1956: The White House Years*. Garden City, N.Y.: Doubleday, 1963.

Erikson, Erik H. *Childhood and Society*. New York: W. W. Norton, 1963.

Esherick, Joseph, ed. *Lost Chance in China: The World War II Despatches of John Stewart Service*. New York: Random House, 1974.

FitzGerald, C. P. *Changing Directions of Chinese Foreign Policy*. Melbourne: Australian Institute of International Affairs, 1971.
————. *The Chinese View of Their Place in the World*. London: Oxford University Press, 1965.
Floyd, David. *Mao Against Khrushchev*. New York: Praeger, 1963.
Freedman, Lawrence. *The West and the Modernization of China*. London: Royal Institute of International Affairs, 1979.
Freedman, Robert O. *Economic Warfare in the Communist Bloc: A Study of Soviet Economic Pressure Against Yugoslavia, Albania, and Communist China*. New York: Praeger, 1970.
Gallicchio, Marc S. *The Cold War Begins in Asia: American East Asian Policy and the Fall of the Japanese Empire*. New York: Columbia University Press, 1988.
Garrett, Banning N., and Bonnie Glaser. *War and Peace: The Views from Moscow and Beijing*. Berkeley: Institute of International Studies, 1984.
Garthoff, Raymond L. *Detente and Confrontation: American-Soviet Relations from Nixon to Reagan*. Washington, D.C.: Brookings Institution Press, 1985.
Garver, John W. *Chinese-Soviet Relations, 1937–1945: The Diplomacy of Chinese Nationalism*. New York: Oxford University Press, 1988.
Gelman, Harry. *The Soviet Far East Buildup and Soviet Risk-Taking Against China*. Santa Monica: Rand Corporation, August 1982.
Ghosh, Partha S. *Sino-Soviet Relations: United States Perceptions and Policy Responses, 1949–1959*. New Delhi: Uppal, 1981.
Gilks, Anne, and Gerald Segal. *China and the Arms Trade*. London: Croom Helm, 1985.
Gillison, Jerome. *The Soviet Image of Utopia*. Baltimore: Johns Hopkins University Press, 1975.
Gittings, John. *Survey of the Sino-Soviet Dispute: A Commentary*. London: Oxford University Press, 1968.
Goldman, Marshall I. *Gorbachev's Challenge: Economic Reform in the Age of High Technology*. New York: W. W. Norton, 1987.
Gottlieb, Thomas. *Chinese Foreign Policy Factionalism and the Origins of the Strategic Triangle*. Santa Monica: Rand Corporation, 1977.
Griffith, William E. *The Sino-Soviet Rift*. Cambridge, Mass.: MIT Press, 1964.
Gurtov, Melvin, and Byong-Moo Hwang. *China Under Threat: The Politics of Strategy and Diplomacy*. Baltimore: Johns Hopkins University Press, 1980.
Haldeman, H. R. *The Ends of Power*. New York: Times Books, 1978.
Halliday, Jon, ed. *The Artful Albanian: Memoirs of Enver Hoxha*. London: Chatto and Windus, 1986.
Hammond, Paul Y. *The Cold War Years: American Foreign Policy Since 1945*. New York: Harcourt, Brace and World, 1969.
Harding, Harry, ed. *China's Foreign Relations in the 1980s*. New Haven: Yale University Press, 1984.

Harris, Lillian Craig. *China's Foreign Policy Toward the Third World*. New York: Praeger, 1985.

——, and Robert Worden, eds., *China and the Third World: Champion or Challenger?* Dover, Mass.: Auburn House, 1986.

Hart, Thomas G. *Sino-Soviet Relations: Reexamining the Prospects for Normalization*. Aldershot: Gower, 1987.

Hayes, Peter, Lyuba Zarsky, and Walden Bello. *American Lake: Nuclear Peril in the Pacific*. New York: Penguin, 1986.

Herrmann-Pillath, Carsten. *Die chinesische Wirtschaftsreform im Spiegel sowjetischer Darstellungen, 1979–1986*. Cologne: Berichte des Bundesinstituts für ostwissenschaftliche und internationale Studien, no. 42, 1986.

Hersh, Seymour M. *The Price of Power: Kissinger in the Nixon White House*. New York: Summit, 1983.

Hewett, Ed A. *Reforming the Soviet Economy: Equality Versus Efficiency*. Washington, D.C.: Brookings Institution, 1988.

Hill, R. J., and J. A. Dellenbrant. *Gorbachev and Perestroika: Towards a New Society?* Aldershot: Edward Elgar, 1989.

Hinton, Harold. *The Bear at the Gate: Chinese Policy-Making Under Soviet Pressure*. Washington, D.C.: American Enterprise Institute for Public Policy Research, 1971.

——. *The Sino-Soviet Confrontation: Implications for the Future*. New York: Crane, Russak, 1976.

Hudson, G. F., Richard Lowenthal, and Roderick MacFarquhar, eds. *The Sino-Soviet Dispute*. London: The China Quarterly, 1961.

Jacobsen, C. G. *Sino-Soviet Relations Since Mao: The Chairman's Legacy*. New York: Praeger, 1981.

Jianguo yilai Mao Zedong wenxuan, 1949.9–1950.12 [Selected Mao Zedong Documents Since the Founding of the PRC, September 1949–December 1950]. Beijing: Zhongyang Wenxian Chubanshe, July 1987.

Jo, Yung-hwan, and Ying-hsien Pi. *Russia Versus China and What Next?* Lanham, Md.: University Press of America, 1980.

Joensson, Christer. *Superpower: Comparing American and Soviet Foreign Policy*. New York: St. Martin's Press, 1987.

Johnson, Paul M. *Redesigning the Communist Economy: The Politics of Economic Reform in Eastern Europe*. Boulder: East European Monographs, 1989.

Jones, Peter, and Sian Kevill, eds. *China and the Soviet Union*. New York: Facts on File, 1985.

Jukes, Geoffrey. *The Soviet Union in Asia*. Berkeley: University of California Press, 1973.

Kanet, Roger E., ed. *The Soviet Union and the Developing Nations*. Baltimore: Johns Hopkins University Press, 1974.

Kapur, H., ed. *The End of an Isolation: China After Mao*. Dordrecht: Martinus Nijhoff, 1985.

Karol, K. S. *Visa pour la Pologne*. Paris: Gallimard, 1958.

Kau, Michael Y. M., and John K. Leung, eds. *The Writings of Mao Zedong, 1949–1976*, vol. 1: *September 1949–December 1955*. Armonk, N.Y.: M. E. Sharpe, 1987.

Kautsky, John H. *Communism and the Politics of Development: Persistent Myths and Changing Behavior*. New York: John Wiley, 1968.

Keal, Paul. *Unspoken Rules and Superpower Dominance*. London: Macmillan, 1983.

Keeble, Curtis, ed. *The Soviet State: The Domestic Roots of Soviet Foreign Policy*. London: Royal Institute of International Affairs, 1985.

Keith, Ronald C. *The Diplomacy of Zhou Enlai*. New York: Macmillan, 1989.

Kim, Ilpyong J., ed. *The Strategic Triangle: China, the United States and the Soviet Union*. New York: Paragon House, 1987.

Kim, Samuel. *China, the United Nations, and World Order*. Princeton: Princeton University Press, 1979.

———. *The Third World in Chinese World Policy*. Princeton: Center of International Studies, Woodrow Wilson School, 1989.

———, ed. *China and the World: Chinese Foreign Policy in the Post-Mao Era*. Boulder: Westview, 1984.

Kimura, Tetsusaburo. *The Vietnamese Economy, 1975–86: Reforms and International Relations*. Tokyo: Institute of Developing Economies, 1989.

Kissinger, Henry. *White House Years*. Boston: Little, Brown, 1979.

———. *Years of Upheaval*. Boston: Little, Brown, 1982.

Klintworth, Gary. *China's Modernization: The Strategic Implications for the Asian-Pacific Region*. Canberra: AGPS Press, 1989.

Klochko, Mikhail A. *Soviet Scientist in Red China*. New York: Praeger, 1964.

Levesque, Jacques. *Le Conflit sino-sovietique et l'Europe de l'Est: Ses incidences sur les conflits soviéto-polonais et soviéto-roumain*. Montréal: Les Presses de l'Université de Montréal, 1970.

Lewis, John Wilson, and Litai Xue. *China Builds the Bomb*. Stanford: Stanford University Press, 1988.

Lieberthal, Kenneth. *Sino-Soviet Conflict in the 1970s: Its Evolution and Implications for the Strategic Triangle*. Santa Monica: Rand Corporation, 1978.

Lin, Chong-pin. *China's Nuclear Weapons Strategy: Tradition Within Evolution*. Lexington: D. C. Heath, 1988.

Link, Werner. *The East-West Conflict: The Organization of International Relations in the Twentieth Century*. Dover, N.H.: Berg, 1986.

Liu Shaoqi. *Collected Works*. 2 vols. Hong Kong: Union Research Institute, 1968–69.

McCauley, Martin, ed. *The Soviet Union Under Gorbachev*. London: Macmillan, 1987.

MacFarquhar, Roderick. *The Origins of the Cultural Revolution*, vol. 1: *Contradictions Among the People, 1956–1957*. London: Oxford University Press, 1974.

——. *The Origins of the Cultural Revolution*, vol. 2: *The Great Leap Forward, 1958–1960*. New York: Columbia University Press, 1983.

McGwire, Michael. *Military Objectives in Soviet Foreign Policy*. Washington, D.C.: Brookings Institution, 1987.

Mao Zedong. *Mao Zedong Sixiang Wansui* [Long Live Mao Zedong Thought]. 3 vols. Hong Kong: n.p., 1967–69.

——. *Selected Works*. 5 vols. Beijing: Foreign Languages Press, 1965–1977.

Marrese, Michael, and Jan Vanous. *Implicit Subsidies and Non-Market Benefits in Soviet Trade with Eastern Europe*. Berkeley: University of California Press, 1982.

Martin, Edwin W. *Divided Counsel: The Anglo-American Response to Communist Victory in China*. Lexington: University Press of Kentucky, 1986.

Mayers, David Allen. *Cracking the Monolith: U.S. Policy Against the Sino-Soviet Alliance, 1949–1955*. Baton Rouge: Louisiana State University Press, 1986.

Medvedev, Roy. *China and the Superpowers*. Oxford and New York: Basil Blackwell, 1986.

Mehnert, Klaus. *Peking to Moscow*. New York: Mentor Books, 1964.

Mitchell, R. Judson. *Ideology of a Superpower: Contemporary Soviet Doctrine and International Relations*. Stanford: Hoover Institution Press, 1982.

Nathan, Andrew J. *China's Crisis: Dilemmas of Reform and Prospects for Democracy*. New York: Columbia University Press, 1990.

Nelsen, Harvey. *Power and Insecurity: Beijing, Moscow, and Washington, 1949–1988*. Boulder: Lynne Rienner, 1989.

Nelson, Daniel, and Stephen White, eds. *Communist Legislatures in Comparative Perspective*. Albany: State University of New York Press, 1982.

Nie Rongzhen. *Nie Rongzhen Huiyi Lu* [Reflections of Nie Rongzhen]. 2 vols. Beijing: Zhanshi, 1983.

Nixon, Richard. *Memoirs*. New York: Grosset and Dunlap, 1978.

Okazaki, Hisahiko. *A Japanese View of Détente*. Lexington, Mass.: D. C. Heath, 1974.

Orleans, Leo. *Professional Manpower and Education in Communist China*. Washington, D.C.: Government Printing Office, 1960.

Park, J. K., and J. M. Ma, eds. *The Soviet Union and East Asia in the 1980s*. Boulder: Westview, 1983.

Perkins, Dwight H. *China: Asia's Next Economic Giant?* Seattle: University of Washington Press, 1986.

Peterson, Sophia. *Sino-Soviet-American Relations: Conflict, Communications and Mutual Threat*. Denver: University of Denver, Graduate School of International Studies, 1979.

Pike, Douglas. *Vietnam and the Soviet Union: Anatomy of an Alliance*. Boulder: Westview, 1987.

Pollack, Jonathan. *China's Potential as a World Power*. Santa Monica: Rand Corporation, 1980.

Prados, John. *The Soviet Estimate: U.S. Intelligence and Russian Military Strength*. New York: Dial Press, 1982.

Pye, Lucian. *The Mandarin and the Cadre: China's Political Cultures*. Ann Arbor: Center for Chinese Studies, University of Michigan, 1988.

———. *The Spirit of Chinese Politics: A Psychocultural Study of Political Development*. Cambridge, Mass.: MIT Press, 1968.

Ray, Hemen. *China and Eastern Europe*. New Delhi: Radiant Press, 1988.

———. *The Sino-Soviet Conflict Over India*. New Delhi: Abhinav Pub., 1986.

Riskin, Carl. *China's Political Economy: The Quest for Development Since 1949*. New York: Oxford University Press, 1987.

Rothenberg, Morris. *Whither China: The View from the Kremlin*. Miami: Center for Advanced International Studies, University of Miami, 1977.

Rozman, Gilbert. *The Chinese Debate About Soviet Socialism, 1978–1985*. Princeton: Princeton University Press, 1987.

———. *Mirror for Socialism: Soviet Criticisms of China*. Princeton: Princeton University Press, 1985.

Rubinstein, Alvin Z. *Soviet Foreign Policy Since World War II: Imperial and Global*. Cambridge, Mass.: Winthrop Publishers, 1981.

Ryan, Mark A. *Chinese Attitudes Toward Nuclear Weapons: China and the U.S. During the Korean War*. Armonk, N.Y.: M. E. Sharpe, 1989.

Salisbury, Harrison E. *War Between Russia and China*. New York: W. W. Norton, 1969.

Schram, Stuart, ed. *Chairman Mao Talks to the People: Talks and Letters, 1956–1971*. New York: Random House, 1976.

———, ed. *The Political Thought of Mao Tse-tung*. New York: Praeger, 1963.

Schurmann, Franz. *The Logic of World Power: An Inquiry into the Origins, Currents, and Contradictions of World Politics*. New York: Pantheon, 1974.

Segal, Gerald. *The Great Power Triangle*. New York: St. Martin's, 1982.

Segal, Gerald, ed. *Arms Control in Asia*. London: Macmillan, 1987.

———, ed. *The Soviet Union in East Asia: Predicaments of Power*. London: Heinemann, 1983.

———, and William Tow, eds. *Chinese Defense Policy*. Urbana: University of Illinois Press, 1984.

Service, John Stewart. *The Amerasia Papers: Some Problems in the History of U.S.-China Relations*. Berkeley: China Research Monograph, 1971.

Shevchenko, Arkady N. *Breaking with Moscow*. New York: Knopf, 1985.

Simmons, Robert R. *The Strained Alliance: Peking, Pyongyang, Moscow and the Politics of the Korean Civil War*. New York: Free Press, 1975.

Sokoloff, Georges, and Françoise Lemoine. *China and the U.S.S.R.: Limits to Trade with the West*. Paris: Atlantic Institute for International Affairs, 1982.

Solodnovikov, V., and V. Boslovisky. *Non-Capitalist Development: An Historical Outline*. Moscow: Progress Publishers, 1975.

Sonnenfeldt, Helmut, ed. *Soviet Policies in the 1980s*. Boulder: Westview, 1985.

Spurr, Russell. *Enter the Dragon: China's Undeclared War Against the U.S. in Korea, 1950–51*. New York: Newmarket, 1988.

Stuart, Douglas, ed. *Security Within the Pacific Rim*. Aldershot: Gow Publishing Co., 1987.

———, and William Tow, eds. *China, the Soviet Union, and the West*. Boulder: Westview, 1982.

Sutter, Robert G. *Chinese Foreign Policy: Developments After Mao*. New York: Praeger, 1986.

Talbott, Strobe, ed. *Khrushchev Remembers*. Boston: Little, Brown, 1970.

———, ed. *Khrushchev Remembers: The Last Testament*. Boston: Little, Brown, 1974.

Tatu, Michel. *Le triangle Washington-Moscou-Pékin et les deus Europe(s)*. Paris: Casterman, 1972.

Timmermann, Heinz. *Peking's 'eurokommunistische' Wende: Zur Wiedereinschaltung der Kommunistische Partei Chinas in das internationale kommunistische Parteiensystem*. Cologne: Berichte des Bundesinstituts für ostwissenschaftliche und internationale Studien, no. 25, 1983.

Thomas, Raju G. C. *The Great-Power Triangle and Asian Security*. Lexington, Mass.: D. C. Heath, 1983.

Thornton, Richard. *Soviet Asian Strategy in the Brezhnev Era and Beyond*. Washington, D.C.: Washington Institute for Values in Public Policy, 1985.

Tsou, Tang. *The Cultural Revolution and Post-Mao Reforms: A Historical Perspective*. Chicago: University of Chicago Press, 1986.

Tucker, Nancy Bernkopf. *Patterns in the Dust: Chinese-American Relations and the Recognition Controversy, 1949–1950*. New York: Columbia University Press, 1983.

Ulam, Adam. *Expansion and Coexistence: Soviet Foreign Policy, 1917–1973*. New York: Praeger, 1974.

U.S. Department of State. *United States Relations with China with Special Reference to the Period 1944–1949* [The China White Paper]. Washington, D.C.: Government Printing Office, 1949.

Van Ness, Peter. *Revolution and Chinese Foreign Policy: Peking's Support for Wars of National Liberation*. Berkeley: University of California Press, 1970.

Vladimirov, Peter. *The Vladimirov Diaries: Yanan, China, 1942–1945*. New York: Doubleday, 1975.

Weigert, Andrew J., J. Smith Teitge, and Dennis W. Teitge. *Society and Identity: Toward a Sociological Psychology*. Cambridge and New York: Cambridge University Press, 1986.

Whiting, Allen S. *China Crosses the Yalu*. New York: Macmillan, 1960.

———. *The Chinese Calculus of Deterrence: India and Indochina*. Ann Arbor: University of Michigan Press, 1975.

———. *Siberian Development and East Asia: Threat or Promise?* Stanford: Stanford University Press, 1981.

——— . *Soviet Policies in China, 1917–1924*. New York: Columbia University Press, 1954.

Wich, Richard. *Sino-Soviet Crisis Politics: A Study of Political Change and Communication*. Cambridge, Mass.: Council on East Asian Studies, Harvard University, 1980.

Wolfe, Thomas W. *Soviet Power and Europe, 1945–70*. Baltimore: Johns Hopkins University Press, 1970.

Wortzel, Larry, ed. *China's Military Modernization: International Implications*. New York: Greenwood, 1988.

Yahuda, Michael. *China's Role in World Affairs*. New York: St. Martin's, 1978.

Yang Junshi. *Xiandaihua yu Zhongguo Gongchanzhuyi* [Modernization and Chinese Communism]. Hong Kong: Chinese University Press, 1987.

Yin, John. *Sino-Soviet Dialogue on the Problem of War*. The Hague: Martinus Nijhoff, 1971.

Zagoria, Donald. *The Sino-Soviet Conflict, 1956–1961*. Princeton: Princeton University Press, 1962.

——— . *Vietnam Triangle: Moscow, Peking, Hanoi*. New York: Pegasus, 1967.

———, ed. *Soviet Policy in East Asia*. New Haven: Yale University Press, 1982.

Zaslavskaia, Tat'iana. *A Voice of Reform*. Edited by Murray Yanowitch. Armonk, N.Y.: M. E. Sharpe, 1989.

Articles

Aslund, Anders. "Soviet and Chinese Reforms." *The World Today* 45, no. 11 (November 1989): 188–91.

Banister, Judith. "Population Policy and Trends in China, 1978–83." *China Quarterly*, no. 100 (December 1984), 717–41.

Bernstein, Thomas P. "Stalinism, Famine, and Chinese Peasants: Grain Procurements During the Great Leap Forward." *Theory and Society* 13, no. 3 (May 1984): 339–77.

Braun, Aurel, and Richard B. Day. "Gorbachevian Contradictions." *Problems of Communism* 39, no. 3 (May–June 1990): 36–51.

Brooks, Karen M. "Soviet Agriculture's Halting Reform." *Problems of Communism* 39, no. 2 (March–April 1990): 29–42.

Brown, Roger Glenn. "Chinese Politics and American Policy: A New Look at the Triangle." *Foreign Policy*, no. 23 (Summer 1976), pp. 3–23.

Chari, P. R. "China's Nuclear Posture: An Evaluation." *Asian Survey* 18, no. 8 (August 1978): 817–29.

Chyba, F. Christopher. "U.S. Military-Support Equipment Sales to the PRC." *Asian Survey*, April 1981, pp. 469–84.

Diamond-Kim, Deborah. "Partners in Austerity." *China Business Review*, May–June 1987, p. 15.

Dittmer, Lowell. "Mao and the Politics of Revolutionary Mortality." *Asian Survey* 27, no. 3 (March 1987): 316–40.

———. "Political Culture and Political Symbolism: Toward a Theoretical Synthesis." *World Politics* 29, no. 4 (July 1977): 552–84.

———. "The Strategic Triangle: An Elementary Game-Theoretical Analysis." *World Politics* 33, no. 4 (July 1981): 485–515.

Federenko, N. "Khrushchev's Visit to Beijing." *Far Eastern Affairs*, no. 2, 1990, pp. 213–24.

———. "The Stalin-Mao Summit in Moscow," *Far Eastern Affairs*, no. 2, 1989, pp. 134–48.

Garrett, Banning. "China Policy and the Strategic Triangle." In Kenneth A. Oye et al., eds., *Eagle Entangled: U.S. Foreign Policy in a Complex World*, pp. 228–64. London and New York: Longman, 1979.

Garver, John W. "The 'New Type' of Sino-Soviet Relations." *Asian Survey* 29, no. 12 (December 1989): 1136–53.

Gelber, Harry. "China's New Economic and Strategic Uncertainties and the Security Prospects." *Asian Survey* 30, no. 7 (July 1990): 646–68.

Goldman, Marshall, and Merle Goldman. "Soviet and Chinese Economic Reform." *America and the World, 1987/88*, pp. 551–74. New York: Pergamon Press, 1988.

Green, Elizabeth E. "China and Mongolia: Recurring Trends and Prospects for Change." *Asian Survey* 26, no. 12 (December 1986): 1337–64.

Halpern, Nina P. "Learning from Abroad: Chinese Views of the East European Economic Experience, January 1977–June 1981." *Modern China* 2, no. 1 (January 1985): 77–111.

He Di. "The Evolution of the PRC's Policy Toward the Offshore Islands (Quemoy, Matsu)." Unpublished paper presented to the Center for Chinese Studies Regional Seminar, University of California, Berkeley, October 31, 1987.

Huan, Guocang. "Sino-Soviet Relations to the Year 2000." Washington, D.C.: Atlantic Council Occasional Paper, 1986.

Joffe, Ellis. " 'People's War Under Modern Conditions': A Doctrine of Modern War." *China Quarterly*, no. 112 (December 1987), pp. 555–72.

Kaser, Michael. " 'One Economy, Two Systems': Parallels Between Soviet and Chinese Reform." *International Affairs* 63, no. 3 (Summer 1987): 395–413.

Kim, Samuel S. "Chinese World Policy in Transition." *World Policy Journal*, Spring 1984, pp. 603–33.

Lampton, David Michael. "China's Limited Accommodation with the USSR: Coalition Politics." *AEI Foreign Policy and Defense Review* 6, no. 3 (August 1986): 26–35.

Lapidus, Gail. "Changing Soviet Perspectives and Policies in Northeast Asia." In Robert Scalapino and Qimao Chen, eds., *Pacific-Asian Issues: American and Chinese Views*, pp. 93–111. Berkeley: Institute of East Asian Studies, 1986.

Lee, Wei-chin. "The Birth of a Salesman: China as Arms Supplier." *Journal of Asian Studies* 6, no. 4 (Winter 1987–88): 32–47.

Levesque, Jacques. "Les 'trois obstacles' dans un monde changeant." *Le Monde diplomatique* 31, no. 361 (April 1984): 1, 6–7.

Li Jingjie. "Sino-Soviet Relations and Their Future Prospects." Unpublished paper presented to Faculty Seminar on Comparative Study of Communist Societies, University of California, Berkeley, 1986.

Liao, Tony Kuang-sheng. "Antiforeignism and Chinese Communism in Mao Zedong's Era." Unpublished paper, Chinese University of Hong Kong, 1987.

Lin Biao. "Long Live the Victory of People's War." *Renmin Ribao*, September 2, 1965.

Menon, Rajan, and Daniel Abele. "Security Dimensions of Soviet Territorial Disputes with China and Japan." *Journal of Northeast Asian Studies* 8, no. 1 (Spring 1989): 3–20.

Meyer, Alfred G. "Theories of Convergence." In Chalmers Johnson, ed., *Change in Communist Systems*. Stanford: Stanford University Press, 1970.

Miller, Robert F. "Doctrinal and Ideological Issues of Reform in Socialist Systems." *Soviet Studies* 91, no. 3 (July 1989): 430–49.

Miyamoto, Nobuo. "Basic Structure of the Sino-Soviet Conflict and Its Prospect: Nexus of the US-USSR-China 'Nuclear' Dimension and Great Power Nationalism of the USSR and China." Unpublished Paper, Woodrow Wilson Center, Smithsonian Institution, Washington, D.C., May 1986.

Naughton, Barry. "The Third Front: Defence Industrialization in the Chinese Interior." *China Quarterly*, no. 115 (September 1988), pp. 351–86.

Nixon, Richard. "Dealing with Gorbachev." *New York Times Magazine*, March 13, 1988, pp. 26–30, 66–79.

"On Historical Experience Concerning the Dictatorship of the Proletariat," *Renmin Ribao*, April 5, 1956.

"On Khrushchev's Phony Communism and Its Historical Lessons for the World." As trans. in *Peking Review*, July 17, 1964, pp. 7–28.

Orleans, Leo. "The Soviet Union's Evolving Perceptions of China's Science and Technology." Paper presented at the Fifteenth Sino-American Conference on Mainland China, June 8–14, 1986, Taipei, Taiwan.

Pillsbury, Michael. "U.S.-Chinese Military Ties?" *Foreign Policy*, Autumn 1975.

Pryor, Frederic. "When Is Collectivization Reversible?" Unpublished paper presented to Comparative Study of Communist Societies Seminar, University of California, Berkeley, February 1990.

Ra'anan, Uri. "Peking's Foreign Policy 'Debate,' 1965–1966." In Tang Tsou, ed., *China in Crisis*, vol. 2: *China's Policies in Asia and America's Alternatives*, pp. 23–71. Chicago: University of Chicago Press, 1968.

Ray, Dennis. "Chinese Perceptions of Social Imperialism and Economic Dependency: The Impact of Soviet Aid." *Stanford Journal of International Studies* 10 (Spring 1975): 36–83.

Remington, Thomas. "A Socialist Pluralism of Opinions: *Glasnost'* and Policy-Making Under Gorbachev." *Russian Review* 48, no. 3 (July 1989): 271–305.

"The Reply of the Central Committee of the Communist Party of China to the CPSU's Letter," *Renmin Ribao*, May 9, 1964.

Rozman, Gilbert. "China's Soviet-Watchers in the 1980s: A New Era in Scholarship." *World Politics* 37, no. 4 (July 1985): 435–74.

———. "Moscow's China-Watchers in the Post-Mao Era: The Response to a Changing China." *China Quarterly*, no. 94 (June 1983).

Scalapino, Robert. "Containment and Countercontainment: The Current Stage of Sino-Soviet Relations." In Douglas Stuart and William Tow, eds., *China, the Soviet Union, and the West*, pp. 173 ff. Boulder: Westview, 1982.

Shaw, Yu-ming. "John Leighton Stuart and U.S.-Chinese Communist Rapprochement in 1949." *China Quarterly*, no. 89 (March 1982), pp. 74–97.

Shen Xiaofang. "A Decade of Direct Foreign Investment in China." *Problems of Communism* 39, no. 1 (March-April 1990): 61–74.

Shi Zhe. "I Accompanied Chairman Mao." *Far Eastern Affairs*, no. 2 (1989), pp. 125–33.

Strong, Tracy B., and Helene Keyssar. "Anna Louise Strong: Three Interviews with Chairman Mao Zedong." *China Quarterly*, no. 103 (September 1985), pp. 489–510.

Su, Chi. "Sino-Soviet Relations in the 1980s: From Confrontation to Conciliation." In Samuel Kim, ed., *China and the World*, 2d edition, pp. 115 ff. Boulder: Westview, 1989.

———. "Soviet China-Watchers' Influence on Soviet China Policy." *Journal of Northeast Asian Studies* 2, no. 4 (December 1983): 26–27.

———. "U.S.-China Relations: Soviet Views and Policies." *Asian Survey* 23, no. 5 (May 1983): 566 ff.

Timmermann, Heinz. "The Communist Party of the Soviet Union's Reassessment of International Social Democracy: Dimensions and Trends." *Journal of Communist Studies* 5, no. 2 (June 1989): 173–85.

Tow, William T. "Nuclear Security Problems in the Far East." *Asian Pacific Community*, no. 19 (Winter 1983), pp. 52–72.

Whiting, Allen S. "New Light on Mao: Quemoy 1958: Mao's Miscalculations." *China Quarterly*, no. 62 (June 1975), pp. 263–70.

Wiedemann, Kent M. "China in the Vanguard of a New Socialism." *Asian Survey* 26, no. 7 (July 1986): 774–92.

Yahuda, Michael. "Kremlinology and the Chinese Strategic Debate, 1965–66." *China Quarterly*, no. 49 (January–March 1972), pp. 32–75.

Young, Stephen M. "Gorbachev's Asian Policy: Balancing the New and the Old." *Asian Survey* 28, no. 3 (March 1988): 317–40.

Zagoria, Donald. "The Moscow-Beijing Detente." *Foreign Affairs*, Spring 1983, pp. 853–73.

Index